Understanding Digital Libraries

The Morgan Kaufmann Series in Multimedia Information and Systems

Series Editor, Edward A. Fox, Virginia Polytechnic University

Understanding
Digital Libraries

Second Edition

Michael Lesk

AMSTERDAM · BOSTON · HEIDELBERG · LONDON
NEW YORK · OXFORD · PARIS · SAN DIEGO
SAN FRANCISCO · SINGAPORE · SYDNEY · TOKYO

ELSEVIER   MORGAN KAUFMANN PUBLISHERS IS AN IMPRINT OF ELSEVIER

MORGAN KAUFMANN PUBLISHERS

Publishing Director	Diane D. Cerra
Senior Editor	Rick Adams
Acquisitions Editor	Lothlórien Homet
Publishing Services Manager	Simon Crump
Project Manager	Dan Stone
Developmental Editor	Corina Derman
Editorial Coordinator	Mona Buehler
Editorial Assistant	Asma Stephan
Cover Design	Frances Baca
Composition	CEPHA Imaging Pvt. Ltd.
Technical Illustration	Dartmouth Publishing Inc.
Copyeditor	Yonie Overton
Proofreader	Daniel Easler
Indexer	Kevin Broccoli
Interior printer	The Maple-Vail Book Manufacturing Group
Cover printer	Phoenix Color

Morgan Kaufmann Publishers is an imprint of Elsevier.
500 Sansome Street, Suite 400, San Francisco, CA 94111

This book is printed on acid-free paper.

Library of Congress Cataloging-in-Publication Data
APPLICATION SUBMITTED

ISBN: 1-55860-924-5

For information on all Morgan Kaufmann publications,
visit our Web site at www.mkp.com or www.books.elsevier.com

Printed in the United States of America
05 06 07 08 09   5 4 3 2 1

Again, this book is dedicated to the late Gerard Salton (1927–1995), a great information retrieval researcher who introduced many algorithms in the 1960s that are only now becoming commercially recognized, whose students have taught and studied in many universities, and who in 1961 first introduced me to computers, programming, and information retrieval.

Contents

14. Future: Ubiquity, Diversity, Creativity, and Public Policy   375

References   387

Index   413

Figures

Tables

Figure Credits

Figure 1.2	Based on data from Leach, S. 1986. "The Growth Rate of Major Academic Libraries: Rider and Purdue Reviewed." College and Research Libraries 37 (Nov) and from Rider, F. 1944. *The Scholar and the Future of the Research Library*. New York: Hadham Press.
Figure 1.3	Based on data from Meadows, J (1993) "Too Much of a Good Thing?" in H. Woodward and S. Pilling, eds. *The International Serials Industry*, Aldershot, Hampsire: Gower Publishing.
Figure 1.5	Courtesy of Mrs. Joan Adria D'Amico, the executor of the estate of Mary Crimi, wife of Alfred D. Crimi.
Figure 1.6	Courtesy of the Public Records Office, London FD 850/234.
Figure 1.7	Based on data from several sources including "Birth of a Chip." 1996. *Byte* (Dec) and "The Personal Computing Industry by the Numbers." 1997 *PC Magazine* (March).
Figure 1.8	Based on data from several sources including Pugh, E. 1995. *Building IBM: Shaping an Industry and Its Technology*. Cambridge, MA: MIT Press.
Figure 1.9	Adapted from Hammann, D. 1983. "Computers in Physics: An Overview." *Physics Today* 36(5).
Figure 2.2	Courtesy of the *London Daily Mail*.

Figure 2.3   Courtesy of the *American Chemical Society*.

Figure 3.1   Courtesy Ann B. Lesk.

Figure 3.2   'Flying' scanner by Bob Kobres, University of Georgia Libraries. Reprinted with permission.

Figure 3.3   (a) 4DigitalBooks.com, (b) www.kirtas-tech.com. Reprinted with permission.

Figure 3.7   From DjVuZone.com, Leon Bottou. Reprinted with permission.

Figure 3.8   The World. *Burney London Daily Journal.* 8.3.1728, PB.MIC.BUR.823B. Used by permission of the British Library.

Figure 3.9   Screenshot of heads. Used by permission of the British Library.

Figure 3.10   Screenshot of heads. Used by permission of the British Library.

Figure 3.11   *The Journal of Physical Chemistry*, Vol.92 No.26, p.7162 (Fig.2). Copyright 1988 American Chemical Society. Reprinted with permission.

Figure 3.13   *The Journal of Analytical Chemistry*, 63(17), 1697-1702. © Copyright 1991 American Chemical Society. Reprinted with permission.

Figure 3.14   *The Journal of Organic Chemistry*, Vol. 56, No. 26, p.7270 (Fig.1) © Copyright 1991 American Chemical Society. Reprinted with permission.

Figure 3.15   (a) Courtesy of the Harvard University Library, (b) Courtesy of the French National Library, Francois Mitterand, Dominique Perrault, Architect, Alain Goustard, Photographer.

Figure 4.2   (a) Courtesy of Anne B. Lesk.

Figure 4.4   Courtesy of www.bberger.net/rwb/gamma.html.

Figure 4.5   Courtesy of EE/CS University of California, Berkeley.

Figure 4.6   Courtesy of EE/CS University of California, Berkeley.

Figure 4.7   "Automatic Image Annotation and Retrieval using CrossMedia Relevance Models by Jeon, Lavrenko and Manmatha," *SIGIR'03*. Reprinted with permission.

Figure 4.8   Courtesy of the Department of Engineering Science, University of Oxford.

Figure 4.9   Courtesy of Department of Engineering Science, University of Oxford.

Figure 4.10	Courtesy of David D. Clark.
Figure 5.1	Based on catalogue sample, courtesy of OCLC.
Figure 5.2	Reproduced with permission of Yahoo! Inc. © 2004 by Yahoo! Inc. YAHOO! and the YAHOO! Logo are trademarks of Yahoo! Inc.
Figure 6.1	Copyright © Internet 2. Reprinted with Permission.
Figure 7.1	Courtesy of Dennis E. Egan.
Figure 7.2	Spearman, F. 1906. *Whispering Smith.* New York: Scribner's. Reprinted with permission.
Figure 7.3	Spearman, F. 1906. *Whispering Smith.* New York: Scribner's. Reprinted with permission.
Figure 7.4	Used by permission of the University of Maryland, Human-Computer Interaction Lab.
Figure 7.5	Courtesy of Marti Hearst.
Figure 7.6	Courtesy of Xia Lin.
Figure 7.7	Adapted from Lin, X., and D. Soergel. 1991. "A Self-Organizing Semantic Map for Information Retrieval." *Proc. 14th Int'l SIGIR Conference,* Chicago, IL, Oct.
Figure 7.8	Courtesy of Aslib, The Association for Information Management.
Figure 9.1	Courtesy of the Library of Congress, American Memory Project.
Figure 9.2	(a,b,d) courtesy of Library of Congress, American Memory Project, (c) MS CSP L75, used by permission of the Houghton Library, Harvard University.
Figure 9.3	K. Top120(13). Used by permission of the British Library.
Figure 9.9	Adapted from Van Bogard, J. 1995. *Magnetic Tape Storage and Handling: A Guide for Libraries and Archives.* Washington, DC: Commission on Preservation and Access, June.
Figure 9.10	Adapted from Van Bogard, J. 1995. *Magnetic Tape Storage and Handling: A Guide for Libraries and Archives.* Washington, DC: Commission on Preservation and Access, June.
Figure 10.1	Adapted from Griffiths, J.-M., and D. W. King. 1993. *Special Libraries: Increasing the Information Edge.* Washington, DC: Special Libraries Association.
Figure 10.4	Adapted from Griffites and King. 1993. Special Libraries.

Figure 10.5   Adapted from Cummings, A. M., et al. 1992. *University Libraries and Scholarly Communication: A Study Prepared for the Andrew W. Mellon Foundation.* Washington, DC: Association of Research Libraries. November.

Figure 11.2   Courtesy of Glenco Engineering Inc.

Figure 12.2   From the University of Maryland, July 2004, (http://www.icdbooks.org). Reprinted with permission.

Figure 12.3   Cotton Vit A.XV f.132. Reprinted with permission of the British Library.

Figure 12.4   Reprinted with permission of the Keio University Library.

Figure 12.5   Reprinted with permission. All rights reserved, Copyright © International Library of Children's Literature branch of National Diet Library.

Figure 12.6   Courtesy of Young-hi Lee.

Figure 12.7   Courtesy of Young-hi Lee.

Figure 12.8   Courtesy of the French National Library, Francois Mitterrand (BNF).

Figure 12.9   Courtesy of the Biblioteca Apostolica Vaticana, Borg. R.F. Messicano 1, p. 56.

Figure 12.10   Courtesy of the State Library of Victoria, La Trobe Picture Collection.

Figure 12.11   Courtesy of the Library of Congress, American Memory Project.

Figure 12.12   Courtesy of Terry Smith UCSB.

Figure 12.13   Courtesy of Alfonso Cardenas.

Figure 12.14   Courtesy of Eckerd College, Dolphin Research Project.

Figure 12.15   Reprinted with permission of the Rare Book, Manuscript and Special Collections Library, Duke University.

Figure 12.16   Courtesy of Sayeed Choudhury.

Figure 12.17   Courtesy of Bill Burmingham.

Figure 12.18   From Informedia Digital Video Library, Carnegie Mellon University, news images copyright CNN. © 2004 Cable News Network LP, LLLP. Used with permission.

Figure 12.19   Courtesy of the Cuneiform Digital Library Initiative.

Figure 12.20   Reprinted with Permission of Marc Levoy, Stanford University.

Figure 12.21   Courtesy of Peter Allen, Columbia University Robotics Lab.

Figure 12.22   (b) Courtesy of Dr. Edgar Bruck, Professional School Wiesbaden.

Figure 12.23   CT reprinted with permission of the University of Texas.

Figure 12.24   Courtesy of Prof. Jezekiel Ben-Arie, E.C.E Department, University of Illinois at Chicago.

Figure 12.25   Courtesy of Princeton Search Engine for 3D Models, http://shape.cs.princeton.edu.

Figure 12.26   Courtesy of the Library of Congress, American Memory Project.

Figure 12.28   Courtesy of the Astrophysical Research Consortium (ARC) and the Sloan Digital Sky Survey (SDSS) Collaboration, http://www.sdss.org.

Figure 12.29   Image provided by the IRIS Consortium, in cooperation with the US Geological Survey and with support from the National Science Foundation.

Figure 12.30   Reprinted with permission from the Merit, Opulence, and the Buddhist Network of Wealth Project.

Preface

Changes Since the First Edition

Digital library research and practice has exploded since the first edition of this book, led by the growth of the Web as an interface and access route for information retrieval on a global basis. Online content has flooded onto the Web from publishers, libraries, museums, undergraduates, and practically anyone else with a keyboard or scanner. Library catalogs, museum exhibitions, and historic manuscripts are now available in this format, along with the ubiquitous advertisements and product manuals. A uniform interface has encouraged the proliferation of online content. For instance, in mid-2003 Google claimed to be indexing more than 3 billion Web pages. The Web has more than 150 terabytes of text today, more than all but the very largest research libraries.

Unfortunately, the economic and legal problems discussed in the first edition are still with us. Since the original publication, we have witnessed the dot-com explosion and crash. Despite the many startups and new ventures devoted to online information, we are still looking for a sustainable way to support digital libraries. The copyright tangle has become yet more difficult as a result of the worldwide extension of the period of copyright by 20 years and aggressive steps by the recorded music industry to enforce online restrictions.

The updates in this second edition focus largely on the impact of the Web, as well as on new digital library research projects. For the first time, the average person recognizes something that comes from a digital library research project: Google. This spin-off from the Stanford University Digital Library project, run by Hector Garcia-Molina, is now responsible for more than half the searches done on the Web—more than 250 million searches per day on average. Other research projects that are currently revolutionizing digital libraries include work with fossils, artwork, new and classical manuscripts, architecture, and an array of other innovative online content. The research frontier has moved beyond text, creating large-scale digitization of sounds, images, and even 3-dimensional models.

Why Digital Libraries, and Why this Book?

In 1938 H. G. Wells dreamed of a world encyclopedia in which all human knowledge would be available everywhere, a "complete planetary memory for all mankind." In 1945 Vannevar Bush (leader of American science during the war) had a vision of a scholar able to consult any book by tapping its code on a keyboard. In 1998 the State of the Union message expressed a similar hope: a society in which "every child can stretch a hand across a keyboard and reach every book ever written, every painting ever painted, every symphony ever composed." Today we can build these systems. A million books are already online, along with tens of thousands of art images and musical compositions. We can read, hear, and see an incredible variety of material. Language students can listen to news in many languages from Internet radio stations. Travelers can locate bus timetables for places ten thousand miles away. Some may be frightened by the quantity of information or the potential threat to privacy; others may be frustrated by the difficulty in getting to the information they want or by the extent to which their children (and others) spend time "surfing the Web." Others see online information as our best chance of education for everyone, all the time. Vannevar Bush wrote that great libraries were only "nibbled at by a few"; today they can be accessible to everyone.

This book is about how such digital libraries are built, what they mean to us, and what remains to be done to achieve them. Both the technology and the impact of the digital library will be given their due. Will digitization be something that expands our choice and availability of information, or something that restricts it? Will digital libraries help educate the world, entertain it, or both? Of course, the outcome to questions such as these is not yet known. By making a few languages (such as English) so dominant, the Web could contribute to the withering away of languages spoken by only a few. Or, by making it easy for those languages to preserve their literature and connect their speakers, the Web could help preserve the world's rarer languages. The path we take will be affected by our intentions. As Alice once asked the Cheshire Cat, "Would you tell me, please, which way I ought to go from here?" And as the cat was known to answer, "That depends a good deal on where you want to get to." At least, we can try to understand our choices.

Digital libraries combine the structuring and gathering of information which libraries and archives have always done with the digital representation made possible by computers. Digital information can be accessed rapidly around the world, copied for preservation without error, stored compactly, and searched very quickly. No conventional back of the book index compares with the text search engines we now have. As with its physical counterpart, a true digital library also includes principles for what is included and how the collection is organized. The Web, the overwhelming example of a shared worldwide collection of information, has been turned into many digital libraries by individuals or groups who select, organize, and catalog large numbers of pages. Unlike earlier generations of online services, the Web is accessible to many without training in information use, which has made digital libraries important to far more people than ever cared about them in the past. The Duke of Wellington opposed railways, because they would encourage the poor to move about. What would he have thought of such free access to information?

Over the centuries the world has changed from one in which few people could even do arithmetic to one in which pocket calculators are given away in promotions. Similarly, information has gone from scarce to so common that some may fear that creativity will be discouraged with so much old material available. When thinking about digital libraries, many mundane questions arise, including how to convert material to digital form, how to deliver it to users, and how to pay for it. But some questions go to the key issues of libraries: What is their value to society? How can that value be preserved in digital form? What will the new organizations look like? and What services should they provide? We need to know not only how to build digital libraries, but why—which depends a good deal on where we "want to get to."

Audience

This book is practical. It addresses the problem of a librarian who wishes to digitize material and needs to understand what kinds of conversion technologies are available, or who wishes to purchase digital material and needs to know what can be done with it. It also addresses the problems of a computer scientist trying to understand the library applications of some of the relevant algorithms. More important, it addresses the practical problems of costs and economics, which are today more of an obstacle than the technology. Looking forward, it helps both librarians and computer scientists answer questions such as Will we be able digitize video economically? and How can we search video on a computer? On the most general level, it points out the issues that will affect libraries and their users as digital technology continues to take over functions traditionally done with paper and printing press.

Approach

In writing a book on digital libraries, one tries to strike a balance between today's "hot topics" and material that is known to be of permanent value. There are many excellent references in the literature on databases (most particularly for digital libraries, Witten, Moffatt, and Bell, 1999), and to avoid overlap, I have not gone into the details of such here. By contrast, the economics of digital libraries and the legal issues around intellectual property are newly developed, rapidly changing, and not as well served by existing literature (although the books by Larry Lessig, 2001, and Hal Varian, 1998, are certainly excellent). Collections and preservation are topics which are fundamentally similar to traditional library activities in these areas and can be discussed largely by analogy. Particularly challenging is any attempt at surveying what is being done around the world in digital library projects. This changes so rapidly that anything will be out of date by the time it is written, let alone read, and so I tried merely to give some examples, rather than pretend to be comprehensive as of any particular date.

The overwhelming motivation behind this book has been a practical one: to give specific details of how things are done or could be done, rather than to speak in general terms. Principles are valuable, and I have included some, but what I have always wanted when searching for information is useful detail about what is going on or how something can be accomplished. A book on carpentry needs to discuss wood, perhaps even some ecology; but if all it does is discuss the threat to the rain forest, it won't help someone build a bookcase. There are other books that discuss the *wonders* of the computer age. This book is supposed to tell you how to help bring them about. There are other books that discuss the *dangers* of the computer age. This book is supposed to tell you how to avoid them.

Content

The text is divided into two parts: the first half is *what* and the second half is *why*. In each half, there is one overview chapter and some detail. Thus, the first half of the book deals with building digital libraries and contains most of the technology. Chapter 1 is the history and overview of both libraries and technology, followed by a set of chapters on the parts of digital libraries: text in Chapter 2, image in Chapter 3, and sound and multimedia in Chapter 4.

How to organize and distribute the information is in the next set of chapters: classification and indexing in Chapter 5, networks and distribution in Chapter 6, and presentation in Chapter 7.

The second half will then discuss the importance and impact of digital libraries and their relationship to other important disciplines: user needs in Chapter 8, preservation in Chapter 9, economics in Chapter 10, and law in Chapter 11. Returning to digital libraries, Chapter 12 is devoted to scientific applications and Chapter 13 to cultural/historical digital libraries. Finally, Chapter 14 addresses future questions and policy issues.

Other Resources

Basically, you find out about new developments on the Web. There are excellent books, but no one book can cover everything nor be revised often enough to stay current. Even journal articles are usually better found online, where newer material is available and quick links between articles are easy. There are few references to specific Web pages in the text; they were deliberately avoided since Web pages change so frequently (the average life of a URL is 100 days) that many would be invalid by the time the book appeared. Instead, readers should rely on the search engines; it's usually faster to find the article online than even in your own office. I may have cited the official form of an article to be sure that a reader 10 years hence would know what was meant, but I nearly always read it online.

Acknowledgments

Half the lines in this book changed from the first draft to the first edition, and half or more again have changed for the second. My thanks to the many people who have helped in this process. This includes both the editor of the first edition at Morgan Kaufmann, Jennifer Mann, whose enthusiasm and comments were particularly welcome and supportive for months, and the similarly enthusiastic, patient, and helpful editors for this edition, Lothlórien Homet and Corina Derman. Thanks also to the production editor of this edition, Dan Stone. The referees of the first edition, including Dan Atkins, Martin Dillon, Dale Flecker, Edward Fox, Marianne Gaunt, Peter Hart, David Levy, Wendy Lougee, Greg Newby, Scott Stevens, Hal Varian, Donald Waters, and Terry Winograd, made many useful comments, as have friends of mine such as Michael Bianchi, who read early versions of the manuscript. For the second edition Ed Fox and Christine Borgman have been most helpful. I thank all for their assistance and remind the reader that those mistakes which remain are attributable to my own stubbornness. Thanks as well to my collaborators over the years and to the many researchers working in the area of digital libraries.

Evolution of Libraries

This book is about the practicalities of making a digital library. Sometimes, however, it helps to know where you are coming from, and not just where you are going. So this chapter will review both library and technical history in an effort to discern what might change and what might survive as we introduce new technology. Santayana wrote, "Those who do not study the mistakes of history are condemned to repeat them," and Engels said that history always repeats itself, the first time as tragedy and the second time as farce.

1.1 Why Digital Libraries?

Users of the World Wide Web are familiar with the ability to find Swiss railway schedules or the list of World Series winners on their screens. To some, digital information is a fantastic resource of new powers; to others, dealing with all this online information is a frightening notion on top of dealing with the 300 pounds of paper used in the United States per person per year alone. Universities worry that undergraduates waste too much time "surfing the Web," and everyone is frustrated by the inability to find what they want when they want it.

The response to these concerns should not be despair, but rather organization. A digital library, a collection of information which is both digitized and organized, gives us power we never had with traditional libraries. As mentioned in the introduction, Vannevar Bush, in 1945, wrote that the great research libraries were only "nibbled at by a few"; he also said that selecting items from them was a "stone adze in the hands of a cabinetmaker." What does digital technology offer us instead? Will digital libraries deal with floods of information? Will they help with the "information glut," the "information war," and the many other buzzwords of the "information age"?

A digital library can be searched for any phrase; it can be accessed all over the world; and it can be copied without error. This is why digital libraries are coming. They address traditional problems of finding information, of delivering it to users, and of preserving it for the future. Digital information takes less space than paper information and thus may help libraries reduce costs. But, more important, they can provide a level of service never before attainable—delivery of information to the user's desk, search capability by individual words and sentences, and information that does not decay with time, whether words, sounds, or images.

What does it take to build a digital library? You need to get stuff *into* it; you need to be able to get stuff *out* of it; and you need to be able to *pay* for it. Beyond that, what will the digital library mean? What are the social effects likely to be when digital libraries are widely used by scholars and researchers, by students and teachers, and by the general public?

First, the digital library must have content. It can either be new material prepared digitally or old material converted to digital form. It can be bought, donated, or converted locally from previously purchased items. Content then needs to be stored and retrieved. Information is widely found in the form of text stored as characters, and images stored as scans. These images are frequently scans of printed pages, as well as illustrations or photographs. More recently, audio, video, and interactive material is accumulating rapidly in digital form, both newly generated and converted from older material.

Once stored, the content must be made accessible. Retrieval systems are needed to let users find things; this is relatively straightforward for text and still a subject of research for pictures, sounds, and video. Content must then be delivered to the user; a digital library must contain interface software that lets people see and hear its contents. A digital library must also have a "preservation department" of sorts; there must be some process to ensure that what is available today will still be available tomorrow. The rogue user with a knife cutting out pages may not be a problem in a digital library, but computer systems have their own vulnerabilities, including some caused purely by neglect.

Libraries also need a way to pay for digital collections, and this is a major issue. Certainly in a transition period, the old services cannot be abandoned immediately, and thus new services must be funded in addition to old. Finding a way to fund digital libraries is the most frustrating problem for librarians today. Although economics is the current hurdle, it may not be the most puzzling problem tomorrow. Digital libraries are going to change the social system by which information is collected and transferred. A digital library is not just a collection of disk drives; it will be part of a culture. We need to decide how the typical citizen will get information, as well as the overall importance of information transfer to democracy; we need to decide how to preserve the accessibility of information while increasing its diversity. Libraries have a key role to play in these decisions.

So with all the needs for digital libraries, why do we not yet have them? In 1964, Arthur Samuel predicted that by 1984 paper libraries would disappear, except at museums (Samuel, 1964). Why hasn't this happened? The primary reason is that we cannot easily find the $1 billion or so to fund the mechanical conversion of 100 million books to electronic form, plus the additional and probably larger sum to compensate the copyright owners for most of those books. The economics of digital libraries are tangled with those of digital publishing, the entire networking industry, and questions of security and fraud. Other reasons delaying digital libraries include the very real preferences of the many people who like books as they are (who even like card catalogs); the issue of access for those who cannot afford computers or online services; the challenges of providing a digital library in an easy-to-use and comfortable form; and the many questions reflecting an arguably sensible reluctance to trade a system that works for an unknown one. To some librarians and users, digitizing books is an example of fixing "what ain't broke." Nevertheless, costs are improving, current publications are becoming widely available in electronic form, and we are exploring economic methods of supporting digital information. These trends will make electronic terminals the route by which first students and scholars and then the general public will obtain information.

1.2   History of Libraries

Today, after all, is not the first time that society has had the opportunity of completely changing the way it passes on information. History tells us that there have been many major changes in both the way we distribute and store information and how it is used in society. The music of Bach has flourished on the harpsichord and piano, on vinyl and CD; it has been used in church services and concert halls, and turned into shopping mall Muzak. Information distribution has moved from asking one's neighbors (still common) to formal classification systems, reviews, advertisements, and countless other ways of arranging information and notifying people about it. Indexing and search systems have been added, first on paper and now in electronic form.

What is perhaps surprising is that technology does not always drive the changes in how information is handled. Technological determinism, the idea that it is hopeless to alter the changes forced on us by new inventions, isn't always right. Sometimes it is new inventions that push us in a particular direction; other times it is changes in society. Books, or more properly manuscipts, were sold before they were printed in quantity. Monks in medieval cathedrals kept libraries and copied books for each other by hand. There was an organized medieval book trade, and when printed books replaced manuscripts as the main item of trade, much of the previous infrastructure remained in place. Moving forward, the eighteenth century saw massive changes in literacy and in the kind of material that was written and published, without a great deal of change in the technology of printing. The nineteenth century saw much greater technological advance, but less change in what people did as a result. What, then, will happen as a result of the current technology changes?

For more than a decade, nearly every word printed and typed has been prepared on a computer. Paradoxically, until very recently most reading has been from paper. Now, digital distribution of email, faxes, and of course Web pages has exploded and is breaking this logjam. We would like digital information to be available to everyone, to be preserved for the future, and to enhance our technology, our commerce, and our societies. Libraries provide us with information in the form of books; they let scholars read the books of centuries past, and they deliver current information to businesses. What will they do with electronic information?

If conventional libraries were just to sit and wait, they would not likely become a major provider of digital information. For universities and libraries to retain their status and relevance, they have to participate in the new digital world, as many are indeed doing. There are many social goals that are important for libraries, beyond the simple ability to pile up books or disks.

Digital technology is making it easier to write books, easier to save their content, and in fact easier to save everything being written. This will mean that more and more information is available. It will render the *ability* to find information increasingly important and the *possession* of it less so. Libraries will find it cheaper and easier to store electronic information, as information drifts from paper to computer format. New material is often available digitally today; it will make up more and more of libraries as time goes on. Digital information can be either easier to generate and fetch, or harder. We have a public choice of which goal to pursue. We can find ourselves either with a limited set of sources, or a much wider diversity of them. Technology can move us to few resources or to many, depending on how we apply it. We, as a society, need to make this choice so that we improve accessibility and diversity. The same argument that Benjamin Franklin used to justify the postal service now applies to digital libraries: for a good democracy, the citizens need access to information.

Figure 1.1, for example, shows the Allston neighborhood of Boston in a 1903 map, a modern map, an aerial photograph, and a Landsat photograph taken from space. Making this level of information available with a few keystrokes has applications in education, historical research, and land use planning. For example, note the wide areas adjacent to the Charles River that were indicated as swamps in 1903 and are now dry land; although filled in, even a modern builder would want to know that this area was once wet. The resolution of the aerial photograph is one-half meter; the Landsat imagery is at about 15 meters resolution. Better satellite photography is now available commercially from the Quickbird or Ikonos cameras.

In building systems, whether of maps or books, we must avoid too much focus just on technology and economics. Libraries are pointless if no one uses them, and Christine Borgman (1986, 1996) of UCLA has explained that even online catalogs, let alone online documents, are so hard to use. Experiments with users have shown that the more someone tells a librarian about what they want, the more likely their quest for information will be successful. Building digital libraries is not just a question of piling up disk drives; it involves creating an entire organization of machines and people, perhaps even a culture, in which we are able to find information and use it. The social implications of a world in which information is distributed almost without institutions are not understood; what does this mean for universities, for education, and for publishers?

Information transport has been a key issue in both the past and present. How we move information from one person to another and how we preserve it from one generation to another are persistent questions. Unfortunately, attempts to manipulate information transport pose another persistent issue, namely, efforts to direct what knowledge will be available to people. Depending on motive and point of view, this may be called defining a curriculum, propaganda, advertising, or censorship. The Chinese emperor Shih Huang Ti tried to burn all books, hoping that future historians would say that all knowledge started in his reign. As a democracy, the United States has held the belief that the widest possible distribution of knowledge is best: "the education of the common people will be attended to, convinced that on their good senses we may rely . . . for the preservation . . . of liberty." [Thomas Jefferson in a letter to James Madison, 1787.]

Oliver Wendell Holmes noted that the First Amendment "would not protect a man in falsely shouting fire in a theater." Imposed limits are normally more restrictive on the most widely distributed media. We accept obscenity limits on

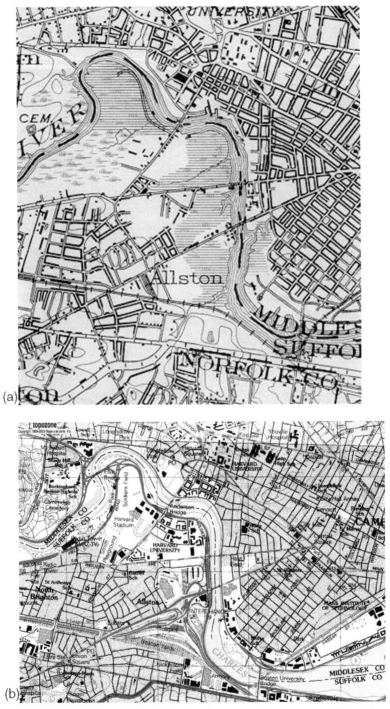

Figure 1.1 The Allston neighborhood of Boston: (a) 1903 map; (b) modern map; (c) digital orthophotoquad (from aerial photography); (d) Landsat space photograph.

Figure 1.1 Continued.

broadcast TV more than on cable TV; we consider a published libel more serious than a spoken slander. Some countries have tried hard to limit information distribution; the former Soviet Union drove its writers to underground publication (*samizdat*). Today, China and Singapore are examples of countries trying to control the spread of electronic information. But electronic media are hard to control and are often private rather than government-owned.

In contrast to attempts at restraints, there have been dreams of widely available knowledge, or at least of making knowledge more accessible. The French encylopedists hoped in the eighteenth century to produce a single compilation of knowledge, as did H. G. Wells, as do more modern futurists attempting to project a model of how people will find information. And, for all time, there has been no single source. It is not enough to know just Aristotle, and neither is it likely that just one source of knowledge on the Internet will do.

The works of Homer have been a part of Western culture for over 2000 years. Once, that meant the presence of a bard who could recite the Iliad and Odyssey from memory. Later, it meant a manuscript, and still later it meant a printed book. Today, Homer (and all the rest of classical Greek literature) is available on the Perseus CD-ROM. Will that become a change comparable to the invention of printing, as is often suggested?

Printing, of course, made books much more widely available. The early presses, however, were still expensive. Through the centuries, technology, most particularly in paper-making, mechanical presses, and typesetting machinery, steadily lowered the cost of books. A single man at a hand-press might print 500–750 sheets a day, while modern printing plants turn out hundreds of thousands of sheets per employee. Paper used to cost a day's wages for 24 sheets; now it is so cheap we have to recycle it to minimize the space taken in landfills. A compositor setting type by hand in the eighteenth century was expected to set 1000 ens per hour, or 3 to 4 words per minute. A Linotype operator could set about 10 words per minute, and a modern keyboarder can do 50 words per minute easily. Combining all of these effects, the *London Daily Journal* of March 4, 1728 cost 3 half-pennies for two sides of one sheet, while the *Times* (London) of 1905 cost 1 penny for 24 pages, or a price per page one-tenth as much. Books and newspapers changed from upper-class luxuries into something accessible to everyone.

As books became more common, large libraries started to include hundreds of thousands of books rather than the dozens of books found in medieval libraries. As a rule, universities become the owners of the largest non-national libraries. In the United States, for example, after the Library of Congress, only the New York Public Library and the Boston Public Library have collections to compare with those of the largest university libraries. Table 1.1 shows the holdings of major university and non-university libraries. For international comparison, the holdings

Table 1.1 Number of volumes held by major US libraries.

	Volumes Held		
Institution	1910	1995	2002
Library of Congress	1.8 M	23.0 M	26.0 M
Harvard	0.8 M	12.9 M	14.9 M
Yale	.55 M	9.5 M	10.9 M
U. Illinois (Urbana)	.1 M	8.5 M	9.9 M
U. California (Berkeley)	.24 M	8.1 M	9.4 M
New York Public Library	1.4 M	7.0 M	11.5 M
U. Michigan	.25 M	6.7 M	7.6 M
Boston Public Library	1.0 M	6.5 M	7.5 M

Table 1.2 Number of volumes held by major global libraries.

	Number of Volumes Held				
Institution	Earlier	1910	1996	2002	Former name, if any
British Library	240 K (1837)	2 M	15 M	18 M	British Museum Library
Cambridge Univ.	330 (1473)	500 K	3.5 M	7 M	N/A
Bodleian (Oxford)	2 K (1602)	800 K	4.8 M	6 M	N/A
Bibliothèque Nationale de France	250 K (1800)	3 M	11 M	12 M	Bibliothèque Nationale
National Diet Library	N/A	500 K	4.1 M	8 M	Imperial Cabinet Library
Biblioteca Alexandrina	533 K (48BC)			240 K	Library of Alexandria

of some of the other major libraries of the world are shown in Table 1.2. Canfora (1990) gives the historical figures, and the library websites give their current holdings. (There are some variations in the definition of "volumes held," such that Table 1.2 includes the holdings of the National Sound Archive in the British Library totals. Note, too, that in counting the holdings of the ancient Library of Alexandria, 24 rolls have been taken as the equivalent of one printed volume.)

Figure 1.2 shows the steepness of the growth in university libraries in the United States around 1900 (Rider, 1944; Leach, 1976).

Although Ecclesiastes said "of making many books there is no end," the concept of the so-called information glut and information overload is mostly a twentieth century idea. Specialization today has destroyed the eighteenth century ideal of an individual who would know everything. William Blake was

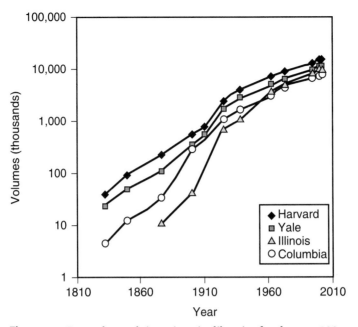

Figure 1.2 Rate of growth in university libraries for the past 100 years.

an example of such: a poet, an artist, and the inventor of copper-plate litho-graphy. "Exceptional" in the nineteenth century might mean excelling in multiple areas: William Morris made exceptional wallpaper, books, furniture, and tapestries, and was best known in his own lifetime as a poet. Today, it can take decades to become an expert in a narrow subdiscipline.

In 1951 there were 10,000 periodicals published; today there are 160,000 (Meadows, 1993, 1998; Kling, 2004), with logarithmic growth expected as shown in Figure 1.3. Kling estimates that today there are more than 100,000 scholarly journals alone.

A more recent set of numbers is available from R. R. Bowker, the organization that issues ISSN (International Standard Serial Number) codes for periodicals in the United States. Figure 1.4 shows the continuing growth in periodical (not just scholarly journal) publication in the United States from 1991 to 2002 (ISSN, 2004).

The concept of being overwhelmed by information was popularized by Derek de la Solla Price (1986). The expansion of the number of journals in recent years and the increase in their subscription costs has been led by the commercial publishers. The effort made by some libraries to collect a very large number of scientific journals encouraged some publishers to charge what would earlier

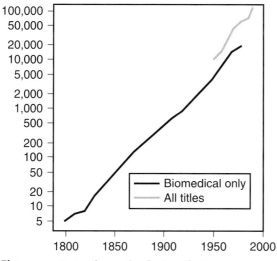

Figure 1.3 Rate of growth of scientific journals.

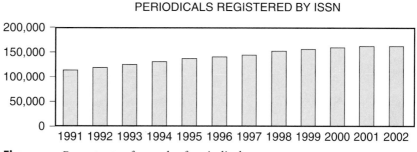

Figure 1.4 Recent rate of growth of periodicals.

have been thought enormous sums for subscriptions. As a result, some journals now cost over $10,000 per year. The increases in price pose continuing problems for libraries. The Andrew W. Mellon Foundation funded a study (Cummings et al., 1992) that documented the loss of purchasing power in libraries over the previous thirty years. Each year during the 1970s, research libraries bought about 1.4% fewer books, while the number of books published increased by more than 2%. These problems continue unabated. Kryillidou (2000) shows that a near tripling of library dollars spent on journals between 1985 and 1999 bought 6% fewer journals. Thus, library collections have more and more gaps.

What is all this information worth? Public justification for libraries has changed over the years. Once upon a time (in the nineteenth century) both education and libraries were seen as important for preserving democracy. Now the idea that encouraging information transfer will help the economy is very popular; state after state tries to attract business by boasting about the advanced telecommunication services that are available. Nevertheless, it is difficult to prove the value of better access to information. Sometimes people think this is obvious. How could one not want access to information? What is the point of piling up books and discs if they cannot be found again? And yet, all library projects today have great difficulty justifying themselves financially. Why should a university spend 4% of its budget on the library (a typical US number)? Why not 2%? Or 1%? For that matter, why not 10%?

Fritz Machlup and Peter Drucker have written of the importance of information and "knowledge workers." But recently there has been considerable controversy about the value of information technology to the economy. This started with Steven Roach (1991), an economist at Morgan Stanley, who suggested that the slowdown in US productivity that started in the mid-1970s, and which most economists attribute to the effects of the oil price increases of 1973, were caused by investment in computers that did not return comparable economic value. Roach argued, for example, that banks which invested heavily in information technology did not show greater profits than banks which did not.

He was refuted by MIT professor Eric Brynjolfsson (Brynjolfsson and Hitt, 1993; Brynjolfsson, 2003), who started by finding that trucking companies which invested in computers did better than trucking companies which invested in trucks, and who has continued to find gains in overall productivity resulting from IT investments. The argument has raged back and forth ever since, with more recent numbers showing better results for computer investment. Thomas Landauer's book (1995) showed that the communications industries made real productivity gains from capital spending on information technology. And Brynjolfsson claims the return on investment in information technology is 54% for manufacturing and even higher, 68%, for all businesses. Of course, all of these discussions reflect investment in computing for many purposes, not just information handling. A recent review by Dedrick et al. (2003) emphasized that "at both the firm and the country level, greater investment in IT is associated with greater productivity growth."

At the end of the 1990s the entire discussion about the value of IT got mixed up with politics and with the dot-com boom. Claims were heard that 30% of US economic growth was the result of the IT industry; the basis for this statement was unclear. The tech-stock collapse of 2000 and on has silenced some of the more vocal assertions for the benefits of IT, but has left the basic argument about productivity without a clear resolution (but see Jorgensen, 2002, and Sichel, 2000).

Arguments about the value of information, unfortunately, have little impact on conventional library operations. Many major public libraries have had budget cuts requiring shorter hours or reduced purchases. And many major universities are reducing their library budgets. Why society values information so little is unclear. On the one hand, the greatest success stories of economic growth over the last 20 years are not based on new innovation, but on adaptations of research done in other countries. Several countries combine an enviable record in Nobel Prizes per capita with a loss of manufacturing industry, as the inventions from these countries are manufactured elsewhere. One would expect information transfer to be essential for business growth. Yet greater commercial success is not found in the countries that have the greatest libraries in the world. Skeptics ask: If the three largest libraries in the world are in Washington, London, and Moscow, but larger economic growth is found in Beijing, Bangalore, and Seoul perhaps having a large library is not all that important for economic success?

Perhaps the greatest boost to the public perception of information value came during the Second World War. Not only were particular devices, such as the bomb, microwave radar, and the jet airplane invented, but entire academic subjects, such as operations research, were created and applied to wartime problems. Nuclear physicists moved in the public image from a group with no public relevance to a status near that of the gods. Computers were also invented during the war, although nobody knew it (see section 1.4).

1.3   Vannevar Bush

During the Second World War the most important paper for digital libraries was written: "As We May Think," by Vannevar Bush. Vannevar Bush (whom we quoted earlier) had been a professor and administrator at MIT, and was the head of U.S. science during the war. Bush published his paper in the *Atlantic Monthly* for July 1945. He wrote about the great scientific progress that had been made during the war and said that this represented our ability to use scientists in teams. Until the war, scientists largely worked alone or in small, independent research groups. During the war, large teams of scientists and engineers working together were able to make enormous strides.

Microwave radar, for example, was invented, built, and actually used during the three and a half years that the United States was in World War II. Compare that with the 10 years that it took in the 1970s and 1980s to introduce a new microwave radar transmission system into long distance telephony. Nuclear physics before the war had the public reputation that Byzantine philosophy might have today: it was considered an entirely ivory-tower subject of no possible practical use. The atomic bomb turned this around (and temporarily resulted in an enormous reputation for physicists). Bush, writing before August 1945, could not mention the bomb, but he had plenty of other examples to write about. He felt the enormous technological progress was a result of learning to organize scientific effort, of changing scientific research from a craft into a factory process and being able to combine the work of many, the mass production of knowledge.

Bush asked to what peacetime purpose we might put this new ability to organize science. He suggested that the best goal would not be another specific engineering goal, such as commercial airplanes, but the general purpose of organizing knowledge. His hope was that scholars could work together themselves. Richard Hamming, inventor of error-correcting codes, once wrote: "Newton said that he saw so far because he stood on the shoulders of giants. In computer science we stand on each other's feet." Bush wanted a breakthrough in accessibility of information, using technology to organize and retrieve books, journals, and notes.

In planning his system, which he called the Memex, Bush relied entirely on barcoded microfilm. He knew about digital computers, but he had grown up with (and made his reputation on) analog computers, which rely on currents and voltages to model quantities, instead of representing quantities as numbers. Bush was never entirely comfortable with digital machines. He did have several very prescient ideas, however. He suggested that individuals would plant links from one piece of knowledge to another, which he called "trails" of information. These trails are the precursors of today's hypertext and the Web. Bush also emphasized the ease with which one could put one's own information into the system. In his article he described how a handwritten page would be photographed and placed into the microfilm archive. Thus, the Memex could include a regular library (he imagined a 1-million-book research library on film), plus one's own notes, plus the notes of one's friends. This range of material was not available in one place until recently, with the invention of the Web; traditionally your notes were in your office, and the library was a big building across campus. Bush also provided a very straightforward interface, based entirely on pictures of pages. Figure 1.5 shows a diagram of the Memex as envisaged by a *LIFE Magazine* artist in 1945.

One thing Bush did not predict was free text searching. In his vision everything was categorized and indexed by people, often by many different people with varied slants on the items they were describing. He talks about the impact of the Turkish bow on Europe; such an item might be on the "trails" of people studying military history, social history, strength of materials, ethnology, anthropology, and so on. But he did not imagine in his first paper people simply keying in "show me every article with the phrase 'Turkish bow' in it." Bush instead envisaged a community of scholars, all helping each other by indexing and relating all the different items published in a library. We have much better technology than he had; we did not have the community he wanted until the rise of the Web.

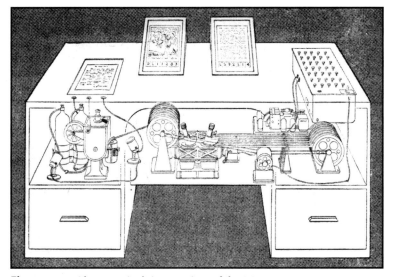

Figure 1.5 *Life Magazine's* impression of the Memex.

The emphasis Bush placed on community and on individual labeling of information was in stark contrast to another leading paper of the late 1940s, Warren Weaver's essay on machine translation. In 1947 Warren Weaver, also an MIT professor, suggested that machines could translate languages; he knew of their cryptanalytic abilities and suggested that Turkish could be viewed merely as an encoded form of English and deciphered by machines.

Now it is certainly possible that foreign language can be used as a code. The United States Navy, during the war, used Navajos as "code-talkers" who relayed messages from ship to ship, talking in Navajo (a language not studied in Japan). But translating a foreign language is much harder than deciphering a cipher message. Although Weaver's essay stimulated a great deal of work on machine translation and an entire field of statistical approaches to language analysis, it has not yet produced widely accepted machine translation software.

Weaver did set up a different thread of development of how material stored on computers would be accessed. Bush, remember, thought in terms of human classification and what we today might call "knowledge structures," while Weaver thought in terms of statistical processing. For the next 40 years, we continued to have research in both areas. Artificial intelligence researchers studied ways of representing knowledge in some fundamental way, while the retrieval groups mostly studied ways of manipulating isolated words and treating them statistically. There were numerous discussions about "understanding," with AI researchers suggesting that until computers could in some sense understand natural language, they would not be able to perform speech recognition or language translation; whereas the IR researchers demonstrated that at least information retrieval could be performed to some degree with programs that were fairly straightforward.

The contrast between Bush's emphasis on human classification and the Weaver strategy of pure statistical analysis has lasted for four decades. For most of that time statistical processing seemed to be winning. It did not look as if the creation of large masses of material with manually defined linkages between subjects was ever going to get the resources, whether volunteer or paid, that would make it possible. Text displays with links from one place to another, like cross-references but appearing automatically when clicked with a mouse, are called *hypertext*. Some of the experimental university hypertext systems found that it was hard to create the hypertext resources and that students did not quickly add to them while taking the courses for which the hypertext system was designed. The rise of the Web suddenly reversed this. After decades of increased emphasis on statistics, we suddenly have a revival of interest in manual linkages and a vast number of them actually implemented across the world. This is a social victory for the ideas of Vannevar Bush.

Bush predicted many other technical changes. He foresaw instant photography, photocopying ("dry photography"), electronic telephone switches, and other hardware advances, nearly all of which have come to pass. He also predicted speech recognition and some other software advances, which have run afoul of the fact that although we can manipulate vast quantities of information with computers, we cannot understand it all. But the basic conception of storing vast amounts of information and accessing it at will, and the identification of this goal as a target for an entire generation of researchers, is Bush's great contribution to the field.

1.4   Computer Technology

Computing technology started fitfully in the late nineteenth century, with mechanical machines such as Hermann Hollerith's punched card sorting devices for use with the U. S. Census. Electronic computers and digital storage, of course, are the key inventions which make possible digital libraries.

The earliest electronic computer was not a "number-cruncher," but a language processing machine. It was a 1943 machine called "Colossus" at the British code-breaking organization, Bletchley Park, shown in Figure 1.6. Colossus was destroyed at the end of the war, but is being rebuilt at the Bletchley Park museum. The popular misconception that computers started out doing arithmetic arose because the success of the Allied cryptanalysts was kept secret for 30 years after the war. Alan Turing, the founder of theoretical computer science, was one of

The original Colossus during the Second World War

Figure 1.6   Colossus—the first electronic computer.

the mathematicians and designers at Bletchley, and many other early researchers knew of the machine and were influenced by it.

Although the existence of Colossus was a secret, the vacuum tube computer ENIAC in Philadelphia was publicized and often considered the beginning of computing. Some of its engineers moved to Remington Rand and there built the first successful commercial electronic computer, the Univac. Univac I filled a room; now, much more powerful machines fit on a chip. Figure 1.7 indicates the progress in transistors per chip over the decades. For comparison, the ENIAC of 1947 had 18,000 vacuum tubes.

Needless to say, there have been many significant advances since then, for example, in computer architecture (notably microprogramming) as well as in device design. The speed of processors has increased as well, although somewhat less dramatically than their complexity. In 1961 the IBM 7090 executed instructions in 2 microseconds; a 1 microsecond instruction timing was still fairly common in the late 1970s. With the rise of better processor designs and smaller features on each chip, speeds have now increased to advertised processor speeds over 1 GHz—superficially a 1000-fold speed increase, although the use of microprogramming means that these numbers are not directly comparable.

Improvements in the technology to store digital information have been among the most impressive in any field. Cheap storage makes digital libraries not only possible, but affordable, and completely changes our view of what is possible. In the 1960s a researcher could just barely take one long text and store it as ASCII (the American Standard Code for Information Interchange is the most common

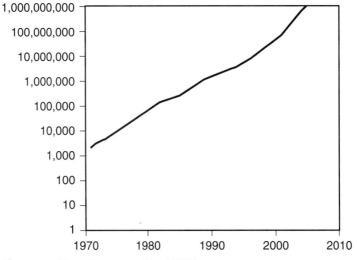

Figure 1.7 Transistors per chip (CPU).

way of representing one letter in one computer byte); today, huge volumes of text are stored commercially and researchers experiment with moderate-sized collections of video.

In general, really fast and accessible memory is more expensive than slower memory. Thus, computers often have hierarchies of memory, with three levels of storage. The best memory involves no large moving objects; it is all electronic, and thus it is 'random-access', meaning that it takes the same amount of time to access any item in memory. Today this is called RAM, and the access time is measured in nanoseconds. The next level is typically built of magnetic disks, and since some physical device (a read head) has to move across the disk to access different portions, it takes substantially longer (milliseconds) to find a particular piece of information. However, once the read head is at a particular point, it can pick up a sequence of bits in times measured in microseconds. Per bit, disks are cheaper than RAM. The lowest level of storage will involve demountable devices, such as disk cartridges. It will have a still lower cost per bit, but it will take seconds to minutes to retrieve a cartridge and mount it in some kind of reading device. Memory is measured in bytes, with large quantities identified as gigabytes or terabytes. Table 1.3 lays out these quantities to help with visualization of common storage amounts.

Primary, random-access memory is now made from semiconductors, while disk drives are now the standard secondary storage technology. IBM built the first magnetic disk in 1956; it held 4.5 megabytes and cost $40,000. Figure 1.8 shows what happened for the next forty years in prices of disk storage.

Table 1.3 Memory sizes.

Unit	Exponent	Amount	Example
Byte	1	1 byte	One keystroke on a typewriter
		6 bytes	One word
		100 bytes	One sentence
Kilobyte	3	1000 bytes	Half a printed page; a tiny sketch
		10,000 bytes	One second of recorded speech; a small picture
		30,000 bytes	A scanned, compressed book page
		100,000 bytes	A medium-size, compressed color picture
		500,000 bytes	A novel (e.g., *Pride and Prejudice*)
Megabyte	6	1,000,000 bytes	A large novel (e.g., *Moby Dick*)
		5,000,000 bytes	The Bible
		10,000,000 bytes	A Mozart symphony, MP3-compressed
		20,000,000 bytes	A scanned book
		50,000,000 bytes	A 2-hour radio program
		500,000,000 bytes	A CD-ROM; the *Oxford English Dictionary*
Gigabyte	9	1,000,000,000 bytes	A shelf of scanned paper; or a section of bookstacks, keyed
		100,000,000,000 bytes	A current disk drive size
Terabyte	12	1,000,000,000,000 bytes	A million-volume library
		20 terabytes	The Library of Congress, as text
Petabyte	15	1000 terabytes	Very large scientific databases
		9 petabytes	Total storage at San Diego Supercomputer Center
Exabyte	18	A million terabytes	
		20 exabytes	About the total amount of information in the world
		5 exabytes	World disk production, 2001
		25 exabytes	World tape production, 2001

Disk prices have been declining rapidly; every 12 to 18 months the capacity available for the same price doubles. As it happens, internal memory prices have been declining at about the same rate. Thus, the justifications for multiple levels of memory, and all the system architecture decisions that go with that, remain the same. Thus, similar database software architectures continue to remain valid.

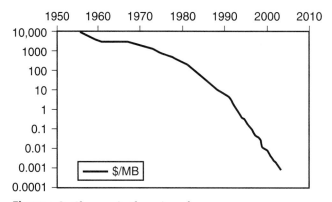

Figure 1.8 Changes in the price of memory.

Were the relative price changes to break step, database systems would have to be redesigned. Relatively cheaper RAM would produce in-memory database systems and favor techniques like OODBMS (object-oriented database management systems); relatively cheaper disks, by contrast, would turn us back to batch-like database system designs. What is changing is that seek times on disks are not coming down as fast as either total capacity or data rate; this is changing disk usage algorithms to be more like tape algorithms.

As recently as 2003, the 300-gigabyte disk drive was announced, and the price of disk storage dropped well under $1 per gigabyte. Consider what this means: in ASCII form, a 300,000-book library, something that would take 5 miles of shelf space, can fit on a 3.5-inch disk drive. Even an off-campus storage facility for such a library would cost at least half a million dollars; the digital equivalent is only a few hundred dollars. It is not surprising, therefore, to hear of corporations that have decided they don't need a paper library and can provide information services more efficiently online. When Wilf Lancaster wrote his book on the paperless library in 1967, people debunked it, but it's here today in many companies.

Disk drive reliability is also increasing, with five-year warranties now commonplace. However, disks are still subject to "head-crashes" which can destroy the entire disk in an instant, and so all data on Winchester disks should be copied to alternate locations. This also protects against inadvertent commands that erase important data.

Many other kinds of storage have been or are used by computer systems. What matters for storage are price, size, and durability. Primary off-line storage has been magnetic tape, which has increased in density until a modern 8 mm video cartridge used for computer storage capacities holds from 5 to 7 GB per cartridge. Still larger capacity drives are coming. Sony announced in 1996 a new 8 mm drive, fitting in a 3.5-inch form factor and holding 25 GB uncompressed.

Yet another cartridge format from Quantum (the DLT 7000, for digital linear tape) will hold 35 GB in a linear-recording format. Still larger capacity tapes are used for digital video in studios, holding up to 165 GB per cartridge. The cost of storage on cartridges, however, is no longer sufficiently below that of disks to make off-line tape systems attractive. Furthermore, magnetic tape can wear out and should have temperature-controlled storage to maximize its life.

The audio CD format looked immediately attractive to computer systems manufacturers, offering a lightweight 650 MB storage device suitable for mass production and extremely durable. CDs, for their first 15 years, could only be written in large factories that had high setup costs, but low costs per disk, making them inherently a mass production device. Recently CD-R disks, or CD-recordable disks have become common. These devices are not physically the same as the traditional CD, since they rely on a different physical mechanism for changing the reflective surface of a disk to encode the bits. However, CD-R disks are read by all standard CD readers. A CD-R device is now under $50 and the blank disks are about 30 cents, making it possible for many people to write their own CDs.

CDs are admirable storage from the viewpoint of a library. Since they are write-once devices, they cannot be overwritten by any kind of software accident. They are physically durable and do not deteriorate with normal use. Philips originally advertised them as "perfect sound forever," and although this slogan is no longer in use, CDs still do not wear out if properly made. They can of course be damaged by sufficiently silly handling (e.g., scratching a label into the wrong side of the disk) or lost by fire or theft, so additional copies are still needed.

Just as CD readers have become ubiquitous on PCs, with the vast majority of nonlaptop PCs now sold "multimedia ready" (an advertising term meaning a sound card and a CD reader are installed), the industry began to design the follow-on device, known as the DVD, or digital video disk, also called the digital versatile disk. The stimulation for the DVD came from the movie industry which could not fit a compressed digital movie at adequate quality into the 650 MB of a CD. Digital video disks hold 4 to 9 GB on a side, depending on whether they are single or double layered, and can also be double sided, which would mean a total capacity of 17 GB (CDs are single-sided). The primary purpose of these disks is to sell movies, for about $20 each. They have been the hot sales item of the last few years in consumer home electronics, and DVD-recordables are now available (albeit in a variety of incompatible formats that has discouraged people from buying the drives). They offer a promise of extremely large and durable storage, ideal for many kinds of digital library applications, once the standards issues are sorted out.

Software technology has also made great strides. Whether software or hardware moves faster is not clear. Some years ago Donald Hammann (1983)

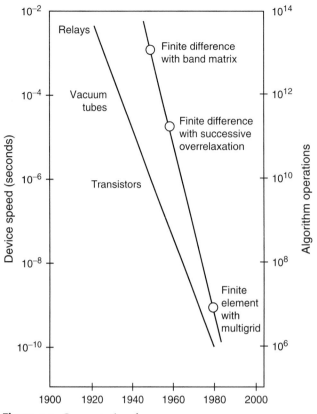

Figure 1.9 Computational progress.

investigated the improvements in algorithms to diagonalize matrices, a standard problem in numerical analysis (the solution of mathematical tasks by iterative methods, an important field for many practical problems). His result (shown in Figure 1.9) tells us if you have large matrices to diagonalize, and you have a choice between 1947 hardware with modern software, and 1947 software running on modern machines, you are better off with the old hardware and new software.

In summary, technology has made enormous advances in processors, input and output, storage devices, and connectivity. In 1962 a good university research computer was an IBM 7090, which cost about $3 million, and a student to program it could be hired for $1.50 per hour, so that the machine cost the equivalent of 2 million hours or the equivalent of 1000 years of work. Not surprisingly, computer time was precious, was shared out among the different users, and was billed by the minute. Today we would buy a better machine for $600 and pay the undergraduate $10 per hour, so that the machine would cost the equivalent of 60 hours or less than two weeks of work. Input is much easier, going directly into an editor instead of via a card punch; output is also much higher-quality, since the machines of 1962 tended to have only upper case printers. Not surprisingly, given the cost changes, libraries can now use computers for many functions, so long as they save even a little time or provide a little help, and we no longer feel we are technically limited in building systems. As Jim Gray (the 1997 Turing Award winner) once said to me, "May all your problems be technical."

1.5   Early Language Processing

Since Colossus was the first electronic computer and was devoted to cryptanalysis, statistical language processing was the very first application of computing. This kind of processing involves calculations on the frequencies of words and characters; the most elementary kind are simple letter-frequency tables. Next, computers worked on the computation of ballistic tables and other numerical applications. But by the 1950s, computers were used to create indexes, including the kind of index/concordance named KWIC (key word in context). KWIC indexes were invented by the late H. P. Luhn, a researcher at IBM. Each significant word was presented in the center of a line of text, with the preceding and subsequent contexts shown. Luhn envisaged them as an alternative to conventional indexes, but they are too bulky to use effectively in this way. They still have applications in literary analysis (concordances and their uses are described in section 2.8). Many literary texts have been entered into computers, partly as a way of making them available and partly for other kinds of literary studies. For example, Michael Hart created Project Gutenberg, in which volunteers have entered hundreds of texts. Hart's goal, which he has been working towards since 1971, was to have 10,000 public domain texts in plain ASCII digital format available online; this goal was attained in December 2003.

Although machine translation work in the early 1950s proved to have only limited utility, work started on syntactic analysis to improve these programs. The syntactic work led to systems that tried to do question-answering, retrieving specific data from tables of numbers in response to English questions. Early promising work by researchers like Daniel Bobrow (then at MIT) and William Woods (then at BBN) has been slow to lead to practical applications in digital libraries. Experiments done by IBM indicated some sobering problems. In the process of learning how to use a traditional query language on a given database, the user learns some important information about the database, such as what questions the database can answer. Users left without any such guidance tend to ask questions which the database system cannot answer, even including such questions as, "What should I do next?" Once it is recognized that users of a natural language query system still have to take a course in the database content, it seems to be less important that they also have to learn a new format to ask questions. Database interfaces have also improved, with systems like QBE (query by example) becoming simple to use.

Over the years a tension developed between model-based and statistically-based techniques for processing language. The origins can be traced to the Bush-Weaver dichotomy mentioned earlier, with Warren Weaver's idea of treating language translation as code-breaking stimulating early work in statistical methods, while more traditional linguists worked away on models of Russian and English to produce automatic translation software.

While one sequence of linguists proposed this or that model for grammar, ranging from context-free grammar through transformational grammar to a dozen other forms, another argued that statistical methods would suffice. Among the early names associated with the models are Anthony Oettinger, Zelig Harris, Noam Chomsky, Martin Kay, and many other linguistic researchers. Despite the large number of models proposed just for English, however, none of them ever produced the kind of reliable and effective software that would convince people immediately of their value. Meanwhile, other linguists, such as Fred Jelinek (then at IBM and now at Johns Hopkins), argued that statistical techniques were the key to processing language effectively. To some extent, their work has been validated by the success of speech recognition programs in the marketplace.

Speech recognition is a problem which must be attacked statistically, since we do not have discrete digital input as from a keyboard, and there tend to be doubtful decisions between phonemes in the form of words and even phrases (consider trying to separate *ice cream* from *I scream,* to give one a familiar example). In the process of using statistical tests to decide which phonemes are the most probable in a given acoustic signal, and then assembling these phonemes into words and the words into sentences, it is easy to plan on using the same kinds of statistical tests at all levels of the process.

The steady improvements in technology also affect the balance between model-based and statistically-based approaches. Statistical methods are likely to require more calculations and more data than model-based approaches. In the days when computation was expensive and data scarce, it could be argued that we couldn't afford to use statistical methods to find linguistic patterns. As computation gets cheaper and data more available, the statistical methods are cheaper and easier to use, and they improve steadily along with the technology. The model-based methods improve with new insights, and those are few and far between.

An interesting analogy to the model/statistical dichotomy in language processing is the same distinction in computer chess. For many years, research on computer chess involved attempts to model "good" moves. Starting with Ken Thompson's "Belle" machine in the 1970s, however, programs which evaluated every move and used specialized hardware to evaluate them as fast as possible started winning the computer chess tournaments. Now a computer is the world chess champion, the Deep Blue machine of IBM beating Gary Kasparov in a very well-publicized challenge match. The winning computers just look at all legal moves. Chess masters do not work this way; they do identify good moves and focus their searching, but computers seem to do better if they don't try to do that. The machines are now so fast that no human can keep up, even if vast amounts of computer time are being wasted evaluating the consequences of bad moves. The researchers in computer chess in the 1950s would not have expected this paradox: a computer is the world chess champion, and we have learned nothing about chess strategy.

There are other games for which the brute force, "search all legal moves" strategies are still impractical. The Asian game of Go is perhaps the most important example. A typical chess position might have 30 legal moves, while a typical Go position at a time when the outcome of the game is still uncertain might have 300 legal moves. A factor of 10 at each move, or of a million to look ahead six steps, is still too much for the computer hardware gains to ignore. None of the model-based approaches to computer Go are close to playing at expert level. On the other hand, computers have played simpler games for years and everyone is quite happy to have them win by simple brute force; nobody complains that we haven't learned about tic-tac-toe strategy.

In the same way we have commercially successful voice recognition and character recognition, but have learned little about linguistics from this software. The verdict is still out on machine translation, which isn't working well enough yet in either statistical or model-based approaches to say which is better.

1.6   The Internet and the Web

Perhaps the most important development of the last decade has been the rise of the Internet, the electronic network between computers mostly widely used today. The development of protocols joined with the use of transmission devices permits large-scale interconnection between computers. The growth rapidly became worldwide; before 2003 the US dominated the Web, in both addresses and pages, but, other countries, particularly in Asia, are now rapidly increasing their presence. Today, only about half the Internet is even in English, and the most wired countries are the Scandanavian countries, not the United States.

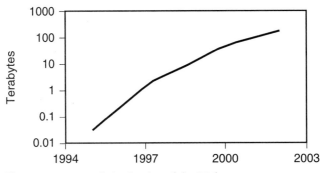

Figure 1.10 Growth in the size of the Web.

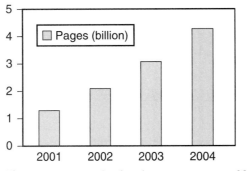

Figure 1.11 Growth of Web pages as reported by Google.

There are about 100 million hosts and nearly a billion users around the world. Figure 1.10 shows the growth and approximate size of the Web.

Another measure of the Web is the total number of pages. Figure 1.11 shows the number of Web pages reported by Google as of the beginning of each year; unfortunately, marketing considerations are probably affecting how often new values are reported.

The most important new software technology for digital libraries, of course, was the invention of the World Wide Web and the Mosaic interface to the Web. The Web was started by Tim Berners-Lee in 1990 (see his 1992 paper); he then worked for CERN and now works for the World Wide Web Consortium (W3C) at MIT. The interface followed five years later; it took a while for enough material to accumulate for an interface to become important. Mosaic was developed by Marc Andreesen at NCSA; he went on to become a founder of Netscape. Mosaic was soon replaced as a browser by programs such as Netscape, Internet Explorer, Galeon, Mozilla, and Opera. The years 1995 to 1997 saw an explosion of public interest in the Internet and of online material and public access.

Berners-Lee created the idea of making it easy for people to accumulate pictures and text for access around the world; Andreesen made the interface that got everyone excited. The result was a phenomenon, as Web pages went from a trickle to a flood over the last two years. There were virtually no Web pages in mid-1993 and by January 1996, there were over 75,000 hosts with names beginning *www;* by the end of 2002 there were 100 million such hosts. The Web is the likely interface for all kinds of information and interaction in the future; we're just not sure about some of the important details, like who will pay. But the Web is the hope for how to deal with the *information glut* of today.

Instead of question-answering, information retrieval of whole texts became common with the boom of the Web. Thousands of people and institutions have posted valuable information on Web pages; the Web now holds about 10 GB of text (something like 10 million volumes if printed out as books). Material on the Web can be found with the search engines run via webcrawlers (Ross and Hutheesing, 1995; Najork and Wiener, 2001). These programs seek out every page they can find on the Web, bring back all the text on it, and compile an index. The earliest such program was the webcrawler of the University of Washington. People hesitated originally to write such programs; it seemed like an enormous demand for computer cycles, storage, and bandwidth. The crawlers and search engines were such an enormous success, however, that they rapidly spread and improved. The University of Washington program was almost immediately pushed aside by commercial ventures such as Lycos and Alta Vista (and the Washington program itself turned into Excite). By August 1996, for example, Alta Vista was indexing 30 million pages from 275,000 Web servers, and it was used 16 million times a day. Today the most-used search engine is Google, which does about half the searches on the Web; it indexes 2 billion pages and does 200–250 million searches a day; second place goes to Overture at 167 million, and then Inktomi at 80 million (see Sullivan, 2003, and Napoli, 2003, for contradictory counts of Google searches per day).

The webcrawlers, or spiders, are programs that spend the evenings retrieving every Web page that they can reach, looking at it for any references to any other Web page, and picking that page up as well. In this way they try to collect every single page, and compete by boasting about how many pages they have found. They make full text indexes to all of this text and provide search services free. High speed is achieved by keeping the index in RAM memory and by using enormous numbers of machines searching in parallel (Google quit saying how many machines it owned after the number passed 20,000).

A more interesting problem is how to find good answers in Web searches, with so many documents from which to choose. Early search engines acquired a reputation for delivering enormous quantities of garbage. Google gained acceptance by figuring out how to show good documents at the top of the retrieved documents list. Its method, invented by founders Larry Page and Sergei Brin while graduate students in the digital library group at Stanford under Hector Garcia-Molina, uses the network of links on the Web as a way of ranking the importance of pages. Pages with a great many links pointing to them are considered more likely to be useful than pages with very few links, so Google promotes the popular pages to the top of the search results.

Unfortunately, the desire of many commercial websites to be listed in response to as many queries as possible, and to be listed as high up as possible, has led to a continual game between the site operators and the search engines. Two primary points of abuse are the use of the *meta* fields in websites and extraneous links. Meta fields were originally designed to provide a way for site operators to add some keywords to their sites that did not need to be displayed to users, but might be useful to search engines. A site might use meta fields to give some synonyms for their content or to elaborate ideas that might be taken for granted by readers. For example, a website mentioning Brooklyn many times, but not New York City, might decide to add New York as a meta tag. However, some site operators put words in meta fields that have nothing to do with their content (the most common such word being *sex* since a great many Internet searches are from people looking for pornography). The major search engines now all have strategies to combat this misuse. Similarly, some people have sites with enormous numbers of self-references, hoping to fool Google and other search engines using similar techniques into overvaluing their site. Again, the major search engines have adopted algorithms to downrate unusually focused or unusually prolific groups of linked pages.

Access to the Web is slow enough that real-time interaction is hard to achieve, giving a strong motivation to the idea of *agents* or *knowbots,* programs that would run around the Web and execute where appropriate. In particular, a Web page could supply a program to run on the user's computer and thus achieve much faster response time, and also offload the computing load from the server machine to the machine of the person who actually wanted to see the result. People hesitated to do this at first for practical reasons (how to get a program which could run on the many types of machines users might have) and for security reasons (how to be sure that this program would not do anything unwanted). James Gosling of Sun Microsystems designed Java, a language which can be interpreted, getting around the problem of which machine it had been compiled for, and which is sufficiently limited in its capabilities (no file reading or writing) to be safe to execute. Java *applets* (the name for a piece of code run as an application inside a Web browser) are now interpreted by software like Netscape, Microsoft Explorer, and other browsers, and can be used to provide interactive services. The Web is clearly the model for the widespread digital library that Vannevar Bush and others envisaged.

1.7 Summary

There seems little sign of any slowdown in the development of storage technologies. Disk prices drop as sizes increase. We see 100-perabyte storage systems now. Perpendicular magnetic recording or other new technologies may produce another factor of 10 in disk capacities. Processors are getting faster and so are networks. The rise of Internet-2 and of experimental 10-gigabit/second networks has increased the standard backbone speeds, so that the United States and Europe are covered by networks with over a 1 GB/sec capacity. Display devices are also steadily improving, albeit more slowly. The 640×480 screen of a decade ago is now more likely to be 1280×1024, with 1800×1440 readily available. Still larger displays are out there, with prototypes of 3000×2000 resolution existing. Much of the very large screen market is moving to either LCD or plasma panel flatscreens, although resolution is not increasing as fast as screen size.

We do not know, however, what people want to do with even the technology we have today. Many questions remain unanswered about how information will be or should be used. These include questions about access methods for finding information and about content and what is or should be available.

How users will choose to find information is a problem which has not been studied enough. Some people search for what they want, knowing fairly accurately what it is; others browse around, looking for something interesting. Some use automatic search tools, while others want to trace manual links (the Bush-Weaver dichotomy is still around). Some would even like formal models or classifications of what is online. How do we continue to cater to all these methods of access? For example, how do we provide searching of images? Or efficient browsing of video and audio?

What content libraries should provide is also unclear. Some material is available as searchable, formattable text. Other information is available only as uneditable images scanned from printed pages, photographs, and illustrations. Users want both, but different retrieval techniques are required, making it hard to provide unified systems. Some of the contents of a digital library will be new material, delivered electronically to the library; other information will be converted from older forms. The libraries need to merge both kinds of collections.

For some materials, digital versions are going to be all the user needs. In fact, for some objects they may be the only form that is created. For other materials, digital versions may serve merely as an aid, with the user eventually getting the original form for deeper study. For example, in traditional libraries, art historians may use books or slides to identify works whose originals the historians would then travel to see. For which users and which materials are digital representations not going to be adequate?

Most important for a library is to have the right content for its users. The Web today contains some 150 terabytes of information, the equivalent of a national library, one of more than 10 million volumes. But is it the most valuable content? And if not, how can we get the right content? Can we even agree on what the right content is? Some wish to exclude some kinds of material (whether it is terrorist information, pornography, or controversial political sentiments). In addition to exclusion, inclusion can represent a problem. Much material on the Web is low in quality. Can we make it possible for people to use the Web effectively to get high-quality answers?

Access to users, as well as to documents, also matters. Not everyone is a computer expert. How do we see that everyone— including those without computer skills and those with less money—still have access to information? We have justified digital libraries and networks with the same arguments for public education and informed voters that we used in the past. In the future, if these arguments matter, digital libraries must be accessible, and systems must be designed to provide information universally, not to isolate people from the information they need.

To begin discussing these questions of how a digital library is used, the next two chapters will deal with the technology of content retrieval for text and images. This will explain how to build a digital library that can find pages and pictures for users. Later chapters will deal with the more institutional aspects of libraries—collections, preservation, and economics. The chapters on usability and on the future of digital libraries will return to some of the social questions we've broached here and will discuss how we might organize information systems for better support of society as a whole.

2 Text Documents

Two basic methodologies support digital libraries today. One is the ability of computers to manipulate text; the other is their ability to manipulate images. A page of text can either be represented as the sequence of characters on the page or as the picture of the page containing the characters. This chapter discusses the technology which handles characters; the next chapter will deal with the technology of images. For a really excellent and detailed survey of methods for searching large text files, see the book *Managing Gigabytes* (Witten et al., 1999).

The ability of computers to manipulate text includes searching, formatting, and other operations. Where once the creation of a concordance, an index of the occurrences of every word in a work or set of works, might have been a life's work, it is now entirely mechanical. Similarly, searching for exact character strings is now trivial. In the mid-1970s the Bell Telephone Laboratories company newspaper started running word puzzles for amusement (e.g. list three words which contain the letters *btl*) and was surprised when a group of people with a machine-readable dictionary proved able to answer these puzzles as fast as they could be typed in. Today, anyone with a personal computer and CD-ROM dictionary can do this.

Vast amounts of text are on the Web. There are fifty thousand French language books, extensive collections of English literature, and everything from physics papers to poetry. In a lifetime, someone reading 10 hours a day for

70 years at 400 words per minute might read 6 gigabytes. Our total knowledge of ancient Greek comes from some 300 megabytes of text. Online we have not just 6 gigabytes, but a thousand times that much text. For the purposes of many digital libraries, online text is all that is needed.

2.1 Computer Typesetting

The most notable success of computing has been in document preparation, with the word processing industry now dominated by programs such as Microsoft Word. Almost nothing in a commercial setting is typed on traditional typewriters any more, let alone written by hand. As a byproduct of this machine conquest, almost everything now written is available in machine-readable form, and its reuse in other ways is easy and widespread.

The new word processing technology has produced vast online databases. These came originally as byproducts of computer typesetting. For some years in the past, it had been possible to control typesetting equipment from paper tape. Monotype machines, for example, typically worked by having the operator punch a paper tape of instructions, which was then used to inform the actual casting machine. The use of computers for typesetting started in the late 1960s, adapted from this process. Standard reference books, which were reprinted and extremely expensive to reset, were early canditates for computer typesetting. *Books in Print*, as an example, was one of the earliest US machine-composed books. Newspapers also led in the use of computer setting; they could take stories from newswires and put them into printed form without editors or compositors.

Technology for computer typesetting has changed over the years. In the early years of computer composition, filmstrips with images of specific letters were manipulated by the computer. As each letter was read into the machine (typically from paper tape), the filmstrip was moved so that a light could shine through the letter, exposing photographic paper, and thus making up the page. Either the paper or the optics had to be moved after each letter in order to get the next letter in the appropriate place, making these typesetters relatively slow. Then CRT (cathode ray tube) screens came into use, with letters placed on the screen, and the entire page exposed as a whole. This saved the time of moving the paper, but a photographic process was still required; the product of this step then went into a chemical developer, finally producing a sheet of photographic paper, which could then be used in offset printing.

Most recently, we have seen the advent of laser printers. These printers, derived from xerographic copy machines and invented at Xerox PARC in the 1970s, dispense entirely with the idea of creating a physical plate. Instead, an optical image of the material to be reproduced is projected onto a drum coated with a material (various forms of selenium) which becomes electrically charged when exposed to light. The image exists as areas of light and dark, creating charged and uncharged regions on the surface of the drum. Electrically charged ink particles are then picked up by only part of the drum and are thus transferred to the page to be printed. The image is initially generated with a laser turned on and off by electrical circuitry, rather than from a CRT or from a page (thus the name *laser printer*). Laser printers started as one-at-a-time output machines, replacing complex chain printers for computer output; but now large machines built on this principle, such as the Xerox Docutech or Kodak Lionheart, can print high-quality (600 dots per inch) multicolor images so rapidly (135 pages per minute) that entire books can be printed on demand. They are still not quite competitive either for the very highest quality printing jobs (1500 dots per inch is easily achieved by the offset industry) or for very long press runs, but they are taking over office applications. The newest developments are in color printing, where color laser printers are still competing with inkjet printers (color laser printers offering somewhat better saturation and speed but at higher cost) and also with dye sublimation printers, which provide extremely high-quality color.

Simultaneous to the development of printing technology, the software to format documents has developed. Starting in the mid-1960s at MIT, programs which let people print formatted documents using electric typewriters were developed. The MIT software led to research progress chiefly through such new programs as *nroff/troff* at Bell Labs, *scribe* at CMU, and *TEX* at Stanford. These programs, originally devoted to justifying right margins and numbering lines (tasks extremely annoying to manual typists), were letting users choose font styles and sizes and other kinds of formatting by the mid-1970s.

Two models of printing software followed. Some word processing software is keyed to the exact appearance of the text: their commands reflect choices such as "italic" or "point size 12" and their output is hard to adjust in format. Nor do they specify whether something is in italics because it is an author name, a title, a heading, a foreign word, or for some other reason. They tend to be simple to edit, following the model of "what you see is what you get" (WYSIWYG) originally developed for the Bravo text processor at Xerox PARC in the early 1970s and followed by most commercial word processing systems. The other model, pioneered at Bell Labs, describes a document in terms of content: text is labeled as "heading" or "footnote" or the like, and a separate set of formatting instructions decides that a heading might be 12 point Helvetica bold or some such description. Such text is harder to type but easier to repurpose (e.g., reformat into multiple columns). The present development of the first model is Postscript and of the second model is SGML, both of which we will discuss later in the text.

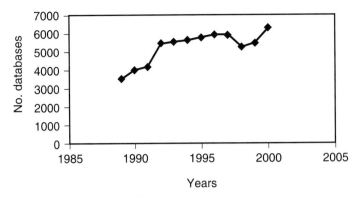

Figure 2.1 Growth of online databases.

Of course, once the text is keyed for printing, it can be saved for many other uses. Large text databases were accumulated fairly rapidly from such sources as online newspapers; for instance, the electronic file of Toronto's *The Globe and Mail* dates to 1964. The text retrieval industry developed based on dialing up large central database systems and phrasing interactive queries. Such systems started with government research in the 1950s and 1960s; for example, Dialog, the biggest such commercial system, derives from a NASA project named RECON.

Figure 2.1 shows that the number of commercial online databases has been growing over the last 10 years (Williams, 2001). Competition from CD-ROMS continues, and of course the Web is now cutting into such databases. In 2000 there were some 15 billion records in the commercial services, each probably 1–5 kilobytes, for a total of perhaps 20 terabytes, or only about the size of the Web (and there is a lot of duplication in both the Web and these commercial services). The commercial services boasted of 90 million searches in the year 1998; this seems trivial compared to 200 million per day on the Web.

The variety of material available online today is immense. The complete text of many newspapers, most abstracting and indexing journals, and a great many current magazines are available in digital form. All of this is a byproduct of the commercial printing industry. For-pay online systems have good coverage of magazines, many scientific journals and in particular those in medicine, all abstracting and indexing services since about 1970, and most major newspapers since 1990. For-pay CD-ROMS include many major reference works including encyclopedias and dictionaries; the many journals available in CD-ROM are usually image-based, although a few are text-driven.

Free resources on the Internet include a great many technical reports, current papers, and a variety of royalty-free or public domain material ranging from student papers to major works of pre-1920 literature. Most books and journals are still not on the Internet in full text form; the hurdle is economic, not technical, and will change in time.

2.2   Text Formats

Text can be stored in a variety of formats. For languages that use only the 26 letters of the Latin alphabet (most notably English), the ASCII standard has won out over alternatives (5-bit teletype code, 6-bit BCD, and 8-bit EBCDIC). ASCII is a 7-bit code, leaving 1 bit of each 8-bit byte unused. However, there are a great many languages which need additional symbols, whether just a few accent marks (most Western European languages) or thousands of new symbols for idiographs (Chinese and Japanese). Standards groups are working on all these questions, and a new Unicode standard is the most generally accepted answer, covering the characters for all major languages with a 16-bit-per-character representation.

Much more important than the character set itself is the method of signalling how the letters are to be handled. In the WYSIWYG style the letters are marked with direct typesetting information: font, size, position, and so forth. This is normally done by putting very specific typesetting codes (in older systems often labeled with codes like "upper rail" from the description of hot-lead machines) around the letters. However, in such environments it is not possible to revise the formats. Publishers have "style manuals" describing the formats of their books and magazines; to convert from one to another would be impossible if only the output format and not the meaning of the input were described in machine-readable form.

Increasingly, therefore, large publishing groups are using higher-level descriptive systems, in which each input character is in some way marked as to the intent of the character. Three main standards are worth discussing: MARC (Machine-Readable Cataloging), SGML (Standard Generalized Markup Language), and HTML (Hypertext Markup Language). In each case it is possible to look at the environment of a character and decide what that character means, not just what it should look like. This point bears not just on publishing convenience, but on the entire philosophy of text retrieval and display: who should be in control? Often the author writes a string of words, the publisher chooses what they will look like on the page, and the reader just reads. Not always, however. Some authors, particularly poets, have cared a great deal about the exact appearance of their words on the page. And if the reader gets the document in a format like SGML, it can be rearranged into a format of the reader's choice. Sometimes this seems all to the good; for example, someone with poor vision can choose to reformat with larger size print, making the document easier to read. Or, someone reading from a screen can adapt the presentation to the size of the screen (or the window in use). However, this limits the control of the author and publisher over the appearance of the material, which can prove problematical: a page design carefully laid out for optimum readability (e.g., with references to pictures placed relative to text or detailed tables) may be destroyed by a reformatting user, leading to a difficult-to-absorb text. So publishers and authors may object and wish to retain control of the appearance of the document. We do not yet know what the socially acceptable solution is going to be: will readers be given complete freedom to rearrange material (perhaps even to the extent of choosing to hear the document read aloud) or will publishers and authors demand some control over the appearance of documents and avoid systems which risk losing it? Each choice might be appropriate depending on context.

Finally, properly tagged text is essential for some kinds of retrieval. You may well wish to distinguish a search for "Tom Stoppard" as an author, a translator, or the subject of a biography. If people searching the file are to be able to search for particular words in the title or for author names as opposed to names mentioned somewhere in a document, it is necessary to have the fields labeled properly in the database.

Of the standards mentioned, the oldest is MARC, designed at the Library of Congress in 1969. MARC is used primarily for bibliographic records, but is typical of a number of record-oriented formats. In MARC each line contains a code identifying what it is, followed by the text. For example, code 100 is a personal author and code 245 is a title. Part of a sample book record might look something like this:

```
100a Lockley, Ronald Mathias.
245a The private life of the rabbit:
245b an account of the life history and social behaviour of the
     wild rabbit
260a London : 260b Corgi, 260c 1973.
300a 174, [8] p. : 300b ill. ; 300c 20 cm.
500a Originally published, London: Deutsch, 1964.
```

The key fields shown are the author (100), title (245, divided at a colon), place of publication (260a), publisher (260b), and date (260c). In addition, the number of pages, size, and original publisher are shown. The full record would also have the Dewey and/or Library of Congress class and other data. MARC, as can be seen, is a very record-oriented language, with very rigorous formats. It is tailored to bibliographic entries for library catalogs and thus does not support many of the features needed in full documents (equations, tables, footnotes, and so on).

By contrast, SGML is a much more flexible standard. In fact, SGML is only a syntax and a philosophy. It essentially says that information is to be tagged meaningfully and that tags are to be contained within angle brackets. Thus, an SGML sequence might look something like this:

```
<title>Huckleberry Finn</title><author>Mark Twain</author>
```

where each field to be tagged is surrounded by two tags in angle brackets, one indicating the start of each field and the other the end. The end tag is the same as the start tag except that it is preceded by a slash. The tags must be nested correctly; for example, the following line is illegal:

```
<title>Huckleberry Finn<author></title>Mark Twain</author>
```

Tags may contain other information. For example, one could have `<author type=pseudonym>` or `<figure graphicfile="F11830.gif">`. On the other hand, a tag can be freestanding without any data (e.g., `<thinspace>`). In addition to information in tags, SGML also deals with the definition of special characters. These are preceded by "&" and ended by ";"as in the example "&pound" for the sterling currency symbol £.

The content of tags is flexible, but there are several popular standards for them. These include the American Association of Publishers (AAP) Electronic Manuscript Standard, the Department of Defense CALS rules, and the Text Encoding Initiative (TEI) standard. Many publishers have defined their own DTD (document type definition) to reflect their particular needs and requirements. Here is a sample of the TEI labeling:

```
<stage>Enter Barnardo and Francisco, two Sentinels, at several
   doors</stage>
<sp><speaker>Barn<l part=Y>Who's there?
<sp><speaker>Fran<l>Nay, answer me. Stand and unfold yourself.
<sp><speaker>Barn<l part=i>Long live the King!
<sp><speaker>Fran<l part=m>Barnardo?
<sp><speaker>Barn<l part=f>He.
<sp><speaker>Fran<l>You come most carefully upon your hour.
```

Some complexities of printing are still settling down in SGML. Notably, *mathematical equations* in SGML are very complex, and I think that a language similar to Unix *eqn* is likely to succeed. Very roughly, *eqn* is a format in which equations are typed as they would be read aloud. The Web doesn't handle equations yet, so the syntax is still to be decided. For *tables*, a format with a great many internal labels such as `<row><cell>xx</cell><cell>xx...` is winning over the Unix *tbl* style of separating the format from the table data. Similarly for *bibliographic citations*, the UNIX *refer* concept that the user should have a separate bibliographic file with just data and specify the format elsewhere is losing to the SGML scheme in which the user tags each item but specifies the order. It is harder to convert from one citation style to another than in *refer* but easier to control the exact appearance as one is typing. At least there are content labels on the fields. For *graphs* and *images,* importing Postscript seems to be the winning strategy.

The formatting language used on the Web is HTML, hypertext markup language. HTML is syntactically a very similar language to SGML, with the same kinds of formats. The major relevant difference is that HTML supports hypertext links. Just as with ordinary formatting tags, these are specified in a format such as

```
<A HREF="http://www.cis.ohio-state.edu:80/text/faq.html">
```

Their meaning, however, is that they point to another document or another place in this document.

Since most word processors follow the WYSIWYG model, it is more difficult to find one that makes it easy to enter SGML labels. Some publishers claim that it can be twice as expensive to enter material formatted correctly in SGML than it is to use an ordinary word processor. Although some aspects of the formats can be converted automatically, there is no way to supply automatically the information about the labels needed for proper SGML.

Clearly, no one has the time to read an entire library. Everyone must use some method to decide which items to read. Although there is much dislike for the searching process, and many users insist they find what they need via browsing or serendipity, searching is really essential for proper use of any library, especially a digital library being accessed remotely with no one at the next table to ask for help. Given a large collection of online texts, how can the reader find what is wanted? This divides into several basic questions:

- What kind of vocabulary is used to describe the content? This may be just the text as it appears, or there may be synonyms, indexing, or other kinds of content labeling.
- What kind of connectives, if any, are used to handle searches which involve more than a single word or term? The most common form is Boolean logic—"ands" and "ors"—but some systems use less logic; they have perhaps more natural forms of multiple-item search.
- How does one actually find a particular item in the text? There are many algorithms, and one important ingredient in digital libraries is knowing how to do the searches. The next few sections will deal with the different search algorithms.
- How does one rank the various items which seem to satisfy the search? Until recently there were no good answers to this question; now Google has demonstrated that one can evaluate the utility of documents by using the number of links to them and thus provided a way to rank-order the results of searches.

2.3   **Ways of Searching**

To understand searching, remember a little bit about computer speeds. It normally takes a computer a few microseconds at most to pick up a single character, examine it, and decide what to do next. By contrast, suppose one needs something from a disk. Retrieving a disk block at random requires waiting for a rotational latency, the time required for the disk to spin around to the place where your data is recorded, perhaps 20 milliseconds. Thus most of the time involved in a retrieval system is spent waiting for the disk to revolve, and minimizing the number of disk accesses is the way to keep the process running fast.

There are several basic search techniques: linear search, inverted files, and hash tables.

Linear search routines start at the beginning, go character by character through the text looking for whatever it is that is wanted, and stop at the end of the text. The entire file is processed. Inverted file search routines make an index and retrieve only the blocks that contain the right matches. Hash table searching algorithms compute a good guess at the location of the items you want. Finally, tries and signature files require a linear scan again, but they condense the material being searched so that the scan is faster. Let us take them in turn.

Linear Searching

Linear scanning is a search algorithm that simply goes through a file from beginning to end looking for a string. On Unix systems this is done by a command "grep," which has become a pseudonym for the process. Linear scanning is slow, but it can be used to search for more than just a single string. In particular, the convention of searching for "regular expressions" has arisen; these can be retrieved without backing up, and a large amount of computer theory has been developed around how to do this. We can afford only a brief explanation here, but detailed coverage can be found in Aho, Sethi, and Ullman (1986). String searching is often extended to a more flexible kind of request called, in computer terms, *regular expressions*. Regular expressions are a limited extension to strings. The simplest form of regular expressions are so-called wildcard characters, in which the period (.) of the extension can be used to match any character. Thus, a search for **a.c** matches any three characters beginning with **a** and ending with **c**. Another common operator is a repeat operator; for example, **a+** matches one or more adjacent instances of the letter **a**. Table 2.1 is a more complete list of regular expression operators.

Regular expressions include strings as the simplest case, so the expression **cat** matches the corresponding word. The expression **[a-zA-Z]+** matches any string of letters, and the expression **(dog|cat)** matches either the word

Table 2.1 Operators and their meanings.

Operator	Meaning
.	Any character
A*	Match any number of **a**s
A+	Match one or more **a**s
A?	Either nothing or a single **A**.
[a-d]	Matches any of **a**, **b**, **c**, or **d**
(a)	Matches expression **a**
a|b	Matches either **a** or **b**

dog or the word **cat**, or nothing. By convention, whenever there is a choice, the longest possible expression is matched.

Searching for regular expressions involves moving through the entire file, character by character, and keeping track of the matches. If there are choices, the computer must know what possibilities the current string might match. For example, a search for **[a-z]+s** (all words ending in s) against the string **mess** will produce a choice at each **s**: is this the final **s** or just another letter in the **[a-z]+** substring? The first **s** is in the substring, the last is the final letter, but this can't be known in advance. If the computer keeps track of both alternatives, the search is called nondeterministic. Usually, the search is converted to a more complex deterministic algorithm in which the set of choices is represented by a state in a finite automaton, speeding up the algorithm. Further details can be found in the aforementioned Aho, Sethi, and Ullman (1986) and forthcoming in Aho et al. (2004).

If you know you are looking for a specific string of letters with no operators, you can do better. The Boyer-Moore algorithm was the first technique that did a linear scan, but did not look at every character. Suppose you are looking for a long word like *aardvark*. The preceding algorithms start looking at each character to see if it is an *a*; if not, they continue with the next character. But suppose the computer looks ahead to the eighth letter. If the word *aardvark* begins at a given point, the eighth letter must be a *k*. Suppose, however, that the eighth letter ahead is a *t*. Then the word *aardvark* doesn't start at this point. In fact, it can't start anywhere in the next eight letters, since there is no place in the word for a *t*. The search can skip eight letters ahead, without even looking at the intervening seven characters.

In practice, this may not be very valuable; it may be that reading the characters takes most of the time and whether they are looked at or not is unimportant.

In other circumstances, especially if the processor has something else to do, the Boyer-Moore algorithm or one of its refinements may be a useful speedup.

Over the years there have been attempts to build special purpose hardware searching devices, usually implementing some kind of string or regular expression matching. They have ranged from the IBM HARVEST system of the late 1960s to more recent systems by GE and TRW. These devices provide a hardware implementation of a finite state machine and a way to load an expression into it. They then stream large quantities of data past the device, which picks off what it wants. This may help in unloading a central CPU, for example, and it is possible to put such a device into a disk controller, providing a kind of searching right off the disk stream. Most of the attraction of these devices is the same as with any other kind of linear search: very flexible searching parameters and no internal storage of the file required to search it.

The most ambitious linear search attempt to date is the use of the Connection Machine, a parallel computer with thousands of simple processors, to do text scanning (Stanfill and Kahle, 1986; Stanfill et al., 1989). So long as the entire file is simultaneously accessible, the Connection Machine could search it rapidly. The main advantage of a system like this is not in single-query search, however; it is in an application where a great many queries are being searched at once, so many that effectively the whole database has to be read anyway (because the set of matches will cover most of the disk blocks used to store the data).

All linear search algorithms have some properties in common. They require no space beyond that used by the original file (except for space proportional to the query size, not the file size). They can use the file the instant it is written, requiring no preparatory work. They can search for complex expressions, not just strings. But they all get slower as the file to be searched gets longer. Even parallel systems, fast though they are, will be slow once the database reaches a certain size.

Inverted Files

All of the algorithms mentioned thus far require performance time proportional to the length of the string being searched. If the file to be scanned doubles in size, they take twice as long. This is acceptable if one is looking through a short file, but is not a good way to search billions of characters in an extensive text database. Instead, the standard technology uses *inverted files*. Inverted files are like the index at the back of a book: the elements to be searched for are extracted and alphabetized and are then more readily accessible for multiple searches.

Thus, given a text such as *now is the time for all good men to come to the aid of the party*, an inverted file program needs a preparatory phase in which it makes a list of each word and where it appears. To break this process down, start by numbering the bytes in the text (blanks are indicated by _ for clarity):

```
Position:  0 1 2 3 4 5      10        15        20        25        30
String:    n o w _ i s _ t h e _ t i m e _ f o r _ a l l _ g o o d _ m e n _
Position: 33  35       40        45        50        55        60
String:    t o _ c o m e _ t o _ t h e _ a i d _ o f _ t h e _ p a r t y
```

Then label the words with their byte position, as in the following list:

Word	Byte Position
Now	0
Is	4
The	7
Time	11
For	16
All	20
Good	24
Men	29
To	33
Come	36
To	41
The	44
Aid	48
Of	52
The	55
Party	59

And this is then sorted into alphabetical order, yielding

Word	Byte Position
Aid	48
All	20
Come	36
For	16
Good	24
Is	4
Men	29

(contd)

Word	Byte Position
Now	0
Of	52
Party	59
The	7
The	44
The	55
Time	11
To	43
To	53

This permits a fast alphabetical lookup of each word, followed by a direct retrieval of the relevant part of the string. On average, to find an item in a list of N items takes $\log_2 N$ steps; this is much faster than reading an entire long file. Even for N of 1 billion (10^9) items, for example, $\log_2 N$ is only 30. To achieve this search time, use *binary search*, start at the middle of the list, and see whether the item sought is in the first or second half of the list. Then find the middle item of that half and repeat until the item is found.

Another possibility with an inverted file is simply to do a two-stage linear scan. Suppose the inverted file contains 10,000 items. Write a new file containing every 100th word and its position in the inverted file. Scan that shorter list linearly to locate the approximate position of the sought term and then scan the 1/100th of the large list. For 10,000 items, binary search should take about 14 probes and two-stage search will take 50 in each list, or 100 total. However, since there are fewer random probes (requiring a disk seek) and more continuous reads, the performance difference is likely to be small. It is not uncommon to find the cost of reading "the next item" off a disk to be, say, 1/30th the cost of reading "a random item" so that 2 seeks and 100 reads require only as much time as 5 seeks, much less than 14.

Inverted files are the basis of the large systems used today. Nothing else can manage files of gigabytes or terabytes with adequate response time. That said, inverted files have disadvantages. They cannot search for arbitrary expressions. Typically, systems based on inverted files can only do searches based on the beginning of words. Thus, one will find options for searching for keys like *plate?*, meaning all words which begin with those five letters (*plated, plates,* and so on). To do the reverse—to find all words which *end* with a particular string—will normally require another complete inverted file with the words sorted on their ends, not their beginnings. Inverted files also must be computed before the searches can be done; this can be a long, slow process. Basically, it is a sort and will take $N \log N$ time units for N words in the file. Most important, it means that updates cannot be accessed immediately; as the file is changed, it must be reindexed to create a new set of inverted files. Often, supplementary files are used to allow updates to be accessed immediately, at the cost of requiring two searches.

Inverted files may take a lot of space. The overhead for inverted file systems ranges from 25–200 percent. Space needs can be lowered by using *stopwords*, typically the 50 or 100 purely syntactic words which comprise about half the word occurrences in English. Assuming that users will rarely wish to search for words like *the* or *and*, a great deal of space in the inverted file can be saved by not bothering to keep track of them. On the other hand, more space is required if information must be stored about the context or position of each word. For example, some systems can search for a word that appears in a book title or for author names (which must be done with field labels since items like *bond* can plausibly be either a name or a word). This is called *fielded searching* and normally is done by indicating with each word occurrence which part of the text it came from. Here is a reason why it is important to have text tagged so that the computer identifies which part of the input file serves what functions.

Today, inverted files dominate all the large retrieval systems and all the CD-ROM systems. They mesh fairly well with user expectations. The low cost of modern RAM allows Web search engines to keep the entire inverted file in RAM memory, greatly accelerating their operation.

Hash Tables

Another form of search that does not involve scanning an entire file is the use of hash tables, or hash coding. The idea behind hash coding is that it would be convenient, given a word, just to compute where it appears in the file. If each letter appeared the same number of times in English, one could just say that words starting with *M* would be halfway through the inverted file. However, this is obviously not the case. One solution would be to keep careful files on the fraction of words starting with each set of letters, but because of the interletter frequencies this is difficult. For example, *Th* is more common than one would expect by looking at the letter frequencies separately, whereas initial *Ts* is less common that one would expect under the same consideration. Simpler to take each word and compute a *hash* function from it. A hash function is similar to a random number generator: it tries to produce a flat output in which each possible value for the function has about the same probability. However, it is reproducible: given the same input, it reproduces the same output. Thus, a hash storage system works by taking each input word, computing its hash function, and storing the word and whatever auxiliary information is needed in the location pointed to by the hash function.

Consider a simple (but not very good) hash function like "add up all the values of the letters in each word." Then taking the same string we had before (*now is the time for all good men to come to the aid of the party*) and assigning $a = 1, b = 2$, and so on, we would get hash values as follows:

Word	Value
now	52
is	28
the	33
time	47
for	39
all	25
good	41
men	32
to	35
come	36
to	35
the	33
aid	14
of	21
the	33
party	80

One problem is immediately apparent. Even for such short words, we find the bucket locations (i.e., number of values) ranging up to 80. To store only 16 words, that seems silly. To make such a list a reasonable length, the easiest thing to do is divide by some number and take the remainder. It is good if that number is a prime, since it will spread out the remainders more evenly. Let's arbitrarily pick 19 buckets in the hash table. Then the hash function is "add up the letters and take the remainder modulo 19." The result is

Word	Value
now	14
is	9
the	14
time	9
for	1
all	6
good	3
men	13

(contd)

Word	Value
to	16
come	17
to	16
the	14
aid	14
of	2
the	14
party	4

So the contents of the buckets are

Bucket	Word
1	for
2	of
3	good
4	party
9	time, is
13	men
14	the, aid, now
16	to
17	come

Already all the standard problems of hash storage have shown themselves. The words *the, aid,* and *now* all wound up at 14—they are said to have *collided.* Meanwhile buckets 5 through 8 have nothing in them. Since the aim is to spread out the values evenly across the 19 buckets, this shows that our hash function wasn't very good. Let's try something slightly better: multiply each letter value by its position in the word. This yields

Bucket	Word
2	time
3	good
4	all
8	men, of
9	is
11	party
12	to, aid

(contd)

Bucket	Word
13	the
14	for
16	come
18	now

There are still two collisions; this is normal for hash storage systems. To search this list, repeat the hash computation on the word sought and look in the resulting bucket. In general, results very close to the desired one-probe-per-item can be obtained. The bucket is normally organized into a "collision chain" of cells, putting the items in other cells which are empty. Either a linear search or a secondary hash function searches through the collision chain for additional items. Hash systems can provide faster retrieval than binary search. They are very common in exact match computer applications (e.g., looking up words in computer languages like Fortran). Surprisingly, we do not know who invented hashing. It was certainly known in the 1960s (Morris, 1968), but although it is not an exact derivative of any noncomputer storage mechanism, nobody has claimed the invention. The hash algorithm described here is not really very good (e.g. just adding the letter values collapses anagrams), and an implementor looking for procedures to code should consult papers on text retrieval by hashing, such as Savoy (1990), Ramakrishna and Zobel (1997), and Zobel et al. (2001).

The disadvantages of hash storage for digital libraries relate to the sensitivity of the storage algorithm to the exact spelling of a word. Since the goal of the hashing algorithm is to spread the words as randomly as possible, variants like *plated* and *plating* will be very far apart (in this last hash table, at 1 and 16, respectively). Hash tables are thus a bad way to search for a set of words sharing a common root. Since many retrieval systems wish to do searches for words with common beginnings, hash tables for words are rarely used in large systems despite their efficiency advantages. Hashing shares with inverted files the need to spend time processing a file before it can be used and the need for storage overhead.

Updating in hash tables shows some asymmetries. Adding an item is straightforward, but deleting an item involved in a collision requires either (a) the reorganization of the collision chain to be sure that everything can still be found (a difficult operation since the list of items that hashed into this chain is probably hard to find) or (b) the abandonment of that memory cell, filling it with a dummy entry that just says "keep looking." The upshot is that hash table systems are not efficient for a database that involves a lot of changes if any large fraction of the changes involve deletions.

There is a variant of hashing called *perfect hashing* in which collisions are avoided, for a particular list of words, by selecting a hash function with no collisions on that list (and which maps the list into one of exactly the right length). Instead of handling collisions at search time, an auxiliary table is made to adjust the hash function so that these collisions do not come up (Cormack et al., 1985).

Unfortunately, perfect hashing requires a stable list of words. Since practical digital libraries get updates, perfect hashing is not usually relevant. Even with perfect hashing, the words still must be stored in the hash table and checked to ensure that the right one is found; perfect hashing still allows the possibility that an incorrectly typed search term may be hashed to the same location as a different word.

Other Text Search Issues

Textbooks on data structures include other forms of file organization; these include *tries* and *signature files*.

Tries, developed by Edward Sussenguth (at Harvard) and others in the mid-1960s are instantly generated inverted files. Moving letter by letter through a list of words, each letter points to a list of items. To begin, one chooses the correct first letter, which points to a list of items by second letter, and so on. Tries have the advantages that updating is easy for both additions and deletions and retrieval is relatively fast. Prefix searches for all words beginning with a given string are also easy. However, both storage overhead and the time required to process the data into the trie are disadvantages. As a consequence, tries are not popular in digital libraries.

Signature files are another data structuring technique that can sometimes be applied to digital libraries. This model is the closest analog of edge-notched cards. Each record is replaced with a short string containing codes reflective of the content of the record, and these are then linearly searched. The codes are generated with hash routines so that they make very efficient use of the available space. Nevertheless, searching any kind of linear file is eventually going to be slower than searching an inverted file.

Since digital libraries are usually searching files of text, the kind of numerical or exact-match technologies used in databases are not sufficient. For example, a search for *library* should probably retrieve documents using the word *libraries* and, similarly, other morphological changes. Roughly speaking, there are something like three variants of the typical English word (albeit perhaps with widely different frequencies). In declined languages such as Russian, there may be many more variants.

Suffixing even of English is more complicated than just matching prefixes. Consider, for example, the following list:

Root	Derived Word
cope	coping
copy	copying, copies
cop	copping (a plea), cops

Other nonregular English derivations include such changes as *absorption* from *absorb* or *slept* from *sleep*.

It is possible to do some of the simpler transformations merely from the complex word; for example, removing final *s* or *ing* but it is much more accurate to do this in the context of a dictionary of stems. Otherwise it is hard not to start turning *nation* into *nate* or to work out that *determination* should come from *determine* but that *termination* comes from *terminate*. See Lovins (1968), Porter (1980), Paice (1990), Hull (1996), or Kostoff (2003) for suffix analysis rules. A common simplification is right truncation: searching for every string beginning with a certain set of letters. This introduces inaccuracies but is adequate for many systems and easily understood by the user.

Prefixes also could be removed, although they are less important in English. Again, a dictionary of word stems is valuable in deciding why *in-* might be removed from *inadequate* or *inaccuracy,* but not from *infer*. Prefixes are more likely than suffixes to change the meaning of a word; removing *in* often reverses the meaning of a word (but do not forget that there are exceptions like *inflammable*). Truncation from the left, a possible alternative to prefixing, is more expensive than right truncation in the typical retrieval system; it will require the entire word indexing software to be redone, with the strings handled in reverse order.

Sometimes users might wish to have variable characters in the middle of words to allow, for example, looking for *aeroplane* and *airplane* by typing something like *a?plane* at the search system. This can be quite expensive to implement and comes up less frequently, so it is often omitted from system design; again, cheaper RAM memory has allowed some of the Web search engines to support this kind of operation.

Other possible ramifications of text search include the ability to search for phonetically similar strings. Although dating from 1916, the best known system for this is Soundex, a translation algorithm which attempts to reduce similar sounding words to the same string. Words are replaced by four-character strings, each of which has an initial letter and then three digits. The letter is the initial letter of the original string; the digits represent successive consonants in the word, grouped into classes:

Class	Letters
1	BPFV
2	CGJKQSXZ
3	DT
4	L
5	MN
6	R
0	—

The zero is used to fill out strings when there are not enough consonants. Note that all doubled letters (including doublings of class members) are treated as single codes. Thus *Jack* becomes J200, as would *Jock* or *Jak*. But *Jacques* would be J220 because vowels are interposed between the *cq* and the *s*.

String matching software also has other applications. Searching databases of genetic sequences using string matching techniques is now of major importance in computational molecular biology. The greater tolerance for insertions and deletions in this context has caused alternate algorithms, such as dynamic programming, to be more heavily used than in text searching.

Free text search systems of the sort described in the last few sections were a rapidly growing business in the 1990s. Some of the leading text retrieval software companies and their revenues are shown in Table 2.2.

The text retrieval industry as a whole grew rapidly until the mid-1990s and then turned into a Web search industry. Currently, the number of searches done on the Web is enormous compared to those done using stand-alone search systems.

Table 2.2 Revenues of text retrieval software companies.

Company	Product	1996 Revenues	2002 Revenues
Dataware	OpenText	$41 M	$152 M
Fulcrum	Hummingbird	$31 M	$180 M
Information Dimensions	OpenText	$29 M	Absorbed
Verity	Ultraseek	$21 M	$93 M
Excalibur	Convera	$19 M	$23 M

2.4   Web Searching

Today, the Web is the search mechanism of choice. Robots scour visible files and copy them back to a central location. Files are then indexed and cached, ready for a user to provide a query, whereupon the results are displayed to the user's browser.

Robots were an unanticipated feature on the Web. When they were first created, there was unanticipated chaos. For example, some very dumb robots simply went through pages clicking every box including "delete" operations in databases. More commonly, they simply overloaded systems by doing continual fetches on the same Web server or by piling up too many bandwidth requests. The Web community felt a need to control these robots, and the convention of a "robots.txt" file appeared. This file contains instructions to visiting robotic systems, specifying which areas they should enter or keep out of. The format is relatively trivial: the *robots.txt* contains lines of the form

```
User-agent: name
Disallow: files
```

where *name* identifies a particular robot, with the "*" character meaning any robot, and *files* gives a part of the filesystem that the robots should not visit, with a single "/" meaning the entire file system. Thus,

```
User-agent: *
Disallow: /
```

tells all robots to go away.

The purposes of robot exclusion have changed, however. The well-known search engines now use well-debugged and more gentle spiders, which avoid overloading a single server. Primary motivations for robot exclusion are now economic, namely, precluding people from accessing a site other than through mechanisms designed by the site owner, typically to force exposure to advertisements or to go through a payment mechanism.

Search engines now often cache the results they have found. Web pages are not very reliably maintained and are often unavailable. The search engine typically wants to copy the page anyway, and by retaining the copy the search engine can supply missing pages.

On the Web, most of the search engine software provides only a relatively simple interface. Frequently, users do not even know that some moderate amount of fielded searching is available, typically by typing strings like `url:xxx` to mean "look for xxx in the url of the page." Most search queries are very simple.

Typical Web searches return one or two pages of results, which then must be improved by page ranking.

2.5 Thesauri

As we will discuss in Chapter 7 under retrieval system evaluation, there are two kinds of mistakes that a retrieval system can make: errors of omission (a relevant document is not found) and errors of inclusion (a nonrelevant document is retrieved). The first kind of error is called a *recall* failure and the second is a *precision* failure. Conventionally, in simple keyword searching, a recall failure can occur when the same concept is expressed in two different words. The user might ask for information on "boats" and the document might talk about "ships" or some other equivalent. Precision failures can arise by the presence of ambiguous words: the user may have asked for "rock" meaning music and be given documents about geology. The use of a thesaurus is a possible answer to these problems.

With a thesaurus, a single label is applied to each concept. The most familiar form is *Roget's Thesaurus,* a list of 1000 concepts with a list of words for each. A variant of this format is used in information retrieval. Thesauri give a single label for each separate idea and then a list of equivalent terms. Most commonly, the label is not a number as in Roget, but a phrase. Thus, for example, in Medical Subject Headings (MeSH), the word *neoplasm* is used for "cancer" and its equivalents. Thus, the same label can be searched for regardless of the word used in the text, improving recall.

As an example of a thesaurus, consider the ERIC (Educational Resources Information Clearinghouse) thesaurus shown in the following excerpt:

```
DEBATE    CIJE: 246    RIE: 240    GC: 400

   BT Language Arts

   RT Persuasive Discourse; Public Speaking; Social Problems;
      Verbal Communication

Debate Judges USE    JUDGES

Deceleration USE    ACCELERATION (PHYSICS)
```

The user starts with the words in the left column (the *entry vocabulary*), and the system recommends or offers the terms in the central column as legal descriptors. The entry vocabulary is alphabetically arranged. In this excerpt **BT** means "broader term," while **RT** means "related term," and **USE** means "use instead."

Each category label is unique in the thesaurus. Each label has one and only one meaning so that a search can be unambiguous within the limits of that label definition. However, there are ambiguities in the best-written texts, and there are certainly opportunities to choose different topics as being worth recording about a document. There are going to be different decisions about what the proper focus of emphasis should be, or about the extent of some label definition. Thus, even the use of a proper thesaurus, combined with professional assignment of index categories, will still leave some retrieval problems.

In addition, it is expensive to use thesauri in information retrieval systems since there is as yet no automatic way of assigning the categories. Manual indexers, as used in the retrieval systems Medline or Westlaw, involve considerable cost and some delay. Only elaborate and well-funded retrieval operations can afford this. Many smaller digital library operations cannot use manual indexing and thus find little use for thesauri. Early experiments by Cleverdon, Salton, and others showed little benefit from manual indexing, causing most online systems to decide that thesauri were not worth the trouble.

2.6   Statistical Language Processing

Could syntactic processing improve retrieval? Surface structure parsers, which identify the correct structure of each sentence, would seem potentially useful for labeling the content of documents. This promise has been held out for decades, but with relatively little progress. What is wrong?

- Surface structure parses are ambiguous. Sentences such as *"Time flies like an arrow"* with its five possible analyses (consider the parse of the sentence *"Fruit flies like a banana"*) are still relatively simple compared with many longer sentences. Given the isolated sentence *"I saw the man in the park with the telescope"*, there is no way even for a human reader to decide whether the telescope belongs to the narrator, the man, or the park.
- Surface structure parses don't tell you what you need to know. For example, *"The pig is in the pen"* and *"The ink is in the pen"* have the same surface structure parse, but if that is all you can say about the two sentences, you are not helping with the actual problem of deciding between the different meanings of *pen*.
- Surface structure does not take account of context. *"John went home; you should too"* may ask you to go home, but not necessarily to the same place that John went. A more common example is the failure of surface structure parsing to deal with pronoun reference. A system may not realize that *car* is the object of *drive* in the sentence *"If a car breaks down, you can't drive it any further"* if it cannot decide the referent of *it*.

■ Surface structure may be too restrictive. Given a query for "optical character recognition," a parser might deduce that the sentence "*Special character sets have been designed for easier recognition by optical or magnetic check-reading machines*" does not contain that phrase, but it is probably relevant to the query.

In their 1975 book, Karen Sparck-Jones and Martin Kay discussed the paradox that linguistics seemed to be of so little use to libraries and retrieval. Sparck-Jones was still pessimistic in 2001. Their discussion is unfortunately still valid (Sparck-Jones, 2002). Part of the problem is that much of linguistics has been devoted to syntax, while many of the problems of information retrieval derive from semantics. Retrieval can work reasonably well with strategies that do not use word order at all, sorting the words in a document into alphabetical lists. By contrast, knowing the syntactic structure of the sentences, without knowing the words, would be useless for finding anything.

An exception was Salton's work on phrase detection. He was able to make considerable progress on identifying phrases for the purpose of improving the precision of retrieval systems (Salton and Buckley, 1991). Salton's later work used weighted term matching for global selection and then local context of the terms to improve precision. Salton used distinguishing words based on the trailing context; thus "Kennedy, elected President in . . ." can be distinguished from "Kennedy, appointed Justice in . . ." to separate articles referring to John F. Kennedy from those referring to Anthony M. Kennedy. This yielded impressive performance numbers using entire articles from *Funk and Wagnall's Encyclopedia* as queries. Working with shorter queries is more difficult.

Others have continued Salton's work on phrases, but progress is slow and somewhat doubtful. Pickens (Pickens and Croft, 2000), for example, writes that "it is still not clear whether phrases can be used to improve retrieval effectiveness." Perhaps more ambitious work such as that of Chung and Schatz (Chung et al., 1999), using phrases and context to create large-scale concept spaces, will make better use of linguistic models in retrieval.

Part of the difficulty with trying to disambiguate language is that much ambiguity is deliberate, left in the text either because the speaker would rather have the ambiguity or because it is not worth the trouble of being precise. For example, spoken sentences with acoustic ambiguities, in which a given sound can be correctly transcribed into either of two words, are called puns (Why did Cinderella buy a Polaroid camera? She was tired of waiting for her prints to come.) There are syntactic ambiguities (British left waffles on Falklands). And there are semantic ambiguities when a given word might be read two different ways (How do you identify a dogwood tree? By its bark.) More often, of course, ambiguity is unintentional but unimportant. Do you care, for instance, that you cannot tell at the beginning of this sentence whether "more often" modifies only *unintentional* or also *unimportant*?

2.7 Document Conversion

How do documents get into retrieval systems in the first place? Overwhelmingly, they arrive from computer word processing systems, as virtually everything written today is prepared on a computer. However, sometimes old documents need to be converted into machine-readable form. There are two general strategies for doing this: keying them or scanning them. Scanning is followed by optical character recognition (OCR) to obtain a character by character text, although accuracy is sometimes unacceptably low without postediting.

It would seem that scanning would generally be much cheaper than keying. Rekeying costs perhaps $1/KB for a single keying and 50% or so more for careful checking or rekeying. The cheapest prices are not likely to be from US-based keying operations. Given that a good typist can do 50 words per minute, at 6 bytes/word the actual input rate is perhaps 300 bytes/minute or 20,000 bytes per hour. However, there are nearly always markup, labeling, and other costs. (The extra cost of markup and tracking is why double keying does not cost twice as much as single keying).

In keying historic materials, often it is desirable to retain the original spelling and any mistakes, rather than correcting them to current standard. To do this, it may actually be effective to have the keying done by people who do not know the language in which the document is written, as they are less likely to replace older conventions by modern forms.

Scanning is in principle cheaper, even for pages that are sufficiently fragile that each one has to be handled individually. Scanning, OCR, and correction for one page (perhaps 2000-3000 bytes) costs about 40 cents per page, or 20 cents per KB, provided that not too much postediting is required. Manually fixing mistakes at a rate of one or two per line can cost as much as rekeying. As an example of how poorly OCR may function on some text that actually doesn't look all that bad to the eye, Figure 2.2 shows an image from the *London Daily Mail* and two different commercial OCR program results.

OCR programs do much better with higher-quality printing on better paper. Figure 2.3 provides such a sample from an American Chemical Society journal. The only mistake is in the footnote.

OCR results have been improving steadily. The University of Nevada, Las Vegas, used to run regular comparisons between OCR systems. In 1996 their test involved 5 million bytes of text from corporate annual reports, newspapers, legal documents, business letters, and magazines. Scanning resolutions ranged from

New Humphrey mystery

HUMPHREY the Downing Street cat, cleared of killing four robins a fortnight ago, is back under a cloud. He has been spotted by police and security men returning to No 10 with a baby duck in his mouth, suspiciously like one of several birds reported missing from Duck Island in nearby St. James's Park. Malcolm Kerr, head keeper, said: "Humphrey is far from innocent." The cat, aged six, is believed to operate under cover of darkness and to be an expert at dodging traffic on his park trips.

New Humphrey mystery
HUMPHREY the DownLng Street cat, cleared of kllll'ig fotir robins a fortnight ago, Ia back under a cloud. He has been spotted by police and security men retilrning to No 10 with a baby duck in Ms mouth, suspiciously like one of several birds reported missing from Duck Island In nearby St. James'5 PariL Malcolm Kerr, head keeper, said: "Humphrey Ia far from Innocent." The cat, aged six, Ia believed to operate wider coe'er of darkness and to be an expert at dodge tram£ on `lie park trips.

New Humphrey mystery
   HREY the Downing Street cat, c
four robim a fortnight ago, is back under a cloud. He has been spotted by PoUce and security men returning to No 10 with a baby d-uck in his mouth, suspiciously Uke one of several b@ reported   ftom Duck Is@d in nearby St. James's Park. Maloolm Kerr, head keeper, said, "Humphrey is far fmm bmocent.' The cat, aged s@ is believed to operate under   of darkness and to be an expert at dodging trame on his park trips.

Figure 2.2 OCR results of newspaper text.

about 200 dots per inch (the typical fax machine resolution) to 400 dots per inch (dpi). They found character accuracies of 97–99% for the different quality documents over several OCR programs. Each year accuracy is improving, albeit slowly. The best 1996 program scored 98.83% accuracy on English business letters; the best 1995 program came in at 98.61%. In some cases speed is decreasing (although faster processors mean that users still see quicker results). The recognition speeds ranged from 25 to 200 characters per second (Rice et al., 1996). With word accuracies of about 95%, there is still a lot of correction to do. A review in 2002 by ZDNet India (Pardawala and Kantawalla, 2002) rated Omnipage at 99.29% and ABBYY Finereader at 99.05%. Currently, a great deal of effort is spent capturing and reproducing the format of the scanned document, which is important for later word processing, but not particularly important for information retrieval. Another major element of progress is the support of additional

increase in shear rate. The thixotropy and the viscoelas-
ticity and non-Newtonian behavior are indicative for
changes in the internal structure of the solution. Those
changes originate from alignment and disruption of the
rodlike micelles by the shear forces.[41,42]

increase in shear rate. The thixotropy and the viscoelas-
ticity and non-Newtonian behavior are indicative for
changes in the internal structure of the solution. Those
changes originate from alignment and disruption of the
rodlike micelles by the shear forces.41~2

Figure 2.3   OCR of journal passage.

languages; Finereader supports more than 100 languages, and others are working
on Chinese and Japanese OCR (Tseng and Oard, 2001).

Fortunately, some information retrieval algorithms are very resistant to OCR
errors. This makes sense, since a word of great importance to the content of a
document is likely to be repeated, and the OCR program may well capture at
least one of the instances correctly. At the University of Colorado, Tom Landauer
performed studies on Latent Semantic Indexing, which showed good retrieval
performance on copy with up to 50% of the words degraded. The experiments
took place on a collection of medical abstracts, and LSI showed a 20% advantage
over plain keyword search, even with half the words misspelled. Similar studies
were done by Craig Stanfill at Thinking Machines, by Bruce Croft (Pickens
and Croft, 2000), and by Claudia Pearce (Pearce and Nicholas, 1996). Croft
found significant degradation in his results, which were word-based; Pearce and
Nicholas, working with an N-gram based indexing system, were able to achieve
remarkably good retrieval even with 30% character errors (meaning that the
average word was garbled). Olive Software, a leader in the conversion of old
newspapers, designs its search software carefully to adapt to the errors made by
OCR systems running on badly printed and badly conserved originals. Similar
problems exist in systems running off speech recognition (Crestani, 2000), those
using handwriting (Nielsen 1993), and in processing a variety of multimedia
documents (Perrone et al., 2002).

Whatever the ability of OCR to cope, scanning old paper has high handling
costs. Considerably cheaper scanning can be achieved either with modern paper
that can be sheet fed or with microfilm. Sheet feeding or microfilm scanning will
cost perhaps 10 cents per page, depending on how much indexing information
has to be keyed along with it.

Any estimate of conversion cost is likely to be grossly low if considerable editorial work is required. The easiest conversion is material which is self-describing
(so that no large number of identification labels must be keyed along with the

basic text), not full of typographic variations that must be tracked, and not requiring careful reproduction of nonstandard spelling. Tables, equations, and other nontext materials also raise scanning costs.

Much literary material has already been converted and made available by commercial vendors. Chadwyck-Healey, for example, sells a set of five CD-ROMS containing all published English poetry up to 1900, the full text of the Patrologia Latina, and other literary information. Other material comes from government-organized projects, such as the full texts of French classic literary works prepared at the University of Nancy at the TLF (Trésor de la Langue Française). Still more material comes from a mix of smaller government-funded projects or university efforts and is deposited in such places as the Oxford Text Archive or in area-specific archives such as the Rossetti file at the University of Virginia. Universities engage in related efforts, such as the CLIO system at Columbia, which attempts to put the material needed for the university's basic courses online. Finally, totally volunteer efforts, such as Project Gutenberg, have put additional items into machine-readable form.

Keeping track of all this material has been a bit chaotic over the years. In the early days of computer-readable texts, *Paradise Lost* was keyed three times by people who did not know it was being done elsewhere. More recently, however, the Center for Electronic Text in the Humanities (CETH) at Rutgers and Princeton has maintained an online catalog of materials for humanists. Since this catalog is on RLIN (Research Libraries Information Network), many people without access to RLIN rely on Internet search systems, which will find many of the works sought. A serious issue, however, is the quality of editing of each of the files. For many humanities researchers, it is important to have accurate, well-edited texts online; versions adequate for popular reading are not sufficient. Insufficient evaluation has been made of the editorial quality of some online texts, particularly those contributed by volunteers. And in some cases, the desire to avoid copyright problems has resulted in the use of nineteenth-century texts instead of modern and more accurate texts still under copyright protection.

Among the earliest uses of computers in the humanities was for the compilation of concordances. Concordances, or alphabetical lists of each word in a given document, had been made by hand over the years for a few books, such as the Bible and the works of Shakespeare. With computers, it suddenly became possible to do concordances rapidly and easily, and they blossomed for many kinds of texts (e.g., the concordance to the works of the Roman historian Livy, done in 1966 by David Packard). Students using either concordances or search tools with full text capabilities can write papers on subjects like "the concept of fire in the works of Galileo" much more efficiently than is possible without a machine-readable copy. It is possible to find each use of the word and then consider the word, the context, and the underlying concept. Computers also facilitate looking at the use of new words in an author's work, or looking at the development of an author's vocabulary over time (if many works are available).

Among other applications for online works, one of the most popularized is stylistic analysis to determine authorship. The original study in this area was done by the famous statistician Mosteller to identify the authors of the Federalist papers (originally published under a pseudonym), based on the use of words by Hamilton, Madison, and Jefferson. Similar studies have been done on parts of the Bible, purported new works by Shakespeare, and various other publications (including an investigation of the authorship of the best-selling novel *Primary Colors*). A related application of computerized text analysis identifies psychologically important terms (e.g., body parts) in texts and counts them, thus producing a kind of characterization of text which is not easy to do by traditional methods. Computers are also excellent at comparing different editions of the same work. Nor do they need the hardware complexity of the machine built by Hinman, which flickered between images of two pages of different copies of Shakespeare's First Folio to detect all changes during printing.

Other applications include the educational use of online text for learning languages. Computer-aided instruction is good at vocabulary drill, for example, and can be extended with the use of full texts to teach syntactic structures in foreign languages. The computation of reading levels, and thus the preparation of texts aimed at particular grade levels, is also easier with mechanical assistance.

It is possible that scholarship will be moved in the direction of extremely detailed textual studies by computer text-processing. It is now relatively easy to count the number of lines of Keats which do not contain the letter 'j,' but not much easier than a century ago to discuss the importance of religion in Shakespeare's plays. We must rely on human judgment to decide whether the first kind of study is worth doing and in what balance compared to the second.

2.8   Summary

Text processing on machines is now a mature industry. We can get giant volumes of current text in ASCII form, and the Web search engines are examples of what can be done with it. Many traditional paper abstracting and indexing services, for example, now see most of their usage online, and there are online versions of many current publications. This chapter has reviewed how such systems are built and what some of the uses of machine-readable text have been. Not only are such systems practical, they are economical and can be substantially cheaper and easier to use than paper storage.

The technology of inverted files currently dominates the industry. We can do as detailed a text search as we wish; modern systems can search up to terabytes

(10^{12} bytes) of text with adequate response time. Even as the Web gets larger (and remember that the current content of the Web in ASCII is already several times bigger than the largest brick and mortar libraries), we can still manage to do the necessary searching for full text. For smaller files, some of the alternative search mechanisms have advantages and are useful in writing programs to manage user files.

Every word can be found with a search engine. This can be good or bad. My name is rare; a search for "Lesk" will find either me or one of a small number of my relatives. Those whose name is Bond have a much harder time with search engines; in addition to the many people with that name, much use of the word is made in chemistry or glue manufacture, not to mention the many Web discussions of James Bond movies. Similarly, some concepts are easy to search for, while others are shadowed under more popular meanings of the same word or may not have a single obvious descriptive term. Nor is simple word searching always enough when what is sought is the relationship between two words, and it may be an outright disadvantage when looking only for authors and getting citations instead.

Progress will have to take the form of more concept-oriented searching, as some search engines are already beginning to advertise. Such systems will have to rely on some combination of detecting word relationships, using thesauri, and otherwise trying to access conceptual ideas rather than just word strings. We will discuss some of these challenges in Chapter 5; others remain open research problems. More immediately, however, libraries must face up to material for which we lack even full ASCII text, namely scanned pages of books and journals.

Images of Pages

Besides ASCII, the other way digital books arrive in libraries is as scanned pages. Some material is either not available as ASCII code or not appropriate to store that way. Most of such content is stored as images, portraying a picture of the original. This chapter discusses how such image files are created and how they can be accessed and used. Image files are the way most digital libraries today store non-ASCII information. Often, for content such as photography, which is basically pictorial rather than textual, this will be the format used for many years to come.

Even for material which is fundamentally made of words, software systems today often provide access to images of text, not to ASCII code. The reader sees a scanned version of the printed page. The advantages are familiarity and ease of creation. The reader sees the same familiar image, down to the headings and type styles. The software is simpler to build since it does not vary with subject matter. The disadvantages of the image format are that searching must depend on other cues than the text itself (often a separate index or OCR file) and that the image is usually much bulkier than the text would be. A typical printed page from a book would contain some 2,000 bytes in ASCII, while the same page as an image will be 30 kilobytes or so, even compressed. For example, Figure 3.1 shows a comparison: the word 'cat' has three bytes; the line drawing is about a kilobyte; and the scanned photograph is 13 kilobytes compressed with JPEG (Joint Photographic Experts Group) compression.

Figure 3.1 A comparison of representations of the word *cat*.

Images are much less adaptable than text: a reader with poor eyesight or viewing a bad screen or under bad light conditions cannot choose a larger character size, for example. Cut-and-paste downloading also makes capturing the material for later use more difficult (although both Xerox PARC and the Bibliothèque Nationale de France have experimented with bitmap editing systems).

3.1 Scanning

Images are often the choice for older material; post-1980 material will be available in machine-readable form, since hot-lead machines had completely given way to computer typesetting by then. A library wishing to convert old material to machine-readable form, however, is likely to have no economic alternative to scanning, since keystroking costs 10 times as much as scanning. Scanning is so cheap, in fact, that its cost is comparable with the cost of building shelf space to hold books.

Scanning technology has improved dramatically through the 1990s in accessibility and usage. Handheld scanners are now available for PCs, and there are over 800 million scanned images on the Web. Much of the improvement has been a consequence of the development of photocopiers and facsimile machines, resulting in widely available hardware to move paper through electronic gadgets and produce digital representations of them.

There are several kinds of scanning machines available. The most familiar are flatbed scanners, which place the image on a glass window and move a scanning head past the image. Typically, scanner windows will accommodate up to 8 × 14 inch paper, although they will accept smaller images as well, and large-format machines do exist (accommodating up to 24 × 36 inches). They will normally scan color, grayscale, or bitonal (one bit per pixel) and will do so at resolutions up to 1200 or 2400 dpi. Flatbed scanners with good quality and interface software now cost under $100. Such scanners do a simple bitonal scan at a few seconds per page or so. They can be equipped with sheet feeders to handle paper of acceptable strength.

Scanning machines are based on CCD (charge-coupled device) sensors and are essentially a linear array of CCD sensors, perhaps with color filters in front of them. The scanning array has many devices, since to achieve 300 dots across an 8-inch page the scanner needs a 2400-element row of sensors, but it is physically small and optics are used to reduce the image to the size of the array. Although flatbeds move the scanner past the image, there are also scanners which push the paper past the imaging device. Flatbeds are preferable for scanning from books or fragile paper, which cannot be moved easily by machine.

As an example of the use of such a scanner, I fed a 900-page book (out of copyright) through an HP Scanjet 4C, at 15 seconds/page; since I needed to change the stack of paper every ten or fifteen minutes and often missed the change, it took most of a day, rather than the expected 2 hrs. Quality was high enough for an OCR program to work quite reliably (it took overnight to do all 900 pages). An automatic deskewing program was used to align the pages. To use the stack feeder, however, meant cutting the binding off the book to turn it into a pile of loose pages. Some items, of course, should not be treated this way, but this means each page is placed by hand. Stack feeders are often not appropriate for old books, even if the book can be destroyed, since the dirt and paper chips common in such books are likely to jam the scanner.

There are also scanners costing $20 K and more; these scan in pages per second instead of pages per minute and are normally used in commercial applications to handle large volumes of standard-format documents (credit card slips, bank checks, and the like).

Other kinds of scanners pass the pages across the scanning head rather than moving the scanning head. Many of these scanners are faster, but they require that the paper be somewhat stronger and in better condition. They may also be double-sided, flipping the paper over and sending it past the scan heads again. Often they are only 300 dpi bitonal (i.e., they are made to scan printed or typed documents and not color drawings or photographs). These scanners might well operate at 1–2 seconds per page, at a cost of $5000 to $10,000. Another kind of paper-moving scanner is a desktop device that feeds a single page through a small scanner, again intended for print-only copy for OCR. These are now cheap enough to be bundled with keyboards.

Better for library use are scanners which mount a sensor above the page and do not touch it at all. The best known is the Minolta PS7000 bookscanner, although others are made by companies such as Leaf Systems. Often the scanner is effectively a digital camera, meaning that there may be no moving parts in the system. Prices for these systems start at $7000 or so; a person must turn the pages, but the book need not be pressed against anything (it still has to open

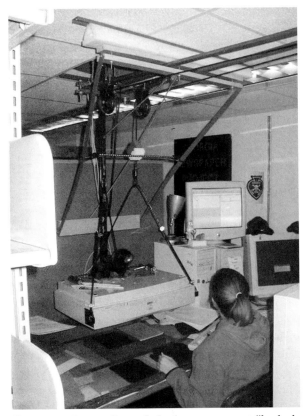

Figure 3.2 Suspending a flatbed scanner to get "look-down" operation.

pretty flat, though). Software may compensate for the curl of the pages at the binding. A remarkable attempt to build a similar system at the University of Georgia is shown in Figure 3.2; this is an ordinary flatbed scanner mounted upside down and hung from the ceiling with cables and counterweights so it can be lifted from the book with a footpedal. Needless to say, this required a library staffer with considerable mechanical skills.

Two different page-turning machines are now on the market, one named the Digitizing Line from 4 Digital Books and the other named the Bookscan from Kirtas Technology. Both are fairly expensive (around $300 K and around $150 K, respectively) and use air pressure to grab and separate the pages (usually vacuum to grab, and a gentle air blast to separate pages stuck together). These devices are shown in Figure 3.3. They can process pages two to four times as fast as a person turning pages, and are believed to turn more reliably and thus produce somewhat better quality. Given their relatively small cost advantage when one

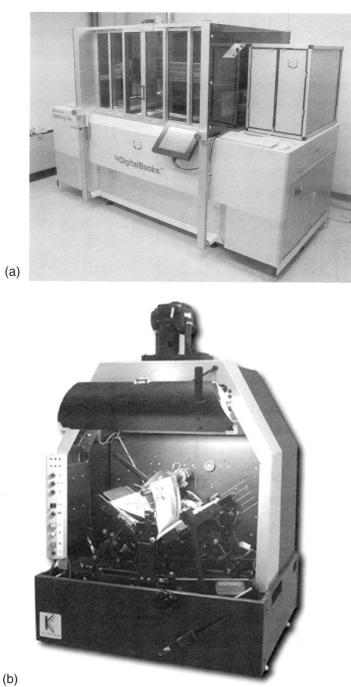

(a)

(b)

Figure 3.3 Page-turning and scanning machines: (a) Digitizing Line; (b) Kirtas Bookscan.

compares the price of the machine to the cost of labor, and the fragility of paper in old books, many libraries are staying with hand operation.

Quality of scanning is normally expressed in resolution, measured in dots per inch. For comparison, fax machines scan 200 dots per inch (horizontally only), while laser printers print at 300 dots per inch. Scanning is inherently more demanding of resolution than printing, since a printer can align the letters it is printing with the basic grid of pixels it can print. It is worth a factor of two in resolution to be able to align the letters with the ink spots printed by the machine. Thus, one would expect to need 600 dpi scanning to preserve the quality of a laser printer page at 300 dpi. Quality that good may not be necessary if the only goal is readability. Figure 3.4 shows progressively poorer resolution in scanning. The readability also depends on the type size; this document was about 6-point type, print about as small as will normally be encountered for library documents. At this type size, the 100 dpi image is almost unreadable. Librarians and others normally consider 300 dpi to be a minimum quality resolution for scanning, and many argue for 600 dpi or even higher.

To understand the type in Figure 3.4, consider that a minimum letter representation as a bitmap for display is about 5×7. This means that 10 bits across the letter are needed for scanning. An average letter printed in 8-point type is about 4 points wide, or 18 letters per inch. Thus, resolution of 180 dots per inch, or about 200 dpi, should be enough to provide readable quality, and 300 dpi should be good enough to provide some margin. So, for example, the Archives Division of the State of Oregon specifies the following in its administrative rules: "(1) Office documents containing fonts no smaller than six-point shall be scanned at a minimum density of 200 dpi. Documents containing fonts smaller than six-point, architectural and engineering drawings, maps, and line art shall be scanned at a minimum density of 300 dpi."

Microfilm scanners, for libraries, comprise an important subclass of scanners. Microfilm is physically strong, and of standard format (either 16 mm or 35 mm). As a result it can be scanned faster than paper, with microfilm scanners running in times measured in seconds per page. Companies such as Minolta, Mekel and Sunrise build microfilm scanners costing tens of thousands of dollars. Libraries have traditionally used 35 mm microfilm; most other users have moved to 16 mm film. Normally, microfilm is black and white, high contrast, and thus only bitonal scanning makes sense. The grayscale or color information is usually destroyed when the film is made. Microfilming can be done in color, but the higher cost of the film, its lower resolution, the scarcity of color illustrations in old books, and the greater care that would be needed in the filming all mean that color film is rarely used.

Although scanners are still essential for conversion of older library contents, new images increasingly come directly from digital cameras. Scanner sales in the

(a)

Adirondack Division	3	5	11
Lv Utica....................	1 50	2 15	§8 55
Ar Forestport...............	f 2 48	f 3 17	§9 44
Ar Woodgate...............	f 2 58	f 3 27	§9 55
Ar McKeever...............	f 3 09	f 3 38	§1008
Ar Thendara..............	3 25	3 55	§1029
Ar Big Moose..............	3 49	4 13	§1052
Ar Beaver River..........	4 06	f 4 25	§1108
Ar Sabattis..............	4 38	f 4 52	§1144
Ar Horseshoe.............	f 4 48	f 5 00	§1155
Ar Childwold.............	5 00	5 11	§1208
Ar Tupper Lake..........	5 21	5 34	§1222
Ar Saranac Inn...........	5 47	5 58	§1245
Ar Lake Clear Jct.........	5 55	6 04	§1250
Ar Saranac Lake..........	6 40	6 45	§1 25
Ar Lake Placid..........	7 10	8 00	.....

(b)

Adirondack Division	3	5	11
Lv Utica....................	1 50	2 15	§8 55
Ar Forestport...............	f 2 48	f 3 17	§9 44
Ar Woodgate...............	f 2 58	f 3 27	§9 55
Ar McKeever...............	f 3 09	f 3 38	§1008
Ar Thendara..............	3 25	3 55	§1029
Ar Big Moose..............	3 49	4 13	§1052
Ar Beaver River..........	4 06	f 4 25	§1108
Ar Sabattis..............	4 38	f 4 52	§1144
Ar Horseshoe.............	f 4 48	f 5 00	§1155
Ar Childwold.............	5 00	5 11	§1208
Ar Tupper Lake..........	5 21	5 34	§1222
Ar Saranac Inn...........	5 47	5 58	§1245
Ar Lake Clear Jct.........	5 55	6 04	§1250
Ar Saranac Lake..........	6 40	6 45	§1 25
Ar Lake Placid..........	7 10	8 00	.....

(c)

Adirondack Division	3	5	11
Lv Utica....................	1 50	2 15	§8 55
Ar Forestport...............	f 2 48	f 3 17	§9 44
Ar Woodgate...............	f 2 58	f 3 27	§9 55
Ar McKeever...............	f 3 09	f 3 38	§1008
Ar Thendara..............	3 25	3 55	§1029
Ar Big Moose..............	3 49	4 13	§1052
Ar Beaver River..........	4 06	f 4 25	§1108
Ar Sabattis..............	4 38	f 4 52	§1144
Ar Horseshoe.............	f 4 48	f 5 00	§1155
Ar Childwold.............	5 00	5 11	§1208
Ar Tupper Lake..........	5 21	5 34	§1222
Ar Saranac Inn...........	5 47	5 58	§1245
Ar Lake Clear Jct.........	5 55	6 04	§1250
Ar Saranac Lake..........	6 40	6 45	§1 25
Ar Lake Placid..........	7 10	8 00	.....

Figure 3.4 Comparison of scanning resolutions: (a) 300 dpi; (b) 150 dpi; (c) 100 dpi.

United States peaked in 2000, at about 9 million, while Infotrends expects that in 2004, 53 million digital cameras and 150 million camera-equipped cellphones will be sold. New, higher-resolution digital cameras are capable of producing adequate conversions, although even a six-megapixel camera does not give as good an image as a 300 dpi flatbed scanner. Scanners are likely, however, to be limited to the conversion of old materials as nearly all new images come in digital form.

3.2 Image Formats

Plain text images can be stored in a variety of formats. Various computer operating systems or display control software systems (such as window managers), for example, have their own standard image representations, designed to be rapidly loaded onto a screen. In most library applications, however, compression is most important. Compression can be either perfectly reversible (lossless), or it can change the image slightly to obtain a higher degree of compression (lossy). Often librarians prefer lossless compression to avoid any information loss—a higher priority than saving on storage, which is becoming increasingly cheap.

Scanning books or journals and wishing to compress bitonal images of printed pages is exactly the same problem faced by the groups standardizing facsimile transmission. Facsimile standards, issued by the international telecommunications groups, have moved through several stages. The most recent version is known as Group IV, issued by a group once known as CCITT (Consultative Committee on International Telecommunications Technology) and now called ITU, International Telecommunications Union. Often the compressed bits are surrounded by a TIFF (tagged independent file format) heading section, which serves to inform programs using the file what the file structure is. TIFF can be used to describe many different kinds of image files; it is not limited to Group IV fax compression.

All image compression algorithms take advantage of some redundancy in the image. The basis of fax compression is that pages are made of letters, which are made up of printed strokes of conventional width. Thus, the normal background is white, with intervals of black of fairly predictable length. Furthermore, consecutive scan lines often have similar black/white patterns. For example, in encoding the letters *l*, *L*, or *T*, all of which have vertical strokes, the same number of black bits will appear in the same place on several successive horizontal scan lines.

Thus, CCITT Group IV fax combines horizontal and vertical compression algorithms. The horizontal compression is based on run-length encoding, using Huffman coding (see chapter 7) separately on the black and white bits of the line. A set of precomputed tables of Huffman codes tuned for the typical widths of letter strokes is written into the standard. Vertical compression is based on adjacent line coding. The standard contains codes for "this section of this line is like the last line," or "... like the last line shifted one bit right or left." Group IV fax is generally the most effective compression technique for printed pages.

Bytes	Format
1,065,016	Uncompressed
293,076	GIF
264,694	LZA (Unix compression)
144,026	Tiff group IV

Table 3.1 An example of bytes in different compression formats.

Table 3.1 shows the number of bytes in a scanned-page image (of a large page covered very densely with relatively small print) compressed in different ways.

With more normal pages, a TIFF image around 25–30 KB per page is common. Given the tape storage cost of $4/GB quoted earlier in the text, this means that tape storage of three copies of a typical library book (30 KB/page and 300 pages, or about 10 MB/book) would be about 10 cents. At these rates the dominant cost is going to be the human and machine time involved in writing the tapes, not the physical costs of the medium.

3.3 Display Requirements

Reading images on a screen can be difficult. The typical resolution for scanning is 300 dpi, but the typical computer workstation screen resolution is 72 dpi. This means that either the optical quality is lowered by a factor of 4 to get the page to have the same size, or that only part of the page will be visible. In terms of resolution, an 8.5 × 11 page scanned at 300 dpi requires 2560 × 3300 bits, and the screen might be 1024 × 768 or 1152 × 900, again far too small. There are several strategies that can be taken to deal with this.

Often the page is smaller than the computer screen. Books are often printed on paper measuring 6 × 9 inches, and a workstation might have a screen 14 inches across and 10 inches high. This permits some expansion. Typically the page has a blank margin which can be trimmed off as well, allowing still more expansion. Various interface techniques let the user navigate around the page, including scroll bars, zoom controls, or a small version of the page with an enlarging lens.

Users can be asked to buy bigger screens. Screen sizes of up to 1800 × 1440 are available today. However, there are still going to be people with laptops (or old computers) who will wish to access the digital library. Antialiasing can be used to improve the quality of the display. Antialiasing is a computer graphics technique which uses grayscale to give apparently better resolution for bitonal images.

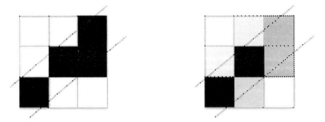

Figure 3.5 An example of antialiasing.

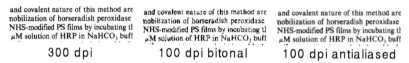

and covalent nature of this method are
nobilization of horseradish peroxidase
NHS-modified PS films by incubating th
μM solution of HRP in NaHCO₃ buff

300 dpi

and covalent nature of this method are
nobilization of horseradish peroxidase
NHS-modified PS films by incubating th
μM solution of HRP in NaHCO₃ buff

100 dpi bitonal

and covalent nature of this method are
nobilization of horseradish peroxidase
NHS-modified PS films by incubating th
μM solution of HRP in NaHCO₃ buff

100 dpi antialiased

Figure 3.6 Examples of antialiased text: (a) 300 dpi; (b) 100 dpi bitonal; (c) 100 dpi antialiased.

When a black and white image is placed on a computer screen, the original image design rarely aligns perfectly with the boundaries of the pixels which make up the screen. Clearly, those pixels which correspond to entirely white parts of the image should be white and those which are covered by black parts of the image should be black. For those pixels which are partly covered by the black part of the image, however, it improves the appearance of the image if they are gray rather than forced to either black or white. To understand this, consider the two representations of a diagonal line shown in Figure 3.5.

Assume that the area between the two diagonal strokes is supposed to be black. Note that in the left-hand figure all pixels are either black or white, which results in a rather jaggy approximation of the line. In the right-hand figure, the use of gray for the partially included pixels gives a somewhat better rendition.

This is shown for text in Figure 3.6, in which the same image is shown scanned at 300 dpi, reduced to 100 dpi bitonal, and at 100 dpi resolution antialiased. As can be seen, the antialiasing adds significantly to the readability and appearance of the text.

None of these alternatives is really a substitute for larger and higher-quality screens. In addition to the dot resolution, screens also differ in refresh rate (the higher the better, with most computer terminals now above 60 Hz) and in color quality, which we will describe later.

Many people, of course, still prefer to read from paper. It is more portable than even a laptop, until one gets to very large books. It is less dependent on electric power and less of a risk in places where either electric shock or theft may be a problem. More important, it is a medium that facilitates ease in moving about and in adjusting one's reading position and, as we've seen, it is higher in resolution.

The problem of generating images from a text file, whether for printing or for screens, would seem straightforward, and for plain text documents it is. For more complex documents it can be difficult, and for years fast printing of routine text conflicted with the ability to print high-quality graphics. In the 1980s Adobe Systems introduced Postscript, a general graphics language adapted to drawing letters from fonts. Postscript is now a standard language for interfacing to many kinds of printers and is perhaps the closest thing we have to a completely accepted standard for materials in machine-readable form. However, it is a graphics language, not a text language. It describes the appearance of a page, with the letter positions and the particular size and style of each letter all specified. Thus, it is more difficult to reuse Postscript-encoded material for other purposes than it is to reuse SGML or other text-coded materials.

Postscript, in principle, is a very powerful and complex language. It defines fonts and logos using software which can generate any kind of graphical appearance. Postscript includes a complete set of control commands in which any program can be written; I once wrote a text justification program in raw Postscript. Postscript also contains procedures for printing characters in various fonts, which are also defined in the same language. These two parts of Postscript are usually kept fairly separate: fonts are defined and then characters are printed from the fonts. Postscript includes color definition and color printing commands.

Postscript also allows the representation of arbitrary bitmaps, as from scanned images. The typical printer, however, is much slower at dealing with such bitmaps than it is with text, and some printers may run out of memory if they are asked to print too many bitmaps, or too detailed a bitmap, on a page. Under some circumstances it may be faster to convert images directly to more printer-adapted languages such as Hewlett-Packard's PCL (Printer Control Language). However, such languages are not likely to be portable across different manufacturers and should be avoided for general-purpose use. Alternatively, companies such as Adobe manufacture hardware and software to assist printers in handling Postscript and at achieving faster rates of printing.

Postscript is the basis of an Adobe software package called Acrobat, which serves as a page-viewing interface. Acrobat displays a format named PDF (Portable Document Format). PDF, like Postscript, preserves a particular page appearance. Unlike languages like SGML or HTML, Postscript and PDF do not let the user decide what the page will look like, so control of appearance stays with the document's author. For the purposes of building a digital library, this makes document entry and display simpler, albeit less flexible.

PDF is not exactly Postscript. PDF lacks the general-purpose programming language, and PDF includes provisions for interactive viewing events (e.g., the user choosing which page to display next). However, Adobe provides software to print PDF or generate it (Acrobat Exchange and Acrobat Capture). The philosophy of both Postscript and PDF is similar: the creator of a document specifies what it should look like and the reader gets that appearance. Thus, neither is suitable for an application in which, for example, people with limited vision wish to reprint everything in type three times the size of the original.

In general, Postscript and PDF are both used to print or display documents that started as machine-readable text, rather than images. Depending on exactly what software you have and where your document came from, you may be able to perform other operations such as exporting text to other systems. PDF attempts to provide controls that the document's owner can set to inhibit printing or copying if that is desired.

Neither Postscript nor PDF stresses the compression of documents which originate with scanning. There are new methods which can produce more compact representations than the general image storage systems. They are called *multilayer* or *multiraster* methods. In general, these work by separating the foreground of the page from the background. The text block (foreground) is usually high spatial frequency (sharp edges) and high contrast (only black or white); the background, whether pictures or the blank page, has fuzzier content and shades of gray. Furthermore, the text block contains many repeated images; the background usually doesn't. Thus, for example, the DjVu algorithm of AT&T (Bottou et al., 1998, 2001; Mikheev et al., 2002) compresses the background with JPEG and the foreground with dictionary compression. The result is 5 to 10 times as good as JPEG for complex pages. In addition, since the text compression relies on identifying repeated elements and noting where they appear, this is effectively OCR, and DjVu thus allows you to search the documents (effectively giving OCR as a byproduct of the compression).

As examples, the images in Figure 3.7 show the background, foreground, and full page for a typical printed page with a slightly colored background.

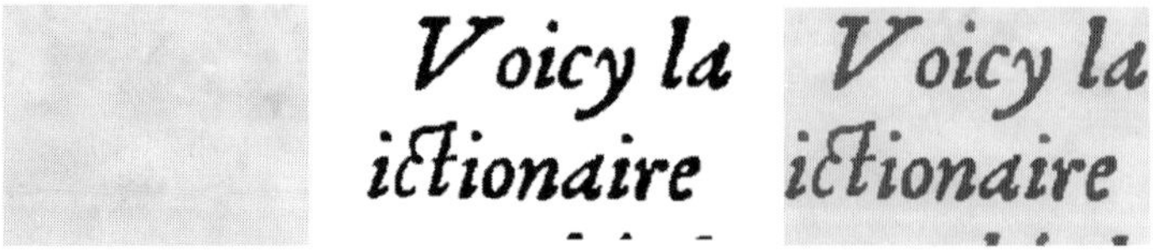

Figure 3.7 Example of background, foreground, and a full page.

DjVu is a proprietary system. Patent rights to the DjVu algorithm went from AT&T to a start-up named LizardTech and now belong to Celartem, which bought LizardTech in 2003. Other, less restricted compression software also uses the foreground/background separation idea. In particular, JPEG 2000 is to be a publicly available compression technique using multilayer methods. JPEG 2000, however, does not include a searching method by default (and we are still awaiting widespread availability of JPEG 2000 software).

3.4   Indexing Images of Pages

How does one find anything in images of pages? Unlike ASCII text, none of the kinds of database construction that we have described are possible with images. The traditional library instance is to write text descriptions of each picture and then index the text. In the context of page images, this means finding an alternate source of index information for the pages. This may, in the worst case, involve library cataloging of the material. If the images are pages in books, this may not be too bad, since a relatively small amount of cataloging will cover a large number of pages at 300 pages per book. However, the difficulty of flipping through a set of computer images, compared with flipping pages in a book, means that users will expect to be able to locate items with a fair degree of accuracy. This means indexing to the table of contents level.

Another alternative is to find an index made for other reasons. For example, the Adonis CD-ROMs (which include page images of some 700 biomedical journals) include journals which are covered by the Medline indexing system. The Adonis images need only be labeled by journal, volume, and page. Users can search Medline, retrieve a page location, and then use Adonis to find the image of that page. Similarly, the IEEE journals in CD-ROM format are covered by a printed index prepared by the society's publishing division, Inspec (IEE). The older the material involved, unfortunately, the less likely it is that such an index will exist. The newer the material, the more likely it is that a full-text searchable version will exist. Thus, the use of alternative index sources may apply in only a limited number of cases.

Typically, with online pictures of people or scenery, users might browse through thumbnails (small-size versions) of the images. But thumbnails of text pages are unreadable. If OCR worked extremely well (or was corrected manually to a high level), recognized page images could be treated as we discussed in Chapter 2. Although OCR reaches an adequate level of performance on very clean modern printing or typing, it is not accurate enough on old print or deteriorated paper to be a replacement for the imagery. What OCR can do, however, is provide a text to be used for indexing and searching. There are search algorithms which are fairly resistant to occasional errors in the text, and these will permit text searching techniques to be used with image databases.

This technique has been suggested for at least two decades. It was first tried seriously at the National Agricultural Library in the mid-1970s and was used in experiments such as the RightPages system of AT&T Bell Laboratories and UCSF (University of California San Francisco) and the TULIP effort of Elsevier; it's also now used in historical newspaper systems such as the Olive Software system. However, it has several practical disadvantages.

- In order to highlight matching terms (often considered a very desirable feature of a digital library system), the OCR program must indicate the exact location of the characters recognized. Few provide this information; AT&T achieved it by writing its own OCR software.
- The OCR errors make it impossible to guarantee performance to the users, and faced with a system making apparently incomprehensible errors, users are likely to retreat from its use.

OCR results are improving, although one still cannot dispense with proof-reading. There is even work being done now on OCR for old printing, by Sayeed Choudhury at Johns Hopkins, and there are some commercial products available (e.g., from Olive Software).

There are still other possibilities for navigating images. For some documents it may be possible to find alternative ways of displaying guidance on reading images. Figure 3.8 shows an eighteenth-century newspaper page. The full page is not suitable for display, because there is not enough resolution on a typical screen to show the entire page and be able to read any of it. In order to read a story, for instance, a page has to be enlarged to a level at which only a small portion will fit on a screen, and thus the user will lose all context about what has appeared where. Some other means of letting the user navigate around the page is necessary.

The answer is to take advantage of the newspaper format. Although the print on the page shown in Figure 3.8 is too poor for OCR, the horizontal and vertical rules used by newspapers can be found and then used to cut the page image into stories. The easiest way to locate such lines in low-quality images is not to look for continuous strings of bits, but to calculate average horizontal and vertical bit densities per scan line. In this case, for example, the first step is to find the vertical lines, which are continuous down the page. For each vertical column of pixels, count the dark ones and divide by the length; this will show the vertical rules despite breaks in them. Then, having divided the page into columns, repeat the calculation for each horizontal scan line within a column. That quickly divides the columns into stories. Images of the first few lines of each story can then be used to indicate what it is, a sort of menu of the paper shown in Figure 3.9.

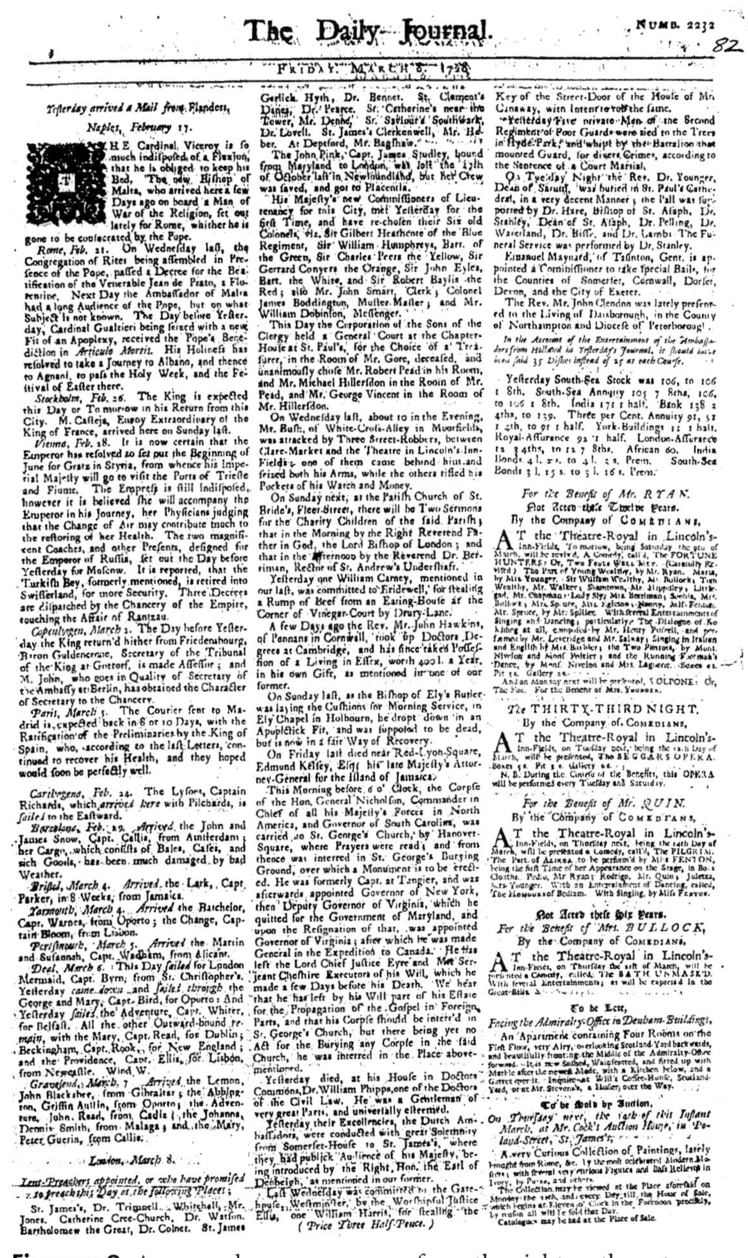

The Daily Journal. NUMB. 2232

82

FRIDAY, MARCH 8. 1728.

Yesterday arrived a Mail from Flanders.

Naples, February 17.

THE Cardinal Viceroy is so much indisposed of a Fluxion, that he is obliged to keep his Bed. The new Bishop of Malta, who arrived here a few Days ago on board a Man of War of the Religion, set out lately for Rome, whither he is gone to be consecrated by the Pope.

Rome, Feb. 21. On Wednesday last, the Congregation of Rites being assembled in Presence of the Pope, passed a Decree for the Beatification of the Venerable Jean de Prato, a Florentine. Next Day the Ambassador of Malta had a long Audience of the Pope, but on what Subject is not known. The Day before Yesterday, Cardinal Gualtieri being seized with a new Fit of an Apoplexy, received the Pope's Benediction in *Articulo Mortis*. His Holiness has resolved to take a Journey to Albano, and thence to Agnani, to pass the Holy Week, and the Festival of Easter there.

Stockholm, Feb. 26. The King is expected this Day or To-morrow in his Return from this City. M. Casteja, Envoy Extraordinary of the King of France, arrived here on Sunday last.

Vienna, Feb. 28. It is now certain that the Emperor has resolved to set out the Beginning of June for Gratz in Styria, from whence his Imperial Majesty will go to visit the Ports of Trieste and Fiume. The Empress is still Indisposed, however it is believed she will accompany the Emperor in his Journey, her Physicians judging that the Change of Air may contribute much to the restoring of her Health. The two magnificent Coaches, and other Presents, designed for the Emperor of Russia, set out the Day before Yesterday for Moscow. It is reported, that the Turkish Bey, formerly mentioned, is retired into Swisserland, for more Security. Three Decrees are dispatched by the Chancery of the Empire, touching the Affair of Rantzau.

Copenhagen, March 2. The Day before Yesterday the King return'd hither from Friedensbourg. Baron Guldencrone, Secretary of the Tribunal of the King at Gottorf, is made Assessor; and M. John, who goes in Quality of Secretary of the Embassy to Berlin, has obtained the Character of Secretary to the Chancery.

Paris, March 5. The Courier sent to Madrid is expected back in 8 or 10 Days, with the Ratification of the Preliminaries by the King of Spain, who, according to the last Letters, continued to recover his Health, and they hoped would soon be perfectly well.

Carthagena, Feb. 24. The Lyons, Captain Richards, which *arrived here* with Pilchards, is *sailed* to the Eastward.

Barcelona, Feb. 19. *Arrived* the John and James Snow, Capt. Callis, from Amsterdam; her Cargo, which consists of Bales, Cases, and such Goods, has been much damaged by bad Weather.

Bristol, March 4. *Arrived* the Lark, Capt. Parker, in 8 Weeks, from Jamaica.

Yarmouth, March 4. *Arrived* the Batchelor, Capt. Warnes, from Oporto; the Change, Captain Bloom, from Lisbon.

Portsmouth, March 5. *Arrived* the Martin and Susannah, Capt. Wadham, from Alicant.

Deal, March 6. This Day *sailed* for London Mermaid, Capt. Byrn, from St. Christopher's. Yesterday *came down* and *sailed through* the George and Mary, Capt. Bird, for Oporto: And Yesterday *sailed* the Adventure, Capt. Whiter, for Belfast. All the other Outward-bound *remain*, with the Mary, Capt. Read, for Dublin; Beckingham, Capt. Rook, for New England; and the Providence, Capt. Ellis, for Lisbon, from Newcastle. Wind W.

Gravesend, March 7. *Arrived* the Lemon, John Blackshire, from Gibraltar; the Abbington, Griffin Austin, from Oporto; the Adventure, John Read, from Cadiz; the Johanna, Dennis Smith, from Malaga; and the Mary, Peter Guerin, from Callis.

London, March 8.

Lent-Preachers appointed, or who have promised to preach this Day at the following Places;

St. James's, Dr. Trimnell. Whitehall, Mr. Jones. Catherine Cree-Church, Dr. Watson. Bartholomew the Great, Dr. Colnet. St. James Garlick Hyth, Dr. Bennet. St. Clement's Danes, Dr. Pearce. St. Catherine's near the Tower, Mr. Denne. St. Saviour's Southwark, Dr. Lovell. St. James's Clerkenwell, Mr. Heber. At Deptford, Mr. Bagshaw.

The John Pink, Capt. James Studley, bound from Maryland to London, was lost the 17th of October last in Newfoundland, but her Crew was saved, and got to Placentia.

His Majesty's new Commissioners of Lieutenancy for this City, met Yesterday for the first Time, and have re-chosen their Six old Colonels, viz. Sir Gilbert Heathcote of the Blue Regiment, Sir William Humphreys, Bart. of the Green, Sir Charles Peers the Yellow, Sir Gerrard Conyers the Orange, Sir John Eyles, Bart. the White, and Sir Robert Baylis the Red; also Mr. John Smart, Clerk; Colonel James Boddington, Muster-Master; and Mr. William Dobinson, Messenger.

This Day the Corporation of the Sons of the Clergy held a General Court at the Chapter-House at St. Paul's, for the Choice of a Treasurer, in the Room of Mr. Gore, deceased, and unanimously chose Mr. Robert Pead in his Room, and Mr. Michael Hillersdon in the Room of Mr. Pead, and Mr. George Vincent in the Room of Mr. Hillersdon.

On Wednesday last, about 10 in the Evening, Mr. Bush, of White-Cross-Alley in Moorfields, was attacked by Three Street-Robbers, between Clare-Market and the Theatre in Lincoln's-Inn-Fields; one of them came behind him and seized both his Arms, while the others rifled his Pockets of his Watch and Money.

On Sunday next, at the Parish Church of St. Bride's, Fleet-Street, there will be Two Sermons for the Charity Children of the said Parish; that in the Morning by the Right Reverend Father in God, the Lord Bishop of London; and that in the Afternoon by the Reverend Dr. Berriman, Rector of St. Andrew's Undershaft.

Yesterday one William Carney, mentioned in our last, was committed to Bridewell, for stealing a Rump of Beef from an Eating-House at the Corner of Vinegar-Court by Drury-Lane.

A few Days ago the Rev. Mr. John Hawkins, of Pennans in Cornwall, took up Doctors Degrees at Cambridge, and has since taken Possession of a Living in Essex, worth 400 l. a Year, in his own Gift, as mentioned in one of our former.

On Sunday last, as the Bishop of Ely's Butler was laying the Cushions for Morning Service, in Ely Chapel in Holbourn, he dropt down in an Apoplectick Fit, and was supposed to be dead, but is now in a fair Way of Recovery.

On Friday last died near Red-Lyon-Square, Edmund Kelsey, Esq; his late Majesty's Attorney-General for the Island of Jamaica.

This Morning before 6 o' Clock, the Corpse of the Hon. General Nicholson, Commander in Chief of all his Majesty's Forces in North America, and Governour of South Carolina, was carried to St. George's Church, by Hanover-Square, where Prayers were read; and from thence was interred in St. George's Burying Ground, over which a Monument is to be erected. He was formerly Capt. at Tangier, and was afterwards appointed Governor of New York, then Deputy Governor of Virginia, which he quitted for the Government of Maryland, and upon the Resignation of that, was appointed Governor of Virginia; after which he was made General in the Expedition to Canada. He has left the Lord Chief Justice Eyre and Mr Serjeant Cheshire Executors of his Will, which he made a few Days before his Death. We hear that he has left by his Will part of his Estate for the Propagation of the Gospel in Foreign Parts, and that his Corpse should be inter'd in St. George's Church, but there being yet no Act for the Burying any Corpse in the said Church, he was interred in the Place abovementioned.

Yesterday died, at his House in Doctors Commons, Dr. William Phipps, one of the Doctors of the Civil Law. He was a Gentleman of very great Parts, and universally esteemed.

Yesterday their Excellencies, the Dutch Ambassadors, were conducted with great Solemnity from Somerset-House to St. James's, where they had publick Audience of his Majesty, being introduced by the Right Hon. the Earl of Denbeigh, as mentioned in our former.

Last Wednesday was committed to the Gate-house, Westminster, by the Worshipful Justice Ellis, one William Harris, for stealing the Key of the Street-Door of the House of Mr. Canaway, with Intent to rob the same.

Yesterday Five private Men of the Second Regiment of Foot Guards were tied to the Trees in Hyde-Park, and whipt by the Battalion that mounted Guard, for divers Crimes, according to the Sentence of a Court Martial.

On Tuesday Night the Rev. Dr. Younger, Dean of Sarum, was buried in St. Paul's Cathedral, in a very decent Manner; the Pall was supported by Dr. Hare, Bishop of St. Asaph, Dr. Stanley, Dean of St. Asaph, Dr. Pelling, Dr. Waterland, Dr. Bisse, and Dr. Lambe. The Funeral Service was performed by Dr. Stanley.

Emanuel Maynard, of Taunton, Gent. is appointed a Commissioner to take Special Bail, for the Counties of Somerset, Cornwall, Dorset, Devon, and the City of Exeter.

The Rev. Mr. John Clendon was lately presented to the Living of Daisborough, in the County of Northampton and Diocese of Peterborough.

In the Account of the Entertainment of the Ambassadors from Holland in Yesterday's Journal, it should have been said 35 Dishes instead of 25 at each Course.

Yesterday South-Sea Stock was 106, to 106 1 8th. South-Sea Annuity 105 7 8ths, 106, to 106 1 8th. India 171 1 half. Bank 138 3 4ths, to 139. Three per Cent. Annuity 91, 91 1 4th, to 91 1 half. York-Buildings 11 1 half. Royal-Assurance 92 1 half. London-Assurance 12 3 4ths, to 12 7 8ths. African 60. India Bonds 4 l. 2 s. to 4 l. 3 s. Prem. South-Sea Bonds 3 l. 15 s. to 3 l. 16 s. Prem.

For the Benefit of Mr. RYAN.

Not Acted these Twelve Years.

By the Company of COMEDIANS,

AT the Theatre-Royal in Lincoln's-Inn-Fields, To-morrow, being Saturday the 9th of March, will be reviv'd, A Comedy, call'd, The FORTUNE HUNTERS: Or, Two Fools Well Met. (Carefully Revised.) The Part of Young Wealthy, by Mr. Ryan. Maria, by Mrs. Younger. Sir William Wealthy, Mr. Bullock; Tom Wealthy, Mr. Walker; Shamtown, Mr. Hippisley; Littlegad, Mr. Chapman; Lady Sly; Mrs. Berriman; Sophia, Mrs. Bullock; Mrs. Spruce, Mrs. Egleton; Nanny, Mrs. Forrester. Mr. Spruce, by Mr. Spiller. With several Entertainments of Singing and Dancing; particularly, The Dialogue of Nothing at all, compos'd by Mr. Henry Purcell, and perform'd by Mr. Leveridge and Mr. Salway; Singing in Italian and English by Mrs. Barbier; the Two Pierrots, by Mons. Nivelon and Mons. Poitier; and the Running Footman's Dance, by Mons. Nivelon and Mrs. Laguerre. Boxes 4 s. Pit 2 s. 6d. Gallery 2 s.

And on Monday next will be perform'd, VOLPONE: Or, The Fox. For the Benefit of Mrs. Younger.

The THIRTY-THIRD NIGHT.

By the Company of COMEDIANS,

AT the Theatre-Royal in Lincoln's-Inn-Fields, on Tuesday next, being the 12th Day of March, will be presented, The BEGGARS OPERA. Boxes 5 s. Pit 3 s. Gallery 2 s.

N. B. During the Course of the Benefits, this OPERA will be performed every Tuesday and Saturday.

For the Benefit of Mr. QUIN.

By the Company of COMEDIANS,

AT the Theatre-Royal in Lincoln's-Inn-Fields, on Thursday next, being the 14th Day of March, will be presented a Comedy, call'd, The PILGRIM. The Part of Alinda to be perform'd by Miss FENTON, being the first Time of her Appearance on the Stage, in Boy's Cloaths. Pedro, Mr. Ryan; Rodrigo, Mr. Quin; Juletta, Mrs. Younger. With an Entertainment of Dancing, called, The Humours of Bedlam. With Singing, by Miss Fenton.

Not Acted these Six Years.

For the Benefit of Mrs. BULLOCK,

By the Company of COMEDIANS,

AT the Theatre-Royal in Lincoln's-Inn-Fields, on Thursday the 21st of March, will be presented a Comedy, called, The BATH UNMASK'D. With several Entertainments; as will be express'd in the Great Bills.

To be Lett,

Facing the Admiralty-Office in Denham-Buildings,

An Apartment containing Four Rooms on the First Floor, very Airy, overlooking Scotland-Yard backwards, and beautifully fronting the Middle of the Admiralty-Office forwards. It is new Sashed, Wainscotted, and fitted up with Marble after the newest Mode, with a Kitchen below, and a Garret over it. Inquire at Will's Coffee-House, Scotland-Yard, or at Mr. Stevens's, a Hosier, over the Way.

To be Sold by Auction,

On Thursday next, the 14th of this Instant March, at Mr. Cock's Auction House, in Poland-Street, St. James's,

A very Curious Collection of Paintings, lately brought from Rome, &c. by the most celebrated Modern Masters, with several very curious Figures and Bass Relievo's in Ivory, by Pusso, and others.

The Collection may be viewed at the Place aforesaid on Monday the 11th, and every Day till the Hour of Sale, which begins at Eleven o' Clock in the Forenoon precisely, by reason all will be sold that Day.

Catalogues may be had at the Place of Sale.

(*Price Three Half-Pence.*)

Figure 3.8 A scanned newspaper page from the eighteenth century.

Figure 3.9 Scanned heads of newspaper stories.

Figure 3.10 Story selected from the page.

Clicking on one of these first headings brings up the image of the full story (by showing the page centered on that story). Imagine the user clicks on "TUBEROSE ROOTS"; the result is Figure 3.10. Using this technique, people can browse the image files without any OCR text. The full newspaper page need not be read. Other cues that can be used to help locate stories include the position of material on the page. In the newspaper pages shown in the figure, for example, major international news is typically at the top right, while the top left is theater reviews and announcements. Systems based on features like this will permit users to scan sets of newspaper pages without any indexing.

3.5 Shared Text/Image Systems

Some systems involve both ASCII and image pages, utilizing the advantages of each. Web pages typically encode the images as GIF or JPG and the text as HTML-encoded ASCII; this lets the user handle them with different software and perform different manipulations on each. For example, a user can change the size of the letters in the text, or convert the picture from color to grey-scale. Formatting systems often move the images around relative to the text, either to save space or avoid ugly pages.

The CORE (Chemical Online Retrieval Experiment) project, on which I worked in the early 1990s, involved extracting the illustrations from the scanned pages. This project had access to the information (derived from the typesetting system) which makes up the database of the American Chemical Society (ACS) and which provided the complete text of the articles. But this did not provide the graphic elements of each page. Although half the pages had no graphics, there was an average of about one illustration per page, and about a quarter of the area of the average page was not text. The illustrations are essential to the understanding of the article; online full text systems which leave out the illustrations are often used merely as finding aids, rather than as replacements for the paper. The CORE project had to get these illustrations by finding them in the page images. Since the total project needed to find 399,000 figures and chemical structural diagrams in 80,000 articles with 428,000 page images, it had to be an automatic process.

Pages can have four things beside text: tables, equations, figures, and schemes (chemical structural drawings). The equations and the tables are in the database derived from keyboarding, so the need is to find figures and schemes. Both figures and schemes are visually similar; they are both line drawings, which in the case of figures may include chemical structures, spectrograms, diagrams of equipment, and so on; schemes are usually chemical structures. They must be sorted out, however, since the schemes and figures can be moved past each other in the course of typesetting; that is, Scheme 1 may be referred to in the article before Figure 1, but may appear after it on the page. Figures are always at either the top or bottom of the page, while schemes can appear in the middle of a text column (but often appear at the edge of a page as well). Despite an attempt to avoid OCR in general, the only really reliable way of sorting figures from schemes is to find the caption by looking for the word *Figure* as a bitmap.

Page segmentation is a well-studied problem which has now advanced to the stage of competitions among the practitioners (Fletcher and Kasturi, 1987; Wang and Srihari, 1989; Srihari et al., 1994; Gatos et al., 2001; Antonacopoulos et al., 2003). Often, however, segmentation involves separating halftones or other

7162   *The Journal of Physical Chemistry, Vol 92, No. 26, 1988*

Figure 1. Schematics of the system used for observing holographic interferometry in BLMs. Ar⁺ = argon ion laser; BS = beam splitter; m = mirror; Q = quartz cuvette; BLM = bilayer lipid membrane; M = microscope; C = camera; HP = holographic plate; f = focus; l = lens; and d = interbeam distance.

Figure 2. Complex interferometric fringe pattern observed in a thick GMO film prior to thinning to a BLM.

Second, advantage has been taken of fluorescence to produce distinct interference patterns of molecules that are incorporated onto the surface of a BLM. The power of holographic interferometry is demonstrated in the present report by showing differences between thick lipid films and true BLMs, as well as by determining the shapes and sizes of cadmium sulfide (CdS) particles in situ generated on glyceryl monooleate (GMO) BLMs. Evidence is also provided here, by holographic interferometry, for the presence of Merocyanine 540 on the surface of GMO BLMs.

Experimental Section

Merocyanine 540 (Sigma), glyceryl monooleate (GMO, Nucheck Co.), cadmium chloride (Aldrich), and hydrogen sulfide (Matheson) were used as received. Water was purified by means of a Millipore Milli-Q system.

BLMs were formed across a 1.00-mm-diameter hole in a thin (0.10–0.15 mm thick) Teflon film, placed diagonally in a rec-

Figure 3.11 An example of a journal column.

material which is locally different from text printing. Nearly all the chemical illustrations are line drawings; and there is a continuum between some tables or chemical equations and some figures or schemes. The CORE project therefore wrote its own programs to deal with graphics extraction, based on the regularity of lines in normal text. Figure 3.11 shows a part of a journal column, and Figure 3.12 plots the number of black bits per scanline moving down the page. Each scanline is one horizontal trace across the page; in the figure the number of black dots in each trace is shown. The column begins with a normal figure (a line drawing), which runs from scanline 200 to 800, with irregular low values of bits per scanline (the bump at 150 is the heading line on the page). A five-line caption follows, the five regular bumps from scanline 800 to 1000. There follows an unusual dark figure (1100 to 1700), with a two-line caption (1700 to 1800). The remainder of the column (1800 on) is lines of text, and regular bumps appear in the plot. The regularity of this density plot of ordinary typeset text separates it from the irregular density characteristic of figures. For speed,

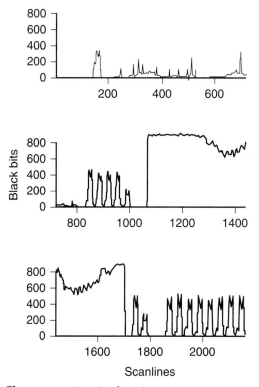

Figure 3.12 Density function.

the CORE project used only overall measures of bit density, not exact character matching (except for the word *Figure* as earlier mentioned).

The first step in graphics extraction is to align the page accurately on the axes. Skew can be produced in scanning, either because the pages have not been cut accurately from the journal or the pages were fed through the scanner on a slight angle. Any correction algorithm must recognize the possibility that the page begins or ends with a figure containing lots of white space. In the CORE project the left edge of each scanline was found, and then a vertical line was run down the left edge of the page and pushed as closely up against the text as possible, to find the skew angle. The page must be within one degree of correct orientation for figure extraction to work. Another method for deskewing was introduced by Baird (1987). Baird takes a set of parallel lines across the page and measures the dispersion of the measurement of the number of dark bits. Where this dispersion is maximum (that is, some of the lines are running through only white space and some through as dark a set of bits as they can find), the lines are aligned with the text baseline. This is a more robust method (it will work with ragged left and right margins) but takes longer. Other algorithms for deskewing are described by Le et al. (1994), Liolos et al. (2001), and Lu and Tan (2003).

After deskewing, the page was broken into double-column and full-width regions. Normally the ACS pages are double-column; however, each could contain one full-width region, either for a title-author block or for a wide table or figure. Looking at the *vertical* density plot (how many black bits in each vertical stripe down the page, taken in thirds) identifies the column boundaries and locates the transitions between double-column and full-width areas. Eventually, the page was cut into at most five regions (two columns at the top, two columns at the bottom, and one full-width section).

Each region was then scanned for figure captions, using exact bitmap matching for the word *Figure* (since the journals use different typefaces, different templates of the word were used for different journals). Each region also had its horizontal densities computed, and the program then computed a function which detects a regular pattern. This function is known as the *autocorrelation function* because it relates the density pattern to a shifted version of the same density pattern. In the same way as one can walk comfortably along a set of ridges (such as a corrugated road) if one's stride matches the interval between the bumps, this function has a maximum value when the shifted pattern differs from the original by one line spacing. Thus, it can be used to detect both the existence of the regular pattern and the distance between lines. Given the line spacing and the autocorrelation function, a threshold is applied to select which parts of the page are graphics. Figure 3.13 shows a sample column with the density function plotted just to the left of the text and the autocorrelation function at the far left. Finally, Figure 3.14 is the result: the figures and schemes were spotted correctly by the program and marked out (using different boxing to represent the figures and schemes separately).

3.6   Image Storage vs. Book Storage

The steady decrease in imaging costs compared with the steady increase in building construction costs raises the question of when they cross: when will it be cheaper to scan books than to build shelves for them? The quick answer is that scanning is comparable in cost to central campus libraries; is more expensive than offsite deposit libraries today; but may be cheaper than physical storage for consortia of libraries today and for individual libraries in a few years. In doing a fair comparison, one should contrast only the cost of the bookstacks; libraries also house offices and reading rooms whose cost may not be related to the book capacity itself.

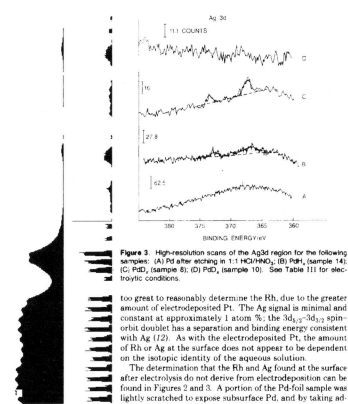

Ag 3d

I 11.1 COUNTS

| 16

| 27.8

| 62.9

D

C

B

A

380   375   370   365   360

BINDING ENERGY/eV

Figure 3. High-resolution scans of the Ag3d region for the following samples: (A) Pd after etching in 1:1 HCl/HNO₃; (B) PdH$_x$ (sample 14); (C) PdD$_x$ (sample 8); (D) PdD$_x$ (sample 10). See Table III for electrolytic conditions.

too great to reasonably determine the Rh, due to the greater amount of electrodeposited Pt. The Ag signal is minimal and constant at approximately 1 atom %; the $3d_{5/2}$–$3d_{3/2}$ spin-orbit doublet has a separation and binding energy consistent with Ag (*12*). As with the electrodeposited Pt, the amount of Rh or Ag at the surface does not appear to be dependent on the isotopic identity of the aqueous solution.

The determination that the Rh and Ag found at the surface after electrolysis do not derive from electrodeposition can be found in Figures 2 and 3. A portion of the Pd-foil sample was lightly scratched to expose subsurface Pd, and by taking ad-

Figure 3.13 Correlation function.

Three different possibilities for library storage are scanning, on-campus storage, and an off-site depository. What do these cost?

- The first good measurement of the cost of scanning books was the CLASS project at Cornell, which found the pure scanning cost to be about $30 per book, or about 10 cents per page (Kenney and Personius, 1992). The CLASS work scanned nineteenth-century mathematics textbooks, and did so by cutting the book away from the binding and placing each page by hand on a flatbed scanner. Other, but very high, cost estimates were given by Puglia in 1999 and also Kingma in 2000 (discussing rare books projects). Currently, companies scanning offshore quote under $10/book for this kind of conversion; a range is reported in Lesk (2003).
- Two contemporary on-campus bookstacks built in the 1990s were the extension to Olin library at Cornell, costing about $20/book, and the extension to Doe Library at Berkeley, costing about $30/book. In both

Dahan and Biali

of the OH groups (δ = 8.19 ppm) as compared with 1 (δ = 10.2 ppm) can be ascribed to the weakening of the hydrogen bond between the OH groups as a result of the presence of the boat conformation in 2.[7] It is interesting to note that whereas there is a large chemical shift difference for the diastereotopic methylene protons of calix[4]arene ($\Delta\delta$ = 0.71 ppm),[8] the $\Delta\delta$ value for 2 is relatively small and therefore under slow exchange conditions these protons appear as a somewhat unresolved AB quartet at 200 MHz.

(b) **IR Spectrum.** The IR spectrum of calix[4]arene is characterized by a low stretching OH frequency (3150 cm⁻¹) due to the presence of a circular hydrogen bond.[2] A marked deviation of the calixarene from the cone conformation into a boat form should result in weakening of the hydrogen bond and a shift of the stretching frequency into larger wave numbers. Indeed, Böhmer and co-workers[9] have shown that the OH stretching frequency of calix[4]arenes bridged at two para positions at nonvicinal rings 3 shifts to higher frequencies with the decrease in length of the bridge and the progressive distortion of the cone conformation. For example, for systems 3 (n = 5-9) the OH stretching frequencies are ν_{OH}(KBr) = 3410, 3340, 3250, 3250, and 3210 cm⁻¹, respectively. For calixarene 2 ν_{OH} (KBr) is 3290 cm⁻¹ and is analogous to the frequencies found for system 3 when n = 6 or 7.

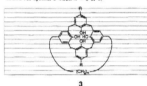

3

(c) **Molecular Mechanics Calculations.** Molecular mechanics calculations of calixarene 2 were performed using the MM2(85) program.[10] According to the calculations, the boat and 1,3-alternate conformations are of similar steric energies and are the lowest energy conformations. The 1,2-alternate and symmetric cone conformations have much higher steric energies and lie 5.3 and 31.2 kcal mol⁻¹ above the boat conformation. It should be noted, however, that the calculations do not take into account properly the hydrogen bonds. Since these hydrogen bonds are likely to contribute mostly to the relative stabilization of the boat and cone conformations, the underestimation of the strength of the hydrogen bonds should result in an overestimation of the steric energies of both conformations. Once this factor is taken into account, it is possible to reconcile the results of the calculations with the experimental result (i.e., exclusive population of the boat conformation).

The calculated structure for the boat conformation of 2 is remarkably similar to the crystallographic conforma-

(7) Wolff, A.; Böhmer, V.; Vogt, W.; Ugozzoli, F.; Andreetti, G. D. J. Org. Chem. 1990, 55, 5665.
(8) Araki, K.; Shinkai, S.; Matsuda, T. Chem. Lett. 1989, 581.
(9) (a) Goldmann, H.; Vogt, W.; Paulus, E.; Böhmer, V. J. Am. Chem. Soc. 1988, 110, 6811. (b) Paulus, E.; Böhmer, V.; Goldmann, H.; Vogt, W. J. Chem. Soc., Perkin Trans. 2 1987, 1609. (c) Böhmer, V.; Goldmann, H.; Vogt, W.; Paulus, E. F.; Tobiason, F. L.; Thielman, M. J. J. Chem. Soc., Perkin Trans. 2 1990, 1769.
(10) Allinger, N. L. QCPE MM2(85). See also: Sprague, J. T.; Tai, J. C.; Yuh, Y. H.; Allinger, N. L. J. Comput. Chem. 1987, 8, 581.

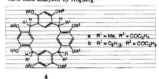

Figure 1. Possible homomerization pathways for calixarene 2. Methyl groups are omitted for clarity.

tion determined for 2·DMF (Table S1 in the supplementary material). The main difference between the experimental and calculated structures is in the O–O nonbonded distances which are overestimated by the calculations by 0.3-0.4 Å possibly due to the partial neglect of the hydrogen bonds.

Dynamic Stereochemistry of 2. Due to the lower ideal symmetry of the boat conformation of 2 (C_{2v} symmetry) as compared with 1 (C_{4v} symmetry), several homomerization pathways of the macrocyclic skeleton are possible for 2 whereas for 1 only the inversion process need to be considered. The stereodynamics of the all-cis stereoisomer of resorcinol-based calixarenes 4 which according to the X-ray analysis also exist in a boat conformation[11] have been analyzed by Högberg.[2,12]

4

Three processes can be considered for the dynamic process operating for 2. In the first process (I in Figure 1) there is an exchange between the "perpendicular" and "coplanar" rings without including the passage of the OH groups through the macrocyclic cavity. This process does not exchange the "axial" and "equatorial" methylene protons. In the idealized transition state a cone conformation of C_{4v} symmetry is obtained. Since the result of this dynamic process is that the molecule looks as if it was rotated by 90°, this process is called pseudorotation.[13,14] The second process (ii) involves the passage of the rings through the molecular cavity (a ring-inversion process)[13] and keeps the identity of the rings ("perpendicular" or "coplanar") unchanged. The third process (iii) can be formally considered a combination of processes i and ii and

(11) Erdtman, H.; Högberg, S.; Abrahamsson, S.; Nilsson, B. Tetrahedron Lett. 1968, 1679. Nilsson, B. Acta Chem. Scand. 1968, 22, 732. Tunstad, L. M.; Tucker, J. A.; Dalcanale, E.; Weiser, J.; Bryant, J. A.; Sherman, J. C.; Helgeson, R. C.; Knobler, C. B.; Cram, D. J. J. Org. Chem. 1989, 54, 1305.
(12) Högberg, A. G. S. J. Am. Chem. Soc. 1980, 102, 6046.
(13) Anet, F. A. L. Top. Curr. Chem. 1974, 45, 169.
(14) It should be noted that in the initial report on the ring inversion barrier of a calix[4]arene (Happel, G.; Mathiasch, B.; Kämmerer, H. Makromol. Chem. 1975, 176, 3317) the ring inversion process was (incorrectly) dubbed "pseudorotation".

Figure 3.14 Classified page.

cases they are almost entirely stacks, but both are underground (and, in the case of Berkeley, built to withstand a Richter force 8 earthquake).

■ The Harvard Depository costs about $2/book, for an off-site storage building with good book storage facilities but no architectural decoration. The Depository is about 35 miles from the main campus and book retrieval costs $4/volume retrieved.

What these numbers say is that for a book which is never or rarely used, off-campus storage is cheapest. Of course, the users may not consider the service good if books require 24 hours to retrieve, but the British Library has managed for a generation with 1-day retrieval for most of its books, partly by an adroit shelving policy which keeps the most used books more rapidly available.

Figure 3.15 (a) Harvard depository; (b) Bibliothèque Nationale de France.

As examples, Figure 3.15a shows the Harvard Depository ($2/book) and Figure 3.15b the 1996 Mitterand (Tolbiac) building of the Bibliothèque Nationale de France ($90/book). Using a large library as an architectural monument may make sense for reasons as varied as a university emblem or political prestige, but money spent on momumentality should not be confused with money spent on library service.

If the choice is between scanning and on-campus storage, the costs are comparable for a single library today. This statement is oversimplified, and several points should be made.

- The CLASS scanning project cost was low as it was done by the library itself; scanning contracted out (as in the JSTOR project, discussed shortly) has been more expensive. Digital images require some kind of digital storage and delivery technology, although with disk space at a tenth of a cent per megabyte and, say, 10 MB/book, the cost is now down to pennies per book. The cost estimates for underground stacks are higher than for above-ground buildings.

■ The CLASS scanning project cost was high, inasmuch as it used books which were old enough that their pages would not go through a sheet feeder. The cost estimates for pure stacks are low since they do not include reading rooms or offices; and certainly to find central campus space for a new library adjacent to an old library will usually require substantial architectural costs (such as underground construction). Most important, multiple libraries can share digital copies (albeit for out of copyright works) without any loss of service quality to any of them, and this is not possible with physical copies (unless the libraries are located near each other).

For comparison, the CORE project, which scanned modern printing on good paper, could use a sheet feeder. The illustrations in the journals we scanned were overwhelmingly line drawings, so we scanned bitonal at 300 dpi. We could achieve about 15 pages per minute through our scanner, which cost about $15,000 back in 1990, and pay somebody about $12.50/hr to stand in front of it. Unfortunately for the economics, we only had about 300,000 pages to scan. As a result, the scanner was idle most of the time, and the cost to us was perhaps $20,000 total, or 7 cents per page, most of which was amortized hardware cost. A scanner with similar performance would be a few hundred dollars today.

Looking at an example of on-campus storage, a more conventional new library is one at the University of Kentucky, which holds 1.2 M books and 4,000 reader seats for $58 M, with construction costs of about $165 per square foot. A survey done by Michael Cooper (1989) gives construction costs ranging from $21 to $41 per book. More recently, *Library Journal* published an article by Bette-Lee Fox (2003) including data for several new academic library buildings, with costs shown in Table 3.2. Some of the more expensive buildings include nonlibrary facilities (e.g., the Bryant College building has a mock trading floor to help teach finance).

Cooper reported that the amortized cost of keeping a book on a shelf for a year is $3. If a book has to be retrieved by library staff, this introduces additional costs. The New York Public Library finds retrieving and reshelving costs of about $2/book. Harvard needs to add another $2 for its Depository, to cover the shipment back and forth for 35 miles.

Don Waters summarized the costs in his report. Waters found the costs for electronic storage and retrieval to be higher (over $2/volume for storage and $6/volume for retrieval), but judged that the costs for the paper library would rise about 4% per year, while the computer costs declined 50% every five years. Under these assumptions, the costs of the digital and traditional library operations cross over in about 5 years. In 1996 Garrett and Waters estimated that in 10 years electronic storage would have a major cost advantage, with access

Table 3.2 Costs of new academic library buildings.			
Institution	Cost	Books Held	$/book
Cal State San Marcos	$48,610,000	840,000	$57
Bryant College	$26,000,000	197,000	$191
Loras College	$17,402,702	455,000	$38
Clarion University	$15,000,000	600,000	$25
SUNY Ithaca	$11,049,000	445,680	$24
Indiana Wesleyan University	$10,600,000	200,000	$53
University of Southern Mississippi	$7,144,147	71,000	$100
Linfield College	$6,793,040	230,000	$29
Interamerican University of Puerto Rico	$5,634,140	52,149	$108
Science Center Library	$3,300,100	87,000	$37

Table 3.3 Comparison of book storage costs.		
Format	Storage/year	Access cost
Book	$5.89	$134.00
Microfiche	$0.16	$7.26
Digital	(no data)	$0.04

costs of $2.70 per book rather than $5.60 for paper. Kingma (2000) compared the costs of paper, microfiche, and digital storage for books and found digital storage already with an enormous cost advantage once the file was available. The results can be seen in Table 3.3. Note that for the digital format, costs were given per image and no storage cost was given. Since the cost of the disk space to store an online book, even in a bulky image format of perhaps 100 MB, is less than 10 cents, the yearly cost is probably in that range ($0.10). The high cost of book access is a consequence of this study being done in a rare book library, with very high staff costs. Getz (1997) reported $6 per book, which seems much more reasonable.

Electronic libraries have some less easily quantified advantages over paper libraries. Books are never off-shelf or inaccessible because someone else is using them (unless publishers adopt per-user license agreements). More important, books do not become inaccessible because they are stolen, and they are not torn or damaged while used. Many users may not be on the premises (reducing the building costs). Access to electronic books can be faster than to paper, although users do not pay for access currently, so it may not be easy to recover cash from them in exchange for this faster access. Most important, access can involve searching and thus much more effective use of the material.

Sometimes electronics have even more advantages. Extremely fragile items which must be provided in surrogate form could be distributed widely once digitized. Many more people can now look at the *Beowulf* manuscript as electronic images than could travel to London and justify to the British Library their need to handle the unique and extremely fragile manuscript. Furthermore, the scanning of this manuscript has been done using advanced photographic techniques including UV scanning and backlit scanning, so that parts of the electronic images are legible even where the corresponding portions of the original manuscript are not legible (the *Beowulf* original was damaged by a fire in the 18th century and further damaged in repair attempts after the fire).

Of course, the most attractive situation is when many libraries can share the costs of digitizing material. The Andrew W. Mellon foundation is funding project JSTOR to implement this strategy. JSTOR began by scanning 10 journals in economics and history back to their first issue, and has now expanded its scanning to over 300 journals. The journals were selected because they are widely held in American libraries. Both page images and cleaned-up text are available. The intent of JSTOR is to see if libraries can in fact relieve shelf space crowding by substituting use of the electronic images for the paper (Bowen, 1995; Chepesiuk, 2000; Guthrie, 2001). JSTOR contracted its scanning to a company in Barbados and paid 39 cents per page for scanning, OCR, and correction. In addition, there are costs in cleanup and quality control in the United States, which are harder to quantify. JSTOR has already noticed an increase in the use of older material (Guthrie, 2000).

Common today is the direct purchase of material from the supplier in electronic form. Publishers issue many journals on CD-ROM, with Elsevier, Springer, and Wiley all offering hundreds of journals electronically. Some industrial libraries already spend more than 50% of their acquisitions budget on electronics; for some pharmaceutical libraries this is approaching 80%.

Lemberg's (1995) thesis goes into digitization costs for all US library holdings in some detail and suggests that over the next 100 years there is a savings of roughly $44 billion to be achieved by digitizing some 22 million documents (and discarding more than 400 million duplicate paper copies of them). The long time period considered makes this result very sensitive to his assumed 8.25% discount rate. Also, he assumes that libraries would make no copyright payments for electronic documents, just as they do not now pay extra to loan a paper document. Only about $2/book on average is available to pay out without destroying the economic benefit of digitization. Another proposal for putting everything online was made by Kahle and colleagues in 2001.

3.7 Large Scale Projects

A number of very large scale projects are now working on making enormous digital repositories. We can expect not just critical mass in some areas, but truly comprehensive collections. The goal of large projects is to provide a base not just for introducing undergraduates to a field, but to permit researchers to do their work and support the education of graduate students.

The first example of completeness may have been the Thesaurus Linguae Graecae project of the 1970s, which converted to machine-readable form the entire corpus of classical Greek literature. However, the researcher in ancient Greek needs commentaries as well, and, though complete, the TLG collection is not a substitute for a classics library at a university. Comprehensiveness will require substantially larger efforts; the TLG is about 300 volumes.

The Gallica collection at the Bibliothèque Nationale de France will include 100,000 French books in image format, added to 10,000 major works of French literature keyed some years ago at the University of Nancy (the Trésor de la Langue Française). About half the books are out of copyright and publicly accessible from the BNF website (*http://gallica.bnf.fr*), while the other half can only be read at the BNF itself.

Several large commercial scanning projects started in the late 1990s, intending to convert books and sell access to them. These included Questia, Netlibrary, and Ebrary. Between them, they probably scanned about 100,000 books—as of 2003, Questia claims 45,000, Netlibrary 37,000, and Ebrary 20,000. The future of these companies is unclear: Netlibrary now belongs to OCLC, and both Questia and Ebrary have seen skeptical news stories about their future (see Hawkins, 2002, for a review).

The largest project now going on is the Million Book Project of Raj Reddy at Carnegie-Mellon University with the cooperation of the Internet Archive, the Indian Institute of Science in Bangalore, and the Chinese Academy of Sciences (St. Clair, 2002). The goal of this project is to provide one million books free to read on the Internet. This would provide a basic collection in all subject areas, albeit one that is fairly old (since it is going to be composed of material that is no longer in copyright). As we've discussed, the actual scanning process is understood and not a real problem. The real issue is the source of the books: this turns out to be a mixture of buying books being weeded from library shelves and borrowing books still on library shelves. The books are then sent to Asia for scanning using manual labor to turn pages, and those in English are converted using OCR so that searching can be provided.

What we do not yet know is the effect that such a library will have. Perhaps the availability of a large amount of material in a common format will stimulate the publishers to put out additional material in this style; other hopeful possiblities include support for large-scale education and research around the world and preservation of quality information from the past.

3.8 Summary

Despite the many positive aspects of electronic libraries, they are not without their disadvantages. Users accustomed to paper may dislike on-screen books, may be intimidated by them, or find the screens difficult to read. If "visitors" to a digital library must provide their own equipment, this may be viewed as an add-on expense (although many colleges already ask every student to buy a computer); and if users have low-quality screens, reading may be still more difficult. If, on the other hand, the library is providing the reading equipment, there may be times when it is overloaded and unavailable without a wait. Similarly, equipment may be broken or under maintenance. Although a single book is never "offshelf" in a digital library, it may well be that a great many books are nevertheless unavailable at times because of a machine failure. One industrial library I used to frequent had an electronic catalog which was initially unavailable on Sundays as a result of maintenance schedules. The idea that the catalog was unavailable even though the room was open would not make any sense to a traditional librarian.

The previous chapter discussed our ability to build libraries of books stored as characters, derived from printing operations or other keying. This has been practical for some time, and large companies sell this service. This chapter concludes that digital libraries of images are also practical today. Collections of hundreds of thousands of printed pages and tens of thousands of photographs have been created and are being used successfully. The costs are not trivial, but they are becoming comparable to the costs of conventional storage.

Part of the question about replacing items with digital media is whether a digital version of some document is entirely suitable as a replacement for the original, or whether it is merely a finding aid. Art historians, for example, usually feel that they must see originals to do their research, and any substitutes (including printed reproductions in books) are just finding aids. Many readers of journals feel the same way; they print out anything longer than a page or so.

For straightforward reading of text, with adequate screens and interfaces, computer versions can be a suitable alternative. Experiments show that reading from screens is as effective as reading from paper. Given the convenience of fingertip access, libraries can look forward to user preference for online rather than paper materials.

Image systems, however, pose more difficulty than text systems in terms of achieving an interface users will like. Image systems need to transmit more data than text systems, and they require greater screen resolution. Many systems today are thus perceived by the users as too slow and too hard to read. Users may be disappointed in a digital library system even if the problem is in their own hardware (e.g., a computer with a screen that is too small).

Whether image representations of printed books are merely a waystation on the road to text systems is not yet clear. Perhaps, as OCR improves, and as the spread of the Web causes the attachment to paper formats to wane, we can expect these page image systems to become less important. However, as an intermediate step in the conversion of already printed material, they are likely to retain their importance until perhaps a few million old books have been converted world-wide.

Multimedia Storage and Retrieval

L ibraries do not just consist of text pages, whether ASCII or image. The current rage for "multimedia" encourages us to plan for collections that include sound, video, software, and everything else imaginable. Unlike the optimistic conclusions in the last two chapters, for which there were suitable methods and successful examples of digital libraries with millions of pages of ASCII and hundreds of thousands of images, building systems for multimedia is harder. In particular, video remains a problem for libraries. The ubiquitous VHS cartridge is fragile and poor in quality. Color photographic film is expensive. And digitizing video today is still expensive and little video is free of copyright restraints; nor do we have good ways of searching it once stored. This chapter will discuss where we stand on handling nontextual material; it may not be straightforward today, but there is active progress. This is probably the area of greatest research interest and progress today.

4.1 Sound Formats: Vinyl, Tape, and CD

The simplest form of nontext material to deal with is audio. Audio has been collected by libraries for years; the Library of Congress even has thousands of player piano rolls. The once-standard vinyl record gave way to cassette tape and then to CD. In one of the faster complete replacements of one technology by another, CD made vinyl obsolete in about 10 years. Cassette tape still survives for the moment since its players are cheaper and, until recently, more standard in automobiles.

There are two common levels of formatting for audio: a high-quality standard for music and a low-quality one for voice. The format for storing music is driven by the entertainment industry, which now uses digital encoding for both studio and consumer formats. Ideally, one would like recorded sound to approximate a live performance in its impression on the listener's ear; a typical person can hear up to 15–20 kHz and a dynamic range of 30–60 dB in loudness. kHz (kilohertz, or thousands of cycles per second) is a measure of frequency. Middle C on a piano keyboard is 0.256 kHz, the A above it is 0.440 kHz, and most people can not hear above 20 kHz, although dogs can usually hear 40 kHz, and cats up to 65 kHz. When digitizing sound, the frequency range in kHz determines the sampling rate, and the dynamic range (the ratio of the loudest sound to the smallest useful difference in loudness) determines the number of bits per sample. Since it requires a minimum of two samples per cycle to give the ear a clue to the existence of a frequency, the sampling rate must be double the highest frequency that is to be captured. Thus, to represent the range up to 15 kHz requires 30,000 samples per second or higher. In other words, a value of the sound wave intensity must be recorded about every 30 microseconds (30 millionths of a second). The decibel scale raises the sound intensity by a factor of 10 every 10 decibels, so that a 65 dB sound is ten times as large as a 55 dB sound. Roughly, 1 dB is the quietest perceptible sound (for someone with good hearing), 30 dB is a quiet room, 40 dB is conversation, 60 dB is loud music, 80 dB is a noisy car, and 100 dB is painful (e.g., an express subway train rushing through a station). To represent the difference between the 30 dB quiet parts and the 60 dB loud parts of a musical performance requires a range of a thousand in amplitude, or at least 10 bits of dynamic range. Music is typically handled by computers in CD format: 44,000 samples per second at 16 bits/sample on each of two audio tracks, comfortably above what is needed to represent what the average ear can perceive. This means that audio CD players must handle 176-KB/second (the standard 1X CD-ROM reader). This format is sufficiently high-quality in terms of both acoustic range and accuracy that most people accept it as a permanent representation, except for a few audiophiles who insist that analog sound has a different and preferable texture. Regrettably, the Audio Engineering Society (2003) is circulating a draft proposal for preservation of old sound recordings which asks for sampling rates of at least 88 kHz and amplitude digitization at 24 bits. This is well beyond the capacity of either the human ear or the equipment on which the original recording would have been made, and will add unnecessary expense to any conversion project; but then, as Flanders and Swann wrote, it will please any passing bat (110 kHz).

Voice, by contrast, is normally acceptable at much lower sound quality. The standard for voice is the telephone line, which clips the sound signal to the range 300–3300 Hz and which has a relatively low amplitude range as well. In fact, digital telephony is normally done at 8000 samples per second with 8 bits of amplitude data per sample, or 8 KB/second. There is also no stereo needed to represent one voice. The frequency range of digital voice in this format is only up to 4000 Hz, which means that many high frequencies (particularly in women's voices) that are quite audible are suppressed. This makes telephony harder to understand than, say FM radio, which can transmit the entire hearing range. The FM carrier bands are 150 Khz wide, divided into three signals with the basic mono signal able to carry up to 40 kHz (the other bands are the stereo sideband which carries the difference of the left and right channels, and a sideband set aside for a separate Muzak-like service which some stations offer). In order to expand the intensity or loudness range, the 8 bits of the amplitude data do not store a plain numerical amplitude (which would mean a range of only 24 dB) but a *companded* amplitude. Companding means that the 8-bit numbers used to code the intensity of the signal are translated to a range of amplitudes that is arranged so that small amplitudes are represented more accurately than large amplitudes. Effectively, the number stored is the logarithm of the actual amplitude. The standard representation is called *mu-law* and is adequate for understanding speech.

Recording and playback of sound are easy since most current workstations include sound digitization and generation cards. The digitization of the telephone equipment business has meant that chips to do mu-law translation are readily available and thus the sound cards are widespread. Nearly every computer is now sold as "multimedia ready" which means, among other things, that it includes a sound card and speakers.

It is possible to compress voice below 8 KB/second while retaining most of the intelligibility. The most common standard is GSM, the compression used in a particular kind of digital cellular telephone system. GSM compression is about a factor of 5 beyond mu-law (160 bytes are turned into 33 bytes). This corresponds to a speech coding rate of 1.6 KB/second. Considerably better compression can be done (research projects for years have reduced speech to 300 bytes/second), but it becomes more difficult to do the compression and decompression in real time, and the compressed sound quality deteriorates, especially as any sounds other than human speech are being transmitted. Thus, they are not acceptable for recording radio programs, for example, which may have incidental music or animal noises. GSM is reasonably tolerant of such nonvoice sounds.

The usual sound formats do not contain any labeling information (audio CDs have a place for it, but only recently started to use it). Thus, libraries attempting to catalog and store sound cannot do so within the sound format itself but must do so outside. In fact, CD cataloging is now possible for amateurs by the use of large online databases which give the track-by-track content of each commercial CD. Audio is also less likely to be self-identifying than printed pages (that is, it is less likely that a cataloger can work entirely from the item itself, rather than requiring information about it from other sources).

In practice, libraries are rarely manipulating collections of commercially recorded music. Music publishers do not usually grant permission for such use, and, as a result, although libraries store and lend audio CDs as physical objects, they rarely have the right to network them or otherwise transmit them. Thus, for libraries, audio libraries often mean speech libraries, which are more likely to have been recorded on cassette recorders, as byproducts of some oral history or anthropological research project. These materials can often be stored at voice quality. At 8000 bytes/second, an hour of sound is about 30 MB. Since a typical conversational speed is about 100–125 words/minute, an hour of talking includes 6000–7000 words, representing about 35 KB of text. Thus, recording sound rather than storing the text spoken requires 1000 times as much disk space. Much more serious, however, is the fact that there is no easy way to search sound recordings. Nor can people browse sounds with anything like the facility that they can scan pictures. Thus, large sound archives typically require detailed cataloging, which is far more costly than the recording and storage of the sound.

Voice on the Internet is now booming with the realization that one can make phone calls across the Internet. Calls can be transmitted for the major length of the transmission across the Internet as packets, and then converted back to analog form to reach the final telephone. Many prepaid phone cards work this way, and companies offer phone service based on this kind of transmission. Quality is now acceptable if not wonderful. For example, the Internet also features CD stores offering samples of many of the CDs (with licenses), and the RealAudio and Windows Media Player formats are used for various kinds of audio libraries. Some libraries, for example the National Gallery of the Spoken Word at Michigan State University, provide voice samples on the Internet. This library, among other works, provides speeches by presidents from Grover Cleveland to Bill Clinton. Voice is easier to store than music; it is hard to search, however, and the copyright problems with music are even worse than those with print. Yet large sound libraries are arriving; Michigan State, for example, has a mixture ranging from Supreme Court hearings to the radio interviews of Studs Terkel.

Users of a sound library would also like to be able to search sounds in many ways. Queries can be imagined to search music by composer, style, instruments that are playing, or even by the musical theme being played. Or one might search for emotional content: romantic music, martial music, or funeral marches. Music searching has developed in the last few years but is still relatively primitive. The major goal is finding tunes that are whistled or hummed.

There are some steps for sound processing that can be taken automatically once a digital representation is available. Perhaps the most common form of sound manipulation is changing the speed of the speech. Normal conversation is about 125 words per minute, but people can understand much faster rates (reading speeds of 400 wpm are not unusual). Thus, it is often desired to accelerate a spoken passage. Simple time compression will also shift the pitch of the sound, making it less intelligible. However, it is relatively easy to accelerate speech while retaining the same pitch. Ordinary listeners can adapt to understand double normal speed. Blind students, who must spend large amounts of time listening to accelerated speech, learn to understand 4X normal speed.

Another easy strategy is segmentation. Particularly with professional speakers (as on the radio), one can expect longer pauses between sentences than between words, and between paragraphs than between sentences. As a result, a computer measuring the amount of silence in a recorded segment (just looking for low-intensity values) can detect interparagraph breaks. By then reading the first sentence in each paragraph, it is possible to give an abbreviation of a journalistic text. It would seem possible to analyze the pitch and intensity of a spoken text and decide what the speaker thought was important, and thus abbreviate it more effectively (excepting perhaps those cases where each paragraph or subsection begins with a summary sentence). Algorithms can be written to do this, however, they are not yet widely available.

4.2   Pictures: GIF and JPEG

The storage of pictures other than images of printed pages introduces other complications. Such pictures are likely to contain color and their use is less predictable. To add to the complexity, there are over a hundred different standards for image representation. The most common, however, are GIF and JPEG.

GIF, the Graphics Interchange File, is a common format, although it has become less so partly due to a claim by Unisys that they had a patent on the Lempel-Ziv compression algorithm used in GIF. GIF uses a 256-element color space, which adapts well to typical computer screens but falls far short of the color range in naturalistic scenes. The compression in GIF comes from two sources: one is the use of Lempel-Ziv compression on the image data and the other is the reduction of the color space to 256 possible values. Since Lempel-Ziv is a lossless compression scheme, this means that GIF is lossless on bitonal or gray-level images (as long as there are only 256 gray levels); it is lossy on color images, for which it reduces the number of colors. GIF is particularly well adapted to computer-generated drawings, since these are likely to use only a few colors. It is not as well adapted to photographs of people or real scenes, since these have a great many colors. To improve GIF compression performance, it is necessary to reduce the number of colors in the scene (below 256). For many scenes, there is little perceived quality loss in reducing to 64 colors (especially on computer displays without good color capabilities).

JPEG, named for the Joint Photographic Experts Group, solves many of these problems. It is also a publicly defined and usable standard, with fast decoding software. The JPEG algorithm is fairly complex and depends on breaking an image into 8×8 pixel blocks, calculating spatial Fourier coefficients to represent the information in each block, and throwing away some of the high-frequency information to compress the image. Spatial Fourier coefficients are a way of describing how rapidly the information in the picture is changing as one moves across the picture. The lowest spatial Fourier coefficients describe features which are flat across the block or across half of it; the highest coefficients describe aspects of the block which are changing back and forth at each pixel. Keeping only the lowest coefficients is an equivalent of viewing the picture from a greater distance or while squinting at it. JPEG is a lossy compression algorithm and also adjusts the color map; JPEG compression of a picture with only five colors will produce a compressed image with many more colors. JPEG is a generally stronger algorithm than GIF and is adapted to a wider variety of pictures and to naturalistic scenes in particular. JPEG is perhaps less well adapted to very sharp computer-generated images, since its Fourier transform methods limit high-frequency detail.

Another image compression technique is ImagePac, the method used in Kodak's PhotoCD (Seybold, 1996; Eastman Kodak, 2003). ImagePac is infrequently used today, since it began as a Kodak proprietary system. Librarians and many other customers are skeptical of any format which is tied to one company; they fear possible restrictions on future use. What's interesting about this system is that it stores different resolutions of each picture so that the user can choose between a low- and a high-resolution version, perhaps using one for display and one for printing. Now this can be done by *progressive transmission* and is part of JPEG 2000 (Taubman, 2001). The Kodak Imagepac system stores luminance data more accurately than chrominance, thus preserving detail better than color. The Kodak PhotoCD format deals with the problem of fast decompression by storing five different resolutions of each picture. Thus, the user can quickly access a low-resolution version for scanning and later access just the high-resolution version. The five resolutions are 128×192, 256×384, 512×768 (considered the base resolution), 1024×1536, and 2048×3072. There is also a higher-resolution version, Kodak Professional PhotoCD, in which the top resolution is 4096 × 6144. Even this, however, does not represent all the detail available in a high-quality 35 mm slide, let alone a larger format negative.

Wavelet compression is the next step forward. Like JPEG, the wavelet algorithms are based on spatial Fourier transforms taken over the picture, but, unlike JPEG, they are taken over the entire picture rather than blocks within the picture. The weighting assigned to different Fourier coefficients decreases faster with frequency, leading to a more efficient use of the code space. Wavelets represent fine detail better than JPEG and achieve high compression. Again, they are lossy.

Figure 4.1 (see Color Plate) shows the effect of reducing, or thresholding, the number of colors in a picture. This photograph was selected to show the effects of color quantization; in a scene with fewer colors (or without natural colors and their variations), color quantization would be less noticeable. The number of colors in image (a) is 7, (b) 20, (c) 50, and (d) 256. Note the effect on GIF compression. Table 4.1 shows the size of the GIF images for the different numbers of color.

One possibility (not used in the preceding examples) for improving image quality is *dithering*. Dithering is a process of representing a color or gray level by using dots of different values which average to the color wanted. For example, newspaper halftoning is an example of dithering: a gray level is suggested by using black dots of different sizes with larger black dots for a darker gray and with smaller dots for a lighter gray.

Figure 4.2 is a comparison of bitonal images dithered and thresholded; as you can see, dithering helps considerably (although typically, it doubles the size of the compressed file). Image (a) in the figure is thresholded, whereas image (b) is dithered. Again, GIF is best for computer-generated images, such as the kind of slides often used in talks, which contain only a few words and very few colors. JPEG is better for normal scenes which contain a wide range of colors, and where color fidelity matters. A suitable retrieval system can be built with any of them, and it is possible to write software that asks in what format an image is and then

Table 4.1 Size of GIF image depending on number of colors.

Number of Colors	Size
2	16,613
4	33,038
7	47,544
10	59,301
20	87,317
50	123,770
256	197,839

Figure 4.2 (a) Thresholding vs. (b) Dithering.

adapts to it, so that the user does not need to know which format was used. For example, the binary computer file containing a GIF image will begin with the characters GIF; and a binary computer file containing a JPEG image will begin with the octal (base-8) value 377 followed by octal 330.

4.3 Color

As with sounds, pictures on screens are not as dramatic in their impact compared with what we see directly in the real world. Computer displays, and all other forms of image representation including photographs, are limited in dynamic range (intensity) and in color gamut by comparison with the abilities of the human eye. For example, the difference in intensity of the light from a scene in a dimly lit room and a scene in bright sunlight is 10,000:1; yet the eye can adapt and recognize colors and shapes in each situation. Photographic paper, on the other hand, can only capture a range of about 100:1. Slide (transparency) film is much better, and in this case computer displays are better also, usually able to display a range of 256:1.

The range of colors people can see is also large compared to many repro- duction technologies. It is not possible today to make devices which reproduce the entire color space; and although it is possible to make systems that are sensitive to infrared or ultraviolet colors beyond what the eye can see, this is not useful for reproducing normal objects. But as Edwin Land (the founder of Polaroid) demonstrated, the eye is extremely good at visualizing colors from a small amount of color information, so it is possible to make computer displays and conventional printing equipment which display only some of the colors that the eye can see, but yet are usable. Sometimes limited displays may appear washed-out, for inability to display sufficiently saturated colors.

Figure 4.3 (see Color Plate) illustrates the so-called 'color gamut' standardized in the 1931 CIE (Centre Internationale d'Eclairage).

The arc-shaped space represents the colors that can be seen. White is in the center; along the edge of the arc are the saturated pure spectrum values from red to blue; and moving towards the center shows the progressively less saturated colors. The eye can see as much of this figure as can be printed. Any system using three dyes or three phosphors will always show a triangular part of the space at best. The marked out areas in the figure indicate different kinds of color production systems and what they can show. A good color film (e.g., Kodacolor or Ektacolor) will distinguish quite a lot of the color space. Computer displays usually show somewhat less than the best color film can, and offset printing (the black triangle in the bottom plate) still less. Newspaper presses can show only a small part of the color space. If you are only doing a few brightly colored items (e.g., cartoons), the lower quality displays may be adequate; for serious color work considerably better effort is needed. For color output the various technologies differ yet again in their characteristics; some printers may lack saturation, while others lack the ability to produce subtle tonal differences. The best digital color printers are dye sublimation printers, but they are both slow and expensive. Color laser printers, working from the technology of color laser copiers, are becoming dominant.

Brightness and contrast of images also cause problems. Often a scanned image, when put on the screen, looks either lighter or darker than the user expected. The problem is that most computer displays are not linear in their intensity; doubling the signal going to the electron gun more than doubles the apparent brightness of the picture. The coefficient of the curve that relates signal strength to brightness is called *gamma*. For some materials, exaggerating the contrast may be adequate; bitonal images, for example, don't depend on shades of gray. But for realistic depictions of normal scenes, it is desirable to have the right relationship between the brightness levels indicated in the image and those seen on the screen. This is particularly true if the user needs to compare brightness levels made by *dithering* with those done with gray-level. As we discussed earlier, dithering is a technique to approximate gray levels with a mix of black and white dots, adjusted to give the right impression. Halftoning in conventional printing is an example of the use of dithering.

Suppose that an area of a scene has 50% intensity (midway between white and black). It can either be printed as a gray-level of 0.50 or as a dithered area in which half of the bits are black. Ideally, these would have the same appearance. In practice, on a typical screen, they will not. Many screen manufacturers correct or partially correct for gamma problems of this sort, trying to make the apparent brightness reflect the intent of the original picture. Figure 4.4, for example, taken from the Web page of Robert Berger at Carnegie Mellon University (CMU), shows the extent to which gamma is represented correctly on the page you are

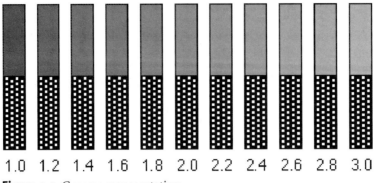

Figure 4.4 Gamma representation.

reading. If you move far enough away from the page so that you see the bottom dot representation as gray, the bars on the left will be darker on top and the bars on the right will be lighter. The bottom half of each bar is a 50% dither. If the gamma correction that went all the way through the printing was correct, the middle bar will look as if the top and bottom are equally dark. To understand whether your workstation corrects gamma properly, find an online image that evaluates gamma (e.g., http://www.scarse.org/adjust/gamma.html) and look at it on your screen.

4.4 Image Search

How can libraries store pictures and sounds? Traditionally, these are cataloged by writing textual descriptions of them and then processing the text. There are thesauri, such as the Getty's Art and Architecture Thesaurus, that attempt to cover some kinds of images. However, there is no generally accepted classification to help with subject searching. Instead, much searching of artworks, for example, is based on the painter's name, the title, or the physical size of the work.

Obviously, art collections are often searched for landscapes showing a particular area, or portraits of a particular person. But in addition, they may be searched for such detail as seasons of the year depicted (a Christmas card publisher will want winter landscapes), style of painting, religious subjects, or even moral messages. For instance, how would someone in a art library who was looking for a painting related to electioneering (and who did not remember Hogarth's work) find this?

We are now familiar with image search engines such as that run by Google. In general, these engines work by finding words in a Web page that include the image and using these words as search terms. If the Web page conforms to "accessibility" standards, every image has to have a label suitable for reading to a sightless person that describes the image; this label can be used for searching. This use of text to describe pictures permits many successful image searches on the Web.

Now imagine doing this without any manual processing or textual descriptions. For many years this did not seem feasible, until the IBM QBIC project demonstrated that it was possible to organize pictures based purely on their bit patterns. QBIC gathers a variety of features about each picture and uses them for search and retrieval. Indeed, effective picture browsing is possible with low-grade attributes of pictures such as color and texture. The QBIC system (Flickner et al., 1995; Niblack, 1998) has now been folded into IBM's DB2 product (Yevich, 2000). This introduced the use of features such as color, texture, and shape.

- *Color.* QBIC computes a histogram of the colors, computing 64 color values, and for each color in the original count, the closest of the color values is counted. A detailed set of examples of searching with color histograms is given by Chitkara and Nascimento (2002).
- *Texture.* QBIC uses texture features such as *coarseness* (how large the features in the picture are, measured by shifting windows of different sizes over the picture), *contrast* (the variance of the gray-level histogram), and *directionality* (the degree of peaking in the distribution of gradient directions).
- *Shape.* QBIC uses the size of items, as well as their circularity, eccentricity, and major axis orientation. This relies partly on manual tracing of features in the picture and partly on color areas to decide which areas represent features. QBIC lets people draw sketches and use them to retrieve pictures.

Continuing from QBIC, other work has involved finding images based on blobs of different sizes and colors and creating rules for finding a particular kind of image. Such work has been done at Columbia (Chang and Smith, 1995; Jaimes and Chang, 2000) and Berkeley (Ogle and Stonebraker, 1995; Forsyth et al., 1996; Forsyth et al., 1997; Belongie, 2002) to cite a few examples. Figure 4.5 is from Berkeley and shows the various images retrieved by a model of "horses." This example was deliberately chosen to show some mistakes; the program works quite well by identifying shapes and using a "body plan" model of each creature. Forsyth and Malik have gone on to attempt to index pictures with words. Given a large set of documents for which one has captions, they attempt to learn which shapes, colors, and textures seem to be correlated with words and thus develop software that can label a picture. Figure 4.6 is an early attempt at recognizing items in pictures. As one can see, there is a good deal yet to be done, but even this kind of labelling may well be valuable in some search situations. Similarly, Manmatha (Jeon et al., 2003) and coworkers have been able to assign keywords to images without attempting to decide exactly which part of the image should be labeled with which word, as shown in Figure 4.7.

Images classified as horses by blobworld

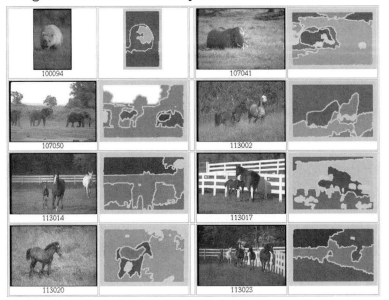

Figure 4.5 Image retrieval of "horses."

Figure 4.6 Recognizing and labelling parts of an image.

Image				
Original Annotation	people pool swimmers water	cars formula tracks wall	clouds mountain sky water	field foals horses mare
Automatic Annotation	water people swimmers pool	cars tracks wall formula	sky mountain clouds park	field horses foals mare

Figure 4.7 Assigning keywords to images.

Figure 4.8 Recognizing the same window in two pictures.

Figure 4.9 Recognizing the same building in two pictures.

If computers are not good at labelling pictures by content, what are they good at? One interesting result of Andrew Zisserman (Schaffalitzy and Zisserman, 2002) tells us that they are very good at recognizing the same object when it appears in two different pictures, even if the pictures are taken from different angles and at different scales. Zisserman identified a function which could be computed for regions of a picture and which was invariant under affine transformations so that viewpoint and size will not matter. He can then sort the images by this value and determine overlaps. Figures 4.8 and 4.9 show examples from his work. Using this kind of technology, it will be possible to make large dictionaries of reference images and find them in other pictures.

4.5 **Automatic Speech Recognition**

Automatic voice recognition has been a goal from the beginning of computational linguistics, and it received a great deal of attention in the 1970s when the Defense Advanced Research Projects Agency (DARPA) sponsored considerable work on speech understanding. At that point in its development, work in the field was still very frustrating. Essentially, there are four parameters that strongly affect the difficulty of speech recognition:

1. Whether speech is normal, continuous speech, or the user is required to speak in discrete words, pausing between each.
2. Whether any user is supposed to be recognized, or the system has been trained on the voice of a single, exclusive user.
3. Whether the dialog can be about anything, or the vocabulary and subject matter (and possibly even the syntax) are restricted to a small number (usually dozens) of words.
4. Whether the speech is over a telephone (which limits the speech to a bandwidth of 300–3300 Hz), or speech is recorded from a quality microphone in a quiet room.

The rule of thumb in the 1970s was that unless three of the four parameters listed were in your favor (the second choice in each item), then your speech recognition task was probably hopeless.

In more recent years there have been great strides. Much of the recognition work is based on dynamic time warping, plus hidden Markov models; see Peacocke and Graf (1990) for details and Stolcke et al. (2000) for an example of continued work. CMU reported speech recognition at 70% word accuracy with continuous, arbitrary speakers. Alex Waibel (1996) discusses systems which accept a large vocabulary of continuous speech from any speaker and have word error rates of 10%. Similarly, IBM (Potamianos et al., 2001) has word error rates of about 10% under conditions where people are unable to do any better. Some of the improvement stems from faster computers and processing, some from improvement in algorithms, and some from a recognition that there are particularly easy tasks to which a system may be tailored. In particular, the job of speaking computer commands, which typically are spoken in a discrete way and are picked from a set of fewer than 100 words, can be done more accurately than typing from dictation. Dictation systems are still usually slower to use than typing (because correcting even 10% of the words may take longer than just retyping a line), but they are gaining much acceptance and are now a standard way of trying to ameliorate the effects of carpal tunnel syndrome. Alexander Rudnicky (Rudnicky et al., 1994) presents improvements in the word error rate (lower numbers are better) for speech recognition systems in Table 4.2.

Table 4.2 Improvements in speech recognition.

Task	Speaker Independent?	Continuous Speech?	Late 1970s	Mid-1980s	Early 1990s
Alphabet	Yes	No	30%	10%	4%
Digits	Yes	Yes	10%	6%	0.4%
Constrained query	No	Yes	2%	0.1%	
Complex query	Yes	Yes		60%	3%
Dictation, 5000-word vocabulary	No	No		10%	2%
Dictation, 5000-word vocabulary	Yes	Yes			5%
Dictation, 20,000-word vocabulary	Yes	Yes			13%

More recently, Koester (2002) has reported word error rates of 6% on large-vocabulary, continuous speech with trained users, and with a total transcription rate (after error correction) approaching 30 wpm. Speech recognition tests were done regularly through the 1990s by NIST (National Institute of Standards and Technology), leading to improvements in technology under increasingly harder conditions (Garofolo, 2000). Experiments have been extended to many languages. Lamel (2002), using broadcast speech (significantly noisier and more difficult than speech recorded with a microphone), found word error rates ranging from 20% for English or Mandarin to 40% for Portuguese.

Note that these error rates are still fairly high. A word error rate of 5% is a rate of about one word per sentence. Furthermore, the programs don't work nearly as well in typical real-world situations, with untrained users in noisy environments, as in manufacturing tests. Broughton (2002) reported word accuracy rates of only around 50%. Mankoff (2000) suggests that after correction, a throughput of 25 wpm is typical (this would be very slow for a typist).

However, we have become adept at finding applications in which the domain of discourse is so restricted that speech recognition can work effectively. A computer program can be designed to use only a few dozen commands, for example, and the names can be chosen to be fairly distinct when pronounced (Church and Rau, 1995). Limited vocabularies of this sort can also be used in dialog systems, as described by Allen (2001). Restricting the subject matter of the dialogue to a specific task greatly helps with interpretation of spoken or written language. An easier task is document retrieval. Audio-based retrieval has recently been explored as part of the TREC program (Garofolo, 2000) with the realization that even 50% word error rates can still allow acceptable retrieval.

Recognizing *who* is talking is a slightly different problem from recognizing what is being said. Voice identification has been studied for years, often with the idea of identifying people for authorization purposes such as unlocking doors, although Wilcox (1994) also looked at it for the purpose of information retrieval. For security applications of speaker *verification*, the speaker can be asked to speak some particular phrase (or one of a number of phrases) which has been recited before. ITT Industries, for example, sells a product called SpeakerKey and points out that users much prefer voice identification to passwords, particularly those passwords recommended by cryptographers, which are hard to guess and thus hard to remember. Other companies with such products include VoiceVault, Veritel, and SpeechWorks. Speaker verification is still sensitive to background noise or other problems. The National Institute of Standards and Technology (NIST) reports show that for one-speaker detection with good microphones and training, the best systems can achieve a 1% false alarm rate with only a 5% miss rate; that is, 1% of impostors are allowed in, while less than 5% of the time a correct person is rejected (Przybocki and Martin, 2002).

On the other side of the law, Alexander Solzhenitzen, in the early pages of his novel *The First Circle*, describes a group of researchers asked by the KGB to identify a potential traitor from voice recordings. This is a harder problem: the person speaking cannot be asked to say something that has been recorded before. Instead, voice properties must be used to decide who it is. Despite various testimony in the courts about "voiceprints," this is still a difficult problem. Michael Hawley's 1993 doctoral thesis, for example, describes algorithms for separating the voices of two radio announcers. Katherine Ramsland (2004) describes the state of this technology in forensic applications.

The ability to identify voices would be useful beyond questions of security and law. National Public Radio correspondents, for example, each have a particular specialty. Someone looking for information about the Supreme Court, for example, would want stories read by the voice of Nina Totenberg. So voice identification would provide a degree of subject indexing of the sound if transcripts were not available.

4.6   Moving Images

The storage of television and the cinema is perhaps the most important question for the entertainment industry. Given the acceptance that the CD format has achieved, abandoning it for the next standard (the DVD) required the strongest technical justification. And that justification was the simple inability to do high-quality moving image storage adequate to hold a full movie on a CD.

The film industry has been seeking to digitize its work for many years. Part of the justification is actually in the creation of movies. To make a movie by pointing cameras at actors costs more than $2500 per second (a typical 2-hour movie, 7200 seconds long, would indeed cost about $20 M). To make a movie by hiring animators to paint cels (single drawings) costs about as much. At 24 frames per second and half a dozen cels per frame, each second requires 100 or so cels, and getting high quality art work painted, even in the Phillipines, is likely to require $250/painting. What about a totally synthesized movie? Suppose each frame is a 3000 × 3000 image (quite high-quality). Each frame is then 10 million pixels, or 2.4×10^8 pixels/second. Suppose 1000 arithmetic calculations were needed to compute each pixel. These must be floating point operations, the kind of arithmetic that is not done on simple integers, but on the kinds of numbers that have many digits of precision. What does a floating point operation cost? It is easy to buy a machine that can do 1 million floating point operations per second (a *flop*) for $10 K; amortize it over 12 months, and for $10 K you can get 3×10^{13} flops (33 million seconds in a year), or 3×10^{-10} per operation. So if each second needs 2.4×10^{11} flops, then computing one second of film would cost $70, or much less than the alternatives.

Synthesized movies began to be practical in the mid-1990s. Looking at the films shown at different SIGGRAPH (ACM Special Interest Group on Graphics) meetings, a viewer of the 1980 conference would have complained about failures in the ray tracing algorithms, while a viewer 10 years later would complain about plot and characterization. *Jurassic Park* was one of the earliest major feature films with a large fraction of computer animation in it, and now entire movies, such as *Finding Nemo,* are computer-generated. Even movies which are primarily made with actors may have long sequences which are synthesized, particularly those involving battles between alien starships and such. Computers still are not good enough at facial expressions to completely replace actors for movies that are supposed to be about real characters.

Even movies that are not created digitally can still be stored and distributed in a digital format. How much space will that take? The preceding pixel numbers were for a very high-quality format that would be suitable for theater projection. Home television sets are much lower quality; in the United States they have 525 horizontal lines and resolve perhaps 350 dots across each line. VHS videotape is of this quality. If we assumed a 500 × 500 image and 8 bits/pixel, at 30 frames per second (broadcast television), that would be a raw rate of 60 million bits per second. There is also much discussion of high-quality television, with a high-quality digital television system to be phased in shortly. The new digital standard is for 1920 × 1080 resolution at 60 Hz frame rates and a 16:9 screen aspect ratio (this is a compromise between current TV and old movie aspect ratios of 4:3 and "wide-screen" movies at 3:2). Superficially, this means 12 times as many

Table 4.3 Disk space for one minute.

Mode	Storage
Script	0.001 MB
Sound recording, mu-law	0.48 MB
Video, H.261 codec	0.84 MB
Video, MPEG-1	11 MB
Video, MPEG-2	40 MB

bits per second. Not all networks claiming to be high-definition TV actually broadcast in the full resolution; some use 720 lines instead of 1080. And there is a general effort in the television industry to use extra bandwidth for more channels rather than higher quality channels; the outcome of this struggle is not yet known.

Video storage demands look particularly large compared with text. In one minute, an actor might speak 125 words, so that even with a sentence or two of stage direction, the script would be under 1000 bytes. Table 4.3 shows how this can expand.

The H.261 algorithm, one of the methods for encoding video (the word *codec* means *coder-decoder*) used at 112 KB/second is unable to do high-quality coding of images with lots of motions; it is best for a videoconferencing application where people are sitting relatively still.

Compression of television is essential; this can rely either on compression within each frame or in addition rely also on the similarity of consecutive frames. Simply sending one JPEG picture per frame, and using 10 kilobytes per picture, would be 2.4 Mbits/second; this is known as "motion JPEG." Such a technology would make no use of frame-to-frame compression. To take advantage of frame-to-frame redundancy, video compression should use the MPEG algorithms, named for the Motion Picture Experts Group. MPEG-1 is the best known. MPEG-1 is commonly used at a data rate of 1.5 Mbits/second and includes compression both within each frame and from one frame to another. At 1.5 Mbits/second, image quality may not be quite good enough for entertainment video; motion is a little jumpy as the program catches up at major scene changes. However, MPEG-1 is adequate for many instructional videos or other "talking heads" applications such as videoconferencing. MPEG-1 starts with 30 frames/second of 352-wide by 240-high pixels, (chosen so that US NTSC at $240 \times 352 \times 60$ fields/second and European PAL at $288 \times 352 \times 50$ fields/second have the same bit rate) and separates the frames into luminance (gray level) and chrominance (color), reducing the color resolution to 176×120, much as is done by Kodak ImagePac.

Individual still-frame coding is very similar to JPEG. However, there are three kinds of frames: I-frames which are encoded entirely as a still image, with no reference to previous frames; P-frames which are predicted from previous frames (by using difference coefficients to give the JPEG parameters), and B-frames which are predicted from both present and future frames (typically interpolating between them). An I-frame must be sent every 12 frames so that the system can start from scratch at least every half-second. In order to use the B-frames, the system must transmit the frames out of order so that when each B frame is received, the bounding frames on each side are known.

MPEG-2 is higher-quality and often uses bit rates of 4–9 Mbits/second. It codes motion at larger block sizes, increases the precision of the JPEG coefficients, and was designed to deal with 720×480 pixel sizes. The practicality of either of these algorithms depends on the amount of material that must be stored. At MPEG-1 rates, a 650-MB CD-ROM can hold about 3000 seconds of video. Unfortunately, that is only about 40 minutes, and a typical modern movie is 2 hours. MPEG-2 requires even more storage; a 2-hour movie would take perhaps 3 GB. Thus, the need for a new kind of storage device, targeted at a few GB; this has produced the DVD.

Improvements on MPEG-2 are likely to require considerable storage and processing capabilities in the decoding device. One way of improving the compression rate of movies would be to start transmitting pieces of the background and asking the display device to save them. Thus, as the camera panned back and forth across a room, it would not be necessary to retransmit the areas of the background that remained static. Today, however, it is not clear what kinds of display devices would have this kind of storage capacity (or the ability to do the real-time computation needed to create 24 or 30 images per second).

If indexing static images is bad, indexing or browsing real-time images would seem to be even worse. Things are not as bad as they seem, however, since the storage system has access to a few pieces of trickery: segmentation, image classification, closed-captioning, and voice processing.

Although people can scan video at faster than normal speeds, much faster than they can listen to speech, it is still useful to divide a video into sections and let people understand the structure of the film or video. This is surprisingly easy. Segmentation can be done by looking at frame-to-frame differences. In one early experiment (Lesk, 1991), I took a 1-hour video, reduced it to 1 bit per pixel, and counted the number of pixels which changed from frame to frame. The number was either about 1% for frames that continued the same scene, or about 30% for a cut (it is not 50% because the frames, on average, are somewhat lighter rather than somewhat darker). A threshold at 10% is quite accurate at dividing a video at the places where the director or editor made cuts in composing the program.

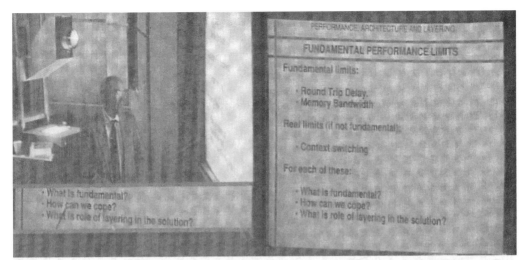

The Limits of Layering in Network Protocols David D. Clark May 18, 1990

Figure 4.10 Video segmentation.

A great deal of later work has been done on segmentation, including research by Zhang (1993), Boreczky (1996), and Qi et al. (2003).

Given a division of a video into a series of scenes, a system can then present one sample image from each scene and use that as a browsable overview of the program. The user can then click on any image and see the full video starting at that point. Figure 4.10 shows an example of this kind of interface, applied to a video of a technical talk in which the cuts are primarily between the speaker and the projection screen. The screen is divided into a top and bottom half. The top half shows two images. On the left is the current image, which changes in real time, as fast as the machine and transmission link can manage, giving the impression of ordinary video. On the right is the most recent viewgraph shown. In the bottom half, four scenes are shown: the present scene, the scene one previous to that, and two forthcoming scenes. That is, the next-to-left-bottom picture will always resemble the top left image, since both are the current scene (although the top left window is video while the bottom windows change only when the scene changes).

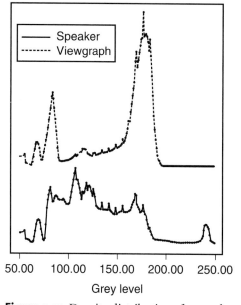

Figure 4.11 Density distributions for speaker and viewgraphs.

In the case of Figure 4.10, still further progress is possible by image classification. There are two basic kinds of scenes in this video: the person (here, David Clark of MIT) speaking in the room, and the viewgraphs that he is projecting. It is relatively easy to tell these apart. Figure 4.11 shows the gray-level distribution of the pixels from frames of these two kinds of scenes. Each curve plots the number of times each gray-level from 0 to 255 appeared in the frame. The top curve shows the viewgraph distribution, with strong peaks (since the viewgraph contains mostly either white or black), while the bottom curve shows the distribution of gray values for a picture of Professor Clark, whose image has the usual range of densities found in a photograph.

As one would expect, pictures of the speaker show a natural distribution of gray values, with a reasonably flat distribution through the middle gray levels. The viewgraph screen is either dark or light and shows a bimodal distribution. Measuring the standard deviation is easily sufficient to tell one of these from the other. In fact, comparing the number of pixels with gray-level at 50% with the number of pixels with gray-level at black is enough to distinguish them. This permits a display only of the viewgraphs or only of the speaker. Similar techniques are used at Carnegie Mellon (Stevens et al., 1994; Satoh, 1999; Jin, 2003) to take a TV news program and sort the studio scenes from the on-location photography.

Segmentation in this way works, the problem is that it is not enough for a modern film. In the 1930s or 1940s, a Hollywood movie would have had scenes of a minute or two in length, and so a 90-minute movie would have had 50 or 75 scenes, a feasible number of images for a viewer to browse through. Today, a movie will have scenes of 1 to 2 seconds in length; it is not uncommon for a 2-hour movie to have 4000 cuts. Viewers can't usefully browse that many scenes. Heuristic techniques can select the ones deemed most important.

Another technique that can produce amazing results is the use of the closed-captioning track that comes with many television programs. Television signals are transmitted with gaps to permit the traditional television set electronics time to move the CRT beam back to the beginning of each scan line and then to move the beam back to the top of the screen after each field. The data in TV fields do not follow immediately after each other; there is a time interval between the last pixel of one field and the first pixel of the next field. This interval is visible as a black bar between frames when the vertical hold on a TV is badly adjusted. On PAL sets, for example, with 625 lines, 580 are used for a picture and 45 lines are left unused. The gap between frames (the vertical blanking interval) made television sets easier and cheaper to build when electronics were less advanced. Now it represents an opportunity to conceal additional information in the television signal.

As a service to the deaf, many television programs transmit, in line 21 of the frame gap, an ASCII version of the dialog of the program. This "closed captioning" is detected and displayed by modern television sets. It can also be captured by computers and used to search or index the material being shown, as demonstrated by Howard Wactlar (Wactlar et al., 1996; Hauptmann and Witbrock, 1998; Myers et al., 2001).

Closed-captioning does not track the actual voice display perfectly, and it sometimes contains spelling errors, but it is an enormous advantage in trying to access television programs. Unfortunately, it is only present on broadcast television (not usually in films or on video), and even then only on some programs (although these are the informational programs most likely to be of interest to libraries). The vertical blanking interval can also be used for data services and will be used, for example, to transmit rating information for sex and violence on TV shows so that the V-chip can limit which programs are watched.

CMU, for example, has used closed-captioning to accumulate a set of pictures of individual faces (Jin, 2003). They look through the closed-captioning for names and then try to link these with faces that they find in the video (faces can be identified by flesh tones). They identify the studio scenes so that they do not constantly get the newscaster's face for each picture. Since the closed-captioning does not track the sound perfectly—and even the broadcast sound may not line up exactly with the image that one wants (as when the newscaster says, "and now we will talk to Alan Greenspan in our Washington studio" before the video cuts to the actual scene)—some empirical scanning is necessary to find the right face. CMU claims to identify faces (i.e., pick the right name from a transcript to put on the image) about half the time. Recently Zhao et al. (2003) have summarized our abilities in face recognition, noting substantial recent progress. It is now possible to make a database of faces from many sources. As an example of this work, Sandy Pentland at the MIT Media Lab built software that finds and recognizes faces, identifying the correct face from a population of several hundred with 99% accuracy and continuing on to recognize expressions as well as faces (Pentland, 1996; Kapoor, 2002). Now there is a boom in face recognition for security applications, with several companies advertising somewhat unbelievable accuracies in finding people walking through airport corridors (Olsen and Lemos, 2001).

There is a regular comparison of face recognition programs, available at the website for the Face Recognition Vendor Test (see Phillips et al., 2003). Indoors, with controlled lighting, the software was able to achieve 90% identification with only 1% false acceptance (imagine a person presenting himself to a camera with the goal of having a door unlock). Outdoors, however, it was not possible to do better than 50% verification while limiting false accepts to 1%. Just as we need good microphones to do speech recognition, we seem to need controlled lighting to do face recognition.

Indexing video is a less critical task than security control; however, there is less control over the images. Again, the CMU experience might suggest that it will be possible to identify the major correspondents and anchors for newscasts but not many of the participants; unfortunately, the correspondents are of less value for indexing. With luck, of course, there will be on-screen or closed-captioned labels for many of the people appearing other than the major anchors.

What can be done to index video programs with no closed-captioning? CMU has used their Sphinx voice recognition software to prepare automatic transcripts. This is a much less accurate transcription than the closed-captioning, although it does have the advantage of better linkage to the actual sound track (although, again, the sound track does not follow the video perfectly). Fortunately, if one wishes to index important topics in the video, it is likely that each topic will be mentioned more than once, giving the voice recognizer several tries at it.

For recent overviews of the situation, one can look at Snoek and Worring (2003) or Hauptmann et al. (2003). Basically, we have a lot of not very reliable tools, but the expense of doing video indexing by hand is so high that we have to pursue all of these methods.

4.7 Summary

This chapter has described indexing of multimedia. Today this technology is still experimental. We can classify pictures very roughly by color, texture, and shape; this is not enough to deal with collections of millions of photographs. We can do speech recognition well enough to be of some use in analysis of voice recordings; we have little technology for searching music. We have various tricks for compressing and browsing video, but only limited technology for searching it.

We can try to rely on browsing. For images, the human eye is extremely good at looking at large numbers of images quickly, so the provision of thumbnail-size images which can be rapidly scanned is a practical alternative to more detailed searching systems. For sound, unfortunately, this is less helpful; it is hard to scan sounds as quickly as we can deal with pictures. Browsing video is a current subject of research, but has not yet led to solutions the typical library can install easily.

To review the last few chapters, we know how to store and search ASCII text. We know how to store, if not necessarily search, pictures and sounds. We can just barely cope with storage of video. Active research in indexing pictures, sounds, and video, however, is likely to produce methods we can use to handle more advanced material in a few years. The practical digital librarian, however, might choose to focus effort on the collections which can be used immediately and look forward to handling multimedia in the future.

Knowledge Representation Schemes

The quantities of material stored in digital libraries, as in all libraries, pose the problem of finding what you want among the stacks, so to speak. In some collections of information, the user is simply overwhelmed. Queries return either nothing or thousands of answers, and users are often baffled about what to do. Attempts have been made over the years to provide a way to find information conveniently, often based on the idea of organizing everything by subject. Often, this was a byproduct of the need to put books on shelves. On disk drives the physical location of any particular byte is irrelevant to the librarian, but the intellectual organization of the collection still matters. This chapter will describe the ways we have tried to organize and arrange knowledge, with the idea of making searching simple.

If we had a single knowledge representation scheme that let us put each idea in one place, and if the users knew this scheme and could place each of their queries in it, subject retrieval would be straightforward. There would still be a need for items at different levels of sophistication, and a need for quality checking, but we could at least imagine a solution to the problem of locating items on a given subject. Is this practical?

Whether knowledge representation can be discussed outside of language processing is unclear. Two famous linguists, Edward Sapir and Benjamin Lee Whorf, proposed what is now known as the Sapir-Whorf hypothesis, which says that language constrains thought. They suggested that there would be cultural differences in the way that different peoples thought about things based on their languages. For example, they felt that the Hopi language would lend itself particularly well to modern quantum physics because of the way it discusses time. In this view there is no independent representation of abstract thought other than a linguistic expression. Most artificial intelligence researchers reject the Sapir-Whorf hypothesis. They believe that there is some kind of abstract knowledge representation in the brain, which is translated to linguistic form when we talk or write, but which could be represented directly in the right mathematical structure. Finding that one best structure is the "Holy Grail" of knowledge representation.

Evidence for abstract knowledge structures comes partly from the study of aphasia, the loss of communication ability, particularly as the result of head injury. Aphasia research started with studies of battlefield casualties in the Franco-Prussian War of 1870. Thus, for about a century, medicine has noticed a distinction between two kinds of aphasia caused by injury to different parts of the brain, Broca's area and Wernicke's area. Broca's aphasics seem to lack syntactic function; they struggle to produce words and have great difficulty arranging the words into sentences of any length or complexity. Wernicke's aphasics, in contrast, lack semantics. They produce "word salad" with great fluency and speed, but cannot produce rhetorically sensible arguments. As these two kinds of aphasia are caused by damage to different parts of the brain, it is tempting to think that "meaning" is somehow created in Wernicke's area and then formed into "language" in Broca's area, implying that they are distinct. But this does not guide us to the form and structure of whatever meaning representation the brain might use.

In practice, it seems unlikely that any single knowledge representation scheme will serve all purposes. The more detailed such a scheme is, the less likely it is that two different people will come up with the same place in it for the same document. And the less detailed it is, the less resolving power it has and the less use it is. Tom Landauer and associates did a number of experiments on the ability of people to give names to concepts. They would ask people to associate a single word with a picture or a concept, for example, the idea of a command that tells you how much money you have spent in some computer system. In Landauer's experiments, people generated so many different words as answers to tasks like this that in order to get 85% coverage of the answers, you need six different words. Of course, many of those words are also answers to different tasks. Thus, asking people to label concepts does not produce unique and reliable answers. Even professional indexers do not produce entirely reproducible results. Humphrey (1992) reports that inter-indexer consistency in Medline (selecting terms from its Medical Subject Heading controlled vocabulary) is under 49%. Voorhees (2000) reports that the overlap between pairs of assessors working on the TREC experiments is 42–49% (see Garofolo et al., 2000, for more on the TREC experiments on spoken document retrieval).

The dream of perfect vocabulary is an old one, although it originated with a slightly different problem. Until the Renaissance, most scholars in Europe wrote in Latin, and they could all read one another's books. With the rise of vernacular literature, scholars became unhappy about their inability to read anything they wanted. Since Latin had been abandoned, some of them thought that perhaps an artificial language would succeed as a common language for all serious thought. An example of this line of thinking is the 1668 publication, *An Essay Towards a Real Character and a Philosophical Language*, by Bishop John Wilkins. There were others, such as Leibniz, who even predated Wilkins in this effort.

5.1   Library Classifications

Perhaps, however, knowledge labelling could be done consistently if it were done by trained librarians. The first step would be to define a formal list of substantives (nouns) describing all subjects. Again, this goes back to Aristotle: we still have courses with names like *Rhetoric*, *Physics*, and *Politics* because these are the titles of his books.

Accordingly, we will take a look at the use of headings in some early library classification systems. The Library of Congress, until 1812, used a system based on the work of Francis Bacon (1561-1626), and then switched to one designed by Thomas Jefferson himself (Table 5.1).

The British Museum Library used 14 headings until 1808 (Table 5.2), some of which still reflected the source of the books rather than their content (Alston, 1986). This was then followed under Antonio Panizzi by an extremely idiosyncratic system in which there were category headings such as "Evidences for and against Christianity," "Total abstinence from liquor," and "Marriage—female suffrage." Perhaps the strangest category was "Morality of war, cruelty to animals, dueling." The top level categories are shown in Table 5.3.

At the end of the nineteenth century, however, the major classification systems now in use were started. These are the Dewey system by Melvil Dewey (founder of the now-defunct Columbia University School of Library Service), first published

Table 5.1 Classification systems used by the Library of Congress.

To 1812 (Bacon)	From 1814 on (Jefferson)
1. Sacred history	1. History, ancient
2. Ecclesiastical history	2. Modern history, except British Isles and America
3. Civil history	3. Modern history, British Isles
4. Geography, travels	4. Modern history, America
5. Law	5. History, ecclesiastical
6. Ethics	6. Physics, natural philosophy
7. Logic, rhetoric, criticism	7. Agriculture
8. Dictionaries, grammars	8. Chemistry
9. Politics	9. Surgery
10. Trade, commerce	10. Medicine
11. Military and naval tactics	11. Anatomy
12. Agriculture	12. Zoology
13. Natural history	13. Botany
14. Medicine, surgery, chemistry	14. Mineralogy
15. Poetry, drama, fiction	15. Technical arts
16. Arts, sciences, miscellaneous	16. Ethics
17. Gazettes (newspapers)	17. Religion
18. Maps	18. Equity (law)
	19. Common law
	20. Commercial law
	21. Maritime law
	22. Ecclesiastical law
	23. Foreign laws
	24. Politics
	25. Arithmetic
	26. Geometry
	27. Mathematical physics, mechanics, optics
	28. Astronomy
	29. Geography
	30. Fine arts, architecture
	31. Gardening, painting, sculpture
	32. Music
	33. Poetry, epic
	34. Romance, fables
	35. Pastorals, odes
	36. Didactic
	37. Tragedy
	38. Comedy

(contd)

Table 5.1   Classification systems used by the Library of Congress (continued).

To 1812 (Bacon)	From 1814 on (Jefferson)
	39. Dialog
	40. Logic, rhetoric
	41. Criticism, theory
	42. Criticism, bibliography
	43. Criticism, languages
	44. Polygraphical

Table 5.2   British Museum Library classification system prior to 1808.

1	Philology, Memoirs of Academies, Classics
2	Cracherode Library
3	Poetry, Novels, Letters, Polygraphy
4	History (ancient), Geography, Travels
5	Modern History
6	Modern History, Biography, Diplomacy, Heraldry, Archaeology, Numismatics, Bibliography
7	Medicine, Surgery, Trade and Commerce, Arts, Mathematics, Astronomy
8	Medicine, Natural History
9	Politics, Philosophy, Chemistry, Natural History
10	Ecclesiastical History, Jurisprudence, Divinity
11	Divinity
12	Sermons, Political Tracts, Kings' pamphlets
13	Acta Sanctorum, Musgrave Biographical Collection, Music
14	Parliamentary Records, Gazettes, Newspapers

in 1876, and the new Library of Congress classification based on previous work by Charles Cutter (replacing the classification designed by Thomas Jefferson), which appeared between 1898 and 1920. These systems are well known; the top level headings of each are shown in Table 5.4.

Note that each book must be put in only one category in each system, since the shelf location is determined by the class number. This is the classification function known as "mark and park." Even if the library owns two copies of a book, it is important for both to be in the same place on the shelf (or the users will get annoyed at having to look in two places to find the book). There may be

Table 5.3 Top levels of Antonio Panizzi's classification system for the British Museum Library.

1	Theology
2	Jurisprudence
3	Natural history and medicine
4	Archaeology and arts
5	Philosophy
6	History
7	Geography
8	Biography
9	Belles lettres
10	Philology

Table 5.4 Dewey Decimal system and current Library of Congress classification system.

Dewey	Library of Congress (LC)	
000 Generalities	A General Works	M Music
100 Philosophy	B Philosophy and Religion	N Arts
200 Religion	C History: Auxiliary	P Language and literature
300 Social Sciences	D History: Old World	Q Science
400 Language	EF American History	R Medicine
500 Science	G Geography	S Agriculture
600 Technology	H Social Science	T Technology
700 Arts	J Political Science	U Military Science
800 Literature	K Law	V Naval Science
900 Geography and History	L Education	Z Bibliography

multiple subject headings, but that does not help the user trying to browse the shelves.

Of course, different classifiers looking at the same book may make different decisions about its primary topic. For example, consider a book of songs about railway accidents, entitled *Scalded to Death by the Steam,* and published in both the United Kingdom and the United States. The primary subject cataloging in the United States was as a book of songs, subcategory railways (LC category number ML3551.L94, Dewey 784.6); the primary subject cataloging in the United Kingdom is as a book about railways, subcategory music (LC HE1780, Dewey 363.1).

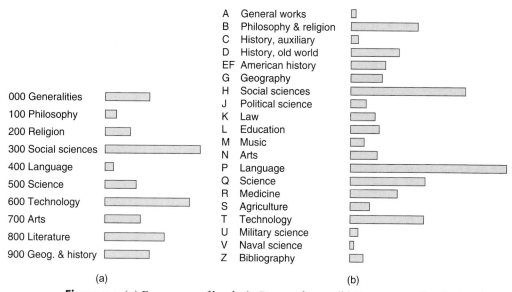

(a)   (b)

Figure 5.1 (a) Frequency of books in Dewey classes; (b) Frequency of books in Library of Congress classes.

In practice, the necessary decisions to select categories involve enough choices that they will not be made the same way by two different people. A book *Selling Mothers' Milk: The Wet-Nursing Business in France, 1715–1914,* which was clearly intended by the author as social and economic history, has wound up (in the United States) being classified under infant nutrition.

Figure 5.1 shows the relative number of books in each of the main Dewey and LC headings, from a sample of over half a million English-language books from the 1970s and 1980s at OCLC, the cooperative cataloging system also known as the Online Computer Library Center. The major reason for the number of books in the language and literature class (P) in LC which are not in Dewey are the large number of fictional works; novels are not classed in Dewey but are classed as literature in LC.

In general, it has been found that Dewey is preferred by public libraries and LC by research libraries. Dewey is perceived as simpler and better suited to smaller collections, while LC provides more detail, which is needed in a very large library. In Europe it is more common to use UDC (Universal Decimal Classification), which resembles Dewey in many ways but is maintained separately. At one point many large libraries maintained unique classification systems (e.g., Harvard and the New York Public Library) but nearly all such libraries have given up their schemes as shared cataloging has become common.

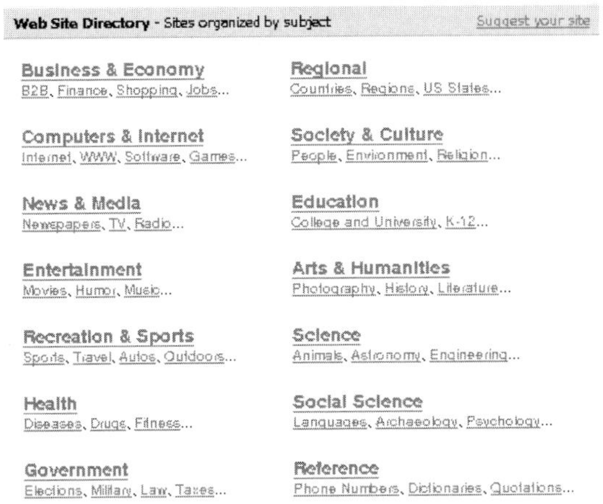

Figure 5.2 Top level classification on Yahoo.

Several Web browsers have also made classifications of the pages they find on the Web. Figure 5.2 is the top level of Yahoo, which originally meant "yet another hierarchical organization." Table 5.5 contains the top level organization of five Web browsers (one now defunct).

Note that a number of Aristotle's labels are still with us. In particular, we still have the same general kind of subject classification, as opposed to classifying items by reading level, genre, document format, or source. The only new element in the online classification is a categorization by *purpose*: employment, hobbies, and so on.

In addition to hierarchical classifications, there are also lists of subject headings, not organized into a structure. Perhaps the best known set of subject categories is that produced by the Library of Congress, not the classification hierarchy (as just described), but their List of Subject Headings (abbreviated LCSH). This multivolume book contains a list of acceptable headings that librarians can use to index books. Many library users are familiar with these headings, for example,

Railroads—Accidents

Railroads—History—United Kingdom

Railroads—History—United States

Railroads—History—United States—New York

Railroads—Subways

Table 5.5 Top level organization of Internet portals.

Yahoo 1996	Yahoo 2003	Excite 1996	Excite 2003
Arts	Arts and Humanities	Arts	
			Autos
Business	Business and Economy	Business	Careers
			Casino
			Celebrities
Computers	Computers and Internet	Computing	Computers
			Dating
			eBay
Education	Education	Education	
Entertainment	Entertainment	Entertainment	Entertainment
			Fashion
			Food & Drink
			Games
Government	Government		
Health	Health	Health and Medicine	Health
		Hobbies	
Internet			
			Investing
		Life and Style	Lifestyle
		Money	
News		News and Reference	News
		Personal Pages	
		Politics and Law	
			Real Estate

(contd)

Table 5.5 Top level organization of Internet portals (continued).			
Yahoo 1996	Yahoo 2003	Excite 1996	Excite 2003
Recreation	Recreation & Sports		
Reference	Reference		
Regional	Regional	Regional	
Science	Science	Science	
		Shopping	
Social Science	Social Science		
Society and Culture	Society and Culture		
Sports		Sports	Sports
			Travel

This kind of classification is clearly not enough. Although it is a long list of unambiguous subjects, it does not include an adequate way to indicate the relationships between them. A book with the subject headings for "armor-plate" and "transport" could be about the building of armored railway trains or about the shipment of steel plate. Nor is there a procedure for indicating the relative importance of different subjects. If a primary and secondary subject heading are indicated, the second could be 40% of the book or 5%. Finally, as with assignment to a particular classed category, different readers of the same book could easily decide that different subjects predominated. However, the LCSH scheme does have the advantage that, unlike classification, a book can have many headings. The classifier must choose whether a book on the history of British education belongs primarily under history, Britain, or education; the subject headings can reflect all three subjects.

The other side of this freedom to assign multiple subject headings is less pleasant. There is no particular need for each topic to appear only once in LCSH. One may ask, "If half the users wishing to look up *refrigerators* call them *iceboxes*, why not index all books on the subject with both terms?" The answer is that not only would it double the length of the index, but one could not distinguish between mechanical refrigeration and iceboxes if necessary. Nevertheless, in a subject heading world, it is tempting to allow multiple names for the same concept.

Efforts have been made to do very precise subject headings. It is possible to indicate relationships between them and to have enormous numbers of subdivisions. Perhaps the most ambitious scheme for extreme precision in this area was the PRECIS system of Derek Austin (Broxis 1976). PRECIS was so named since it was in effect a small abstract, formally described. Each term in a subject indexing entry had a unique meaning, and its role with respect to other terms was formally coded. The roles followed syntactic relationships with such roles as "action," "object," "agent," and "location." However, even with careful supervision of the indexers, the more detail that each indexer must provide for the indexed documents, the more likely it is that two indexers handling the same document will disagree somewhere.

5.2   Indexing: Words and Thesauri

Is it adequate simply to rely on ordinary words for the description of content? This is what most systems do today, and it seems adequate for many tasks. But words fail in two respects. First, there are often many words used to describe the same idea; users looking for *scanning* may not search for *facsimile* or *imaging*. This produces *recall failures*; material that should be found is not. Second, the same word can mean two different things in different contexts. Users typing *grain* at a search system might get articles about wheat and articles about wood grain, and it is unlikely that they wanted both.

Sometimes it is possible to sort out the meanings by knowing the part of speech of the word, as mentioned in Chapter 2 (Section 2.6). *Time flies like an arrow* cannot be about houseflies if *time* is a noun and *flies* is a verb. It is possible to guess parts of speech fairly accurately without doing a complete syntactic analysis. Geoffrey Sampson and coworkers developed statistical methods based on the probabilities of certain word sequences. They started with two kinds of information:

1. A dictionary that gives all the possible parts of speech each word might have. Thus *fly* may be either a noun or a verb; *fat* may be either an adjective or a noun.
2. A corpus of parsed English giving the parts of speech of each word, from which probabilities of different sequences could be computed. Thus *adjective-verb* is impossible while *pronoun-verb* is very common.

Then, given a sentence, they would make a list of the possible choices for each word and look for the selection that would give the best overall probability for the sentence. Garside (1987) worked with pairs of words at a time; Ken Church (1988) got better results later by working with trigrams.

Church used the Brown corpus (1 million words of tagged English) as a base and then tagged 15 million words of wire service text, claiming better accuracy than any other tagging system. A similar program is now available at Collins which will tag anything sent in email. Sampson (Sampson et al., 1989; Haigh et al., 1988) later extended this kind of work to an entire parser that used statistical techniques to assign structures to sentences.

Sometimes knowing the part of speech of a word is enough to settle some question regarding it. But many of the semantic ambiguities are still there even if the part of speech is known. If *wing* is a noun, it won't typically mean "to try," but it can still be part of either a bird, a plane, or a building. Are there similar statistical tricks for deciding on the meaning of a word within one part of speech?

One possibility is simply to average statistics across a document. Knowing whether a document is about astronomy or Hollywood will probably tell you the meaning of *star*. This can be handled by looking up each word in a thesaurus and counting the category occurrences; whatever category is most frequent in the document as a whole is the best choice for a word which could be in more than one category (Amsler and Walker, 1985).

Is it possible to do something more precise? One answer is to use a dictionary, rather than a thesaurus or a grammar, and to count overlaps between the definitions of different senses of nearby words (Lesk, 1986).

Consider, for example, the problem of knowing what the words in the phrase *pine cone* mean and distinguishing them from the meanings in phrases like *ice cream cone*. Look at the definition of *pine* in the *Oxford Advanced Learner's Dictionary of Current English*: there are, of course, two major senses, "a kind of evergreen tree with needle-shaped leaves . . ." and "waste away through sorrow or illness. . . ." And *cone* has three separate definitions: "solid body which narrows to a point . . . ," "something of this shape whether solid or hollow . . . ," and "fruit of certain evergreen trees . . . ." Note that both *evergreen* and *tree* are common to two of the sense definitions. Thus, a program could guess that if the two words *pine and cone* appear together, the likely senses are those of the tree and its fruit. Here is the output for such a situation:

Word	Sense	Count	Sense Definition
pine	1*	7	kinds of evergreen tree with needle-shaped evergreen(1) tree(6)
	2	1	Pine pine(1)
	3	0	waste away through sorrow or illness
	4	0	/ pine for sth; pine to do sth.

(contd)

Word	Sense	Count	Sense Definition
cone	1	0	solid body which narrows to a point from a
	2	0	sth of this shape whether solid or hollow
	3*	8	fruit of certain evergreen trees (fir, pine, evergreen(1) tree(6) pine(1)

What are the advantages of this technique? It is nonsyntactic and thus a useful supplement to syntactically based resolution. Syntax can distinguish *foot* in *foot the bill* and *one foot six inches*, but there are three different meanings of *mole* as a noun: *I have a mole on my skin; there is a mole tunnelling in my lawn;* and *they built a mole to stop the waves.* This technique successfully finds the correct meaning in each of these sentences.

Another major advantage is that such a method of discerning meaning is not dependent on global information. Here is a sentence from *Moby Dick* (with only the pertinent sense definitions listed):

Word	Sense	Count	Definition
There	—	—	
now	—	—	
is	—	—	
your	—	—	
insular	1*	4	of or like islanders; narrow-minded
city	2*	9	(attrib) city centre/ central area
of	—	—	
the	—	—	
Manhattoes	—	—	??
belted	2*	86	any wide strip or band, surrounding
round	4*	28	(compounds) round-arm, adj, adv
by	—	—	
wharfs	0*	1	(or wharves) wooden or stone structure
as	—	—	
Indian	2*	16	(various uses) Indian club, /
isles	0*	3	island (not much used in prose, except)
by	—	—	
coral	0*	15	hard, red, pink or white substance
reefs	1*	9	ridge of rock, shingle, etc just below
commerce	0*	1	trade (esp between countries); the

(contd)

Word	Sense	Count	Definition
surrounds	0*	0	be, go, all around, shut in on all sides
it	—	—	
with	—	—	
her	—	—	
surf	0*	5	waves breaking in white foam on the

Note that it got the correct meaning of *reef*: the alternative meaning is that in *all hands to reef topsails*. If one depended on global information, one would conclude that since *reef* appears nine times in *Moby Dick* and seven of those are related to sails, that should be the meaning chosen; and the two instances of *coral reef* would be mistakes.

On average, this technique seems to be about 50% accurate in finding word senses. It is difficult to measure this, since there is no agreement among dictionaries as to the possible meanings of each word. Furthermore, although the examples here are chosen from words with widely varying meanings, many of the sense definitions in a dictionary are very close together, and retrieving one when another was intended might represent an acceptable margin of error.

Just as some syntactic ambiguities cannot be resolved because the speaker or author did not provide enough information, there are some semantic ambiguities which must be left unsettled. In the previous sentence from *Moby Dick*, "your insular city of the Manhattoes," did Melville write *insular* to mean that Manhattan was "surrounded by water" or to mean that its inhabitants were "narrow-minded"? Of course, he meant both.

Ken Church and David Yarowsky continued such work, using more sophisticated statistical techniques akin to earlier work on parts of speech tagging. For straightforward cases, such techniques get excellent results, with over 90% correct choices between widely separated meanings such as *plant* (grows in the ground) and *plant* (industrial machinery). More recently, Florian has reported disambiguation accuracies over 70% in multiple languages. Unfortunately, there are no standard definitions of sense categories to use for disambiguation, and retrieval is often not improved by reducing the number of overlaps when similar albeit distinct senses are separated. For example, *plant* (verb), meaning "to dig a hole and put a seedling in it," and *plant* (noun), in the ordinary sense of trees, bushes and flowers, are clearly different, but a document about one is more likely than not to be somewhat relevant to the other. See further discussions of sense disambiguation by Gale et al. (1992), Resnik and Yarowsky (1999), and Florian and Yarowsky (2002).

The Wordnet project (Fellbaum and Miller, 1998) has assigned about 150,000 words to about 115,000 semantic classes. For example, the word "cat" has eight classes, ranging from the domestic pet through bulldozers made by a company named Caterpillar to medical computerized axial tomography scans. All the classes (word senses) are arranged in a hierarchy. Again, this forces decisions that might depend on the intended use of the system: are the closest animals to cats wild felines or other kinds of domestic pets? Linguistic researchers have made wide use of the system; it is less commonly applied to information retrieval or digital libraries (Fellbaum and Miller, 1998).

In processing texts, many systems apply a *stoplist* of words which are not significant for semantics, such as purely syntactic words like *the* or *and*. More generally, words may be weighted according to patterns of appearance. The most common weighting is *inverse document frequency*, which assumes that a word is more significant if it appears in few documents. This reflects the tendency of vague words to appear in a great many documents. Classified collections systems can even distinguish between words that appear mostly in one part of the collection and words that appear evenly distributed across all subject areas, assigning lower weight to the evenly distributed terms.

If words, whether from the original document or from subject headings, are not enough, what about thesauri? Earlier in this section, we touched on the use of thesauri for indexing. An indexer in a traditional thesaurus-run system has two tasks. One is to identify which topics in the document are important enough to index; the other is to assign the thesaurus entries for each of these topics.

Thesauri, unlike subject headings, do try to have only one place to put a single item. In Medline's *Medical Subject Headings* (MeSH), to take one example, the word *cancer* is normally replaced by *neoplasm*. There is an *entry vocabulary* to tell you about this synonym. The ideal thesaurus would have one term for each concept and one concept for each term, and there would be minimal overlap between the concepts. This is the mathematical idea of "orthogonality" as a set of dimensions, none of which can be expressed in terms of any of the others. For example, maps have scale, location, and features shown. Any of the choices:

- scale: 1:24,000, or 1:62,500, or 1:250,000
- location: any point in the United States
- features shown: roads, land cover, topography, buildings

make a sensible map. None can be deduced from the others. Ideally, indexing of documents could be like this, but language is not so neatly laid out.

In addition, there can be ways to express relationships between the terms. In MeSH, for example, it is necessary to distinguish between *tamoxifen* as a treatment for breast cancer and as a potential cause for ovarian cancer.

This would be expressed as *Tamoxifen—Therapeutic Use* for the treatment and *Tamoxifen—Adverse Effects* for the possible carcinogenic role.

Although thesauri such as MeSH are used by trained indexers, that does not mean that everyone agrees on how to index documents. The National Library of Medicine (which produces MeSH) keeps track of inter-indexer consistency as part of their quality maintenance program and accepts that 50% agreement is a practical measurement. This means that half the time the indexers disagree on which term to assign. This is a lot better than the 85% or so that Landauer would expect for disagreement among novice indexers, but it is certainly not perfect.

Indexing thesauri are not the whole answer to any of these problems, largely because they require trained searchers and indexers. But they anticipate many of the suggestions for complex knowledge representation languages, and they actually do support large, operating information retrieval systems.

5.3 Metadata

Traditional cataloging is an example of what is now called "metadata." Metadata is information added to a document or object to help describe it. Why would we want metadata when we have all the data in the original object? Think about the purpose of the card catalog in a traditional library setting. Originally, they were used as an alternative to having to walk the shelves looking at books. Today, especially for online subjects, for which we are likely to be able to do a full text search, it may be less clear why metadata are needed. What functions can be served by metadata?

- Metadata can expand the description of an object, either because the words in it are inadequate or there are no words at all (the object may be a picture, a sculpture, a sound recording, or something else not easily searched).
- Metadata can provide information about the object, such as where it can be found or what its uses might be, thereby extending the idea of "content."
- Metadata can provide historical information which may be important to the organization holding the object, such as its provenance or its size and weight.
- Metadata can summarize some property of the object.
- Metadata can provide a description of the object in a standardized form.

A traditional library catalog entry served all of these functions. The description was typically expanded by adding subject headings; the record gave the shelf location; it gave the size of the book; it gave a title and perhaps a brief summary (e.g., a list of chapter headings for a book); and the classification number was taken from one of the detailed structures described earlier in the chapter.

All of these functions still make sense in the world of Web pages. In fact, early in the definition of the HTTP syntax, the "meta" tag was provided to let people add additional data that would not be displayed as part of the normal page. However, the library catalog used the elaborate and tightly controlled MARC record format for its metadata, and it was recognized quickly that MARC records were too complex and expensive to make for Web pages. Furthermore, they were not directly relevant to the new world of Web pages; for example, Web pages don't have a size in inches or centimeters, but they do have a size in bytes.

Originally people thought of the "meta" tags as being provided by the page owner. Unfortunately, abuse of metadata by commercial page owners started almost immediately. People who wanted to attract attention to their Web page, typically because they were being paid per view by advertisers, started putting popular search words in meta tags, whether or not they had anything to do with page content. They sometimes put multiple copies of words in the tags, hoping to swamp some ranking algorithm. The result was to discredit the general use of meta tags and cause the search engines to ignore them. One now finds irrelevant words carefully printed on the page but in the same color as the background, so that the viewer doesn't see them but the search engines will (although the search engine coders have learned this trick). The serious catalogers were driven to keeping their data separately.

In any case, the meta tag had no accepted substructure, and the catalogers needed some way to add fielded data. One wishes to distinguish books *about* Henry James from books *by* Henry James; one wishes to distinguish the LCSH subject heading *Yogis* from a title *Yogi* (especially if the latter book is by Lawrence Berra). Just taking over MARC format was not an answer, partly for the reasons already mentioned and partly because MARC records were designed specifically for libraries. And on the Web there are many Web pages to be described that are from museums, archives, commercial organizations, and other groups, with different kinds of content. One proposal for a new kind of metadata format is the "Dublin Core" effort, an international cooperation to define a simpler, light-weight metadata record.

Dublin Core descriptions of objects have fifteen slots. These are

1. Title
2. Creator
3. Subject
4. Description
5. Publisher
6. Contributor
7. Date
8. Resource Type
9. Format

10. Identifier
11. Source
12. Language
13. Relation
14. Coverage
15. Rights

Some of these are relatively free-form, e.g., Description; others are expected to be filled from standard abbreviations, e.g., Language (which is expected to follow the codes in ISO 639, an international standard defining which languages are considered distinct and how their names should be abbreviated).

Dublin Core, however, has had a fairly rough road for acceptance. To keep the cost of defining these entries down, the descriptions of the 15 properties has to be kept short, and the use of long and complex dictionaries minimized. As a consequence, some catalogers complain that Dublin Core is inadequately precise and request more details and ways of subclassifying the various sections. Even for such a presumably well-defined area as "language," for example, is it enough to have "en" for English? No, even ISO accepts "en-gb" for British English. Do we need further subdivisions for all the dialects within the United Kingdom? Are Cockney, Scouse, or Geordie to be separate languages, subdivisions of "en-gb," or a "format" for spoken English? One can argue about this for a long time without getting anything useful done.

This is a problem that repeats thoughout the idea of retrieving information. Should we spend a lot of effort defining a structure and insisting that everything fit in that structure, or rely on vague language or (even worse) pictures and hope that search systems will solve the problem in the future?

5.4 Knowledge Structures

Artificial intelligence researchers have attempted to define formal knowledge languages, with the goal of permitting knowledge to be expressed with such detail that it can be manipulated automatically. As in indexing thesauri, a typical knowledge representation language will have a hierarchy of concepts and then store relationships between them. For example, animals might be grouped into the traditional Linnean hierarchy, giving us

- animal
- mammal
- carnivore
- dog
- Fido

Looking carefully at this, the relationship between "Fido" and "dog" is not really the same as that between "dog" and "mammal": *isa* and *subset* are typical names for these two distinct semantic relationships, *isa* meaning that the object is a specific example or instance of the related concept, while *subset* means that the object or objects are restricted examples of the concept. Formal knowledge structures exist only in a few areas of research. Chemistry, for example, has an elaborate and complete system of substance names, but nothing similar for reaction names. There is a taxonomy of biological organisms, but much less agreement on the arrangement of diseases. In general, these structures are limited to the equivalent of thesauri; it is difficult to formalize the relations between them. We seem better, at least in Western culture, at organizing nouns than we are at organizing verbs.

The relationships between items can be of varying degrees of complexity. Once one gets beyond the defining hierarchy, there are many obvious relationships that can be used in writing down information. To understand the use of such relationships, remember the relationships in MeSH. If one wishes to distinguish not just the question of whether a particular substance causes or cures a particular disease, but all possible relationships between nouns, a great many relationships might be needed. Virtually every verb in the language might be needed as a link name between substantives. Normally, a somewhat smaller set is used, since a knowledge representation structure is supposed to be something more systematized than a parse tree. Often they seem similar to the cases used in linguistics: agent, object, location, and so on.

By organizing the nodes of an artificial intelligence (AI) language into a hierarchy, each fact can be stored at an appropriate level. The statement that canaries are yellow is stored with "canary," that they fly is taken from a statement about birds, and that they breathe from a statement about all animals. Of course, life is not always so simple. In a knowledge representation language, one could easily write, "All cats have a tail." But what about Manx cats? Does the node for "cat" have to be divided into "Manx" and "non-Manx" cats? Pretty soon there will be so many divisions that the gain from having hierarchies will disappear.

Something more tractable is the use of *frames*. Frames were invented by Marvin Minsky (1975) and represent specific lists of attributes ("slots") to be filled in for specific nodes so that everything is not linked to everything else. Thus, a frame for describing a cat might have slots for weight, color, sex, and so on, while a frame describing a theatrical performance would have slots for playwright, director, cast, and so forth.

This is more reasonable for a large knowledge area. For example, Susanne Humphrey (1989) has built a system named MedIndEx which uses frame structures to provide aids to medical indexers. The frames encode information about what medical subject headings can be used in which parts of the index entries.

For example, the site of a disease must be coded with a term which comes from the Anatomical-Structures part of the MeSH hierarchy. The location of some conditions is even more restricted; a bone neoplasm, for example, must be coded with a term from the skeletal section of the hierarchy. And the frames can make use of the slots that are filled to improve the indexing. Humphrey explains, for example, that if an indexer codes *Bone Neoplasm/Anatomical Structure/Femur*, the system will suggest that the top-level term should be *Femoral Neoplasm*. This system is very detailed and encodes a great deal of medical knowledge. It is unusual in the breadth of its coverage.

Translating all written English into a knowledge representation language requires, in principle, the need to disambiguate every ambiguity in the original text. Clearly, this is not practical. For many ambiguous sentences, the speaker has been willing to say something with an ambiguity because it is not worth the trouble to resolve it; it will make no difference to the listener. We are accustomed to ambiguity that can be resolved and that which cannot be resolved. The sentence "John drove away in a fury" could mean either "John drove away angry" (John was angry) or "John drove away angrily" (the manner of his driving displayed anger). This does not bother a listener since the meaning is basically the same in either case, and unless John then got into an automobile accident it is probably not important which was meant. The work of disambiguating each such possibility is totally impractical. And things get worse if translation is the goal. Martin Kay mentions that when you board a bus in Switzerland, you put your ticket into a machine which, in the French parts of the country, validates it (*valider*), but in the German parts of the country, invalidates it (*entwerten*). There are many stories about widely hyped systems making mistakes, such as translating the name of the late Israeli prime minister Menachem Begin as "Monsieur Commencer."

However, the designers of AI systems do not necessarily need to imagine converting all of an English text into a knowledge representation language. Two choices are converting some of the knowledge of a text into the formal language, or writing the knowledge directly in the formal language, instead of in English.

The conversion idea was perhaps pursued most ambitiously by Roger Schank and his students at Yale. They worked on what were first called "scripts" and then called "MOPs" (memory organization processes) and which represented certain standard scenarios for common situations. For example, there was a "restaurant script" involving the standard actions of seeing a menu, placing an order, getting food, eating food, and then paying the bill. Another was the "natural disaster script" of an earthquake or hurricane, in which some event happened, at some place and time, and caused a certain number of deaths and injuries. Schank produced programs which went through the United Press newswire and tried to list the basic elements from each story that matched one of the scripts. In some ways this was a basic data extraction task—to take a text that contains specific data elements and pull them out for a database.

The most elaborate attempt to produce an enormous body of codified knowledge is the CYC project of Doug Lenat in Austin, Texas, first at MCC and now at Cycorp (Lenat and Guha, 1990). Lenat set himself the goal of writing down all common-sense knowledge in a formal way. He suggested that the problem with machine learning was that computers lacked the more elementary parts of the knowledge that people have. For more than two decades Lenat and associates have attempted to encode everything from elementary biology to time series. They used 100 kilo concepts and wrote down 1 million rules. They ran into several practical difficulties. One was that a great deal of skill in logic was needed to enter the knowledge; despite a goal of entering very simple knowledge, it was not possible as originally hoped to use high school students to do it. Another difficulty was that different people entering similar concepts would choose different ways to do it, as has happened in other experiments of this sort. Most serious was Lenat's discovery time and again that the basic principles of CYCL, his knowledge representation language, had to be adjusted as new areas of knowledge were studied. Initially, for example, Lenat tried to assign probabilities to each rule to indicate degrees of certainty, but was unable to do this in a consistent way.

CYC has no unifying overall ontology, since CYC is broken down into a number of "microtheories," each of which is created specially for its domain. Time will have to tell whether CYC will ever achieve its goals of having the common-sense knowledge of a human being (Stipp, 1995). Sanguino (2001) writes, "In general, CYC still has a long way to go."

5.5 Hypertext

If it is not going to be easy to translate all text manually into formal language, is it possible to rely on specific links for specific document to document queries? This is the model of "trails" suggested by Vannevar Bush in 1945 (see Chapter 1, Section 1.3). Theodor (Ted) Nelson rejuvenated this idea in 1960 and coined the name *hypertext* for it.

In a hypertext document collection, there are pointers from one place in the text to another. Hypertext links, as commonly used, are asymmetrical: there does not need to be a link in the reverse direction for each forward link. They are also modeless: all links are the same kind of link, rather than being labelled with types.

There were various experiments with hypertext systems in the 1970s and 1980s. Perhaps the best known are the systems at Brown University (IRIS) which attempted to use hypertext for teaching courses, and the programming systems like Hypercard (Apple) and Notecards (Xerox). In these experiments it was found that hypertext was frustrating both to write and to read. In terms of writing, the author has great difficulties writing something if the user need not have read the paragraph immediately preceding the one being written. A world in which readers jump from one place to another is one in which the author never knows what the reader already knows, and it becomes difficult to carry through a logical argument. Brown found it very time-consuming to create their hypertext courses, and the students in the courses contributed less than the researchers expected.

The readers have the converse problem. They can easily get lost, and not know how to get back to something they have read. *Navigation* quickly became the big problem in hypertext, and it became commonplace for each hypertext document to have one page which functioned like a traditional table of contents or index, providing pointers to every place in the hypertext and being pointed to by every page as well. That way, users always had a place to which they could return and from which they could find any other point in the text.

Several evaluation studies of hypertext, in fact, found that it was more difficult for people to deal with than were traditional paper texts. Gordon et al. (1988) at the University of Idaho, for example, converted four short magazine articles into a hypertext system and tested students on what they learned from the articles.

Half the articles were general interest and half were technical. Both the linear (traditional) and hypertext versions of the articles were read on the same computer screens. The students remembered more of what they read in a linear format, although the time taken to read either version was about the same. The students also preferred the linear version. Similarly, Shneiderman (1987) compared the ability of people to answer questions from a 138-page set of articles which was available both on paper and in his system, Hyperties. For information at the start of an article paper was better; for information buried in an article or requiring references to more than one article, the formats were equivalent. A more dramatic instance was an experiment done by McKnight et al. (1991) in which the text used came originally from hypertext format rather than paper. Again, the results failed to show an advantage for hypertext.

Despite these early difficulties (Nielsen, 1990), hypertext has now exploded on the world. Today's famous hypertext system, of course, is the Web. Created by Tim Berners-Lee at CERN in 1990, the Web as of April 2003 contained about 20 terabytes of material in some 2 billion documents, with perhaps 30 pointers on each Web page, or a total of 60 billion hypertext links. Much of the Web consists of organizations of other people's pages: there are innumerable hot lists, bookmarks, and other ways of keeping track of what has been seen. There are also, of course, the search engines, and finding things on the Web is partly handled by search engines and partly by the hypertext links.

Part of both the glory and the frustration of the Web is that it has no maintenance organization whatsoever. Individuals add and delete things at will, making it easy for material to appear but also for it to disappear. The ability of individuals to place what they want on the Web has also produced problems, since some Web users want attention for their pages and do things like place irrelevant words on their page to attract the attention of search engines. Libraries will have to try to decide which items are relevant and useful and which are not.

Web pages can not only appear without any organizational approval, but also can and do disappear. The average life of a URL was 45 days in 1996 and has now crept up to 100 days, and with such short lifetimes, the Web is full of pointers to files that no longer exist. This means that somebody who sees something good on the Web must make a judgment as to whether it is likely to still be there if it is wanted again. If it does not appear to be from a source such as a university library or other permanent organization, the only safe thing to do will be to copy it, given permission. Not all URLs are short-lived; Spinellis (2003) reports that half of the URLs he found in reports were still valid after four years. There's no inconsistency here: there are a large number of URLs that turn over very quickly and then some more that are long-lived, and what Spinellis found is that URLs cited in reports tend to be drawn from more durable pages.

Whether, in the long run, libraries can rely on hypertext links as a way of accessing information is doubtful. Unorganized and amateur indexing has been tried in the past with "author-assigned keywords" and such proposals and has been inadequate. Relying simply on citations in known papers is effective but inadequate for complete coverage; a surprising fraction of published papers are never cited at all. Thus, sole reliance on volunteer-built hypertext may not be an adequate method of achieving general library coverage.

Various libraries have attempted to collect Web sites professionally and provide guidance to users; such Web pages are often called "gateways." For example, *www.agrifor.ac.uk* is a gateway site to agricultural information maintained by the University of Nottingham. The creation of such sites is expensive: it costs as much or more to catalog a Web site as to catalog a book. Many Web sites lack the equivalent of a title page telling you the author and publisher name; the cataloger must search around for the information. And a normal library doesn't have to check back on each book in its catalog regularly to see whether it has changed this week.

5.6   Vector Models

If reliance on manual methods is not going to be enough for digital libraries, what can be done mechanically? In the SMART project, Salton introduced the idea of the *vector space* as a way of handling documents in retrieval systems. In vector space mathematics, each different word in a document can be viewed as a direction in a very-high-dimensional space. The number of dimensions is equal to the number of different words in the document collection. The strength of the vector in each direction is the number of times that word (since each word is one dimension) appeared in the document. Thus, each document can be viewed as a vector in this high-dimensional space, and the similarity of two documents can be judged by looking at the angle between the vectors. Documents on very similar subjects should have a small angle between their vectors; very dissimilar documents should have a large angle between their vectors.

Salton also considered the use of a thesaurus in this model. In this case, each word was replaced with the thesaurus category to which it belonged, and the number of dimensions was the number of categories rather than the number of different words. This still leaves, however, an enormous number of dimensions. And that large number of dimensions means that it is often going to be the case that a particular document will not be found in a search for a particular concept, because a related concept was used to describe the document. A document relevant to *dogs* might be missed because it used the word *canine* or *pet*, for example.

Attempts were made over the years, beginning with Vince Guiliano in 1961, to identify related terms on the basis of their overlaps in documents. Statistical methods for word associations looked for words which appeared together. In fact, early suggestions directed one to look not for words which actually occurred together, but for those which occurred with similar word neighborhoods. For example, if we imagine that all documents are spelled with either consistent British or American spelling, the words *airplane* and *aeroplane* will not appear together, and their synonymy will be missed; a searcher who asks for only one word will not find documents containing the other one. But both of these words will appear in documents containing words such as *jet, propeller, wing, rudder, cockpit,* or *carry-on.* Thus, their relationship could be detected. The irregularities of word statistics in small collections, however, caused most such experiments on small test databases in the 1960s to yield unsatisfactory results. And most examples of synonymy are much less clear-cut than this one.

Landauer, Furnas, Dumais, and Harshman thought of trying to mechanically condense the vector space into a space of fewer dimensions using standard mathematical techniques (singular value decomposition). They called this technique Latent Semantic Indexing (Deerwester et al., 1990; Dumais, 2004). LSI, since renamed LSA (latent semantic analysis), operates on a term-document matrix for a text collection, which has rows and columns labelled, respectively, with each word that appears in the collection and each document that is in the collection.

The value of the element at any position in the matrix is the number of occurrences of that word in that document. Thus, given a collection of 10,000 documents with 50,000 words appearing in them, the matrix would have 500 million cells. This might seem much too large for any kind of practical manipulation, but fortunately the matrix is very sparse (the average word does not appear in the average document). Thus, special matrix techniques can be used to accelerate the calculations. What LSI/LSA does is to find a smaller set of dimensions and values which can be used to substitute for the original matrix. Instead of a document being represented by a vector in a 50,000-dimensional space, with almost all elements zero and little chance of finding overlaps, it is represented by perhaps a 100-dimensional vector in which it is likely to have *some* weight on each element.

Imagine two groups of documents, one set about mathematical theory and another about human factors. Terms such as *interface* and *ergonomics* might not appear in the same document, but as long as they both appear with terms such as *display* or *format*, they will be connected by the process. Thus, LSA can make significant improvements in recall as well as precision.

Tom Landauer and Michael Littman (1990) also used LSA to do cross-language retrieval. Earlier, Salton had done cross-language retrieval by creating a bilingual thesaurus, in which words in both languages were mapped into one concept space (Salton, 1970).

Landauer and Littman realized that by obtaining a collection of documents in two languages, and performing the term/document overlaps using both languages, they could make vector spaces into which terms from each language could be mapped. This eliminated the need for manual construction of a bilingual concept thesaurus, although a translated collection was still needed to start the process. For example, here is a passage from the Canadian Hansard (i.e., parliamentary proceedings) in English and French for May 12, 1988:

> Mr. Speaker, during the 1980 election campaign the Rhinoceros Party promised Canadians that if elected they would make us drive on the left hand side of the road instead of the right hand side, and that this new system would be phased in starting with buses in the first year, followed by trucks in the second year, and cars later.
>
> Monsieur le Président, pendant la campagne électorale de 1980 le parti rhinocéros avait promis, que s'il était élu, il nous obligerait à conduire du côté gauche de la chaussée plutôt que du côté droit, ajoutant que ce nouveau système serait appliqué graduellement, en commençant par les autobus la première année, les camions la deuxième année, et les voitures par la suite.

By treating these paragraphs (and all other translated pairs) as the same document for purposes of building the vector space, the words that are consistently paired will be found to be related. Thus, in this case, if *camion* and *truck* usually appear together, they will get very similar representations in the LSA space, and a search for either word will retrieve the same documents.

The word relationships found are not necessarily those you would find in a dictionary, since they combine aspects of the basic word meaning with the context. In the Canadian Hansard, for example, the word *house* is most closely related to *chambre*, not *maison*, because the contexts for these words are typically *House of Commons* and *Chambre de Communes*. If one is doing a search in the Hansard on a topic like "What did the House say about traffic in Ottawa?", the word chambre is indeed the most useful translation.

Landauer and Littman (1990), in an early experiment, used a sample of 2482 translated paragraphs, with at least five lines in both French and English. They trained the LSA system on 900 such paragraphs and computed a 100-dimension space. Then, using other monolingual paragraphs as queries, they would find the translation as the best document over 90% of the time, as one would hope. LSA cross-language works extremely well in assigning these documents to the same positions, despite imperfections in either the translations or LSA and despite the great similarities between many speeches.

An interesting subquestion is the determination of *which* language an unknown text is written in so that a system can decide what software to put it through. One would not wish to index French or German under the misunderstanding that they were English. There are various techniques to solve this—by looking for specific words that are very frequent in a particular language, or by looking at the letter frequencies in the language. A short text in any language, however, may be missing particular cue words. However, there is a cheap trick that works well: given known samples of the different languages, append the unknown text to each sample and run any standard compression algorithm that detects repeated strings on the combination. The one that compresses best is the right language. The compression program will do all the statistics for you.

Another technique for finding information is based on what has been used before. There is strong clustering in citations, in photocopy requests, and in library circulation. Digitally, it will become much easier to gather such information and use it. Clustering phenomena in library usage are well known. A few items get heavy use, and many more are not used at all. The average item in a large research library does not circulate in an average year; one suspects it is not touched (Burrell, 1985). Typically, 80% of the circulation of books comes from 20% of the titles.

Can the bunching of requests be used as a way to help retrieve information? Some years ago in an experiment at Bell Labs, the usage of an Associated Press wire service was tracked. The screen display of stories is shown in Figure 5.3. At the top is the list of stories, each identified by its "slug" (the hyphenated phrase);

```
 1: (f0055) Indexes [1]           11: (f0050) TimeWarner-Turner
 2: (a9510) WEA--USTempsSN.usw10  12: (a0550) China-Fire [5]
 3: (a0554) TourdeFrance-Basques [3] 13: (f0049) Austria-Supermarkets [1]
 4: (f0054) Transactions [1]      14: (f0048) Austria-Supermarkets [1]
 5: (f0053) DJ10 [1]              15: (a0549) Lite-WifeWanted [2]
 6: (f0052) Sema-Olivetti [1]     16: (a0548) TimeWarner-Turner [2]
 7: (a0553) UN-GlobalWarming [3]  17: (f0047) LateNewsAdvisory [1]
 8: (a0552) TimeWarner-Turner [1] 18: (f0046) TimeWarner-Turner [1]
 9: (f0051) Earns-Ford [1]        19: (a0547) Breast-feedingSwitch [5]
10: (a0551) Pint-SizedSpeedster [3] 20: (f0045) OddLots [1]
 3

 r i PM-TourdeFrance-Basques      07-17 0231
^PM-Tour de France-Basques.0234<
^Basque Separatists Harass Riders, Protest as Race Enters Spain<
     PAMPLONA, Spain (AP) _ Basque separatist protesters walked onto
the path of cyclists in the Tour de France race today, forcing the
riders to slow almost to a stop as they climbed a steep ascent.
     About a dozen protesters held a Basque-language banner and
yelled slogans at Tour leader Bjarne Riis and several other
cyclists on the highway in France, about 15 miles from the Spanish
border.
     The Tour cyclists today were entering Pamplona in the Navarre
region of northern Spain.
     The armed Basque separatist group ETA, which wants Navarre and
six other provinces in Spain and France to be united as an
```

Figure 5.3 Screen display of news stories.

picking a number gives that story. The system doled out the actual stories in 10-line screens. It tracked the number of such segments that people read. The number to the right of each identifying phrase is the average number of screens that people who have read this story have gone through (up to 5). So a story with 4 or 5 to its right is one that the average reader has read 40 or 50 lines of; while a story with a 1 is a story which readers have stopped reading immediately; and a story with no number next to it has not been read by anyone. Thus, a story like number 12, "China-Fire" with a 5 rating, is one that somebody has read through; whereas nobody has looked at the "TimeWarner-Turner" story. In this particular display the user picked story 3, on the Tour de France, and the first dozen lines are shown in the figure. Given this data, one could search for stories that had ratings of 3 or above, for example. This would produce a set of stories which other people found interesting. In practice, this would in fact distinguish stories in a useful way. With no names attached, this did not cause a worry about invasion of privacy.

5.7   XML and the Semantic Web

A recent effort to deal with the flood of Web pages has been a more systematic effort to encourage Web page creators or maintainers to supply additional information about their Web page and the information on it. This is partly an attempt to address the inability of search engines to deal with numbers. Words are fairly precise compared to numbers. Despite all the preceding discussion about disambiguation, we have plenty of words like *rhinoceros* and names like *Ayckbourn* which are unlikely to be misunderstood. For numbers, things are much worse. Yes, 2003 is probably a date; but if you find 75 in a document you have no idea whether it is a page number, a temperature, a time interval, or what.

XML is an attempt to extend "tagging" so that the user, or more typically a user program, could know what a data item means. Actually, XML is a syntax, like SGML, that lets you label items. Thus, instead of just putting 75 on a page, the user could have

```
<temperature>75</temperature>
```

or

```
<time-interval><minutes>75</minutes></time-interval>
```

or

```
<price><euro>75</euro></price>
```

to clarify what this particular 75 means. Note that XML uses the same form of bracket notation as SGML. Because XML is a syntax, the knowledge of whether to use "temperature," "temp," "degrees," or "degrees-Farenheit" as a tag within the brackets has to come from somewhere else.

So to achieve the grand vision, in which programs acting for a user read Web pages and make conclusions from the data on them, we need more than just the idea of tagging the data; we need, in addition, some agreement on the tags to be used. This has become known as the *Semantic Web* and is one of the buzzwords of the early twenty-first century. The Semantic Web is an attempt to merge the database area with the Web, so that we can have data schemas and data files stored on Web pages and accessed by programs. Where the Semantic Web parts company with traditional databases is in worldwide intelligibility. Traditionally, databases were isolated items, and each one was interpreted by specific queries and software just for that database. The Semantic Web is intended to be general, so that everyone can write agents that visit Semantic Web pages and work with them.

The Semantic Web vision is very dramatic. Users will have agents that know their preferences for hotel rooms or airline flights, access databases directly, retrieve the options, and make decisions. For this to work, however, we need more than a technical vision: we need a level of economic and technical cooperation that may be hard to come by. Consider the requirements for the Semantic Web concept to succeed:

1. Each user has to post a "data schema" for their data.
2. Each user has to define each data element in terms of that schema.
3. Each user has to define the data elements in a controlled vocabulary.
4. Each user has to define the data relationships in a controlled vocabulary.

Again, a "controlled vocabulary" indicates an ontology, giving precise definitions of the actual items to be used. Thus, such a program might insist on "tan" rather than "beige" as a color. It's not clear yet how these ontologies are going to be created or defined: lots of people would like to make the decisions, few understand the incentives for using them.

If the users don't cooperate, other people's programs won't know what to make of their Web pages. If your program to choose a jacket has to interact with my Web page of clothing for sale, for example, it must understand all the properties of the implied database on the Web page. Thus, to apply our four requirements for a successful Semantic Web to a store selling jackets, consider the following questions:

1. What information comes with each jacket? This is the data schema, informing your program that the items include price, style, size, color, weight, and so on. The schema may have multiple levels; for example, there might be a category "fabric" divided into "lining" and "shell."
2. How is the information linked to the items? This is the definition of the elements, so that we look for tags like `<color>` or `<price>`.
3. What are the names used for the different data properties? For example, price might be specified in dollars; fabrics and colors might be chosen from a list; but what kind of ontology is going to cover all the styles of jackets one might wish to put in a catalog?
4. What are the relationships between these items? Are the fabric choices connected to the color choices, or can you get the same range of colors whether you order the wool lining or the cotton lining?

Will people try to do such labelling well? The history of metadata on the Web is not good; plenty of sites use "meta" tags to try to deceive search engines. Will people agree on the ways they do this labelling? It's not straightforward to define data schema and to define fields in a way that will simplify the way other people will be able to access them. Historically, only very simple schemes (such as the original HTTP formats) are likely to be quickly picked up by many users. Complex schemes are less generally accepted; look at the FGDC (Federal Geographic Data Committee) metadata standard for an example. The more complex the data organization, the fewer people use it and the less likely it is that two different people looking at the same piece of information will describe it the same way.

To start to address the complexity of defining data in XML, note that XML should be used in conjunction with a *document type definition*, called a DTD. A DTD describes the data schema of an XML-encoded document: the legal components and labels that can be included. For example, you might think that a year could be specified as being made of 4 digits. That would be straightforward, but what you find in real documents are times expressed as "ca. 1920," "before 1910," "during the 1930s," or even "two years after Pearl Harbor." So, in fact, the year is going to have to be an arbitrary field, which pushes off to the searching or analyzing system the job of deciding whether "two years after Pearl Harbor" is exactly 1943 or also includes at least part of 1944.

DTDs certainly look forbidding. Here is an example of a part of a DTD that should cover some examples of Shakespeare's plays:

```
<!ELEMENT PLAY (TITLE, FM, PERSONAE, SCNDESCR, PLAYSUBT, INDUCT?,
                              PROLOGUE?, ACT+, EPILOGUE?)>
<!ELEMENT TITLE (#PCDATA)>
<!ELEMENT FM (P+)>
<!ELEMENT P (#PCDATA)>
<!ELEMENT PERSONAE (TITLE, (PERSONA | PGROUP)+)>
<!ELEMENT PGROUP (PERSONA+, GRPDESCR)>
<!ELEMENT PERSONA (#PCDATA)>
<!ELEMENT GRPDESCR (#PCDATA)>
```

What this says is that a play is made up of a title, front matter, personae, scene description, and so on. The title is "PCDATA" which officially means "parsed character data" and in practice is the typical entry to mean "actual content." Personae is a title, and then a list of items which are either a character or a group (note the difference between PERSONAE and PERSONA), and then each of those is again PCDATA. In principle, if you type in the text according to this DTD, you can then search for words in a title, or names in a cast list, without getting extraneous retrievals.

A somewhat fuller example (Pagotto and Celentano, 2000) has to do with cars. The XML document and the corresponding logical structure are shown in Figure 5.4.

The DTD that corresponds to this is

```
<!ELEMENT Vendor (UsedCars,NewCars)>
<!ELEMENT UsedCars (UsedCar*)>
<!ATTLIST UsedCar number CDATA #REQUIRED>
<!ELEMENT UsedCar (Model,Year)>
<!ELEMENT Model (#PCDATA)>
<!ELEMENT Year (#PCDATA)>
<!ELEMENT NewCars (NewCar*)>
<!ATTLIST NewCar number CDATA #REQUIRED>
<!ELEMENT NewCar (Model)>
```

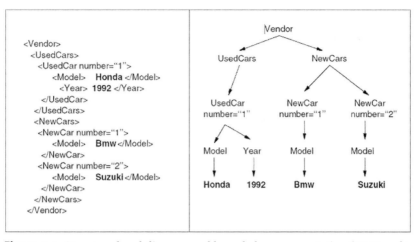

Figure 5.4 Structured and diagrammed knowledge representation (XML and tree).

You might well feel that it is hard to see how this formality is worth the trouble. Sometimes artificial knowledge representations seem to be a way of saying obvious things in obscure ways.

Even the structure shown in Figure 5.4 is still simple in XML terms. It does not exploit the power of named relations. Specific relations could, in principle, help in understanding the differences between phrases such as:

Low-fat food (food made up of low-fat ingredients)

Dog food (food to be fed to dogs)

The distinctions between phrases can become quite complicated. Rosario and Hearst (2001) distinguish *headache specialist, headache patient, headache interval, headache onset, headache relief,* and *headache drug* as noun phrases with different meanings. Indeed, they are, but it becomes difficult to actually assign correct labels to them and process large quantities of documents. Things become even more complex when numerical data is involved, and *headache interval* as a number might come in anything from minutes to weeks. Even people balk at some of the processing involved; I wrote a paper including a table showing trends in costs of disk drives over the last few decades and sent it to a journal in the United Kingdom whose editor suggested that she would change a chart giving prices in dollars into sterling. I asked if she was going to do this at the current exchange rate or the appropriate exchange rate as of each past date, and whether we should use historical US or UK inflation tables; she gave up and published the chart in dollars. Adding labels without solving the underlying problems doesn't help; it just adds another level of obscurity to an already difficult situation.

Will there be combined text–data search engines that use XML? Yes, the industry is moving to supply these. In such systems, people would be able to pose the kinds of queries that are difficult in Web search engines, such as "title includes the word *dog* and publication date is after 2001." Some online search engines (e.g., Dialog) have supported queries like this for years, but most Web data bases don't. Vianu (2000) provides a good discussion of the theory of XML databases for those looking for more technical detail.

Shah et al. (2002) have looked at how information retrieval would work in the Semantic Web environment. They imagine not just the document retrieval of today, or the fact retrieval enabled by XML, but deductive logic to allow agents to combine information retrieved from different documents. They hope for formal ontologies to standardize vocabulary and natural language processing to extract specific information units from plain text.

Now in the works are plans for widespread data mining services that would go around the Web looking for combinations of text and data to extract important and interesting information. For example, Cannataro (2003) described the "Knowledge Grid," a design for distributed knowledge discovery, in which multiple computers would perform data mining in parallel.

All of these structures suffer from the general problem that they must trade specificity and power for generality and ease of use. As one starts to enforce standardized vocabulary, and encoding of facts in standard relations, it becomes harder and harder to enter material into a system (or to categorize what is already there). As one demands more and more specific relations, it becomes less and less likely that one will find a match to any specific relation. And thus the more work you put into categorizing, ironically, the less you may find as a result.

5.8 User-Provided Links

Historically, specific links provided by users have been important in the use of libraries; they came in the form of literature references. This is the basis of citation indexing. For some years, Science Citation Index (from the Institute for Scientific Information, in Philadelphia) has indexed papers based on the other papers they reference. As an alternative to keyword-based indexing, this can often turn up quite different documents. On the Web, it is similarly possible to track through hypertext links to a given page.

Don Swanson has done some particularly provocative work on the results of studying term and citation networks (Swanson, 1987, 1991, 1997, 2001). He hypothesized that if topic A and topic B are not connected by citations, but topic C is strongly connected to both, it is worth considering whether A and B should be related. In the important example he gave, he found 25 articles arguing that fish oil causes certain blood changes and 34 articles showing how the same blood changes would alleviate the problems of Reynaud's disease, but no articles discussing fish oil and Reynaud's disease. And, indeed, later experiments showed that fish oil appears to be of some use in treating Reynaud's disease. Similarly, he found that there is considerable literature about migraine and epilepsy and about epilepsy and magnesium deficiency, but no papers about dietary magnesium and migraine. After Swanson's publication, several papers appeared with evidence that magnesium alleviates migraine. Despite these examples, it has proved difficult to follow up this work. Neither Swanson nor his followers have been able to mechanically find other examples of this sort.

Will usage-based searching be important in digital libraries as well? Digitally, it is much easier to track usage of different items. As yet, there are no systems that say, "Show me things lots of people have liked," or systems that say, "Show me things other people have overlooked." Such a system is called *community-rated* information. The idea here is that you can model the search you want to do by looking at what other people have done. This is the logic of "Anything Joe recommends, I will like," done mathematically and with a large set of people.

An early example was the "video recommender" of Will Hill and Mark Rosenstein at Bellcore (Hill et al., 1995). They set up an email address which asked people to rate movies from 1 to 10. They sent out a list of 500 movies; amazingly, the average person who returned this list rated about 200 movies. They wound up with a database of about 25,000 ratings. When a new person entered ratings, the database was searched to find the 10 people with the closest agreement. This new person could then be modelled as a linear combination of the best 10 matching people. Given this way of modelling the person, the system could then suggest movies that the model predicted the user would like, but that the user had not rated (and presumably had not seen).

Tests showed that this was a very effective way of recommending movies. Table 5.6 shows different methods of suggesting what videotapes you might want to rent. The correlation coefficient is between the actual rating and the rating predicted by the method given.

Similar work has been done for audio (popular music CDs) by Patti Maes and her group at the MIT Media Lab (Shardanand and Maes, 1995). The technique

Table 5.6 Effectiveness of recommending movies.

Method	Correlation
Choosing movies at random	0.16
Using recommendations of published movie critics	0.22
Community-rating, as described	0.62

is now familiar from its use in systems like Amazon.com ("other people who bought the book you are looking at also bought . . .").

The technique depends on having a large number of items which many people have seen. For rarely read scientific papers, for example, it might be hard to find any data, since nobody would be prepared to rate them. Movies and TV series have the property that a surprisingly large fraction of your friends and colleagues have seen the same programs; there is not the same shared experience for most books, and certainly not for scientific journal articles or most Web pages.

However, popular Web pages are seen by many people, and the "page ranking" systems of Google and its competitors rely heavily on links between pages to decide which are most important. This is a less demanding application than recommending specific pages; the goal is only to rank different pages on a search results list. It's been very successful: getting a small amount of information from a very large number of sources seems adequately accurate, while much faster and cheaper than having professionals rate Web pages.

5.9 Summary

What should librarians in digital libraries do for knowledge representation? This chapter has reviewed several possibilities. The first four choices offered were manual. Three of these forms of knowledge organization are typically created by paid experts: library catalog headings, thesauri, and artificial languages. Cataloging requires the least manual work, while the use of thesauri or artificial languages require more work in exchange for more detailed representations. Since even manual cataloging is fairly expensive at $17 per book (Wilhoit, 1994), it is unlikely to be used for the majority of small Web documents. Hypertext is a manual method which spreads the work around a great many unpaid volunteers, and is thus more practical while less reliable. Additional mechanical possibilities involve vector models, retrieval histories, and community-rating. These all seem to work, and vector models are widely used today. But the history and community techniques rely on enough people seeing each item to obtain useful judgments, which may not be the case.

Compared with all of these methods for organizing information, it seems likely that text searching will be the major method of accessing materials in digital libraries. Text searching, however, works best with items with particularly precise word definitions, such as unusual author names. If we want to search by concepts or browse in general subject areas, there may be a place for classifications and conceptual representations. They may also be of assistance with collections in multiple languages. Research is needed on the most effective ways of using representation languages and on their applications to digital libraries.

Research is also needed on the ways to combine information on genre (e.g., works aimed at children) or quality (e.g., refereeing) with cataloging. The biggest technical problem is extending any of the automatic search methods to sounds and images; as we've seen, some of this is being done, but the selectivity is still primitive compared with text searching.

Ideally, we will be able to combine information derived from classification, from hypertext links, from text and image searching, and from users. We use all of these sources in today's libraries, albeit informally, and we would like to continue using them in the more mechanized future.

6 Distribution

T he last few chapters have covered how the contents of a digital library are stored and organized. This chapter asks how those contents get to the readers. How is information to be moved from creators to receivers? Originally, it came via direct physical transmission: one person talked to another. This kind of transmission has advantages and disadvantages. It can be tailored to the individual listener, for example. It offers the chance for the listener to ask clarifying questions. But it doesn't travel very far, nor can it reach many people at once (the best opera singers without amplification fill a hall of 3,000 people). The listener can't "back up" (without asking the speaker); there is no permanent record; the speaker has limited ability to use aids such as pictures or sound recordings; and the listener and speaker must be present at the same time in the same place.

6.1 Books, CD-ROMs, and DVDs

Writing, of course, made it possible to have a permanent version of information, and writing on papyrus, parchment, and paper (rather than carving on stone walls) made it possible to move texts from place to place. In the Middle Ages there was an active market in copying manuscripts and selling them; this market was taken over by printed books when they arrived.

Category	University Press Journal	Commercial Publisher's Journal
Content creation	30%	26%
Sales, overhead	28%	33%
Manufacturing (paper, printing)	25%	26%
Distribution, subscription handling	17%	15%

Table 6.1 Cost breakdown for producing a journal.

Turning to the present day, the costs of producing a scholarly journal, as summarized by Waltham (2002), are typically only about 25% physical production. Costs are not that different for commercial and noncommercial journal publishers, as shown in Table 6.1. Similarly, John Edwards (2001) of Edwards Brothers Printing reported that the revenue from a $25 book sale is divided with $12 to the retailer, $5 to the author, $2 to the printer, $2 to the publisher, and $1 in profit; similar comments can be found in *Publishing Trends* (2003).

The economies of scale in modern publishing are such that it is difficult to issue a book today in a small press run. University presses are pressured by authors who wish to see their books in print in order to get tenure; but their main market is university libraries, none of which have budget increases adequate to keep up with the inflation in book prices. University presses collected under 2% of US publishing revenues during the 1990s (Greco 2001) and had not gained much by 2002, but nevertheless increased their title count by 10% during the decade (*Publishing Trends*, 2003). Since so many of the costs of printing a book are incurred before the first copy comes off the press, a small press run means high costs, and thus high prices, which further cause libraries to reduce purchases.

Marlie Wasserman (1997) of Rutgers University Press presented some detailed statistics of the cost of publishing a standard monograph in university press quantities. In her numbers, a 288-page book selling 600 copies at $40 would bring in $15,200; but would cost $6,700 in per-copy costs and $22,000 in per-title costs, for a loss on the book of $13,600. The per-copy overhead is $18,000, which for a book selling only 600 copies is prohibitive; it represents $30/copy, more than the publisher is getting for each copy from the bookstores. Wolff (1999) similarly reports that the overhead cost of a university press title is often $15,000 or more. Over the last few decades the average press run of a scholarly book has declined from perhaps 1500 to about 200 copies, and all university presses have been forced to do less publishing of scholarly monographs and more publishing of local history and other books sold to the general public. In 2000, university presses printed some 31 million books, but only 5 million went to libraries.

Scholarly journals are even more affected by the push from authors to see their names in print. Their prices have been raised to levels that no one could have imagined 30 years ago; today a journal subscription can cost as much as a new car. One particular journal, as of 2003, costs $16,000 per year. Since the authors are not being paid for their contributions, and since journals do not carry a retailer's markup, these prices reflect the very small number of libraries which are still willing to subscribe. Ann Okerson (1992) reports that book purchases dropped 15% in the 5 years to 1991, and journal purchases per faculty member in universities went from 14 to 12 in the same period. Association of Research Libraries' statistics for 2002 show that in the 15 years from 1986 to 2001, monograph purchases declined 26%, while unit cost of books went up 68%. Okerson extrapolated to show that in 2017 libraries would buy nothing at all, and we're on the way there (at least on paper).

The publishers react to statistics on the increasing costs facing libraries by pointing to the general consumer price index increase plus the increase in the number of pages per journal issue; together these effects dominate the journal price increases. The libraries, however, have no way of enforcing greater selectivity on the publishers to keep the sizes down, and there is a residual increase in inflation-adjusted price per page, especially for non-US publishers (Marks et al., 1991). The University of Washington reported (Carey and Gould, 2000) that the average cost per page of atmospheric science journals from Springer-Verlag is $1.86, from Elsevier $1.24, and from Kluwer $0.80; nonprofit publishers averaged $0.16 per page.

Traditional publishing and distribution have accelerated substantially in recent years. Time-to-market is everything on instant books such as those published during the O.J. Simpson trial, and publishers have learned to speed up printing and distribution even for ordinary books. Libraries wishing to exchange items can take advantage of a wide array of new delivery services specializing in overnight package handling, and of course the fax machine has made interlibrary copying of journal articles a very rapid process.

The greatest recent change in book distribution has been the great increase in the variety of titles available to the average reader. The rise of the chain bookstores, with enormous stores replacing smaller, individual booksellers, was the first step; then came Amazon.com and its competitors, offering essentially every book in print. This is a welcome contrast to the tendency to concentration; although it is still the case that even in a bookstore with 100,000 titles, most of the sales are best-sellers.

For a period in the early 1990s, it looked like CD-ROMS might become a major publishing medium. CD-ROMs share many distribution properties with books. The CD manufacturing process, like the book publishing process, is most economical at large production runs. It was designed for high-run popular music disks, and the signal can be read as digital or converted to analog sound. CD-ROMs cost, in quantity, well under $1 each to produce, much less than a book. Their distribution began in the mid-1980s, some half dozen years after the audio CD started. Through the late 1980s, most libraries bought CD-ROM drives and began to purchase CD-ROM versions of the abstracting and indexing journals. These purchases displaced online searching on a pay-per-minute basis; libraries realized that if they were spending large amounts of money on online searching, they could save money by purchasing the same database on CD-ROM.

Soon most databases started appearing on CD-ROM, which pushed out magnetic tape and competed effectively with the very expensive online services then common. Then, in the early 1990s, the individual CD-ROM business exploded. CD-ROM drives dropped in price (every new PC now comes with one) at the same time that software distributors realized they wanted to distribute much larger programs. When PC computer RAM memory was limited to 640 K, a 1.4 MB diskette was an adequate distribution mechanism. Now that PCs with 500 MB of internal memory are common and software comes with manuals, options, and elaborate background images, we cannot deliver software in units of 1.4 MB. Many CD-ROMs came on to the market, with the market doubling every year up to early 1995, including in particular the home reference market. CD-ROM encyclopedias more or less destroyed the market for print encyclopedias. Other important categories of reference CD-ROM publishing were atlases, phonebooks, and educational aids for children.

CD-ROM publishing was unusually concentrated by the standards of normal publishing. The distribution channels were harder to break into than for books; stores sold relatively few titles and most of those were from a few major publishers (most obviously Microsoft). Unlike audiobooks, which are sold in normal bookstores, CD-ROMs are sold largely through computer stores, which don't have the same traditions of special orders and generous stocking policies. Consumers got tired of CD-ROM books rather quickly as the Web became available, and the CD-ROM market collapsed.

Now we have DVDs and the possibility of a new set of businesses in DVD publishing. This will certainly make sense for selling large databases to libraries, since the number of disks in a set will drop by a factor of ten or so. However, the possibility of a consumer market seems low, especially given the disagreements on format and standards and the sour taste left in the publishing business by the CD-ROM flop.

6.2 Computer Networks

The digital world allows much faster alternatives to faxes or postal mail for sharing information between libraries. Computer networks now link almost every country in the world. Of course, computers have always exchanged bits with their peripheral devices. These exchanges typically follow a protocol in which one device is in charge and the other is responding. A key difficulty in designing intercomputer protocols, and part of the reason why they are different from protocols used within a single computer, is that they must anticipate that the two machines are of equal status; neither can be assumed willing to just wait around for the other one. Also, of course, the longer delays involved in transmitting over distances and through phone lines means that the protocols cannot assume immediate responses to all messages. The winning network has turned out to be the Internet, running IP (the Internetworking protocol).

There are several basic choices to be made in network design. These include the choice of *packet* or *circuit* switching, and the choice of *bus* or *star* physical arrangements. In a packet network, each batch of information is handled separately. The analogy is postal mail or the telegram; in fact, packets are often called datagrams. Packet networks are like adding soil to your garden, bucket by bucket. In a circuit network there is a preliminary negotiation to set up a route and then information flows along it. An analogy is the telephone system or the way that water flows along a hose; the faucets are turned and then the water moves. Roughly speaking, a circuit network involves overhead to arrange a path, but may recover the cost of the arrangements by being able to move information faster. A packet network is simpler since each packet is completely independent, but there is no opportunity to save routing arrangements that have been set up for one packet to use for future ones.

To run wires around a building, two different topologies can be used. One wire can be threaded through each place that needs one, and everything hung off that wire, like the lights on a Christmas tree. This is called "bus" wiring: one wire passes every place that needs service. The alternative is to have each spot that needs a wire connected to a central location, like a fusebox, for example. This is called "star" wiring since a map of the wires looks like a star, with lines going from one central point to each spot that needs service.

Bus wiring requires less total wire, but requires everybody to share the same wire. It is thus appropriate for a system in which expensive but high-capacity wire is used. Some early computer networks relied on coaxial cable and leaned towards bus wiring. However, bus wiring creates some administrative problems. Since everyone is sharing the same physical cable, if one machine on the cable malfunctions, everyone may suffer loss of service. Similarly, a cable break necessarily affects a great many users. Thus, there has been a tendency to use star wiring, made of cheaper wires, but meaning that each machine has its own connection to some kind of data closet or local switch. This kind of system is easier to manage and usually cheaper to install and—in the form of the 10-base-T standard using twisted pairs of copper wire—has replaced the thick coaxial cable Ethernet. It also simplifies administration of the network, since users are less likely to interfere with each other.

Wireless networks are now coming to prominence. Each computer has a radio antenna, transmitter, and receiver; thus, even though there is no cost for "wire", the network is likely to be more expensive in hardware than a wired network. However, installation is much easier, with no holes to be drilled in walls or cables to be run. Wireless networks, like bus networks, can be overloaded or interfered with by one user. And, like a bus network, one user can overhear the packets transmitted by other users. Wireless is thus a kind of bus.

Originally, different vendors developed different computer network systems and protocols. IBM was known for its SNA (system network architecture) linkages between machines, while Digital had DECNet. The most important development, however, was that of Ethernet at Xerox PARC, invented in 1976 by Robert Metcalfe and David Boggs. The basic idea of an early network of this type was the Alohanet protocol: any system which wishes to transmit simply puts out a packet on the bus with a header saying from whom it has come and at whom it is aimed. Each system listens on the bus and picks up all packets meant for it. Any system wishing to send merely sends a packet and hopes nobody else is doing so at the same time.

This extremely simple Aloha protocol cannot use much of the bus throughput, since as usage increases, the chance increases that two computers will transmit at once. One improvement was the so-called slotted Aloha in which trasmission occurs at fixed intervals, instead of transmitting at will. Ethernet improved this further while retaining the passive medium of Aloha. The Ethernet fabric is a plain coaxial cable with no active parts, and thus fewer chances to fail. As in Alohanet, machines communicate by putting addressed packets on the bus fabric. What Ethernet adds is the idea that machines listen as they are transmitting. If, before it starts sending, a computer hears some other machine transmitting, it does not transmit. And, should two machines start transmitting so closely together in time that neither hears the other before starting to send, they both stop as soon as they detect the collision. Each then waits a random time before trying again, so that the next try will not produce a collision. This is why Ethernet is called CSMA/CD (carrier sense multiple access, collision detection). It is still not possible to use all the capacity of the cable, but it is a great improvement over the original Alohanet. In the Ethernet protocol, each machine needs to be able to hear every other machine in a time shorter than that required to transmit an entire packet. This limits a single

Ethernet to perhaps 100 meters, depending on the transmission speed on the cable.

The simplicities of the basic Ethernet idea are sometimes disadvantages. Every machine can see every packet on the cable, no matter to whom it is addressed. Unless packets are encrypted, sniffing machines can cheat and pick up all sorts of information not intended for them. Also, there are no constraints on the ability of an individual machine to transmit. If a machine on the cable goes haywire and starts transmitting constantly, ignoring all collisions and all other machines, there is nothing the other machines can do. Fortunately, a single Ethernet is limited in length and is likely to be contained within a singly administered domain, so something can be done to bring pressure on the operator of the haywire machine to fix it or at least shut it down.

Since a single Ethernet is only 100 meters long, Ethernets have to be connected to build larger networks. At first, this can be done by *bridges* which simply sit between two cables and copy every packet from one of them onto the other one. This doubles the traffic on the cables, however, and is not an adequate answer for large networks. Larger networks need *routers*. A router is a device that sits between two networks and, like a bridge, moves packets from one to another. But a router does not move every packet across the network. It knows which addresses are on which side. In the simple one-bus Ethernet, machines can be very sloppy about addresses because as long as each sender and receiver know who they are, it doesn't matter if any other machine does. Once routers are introduced, however, addressing matters. Each router looks at each packet address and decides whether it belongs only on the cable it came from or should be sent to a different cable.

What does a router do if it wants to put a packet on an Ethernet cable but suffers a collision? It must wait and try again, just like a normal computer. And this means it must have some memory to save up packets which it has to retransmit. Packet networks with routers are thus store-and-forward networks in which information flows with somewhat unpredictable timing towards the destination. And packet networks need some way of sending back to the originator a message of the form "Your packets are coming too fast, please stop sending."

Of course, a network with routers in it is no longer totally passive. Nevertheless, the basic notion that computer networks have a cheap, dumb fabric and intelligent devices persists, and contrasts with the idea of the telephone network as containing expensive switches and dumb telephones as peripheral devices. In 1996 a digital telephone switch cost about $200/line (world average price) and the phones were $10; East Carolina University revisited these prices (2003) and found carriers quoting average costs of $150–200/phone line/year for analog circuit switched service. By contrast, hubs and routers connect $500 computers, and the Ethernet card, if not included, costs maybe $20. The cost of the hubs and routers is down to $5 per line. The central cost of the traditional telephony service is much higher than that for data switching, and nowadays even the distributed cost of the data switching is lower. Stringing the wire, now the same unshielded twisted pair for either voice or data, is more expensive: wiring may cost $350 per line within a typical building.

It is now common for even residential customers to consider routing their phone calls over the Internet, with "VoIP" (voice over IP) now a growing business. Typically, residential customers are charged $35/month for unlimited US calls (Chamy 2003), and the total VoIP business was $934 M in 2002 (McKay 2003).

Table 6.2 shows the conventional transmission speeds (bits per second) found in computer networks.

The ATM speed of 155 Mbits/sec is a common choice for very high-speed connections, despite the inconvenience of translating to virtual circuits and back, and the unusual design of ATM packets. They are 53 bytes long; 48 bytes of data and 5 bytes of header. The choice of 48 bytes of data length was a compromise across the Atlantic, with the US wanting 64 bytes and the Europeans wanting 32. Today the packet size looks too small, but a great deal of equipment has been designed and sold for this protocol.

The way beyond 155 Mbits/sec was pioneered by experiments such as the gigabit experiments run by the US government, running at 600 Mbits (the "government gigabit") and simultaneous telephone services at 1600 Mbits and 3200 Mbits under the name SONET (Synchronous Optical Networking). There is enormous basic transmission capacity available on fiber, which has raw transmission capacities well into the gigabits and is commonly laid in batches of at least 12 fibers at once. It is now possible to buy 10-gigabit service and the

Table 6.2 Transmission speeds.

Speed	Device and Comments
110 baud	Model 33 teletype, 1950s
1200 baud	Common 1980s variety modem
56 K	Modern modem
500 K	Typical cable modem
1.5 Mbits/sec	T-1 or DS-1 speed
45 Mbits/sec	DS-3
155 Mbits/sec	ATM (asynchronous transmission mode)
622 Mbits/sec	OC-12 optical fiber speed
10 Gbits/sec	OC-192

Figure 6.1 Abilene network links in the United States.

problem perceived by the suppliers is overcapacity, rather than an inability to keep up with bandwidth demands. In South Korea, as of 2003, some 20% of households have broadband (>56 Kbits/sec) data service; this is the highest use of broadband in the world. Figure 6.1 shows the Abilene network links in the United States; note that the high capacity links are up to 10 GB. UUNET has an even larger (commercial) network; its network map is too complex to reproduce easily. The rate of increase in international bandwidth capacity was "only" 40% in 2002; it had been more than doubling every year.

The real precursor of the networks we have today was the Arpanet, started in 1969 by Larry Roberts. Arpanet was a connection between computers doing military research and was provided to these sites by the Department of Defense. ARPA was then the Advanced Research Projects Agency of the Department of Defence; it's now DARPA, with Defense added to the acronym. The Arpanet was high-speed: it started with 56 K lines at a time when 300 baud modems were still standard. Arpanet was intended from the beginning to be real-time, since it was to support remote computing facilities so that users at RAND could log into computers at MIT or at military bases (for example).

The Arpanet introduced a protocol and addressing system for a worldwide computer network. On the networks today, each machine has a four-byte address, with each byte representing a separate parsing step in the routing. For example, a machine address might be 128.253.78.249, in which 128.253.78 specifies a particular Ethernet at Cornell, and 249 is the address of the particular workstation. Normally, such addresses are given symbolically. In this case the machine was named `woop.mannlib.cornell.edu`, which is interpreted from right to left, like a post office address (from specific to general locations). The `edu` string is the `domain` of educational institutions in the United States; alternatives include com (commercial), gov (US government), org (organizations) and net (miscellaneous). So, for example, in addition to cornell.edu we have universities such as rutgers.edu or umich.edu, companies such as ibm.com or sun.com, government agencies such as loc.gov (the Library of Congress) or nasa.gov, and miscellaneous organizations such as acm.org (Association for Computing Machinery) or npr.org (National Public Radio). Non-US addresses normally end with a two-letter country code; thus, inria.fr (the French research organization INRIA) or ox.ac.uk (Oxford University, academic, United Kingdom). Before the domain name come other names describing a location within an institution; thus mannlib.cornell.edu is the Albert Mann Library at Cornell and is distinct from cit.cornell.edu, which is the Computing and Information Technologies organization at Cornell. Finally, woop was a particular computer in the Mann library. Figure 6.2 shows some of this, partially expanding out the sections for Cornell and University College London (ucl.ac.uk).

Over the years, more and more machines joined the Arpanet. Fewer and fewer of the institutions running these machines had military research as their primary

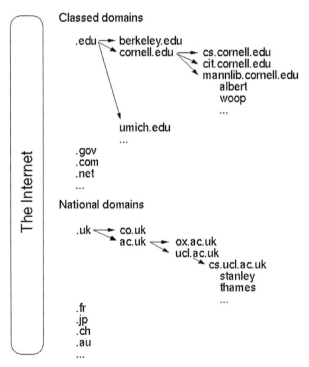

Figure 6.2 Structure of Internet address names.

purpose; at the same time, the military was starting to use the Arpanet for more critical appliations than research and became less comfortable about sharing the net with other users. In the mid-1980s, the Arpanet was split and divided into MILNET, a purely military set of machines, and the civilian machines. NSF took over the administrative and funding responsibility for the backbone of the civilian networks, called NSFNET. NSFNET connected the key supercomputer centers and other users bridged into those centers. The funding NSF provided was relatively small ($10 M/yr) but enabled the backbone to stay up without complex ways of allocating its costs. Users paid much more (perhaps $600 M in 1993) to buy computers and connect them to the backbone.

Since many of the people now wishing to connect to the network had nothing to do with the United States, let alone US military research, other ways of constructing the network were needed. Commercial and semi-commercial nonprofit groups started building regional networks, which then linked up through the internetworking protocol (IP) designed for the Arpanet. This gave rise to the name Internet: a network which connects other networks. Many corporations have internal networks which link up local networks in different laboratories, research groups, or buildings. The number of Internet hosts grew rapidly through the 1990s; it has now slowed down in the US but continues to grow internationally (Figure 6.3).

As traffic on the Internet exploded in 1994 and 1995, more and more commercial companies started connecting customers to the NSFNET backbone. Since NSF had a goal of supporting university research, and for years maintained an "acceptable use policy" which limited what the commercial organizations were allowed to do on the net, the commercial organizations began building their

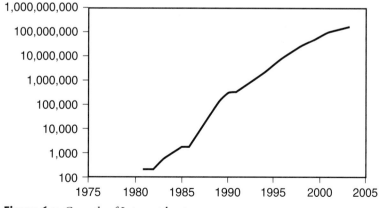

Figure 6.3 Growth of Internet hosts.

own backbones, and as a result the Internet is no longer receiving NSF support. This change was transparent to most users, as the commercial companies interchange traffic without regard to which one of them owns the link to the end consumer.

Most libraries are now connected to the Net, as are most schools. As the costs of Internet connection decline, the actual connection is much less of a question than the need for staff that knows what to do with it. Libraries are also, in some communities, seeking the role of providing Internet access to people who do not have their own connection at home. Within most advanced countries, however, the spread of Internet connectivity into homes is moving so fast that there will be little role for libraries to do this. The United States is not even the leader in connectivity; South Korea has a greater broadband penetration than any other country, with more than 20 broadband connections per 100 citizens (given typical household size, this means that more than half the households in South Korea have broadband connections). Canada, Iceland, Belgium, Denmark, and Sweden also rank ahead of the United States, which has only about 6 broadband connections per 100 people; see Table 6.3, with data from Ismail (Ismail and Wu, 2003).

Estimates by Hough in 1970 and Noll in 1991 suggested that voice telephony would dominate into the indefinite future. In fact, the Internet and data traffic are now larger than voice telephony traffic; data traffic first took the lead on international links, especially trans-Pacific, but data traffic passed voice even within the United States in 2002. Consider, for example, that even though only about 20% of American homes have broadband service, 500 kbits/sec is ten times the bandwidth of a voice circuit, and most of these homes are browsing the Web 1.5–2 hours per day, substantially more time than they spend on the telephone. Internet telephony is now common: witness the use of packets to transmit ordinary voice calls. As we mentioned earlier in the section, this is called VoIP (Voice over Internet Protocol, or more commonly Voice over IP).

Table 6.3 Comparision of international Internet broadband growth.

Country	Broadband/100 People	Growth Rate (2002)
South Korea	21.4	24%
Canada	11.7	31%
Belgium	8.5	93%
Denmark	8.3	84%
Sweden	8.1	53%
USA	6.9	48%

Many people aren't even aware they are using it; they buy prepaid phone cards and have no idea that the vendor is using the Internet and packets to handle their international call.

6.3   Information on the Internet

Given the success of the Internet, how is information provided on it to be made available? The two original services were remote login and file transfer. These have since been encapsulated so that the user does not perceive what is being done, but the basic rules are the same: a user connects to a machine (called a server), and then bits are transferred to the user's remote machine (the client).

The earliest service was remote login. Here, all the computing and data are actually on the server machine. Effectively, the client machine is merely a remote terminal. It has no computing to do other than to provide the screen display, and it need have no copies of the data being transmitted. Often, however, the user wishes to obtain actual data files from the server machine and keep these. For example, the server may not be providing catalog access, but may be providing a library of "freeware" software or freely available text that users may be welcome to download.

For file transfers, the standard protocol was `ftp` (file transfer protocol). Quite large arrays of information became available on some servers using `ftp`, including, for example, the literature texts held by Project Gutenberg (see Chapter 1, Section 1.5), the software distributions at many sites, collections of images posted by people, and many other kinds of information. Inherently, `ftp` involves people making copies of files, resulting in problems distributing updates and old versions proliferating around the world.

The `ftp` archives, scattered over a great many machines, became quite large, and a searching system called `archie` began as a way of finding particular files. The `archie` system relied on searching file names and directory titles, since most of the material on `ftp` was not suitable for free-text search (computer programs and binary images). Note that this basic idea—many files stored by many people in different places, and some kind of scattered searching mechanism —is exactly what turned into file-sharing for music and the Napster idea.

The `ftp` interface was not easy to use, and widespread acceptance had to await the `gopher` system from the University of Minnesota. The `gopher` interface was based on the concept of hierarchical menus and was text-only. It was overrun by the Web and the browsers: first by Mosaic, designed by Marc Andreesen (then at the National Center for Supercomputer Applications at the University of Illinois) and later by Netscape and then Internet Explorer.

Web browsers do not rely on a strictly hierarchical organization. Instead, hypertext links stored anywhere within a document can link to any other place on the Web. Here is an example of a bit of text set up for Web use:

Click for information on `<a href=http://www.seagate.com>` Seagate disk drives `</a>`.

When displayed, this will appear as follows:

Click for information on <u>Seagate disk drives</u>

The underlining (and on color displays a color change) indicates that the words *Seagate disk drives* represent a link. The phrase representing the link is shown within `<a>...</a>` brackets as in SGML syntax. The `href=...` string within the opening `<a>` denotes the location to which the browser should go if this item is clicked. In this case the location, called a URL (uniform resource locator) is `http://www.seagate.com` which is interpreted as: (a) `http` signals that this is a file which is to be interpreted as `http` protocol (as opposed to locations that might begin `gopher:` or `ftp:`); (b) the double slash, which indicates that what follows is a machine name rather than the name of a file on this machine; and (c) the machine name `www.seagate.com`, which is the name of a computer on the Web to which the `http` request should be addressed. There can also be a following file name; for instance, the URL `http://www.cs.ucl.ac.uk/External/lesk` asks first for the machine `www.cs.ucl.ac.uk` and then for the file (relative to the root of `http` files) named `External/lesk`.

The Web browsers can display pictures, play back sound recordings, and even show multimedia. For text, they have access to a few typesetting options, such as italic and bold text display, paragraph breaks, and a limited number of type sizes. Some browsers can also do tables, and the capacity of HTML (hypertext markup language) to do typographic display is increasing. Features in HTML permit a Web page to contain enough decoration and formatting to permit attractive graphic design and thus attract users to this format.

The reader of the Web page also gets to make certain choices about appearance. HTML, as now defined, does not specify exact point sizes or typefonts. Instead, the author specifies normal size, larger, or smaller and typefont as normal, bold, or italic. The client software in the browser chooses whether the overall type is to be small or large, and in principle could make choices about the font as well. For some publishers and authors, this is inadequate control of the format, and they push constantly to have HTML extended to support double column text, equations, and a choice of typefonts. For some readers, on the other hand, it is convenient to have a way to enlarge the print; one advantage seen in digital libraries is the ease with which those with failing vision (or even those reading on poor-quality screens) can choose the presentation format to their taste.

Another option with browsers is the use of links in Web pages, which is unconstrained. As in the tradition of hypertext, anybody can put a link to anything. The collection of all such pages is called, of course, the World Wide Web, and Web pages can be found in virtually all the ways described so far.

- There are free-text search engines that retrieve everything on the Web at regular intervals and index it; Google is the best known.
- There are lists, arranged by subject, of pages on particular topics; the best known are those of Yahoo (yet another hierarchical organization) and AOL.
- There are hypertext pointers on most pages, creating a great chain of references which can be followed.

Most users supplement these public techniques with bookmark lists of pages they like and sometimes with pages of their own containing lists of pages of interest.

A quickly adopted extension to static Web pages was the idea of providing information in the form of programs that would execute on the user's machine to provide fast, tailored interaction. The programming language that made this possible was Java, designed by James Gosling at Sun Microsystems. Java has limitations that reassure the user that it will only handle the Web display and not do damage to the user machine (e.g., Java programs can't erase the user's files or folders). By moving the computation involved in Web operations from the server machine, often overloaded, to the user machine, Java made fancier and more elaborate Web pages possible. Java programs downloaded to the user machine are called "applets" (little applications). They permit extensive creativity and variety on the part of Web page designers, thus extending the applicability of the Web.

Web page enhancements are more than locally executed graphics routines; there are also straightforward downloads of little videos or sound recordings, using languages such as Quicktime. It is now straightforward for a Web page designer to include a multimedia presentation and provide the software to interpret it as a "plug-in" to the Web browser. Over time some of these enhancements, such as Macromedia's "Flash" and Real Networks, "RealPlayer" have become common; some commercial websites now tell users that if they haven't installed the right plug-in, they can't access the site.

The longer-range hope is that Web browsing might be turned over to "agents," which operate in the user's place. These agents would do searching, retrieval, and display of information which the user might want. As a simple example, an agent might understand different protocols, such as the formats of documents in PDF or Word or LaTex, and invoke the correct "viewer" as needed. Most Web browsers already do something like this. More complex agents might maintain standing queries to run against news sites every day and forward interesting stories; again, this is a service readily available from portals. Someday, the marketers hope, agents will shop for you, maintain your calendar, and schedule your entertainment. How accurately they can do this and how much they will be distorted by commercial advertising is not yet clear.

Essentially, every digital library today is on the Web. It is the standard way for distributing material and it is what everyone expects. Today, a service with its own non-Web interface would be considered unusual and frighten off users. Even if your digital library is going to have a peculiar and idiosyncratic access method, it will almost certainly be wrapped in a Web page. Online book catalogs, for example, often predated the Web and used "telnet" or "gopher" as their interfaces, but have nearly all become Web pages. The Web is now the overall space of online information; digital libraries are specific collections within that space.

6.4 Grid Computing

Given a large number of computers connected together, it is possible to distribute jobs among them and have computations done by many computers in parallel. The largest computation jobs these days are not done by single supercomputers, but by collections of smaller machines. In fact, even the architecture of a supercomputer today is likely to be that of multiple processors, rather than a single super-fast device. What does vary is the distance between the machines and their administrative control.

- Sometimes there are single, giant boxes, which contain thousands of processors. These are correctly called supercomputers even though no individual processor is that much faster than what you can buy in a desktop. Such machines now dominate the commercial supercomputer business, having replaced the machines that one hoped different kinds of electronics (ECL logic rather than CMOS, or gallium arsenide rather than silicon) would give the main advantage.

- Sometimes there are multiple boxes, but connected locally and under the control of one administrator. The most common architecture for these is called "Beowulf," and the machines can either be bought or locally designed.

- Sometimes the machines are all over the world and the problem is parcelled out. Each machine gets a bit of the problem and reports back its result over the Internet. There need not be any common management or administration of the machines.

The most famous success of multiprocessor machines was the defeat of the world chess champion Garry Kasparov in 1997 by the IBM Deep Blue machine consisting of multiple RS-6000 processors plus multiple special-purpose chess hardware. Perhaps more important as a model, however, was the factoring of a 140-digit number, a challenge posed by the RSA corporation. This was done in a month by about 200 conventional computers (some PCs, some Sun workstations, and some SGI workstations) and a team of people around the world, led by Peter Montgomery and Arjen Lenstra.

The website `top500.org` presents a list of the 500 most powerful computers in the world each year. In 2002, for example, the number one machine was the Earth Simulator computer in Japan, with spots 2 and 3 belonging to the ASCI Q machines at Los Alamos National Laboratory (the US government has expressed its desire to take back the number one position). More important perhaps is the breakdown of the top 500 machines by architecture. Ten years ago, 90 of the top 500 machines were single-CPU machines; today none are. Only about 200 are multiprocessors in a single box; 300 are clusters or "constellations" (clusters of multiprocessors). The amount of computing power available by multiplying machines far exceeds what you can get by making one machine faster.

Most desktop machines, of course, are idle most of the time. This has led to an interest in using the idle cycles on single large problems, and the cracking of the RSA challenge was done this way; the users of the workstations continued to do their job, but while they were asleep or not driving their computer full speed, spare cycles were spent on factoring. There are now a series of problems being attacked through the use of donated cycles, beginning with the SETI@home project. SETI, which stands for "search for extraterrestial intelligence," requires lots of cycles to go through the recorded radio spectrum from space, looking for something that might be a signal. Since the SETI funding is not going to support a supercomputer, the job has been parcelled out among the desktops of anyone who is willing to help. Similar activities are searching for drugs that might be useful against AIDS or cancer; these programs are trying three-dimensional structure matching to find a chemical compound that might bind to substances important in these diseases. Related projects are looking for drugs against smallpox, anthrax, or other terrorist threats. About two million people now volunteer left-over cycles for these projects.

The general idea of using large numbers of machines with loose connections to attack big problems is called "grid computing." We don't have a good understanding of which problems can be subdivided easily and attacked this way, as opposed to which problems really require a more tightly bound architecture. In addition to issues of efficiency, there is a problem of trust: vandals might attempt to subvert a large computation by sending in inaccurate results. In some problems, it is easy to check what is being reported; more generally, each subproblem has to be assigned multiple times.

Digital libraries use multiple computers typically for storage, not computation. A library can protect against loss of information by sharing its files with another library so that any files lost through a head crash, fire, earthquake, or erasure, whether accidental or malicious, can be retrieved from the other site. This sort of task raises the same issues of trust and organization that sharing cycles requires. So far, most libraries have only stored their copies on computers belonging to other libraries; although there is a lot of empty disk space on desktops, we don't have a "preserve your library at home" group, partly because disk space is now so cheap that we don't really need it.

6.5   Open Source and Proprietary Systems

Some computer code is proprietary, and some is given away. In the early days of computing: (a) hardware was so expensive that software costs hardly seemed to matter; and (b) software normally ran only on one kind of hardware, so you made your software and hardware choices together. In 1961, when I started working with computers, I was paid $1.25 per hour and the IBM mainframe I soon used cost several million dollars. The cost of the computers I used was equivalent to more than a thousand years of my working salary. In those days there was really no such thing as "portability;" programs came from, or were written for, one particular manufacturer. Software was often just given away as an incentive to buy the hardware. Today, all this has changed. Even at undergraduate salary rates, the cost of a computer (and a much faster and better one) is equivalent to only a week or so of salary. Much software runs on multiple platforms, so that I am writing this book sometimes on a Linux system, sometimes on Microsoft systems, and sometimes on an Apple system. Now software has become a large industry, more profitable than hardware manufacturing. Hardware diversity has decreased, with Intel and Intel-compatible machines representing the overwhelming majority of the machines sold. So the user choice today is not so much which machine to buy, but which software platform to use.

Among platforms, the main tension (as of this writing) is between Microsoft operating systems and the Linux open-source system, although some use of larger machines (Sun, SGI, IBM, and others) still remains in the digital library world. Although most software is written with the expectation that it will run on Microsoft Windows, there are many devotees of open source, and the Greenstone open source system is particularly important for digital libraries.

"Open source" refers to the idea that everyone is allowed to inspect, and thus to change, the software which is being distributed. Usually, open source is distributed free, either with no restrictions on use or under the "GNU Public License" (GPL). The use of open source has in its favor that many people contribute to and improve it, you can assure yourself of what it does and doesn't do, and of course it is free and not constrained by complex contracts. Disadvantages are that you may have to do your own support, not as many other people use it, and it changes more often and in unpredictable ways.

The best known open-source system is the Linux operating system, written originally by Linus Torvalds based on the design of Unix, and now maintained by a large community (although Torvalds is still the leader). Linux, effectively, competes with both Microsoft Windows and with various flavors of Unix (including other free versions such as FreeBSD). Nobody knows how many users of Linux there are: you can download it free and you don't have to report to anybody that you have it. Some estimates are that under 10% of servers are now Linux-based; others indicate that 30–40% or more of new servers are Linux (Gulker 2003, and Ewalt 2001). However, only about 1% of the machines accessing Google identify themselves as Linux, whereas about 90% say they are a variety of Microsoft Windows. Microsoft software, which comes bundled with almost all PCs sold, still dominates the end-user market. Compared to Windows, Linux users argue that their platform is more flexibile, less likely to crash, less vulnerable to viruses, and offers greater power and control to the users. Support is available from companies such as RedHat, and a lot of device-controllers and software are available for Linux. Microsoft would counter that far more software and device-controllers are available for Windows, and of course support for Windows is much more organized and well known. Perhaps the best evidence that Microsoft fears Linux, however, is that they helped fund a lawsuit by SCO which threatened to interfere with the sale and use of Linux (alleging that Linux contained lines of copyrighted code now belonging to SCO through a set of purchases of the original Unix code from AT&T).

Perhaps more important to the digital library community is the Greenstone open source package, available at `www.greenstone.org` in multiple languages and for multiple platforms. Like Linux, Greenstone code is open and available for inspection or use without charge. The owners of Greenstone do not charge per-seat fees, impose complex procedures for using their code to be sure that you are not exceeding the number of licenses you have, or engage in any of the other somewhat constraining activities which software companies feel they must do as a way of reducing software piracy. Greenstone was originally written by the University of Waikato in New Zealand; the leader of the project is Ian Witten.

Greenstone is distibuted under the GPL (GNU Public License), which basically says that you can use it freely, but if you redistribute it you must give others the right to redistribute the code you are sending them. The intent of GPL is to prevent a situation in which companies take open source code and resell it with limitations on the use and further distribution of the code. GPL has been around since 1991 and has been successfully used by a large number of projects.

Greenstone provides many facilities that a digital library would need. For details, you should read Witten's book (Witten and Bainbridge, 2003). To summarize, however, Greenstone enables users to build digital library collections and make them accessible to users, either locally on CD-ROM or over the Web. It includes text search, image display, hierarchical browsing, fielded data, and many other capabilities. Many projects around the world are using it. As with all open source projects, you can make whatever changes you want, you can find out exactly what the software does, and you will not be hassled about exactly how many people you have using it.

The alternatives to Greenstone as a way of distributing data are likely to be commercial database systems, not specific digital library systems. There really isn't any commercial software sold only for the purpose of supporting digital libraries, although a variety of data base packages can be used, and some library OPAC (online public access catalog) systems can be generalized to include full text. There are some specialized systems; for example, Olive Software is a leader in the problems relating to digital versions of historical newspapers. Perhaps the most significant, albeit very recent, commercial alternative is IBM DB2 Content Manager. For example, in June 2003, the Australian Broadcasting Corporation agreed to a \$100 M deal with IBM to use DB2 Content Manager to store 100,000 old tapes of broadcast programs (see also Meserve, 2003).

Given the advantages of free software and unrestricted use, why hasn't open source spread more rapidly? One answer is simply the lack of advertising; Microsoft has recently announced that there will be a \$150 M campaign for the 2003 version of Microsoft Office software. Nobody puts anything like the same effort into persuading people to use Linux, or OpenOffice, or Greenstone. Libraries planning to use open source also generally have to have a slightly higher level of technical sophistication, even with the advent of companies like RedHat. As with indexing, the more power you have, the more opportunity you have to dig your own hole and fall into it. Nevertheless, for many of us, falling into a hole we dug ourselves is less threatening than running into somebody else's brick wall, because you are more able to fix the situation by yourself.

6.6 Handheld Devices

In addition to networked computing, information can be distributed by putting it on special-purpose handheld devices. During 2000 there was a brief flurry of interest in the "e-book," the idea that people would read full books on special purpose machines. Online reading of whole books had not been popular, and among the reasons given was lack of portability. So a few startups explored the idea of selling a device that somebody could carry around and read from, downloading books into it. Others worked with the pocket organizers (PalmPilots, PocketPCs, and their ilk) to provide books for reading on these devices.

In general, this was a failure. The publisher ventures, such as AtRandom, MightyWords, or iPublish, have largely folded up. Is this a fundamental problem, or a marketing issue? Are people not interested in reading from screens? Are the screens not quite good enough yet? Was the content not interesting enough? Or is it a question of price and availability?

Certainly, the small size of the screens made many books less convenient than paper, along with issues of lighting and battery life. Late in 2002, Microsoft announced the "Tablet," trying to see if a screen size more like that of an ordinary sheet of paper would be more attractive to users than a conventional laptop or pocket organizer. At least as of summer 2004, this does not seem to have made a significant difference; obviously, a larger machine introduces a penalty in size, weight, and battery life which offsets the gains in readability.

Some of the nonprofit sites, distributing out-of-copyright material for free, are still getting lots of use. These include, for example, the Electronic Text Center at the University of Virginia, which has distributed millions of free e-books (from a library of 1,800 titles). Virginia reported for one period that they were sending out more than a book every 10 seconds. The list of most popular books from Virginia is interesting: many of the titles are familiar (*Alice in Wonderland, Aesop's Fables*) but in one month in 2001, they sent out more than 800 copies of *A History of the Warfare of Science with Theology in Christendom*, written by the president of Cornell in the nineteenth century.

Some of the marketing practices of the e-book companies undoubtedly discouraged customers. There is a tradition of providing a device cheap in order to sell the consumable it needs later—historically, a shaving company made its money on blades, not razors. Thus the e-book companies would not subscribe to standard formats, but tried to force the user to buy all their e-books from one vendor. Prices were typically comparable to those of paperback books. The selection of material available from publishers varied widely.

Will we see a revival of handheld reading devices? Screens are still getting cheaper and better, and we're learning how to extend battery life. Someday, we should have devices that are comparable in weight and readability to a sheet of paper, and which will still have the advantages that one can search the book one is reading, or store many thousands of books in one device. But, at that time, it is also likely that the general-purpose Web browser will be a similar device; all it will take is a wireless connection in addition to the screen, memory, and CPU. So why would somebody want to buy a special-purpose device just for reading a particular book format?

Perhaps the marketers can come up with a package that gives the reader access to a wide selection of published material at a reasonable price, without the user feeling like an unwilling captive of some "book dealership." If so, we might see a revival of the handheld electronic book, but I am skeptical. I suspect that generally accessible Web services with some way to buy current publications will arrive first.

6.7 Security and Cryptography

Is it safe to put information on the Web, or even to connect a computer to it? Computer viruses and computer crime have given a bad reputation to many kinds of computer connections, and the Web is no exception.

Fortunately, the kind of viruses that infected MS-DOS computers and are based on special file extensions on diskettes are not relevant to the Web. Nor is the current favorite virus—the attachment to email which turns into an executable file and wreaks havoc—relevant to most Web programming. However, the presence of servers that respond to outside commands does offer possibilities to vandals and criminals, and Web servers need to be careful about the steps taken to protect their programs. Users are now accustomed to seeing messages that ask them to download and install some particular viewer program in order to see some particular Web page; it is important that these programs be trustworthy in order to preserve computer files.

There is no substitute for basic security and sensible administration on the server machines. Each user should have a password, and each password should be checked to see that it is not easily guessed (i.e., that it is not a common English word or name, or obvious string of letters). Each user should have a separate password, and each reminded to keep it private. There are many administrative decisions to be made which enforce security. For example, at one point, a major workstation manufacturer was shipping machines configured so that any remote machine could log in without any authorization check. Reasonable systems administrators would change this configuration before connecting the machine to the Internet.

In this context, it is important to remember that in line with the general behavior of Ethernets, it is possible for people to snoop on nets and collect packets. They can then look through these packets with programs for login and password sequences, or numbers that appear to be credit cards, and attempt to misuse them. This is not as bad as, say, cellphone conversations, where (as the British royal family found out to its discomfort) there are so many people spending their spare time listening to scanners that perhaps half of all cellphone conversations are overheard. But it does pose risks against which server operators should protect themselves.

One obvious danger comes from the *telnet* connections, which allow outsiders to log in. Computer vandals regularly probe machines on the Internet looking for chances to log in to the computers, trying various names and passwords that have been found by eavesdropping or by other means. *Telnet* has now been abandoned by many organizations in favor of *ssh,* "secure shell," which does not transmit passwords in the clear. Another protection is the use of *firewalls* to separate machines from the outside Web.

A firewall machine is simply another server computer which bridges packets between the outside Net and the computers inside an organization; it is a kind of router. It decides which packets to let through based on various principles and authorization rules. For example, it may allow only connections to the `http` port, except for authorized users. The trick is to decide whether someone sending in packets is indeed an authorized user. Relatively little information comes with the packets that is of use; in particular, the identification of the sending machine cannot be relied on, since it is possible to send messages with fake identification. One feature that a firewall router should have is a little bit of knowledge about possible sources of packets, and it should reject packets that are obviously mislabelled as to their origin (e.g., if they are labelled as coming from a machine inside a corporation but have appeared on the outside of the firewall).

The simplest way to verify the legitimacy of a packet source is a password. The problem with passwords that do not change is that if a vandal snoops on the net and picks up a password today, the vandal can use it tomorrow. Attempts to print out a sequence number for each logon or the date of the last logon, hoping that the legitimate user will notice if these are wrong, are not really reliable. Thus, good systems rely on identification strings that are never used twice. Two such schemes are the SecurID cards marketed by Access Control Encryption, Inc., and the S/Key system invented at Bellcore.

The SecurID card is a credit-card-sized computer with battery, clock, and a display window that shows a six-digit number. Inside the card, an algorithm computes a new six-digit number every minute. The company supplies a program for the firewall machine that can run the same algorithm and thus know for each card what number it should be displaying at any time. A user identifies the card (not using any number printed on the outside) and enters the six digits it is displaying; the firewall compares this number with what it should be, and, if they match, the user must really be in possession of that card. The cards cost about $75 each and are programmed to expire after three years.

The S/Key system is distributed as freeware. It is modelled on the one-time pad of conventional cryptography. The user has a sequence of strings, each of which is used once. At any attempt to claim to be an authorized user, the firewall asks for the next string in sequence. As before, the firewall router has a computer program that can compute a sequence of valid strings. The user either prints out and carries around the strings, or has a computer that can also generate the sequence. Each string is only transmitted once, and there is no way for an outsider to guess from one string what the next one might be. The strings are actually numbers, but, to make them easier to type, are conventionally converted into strings of words. For example, suppose a dictionary of 2048 short words and names is available. Then a 66-bit number can be selected by choosing six of these words, each of which gives 11 bits of the number.

Another danger of vandalism comes from the server programs themselves. As mentioned earlier, Web browsers rely on programs sitting on the server computers which execute when they receive packets. If the only thing they can do is to pick up entries from their databases and forward them as they are designed, then they are no risk. But what if one of these server programs could be persuaded to execute arbitrary programs? Then there would indeed be a risk. This was demonstrated in the case of the `finger` program by the Morris "worm" in 1988. The `finger` program was merely supposed to be a form of directory assistance; given a userid or a name, the finger program would return the userid, name, and phone number of that person on the server machine. Robert Morris, a student at Cornell University, made use of a bug in the `finger` program to write a program which would try to run on as many machines as possible and collect user names and encrypted passwords. As it happened, this program generated so many copies of itself on so many machines that it effectively brought the Internet to a halt on November 2, 1988. Since that time, the recognition of the danger has prompted many security improvements in Internet software.

Since programs like `httpd`—the interpreter of requests for Net browsers—are much more complex than `finger`, it is hard to be sure that they contain no similar risks for libraries. At least, they have been subjected to much greater scrutiny. There is now an organized group called CERT (Computer Emergency Response Team) at CMU which looks for security holes and collects and redistributes information about them. One problem, however, is to be sure that the information about the holes gets to the system administrators *before* it gets to the hacker. Regretfully, CERT sometimes has to use telephones rather than the Internet to keep its own communications private. No incident as serious as the 1988 problem has occurred, however, and the Net infrastructure seems to be relatively robust compared with the viruses spread through the Microsoft Outlook program. Unfortunately, the capacity and robustness of the network infrastructure has led to its use in "denial of service" attacks, in which viruses are used to get many computers to bombard one target computer with millions of messages, in the hope of crashing that target machine or at least keeping anybody else from using the service it provides.

Computer messages come with very little context and have very little security. There is a real danger of eavesdropping on the Net, and there is also a danger of impersonation (sending messages with false indications of their origin). Thus, electronic messages are more likely to need enciphering compared to Postal Service messages, which come in sealed envelopes. Electronic messages are more like postcards.

Encrypting a message requires a `key`. The key traditionally tells you how to encode or decode the message. For example, suppose the cipher system is "Move n letters along in the alphabet." Then the key is the value of n. Suppose the key is 2 so that the cipher is to move two letters along: thus, `cipher` becomes `ekrjgs` and we have an example of the Caesar cipher. It is not considered secure today, although it was apparently good enough for the Romans. Note that the decoding process is to move two letters back in the alphabet; the key for decoding is the same as the key for encoding. If two people both know a key, they can send messages to each other and read them. In fact, since the key to a Caesar cipher is always the same for encoding and decoding, anyone who can read a message can send one and vice versa.

In order to communicate safely in a single-key system like this, both sides of the conversation must have the key, and the key must be distributed in some secure fashion. For years (and it may still be going on), couriers went around carrying keys from one government to its embassies and military installations. Maintaining key security is critical to this kind of cryptography and can be quite tedious. It means that both sides to the conversation trust each other, since either side can divulge the key through either incompetence or treachery. For computer messaging systems, this is a major problem. Since we often send email to people we barely know, we can hardly use the same key all the time, but if we imagine using a separate key for every pair of correspondents, or for every day, the distribution of keys in a single-key system would be an enormous problem.

In 1976 it became publicly known that there were enciphering systems that had separate keys for encryption and decryption, and in which one key could not be found from the other. The technique was apparently invented in 1973 within the United Kingdom security establishment but kept secret These systems are based on the idea of one-way functions; mathematical procedures which can be carried out in one direction, but not reversed. To a typical fifth-grade student, for example, computing a square is a one-way function; the student knows how to multiply 15 by 15 to get 225, but has not yet been taught a method (other than trial and error) to start with 225 and discover that it is 15 squared. One-way functions permit *asymmetric cryptography*, in which I can encode messages that you can decode, but you cannot encode messages yourself.

Consider, for example, use of a one-way function for identification. Suppose we accept squaring a number as a one-way function and I wish to assure you of my identity or, more precisely, assure you that a second message from me has, in fact, come from the same person who sent you the first message. I could send the string 361 in the first message, and in the second one send you 19. You could multiply 19 times 19 and verify that it is 361. Since, in our hypothetical example, nobody can compute a square root, I must have started this process by picking 19 and squaring it to send you the 361 in the first message; no one else could have arranged to know to pick 361 as the number to send first.

In asymmetric cryptography, there are two keys, one for encryption and one for decryption. Usually, one of these keys is kept secret, and one is disclosed, thus the alternate name *public key cryptography*. Either the encryption or the decryption key may be public, leading to two different functions, as follows.

- If I disclose my *encryption* key, then anyone can *send* messages to me, knowing that only I can read them.
- If I disclose my *decryption* key, then anyone can *receive* messages from me and know that I had sent them.

Again, to explain this, let us assume that some simple arithmetic is not reversible. Suppose that multiplication is easy, but nobody can do division without special tricks. Let us suppose that I know something about the number 17, for example, which lets me divide by 17, but no one else can divide by 17. I can then publish 17 as my key and ask you, whenever you wish to send me a message, to multiply it by 17 and send the result. If you wish to send me the sequence of numbers 2, 3 (which might mean that you were sending me the second letter of the alphabet followed by the third), you would send 34, 51. By hypothesis, nobody else can divide by 17, so this is perfectly safe. I can do the division, so I can recover the 2, 3 sequence. No eavesdropper is able to do this.

Conversely, I can send a message which must have come from me. Suppose I wish to send you the message 85. I divide it by 17 and send you 5. You (or anyone else) can multiply 5 by 17 and get back the original 85; but, in this imaginary world, I am the only person who could have done the division to discover the 5, and so the message must have come from me.

The actual mathematical function that is hard to reverse is factorization of integers. It is relatively easy to find that $17 \times 19 = 323$. There is no direct way to start with 323 and determine that its factors are 17 and 19; all methods for doing this involve considerable trial and error. For large enough numbers, numbers with perhaps 150 digits, it is in practice impossible to factor them; and yet it is relatively easy to start with two 75-digit primes and multiply them together.

The cryptographic technique that uses this method is known as RSA after the three then-MIT professors Ron Rivest, Adi Shamir, and Leonard Adelman.

To repeat the main point of our discussion, with asymmetric cryptography either key can be public. If my encryption key is public, then anyone can send me messages knowing that nobody else can read them (*privacy*). If my decryption key is public, then I can send messages that must have come from me (*authentication*). Both are valuable functions for different purposes. The details of modern cryptography are widely available; see for example Stinson (1995) or Delfs and Knebl (2002).

Cryptography also has other uses:

- *message integrity.* If the encryption key is private, no one but the sender can change the message and still send it in the correct code.
- *non-repudiation.* If a message comes encoded in my private key, no one without the key can have encrypted it. Variants of cryptography are used to create digital signatures that can only be applied by the holder of a key (but can run faster since there is no need to recover the message from the signature).
- *digital cash.* Banks can send strings in exchange for money, which they are willing to change back. Again, nobody but the bank can create a valid string, although anyone can verify that the bank created it.

Asymmetric cryptography, although elegant, is about 10 times slower than private key cryptography today. There are many good algorithms for private key encryption, including most notably the standard DES (Data Encryption Standard); those too suspicious to trust the NSA (National Security Agency) can use alternative cryptographic algorithms. Even on a 1990 vintage machine, symmetric cryptographic systems could encrypt 3 Mbits/sec. Since asymmetric cryptography is much slower, it is customary to use it to exchange a "session key" generated randomly for the next session of traffic, and then send the actual traffic with the new private key.

Libraries need to worry to some extent about security both with respect to the privacy of their transactions and also with respect to any charged services they use or sell. Much more attention has been paid to security since interest in electronic commerce has increased. People wish to order across the Internet, and to do this they need to give some kind of authorization number or credit card number. In principle, one would wish to encrypt packets containing such numbers for transmission. It is difficult to agree on a method for doing this within the confines of US government laws regarding cryptographic technology. Cryptography laws are confusing and changing. The United States prohibits the export of technology with really strong encryption, but has relaxed the rules that used to limit exports to 40-bit keys. Nowadays, the key lengths allowed in US products are long enough to be suitable for current applications. The US government does realize the contradiction in the present laws, which allow export of cryptographic technology to NATO countries such as Holland, which have no laws themselves restricting the export of this technology. Other NATO countries may have even stricter laws than the United States, and in France any nongovernmental use of cryptography is illegal. Most important, it is becoming clear that US cryptography laws were pointless, as the industry was moving to countries such as Finland or Switzerland. As of 2003, the export laws have become less of a cause celebre.

A variant on cryptography is the question of dating and notarizing electronic documents. Electronic messages lack the physical attributes that would let them be dated, and of course any date shown on them can be edited. As a result, it is not clear how to establish priorities and dates for electronic messages. Some government organizations require printed documentation instead of electronic documentation in order to be sure of the dates. The dating problem was solved by Scott Stornetta and Stuart Haber of Bellcore when they invented *digital time-stamping* as a way of running an absolutely secure electronic notary system.

Their algorithm makes it possible for someone to operate an electronic notarizing system that is invulnerable to corruption. In a simplistic notarizing system, users send the operator messages and the operator dates them and digitally signs the message. However, this leaves open the possibility that the operator could be bribed to falsely date messages. What Stornetta and Haber realized was that dishonesty by the system operator could be stopped if each certificate of notarization was linked to the previous and next certificates issued.

The basic idea is that users submit hashed codes for the documents they wish to notarize, using a good one-way hash function, so that no one can create a document matching that hash code. The notarizer adds a date, rehashes, and sends back the hashed string. But the new hash is not just based on the date and on the hash code from the original document. Instead, it also includes the hash codes of the previous document sent in, and the next one. In order to be deceptive, it would be necessary not only to create a fake hashed code for the original user, but to create an entire chain of fake hashes involving everything submitted to the hashing authority. This is not possible. The practical implementation of this system, done by a firm named Surety, is to link each week's notarization requests not into a linear chain as described here, but into a tree. The root note of the tree is published as a classified advertisement in *The New York Times* each week. Any individual can verify their notarization certification against the number published in the *Times*, and nobody can create a fake certificate without the ability to change all the printed copies of the *Times* in all the libraries of the world.

6.8   Privacy

One major security issue is the extent to which personal information will be gathered and misused online. Individuals face a complete range of information gathering, some of which is clearly helpful and some of which is clearly threatening. Few of us object to a weather site asking for our location so that entering the site will immediately display the relevant weather forecast. Most of us, on the other hand, would object to a pornography site trying to buy a list of male high school students so that it could send them ads. This area is so new that little has yet been decided, either by law or by code of good practice. Some of the considerations are

- Where is information stored?
- Does the information have to be personally identifiable?
- How long should records be kept?
- Who should have access to them?

Storage Location

The weather site, in fact, doesn't actually have to collect and store anything about me on its site. What it will typically do is create a "cookie" on my own computer. Cookies are bits of information stored in a directory accessible by the Web browser. When my browser goes to the weather site, the site will retrieve its cookie, which tells it the relevant location, and then it can deliver the right piece of weather data. It doesn't have to keep the cookie information outside my own computer. On the other hand, it has that capability, and some people object to this, especially because you rarely know whether the information is only stored locally.

One option for the worried is to use "proxy" servers, which simply reflect your request to the remote site and do not pass through any cookies that show up. The remote site only knows the address of the proxy; it has no idea who the ultimate requestor might be. A properly configured proxy, if you trust it, can retain your cookie and deliver the right information to the weather site, even though the connection to your identity is completely lost.

Personal Identification

Typically, a desktop computer need not tell a website the name of its owner. In principle, the name of the owner doesn't have to be stored anywhere on the computer. However, in reality, everybody wants to know the user's name. When the computer was installed, the vendor almost certainly asked the user to type in his or her name as a way of registering for warranty service. Many sites, even free sites, require their users to register, either to send advertising or to gather demographics about their users so as to attract advertisers. However, a large fraction of people asked to register refuse (for some sites, 80%); they leave the site instead.

A system that collects money from its users is going to have to collect personal information. We do not yet have any anonymous way of paying online with any general acceptance, so the usual way of paying is by a credit card with a name and address. Nowadays such sites typically have "privacy policies," but these are often presented in the form of a long window of text you are supposed to read and then acknowledge with a mouse click. Rarely does a user read the entire window, and even more rarely will the user notice the bit about "we may share your information with our marketing partners" that implies permission to sell your name to anyone they care to.

The European Union has much stricter laws about the collection of personal information than the United States does. In 1998 a European "directive" (not quite a law, but something that must become a law in 3 years) required, for example, that all databases containing personal information must provide a way for the individuals included to review and correct their entries. Some kinds of data (e.g., religious or political beliefs) may not be collected at all. Other rules restrict the sale of data to marketers. Considerable discussion has taken place about these rules in an international context; anyone affected should consult a lawyer. So far, at least, the United States has not enacted similar laws, despite pressure from Europe to do so.

Duration of Records

Some organizations wish to retain records; many individuals would like to think that after some period of time, they could forget about things they had done in the past. Once a transaction is complete, how long should records of it be kept? Financially, for example, a seller clearly must keep records long enough to deal with returns and exchanges, warranty claims, tax issues, and the like. Similarly, libraries have to keep records of borrowed books, at least until the book is returned. But should records be kept after the active need for them is gone? Some information seems entirely transitory, such as the records of my Web searches or Web browsing. How long does a search engine need to retain records of my previous searches? How long will my name stay on somebody's email list?

Again, there is no agreed-upon standard for any of these issues. Most data collectors want to retain data forever. I checked a dozen cookies on my own browser and most had expiration dates many years into the future; I will acknowledge that *The New York Times* and eBay had cookies with short-term (a few days) expiration dates.

Who Should See Records?

This is the largest and most complex question. The basic approach in the United States has been to require that users be notified of the privacy policy of each website, and most sites have responded by sending extremely general legal statements giving them wide authority to resell names and addresses. Europe has a similar problem despite its more restrictive laws. Users would like to think that the only viewers of their personal information are people in some sense trying to help them, as when a patient agrees that his primary physician may send medical records to a specialist. But rarely do we know what use is being made of records and by whom. Many families have "affinity" cards or "club" cards with a local supermarket, allowing the market to track every food purchase. Since, in general, the only effect of these cards is to give the holder a dollar off on a pound of fish now and then, people tend to think of them as innocuous. If they suddenly find medical insurance companies complaining that they bought too many cigarettes or chocolates, they might have a different view. There have been some publicized scandals involving drugstores selling lists of people who, based on their drug purchases, are probably suffering from particular medical conditions.

The lists of records that might be of interest goes on and on. During the McCarthyism period of the 1950s, the FBI tried to find out who was borrowing certain books from libraries, and libraries developed a principle that records of book borrowing should be private. During the confirmation hearings of Robert Bork, a newspaper published records of videotapes he had rented, and as a result those records are now private. During the Monica Lewinsky scandal, an effort was made to find out what books she had bought at Kramerbooks in Washington, DC. Some of these efforts are a joke to an outsider: can it really have been worth publishing that Bork had rented the Marx Brothers movie *A Day at the Races*? But I know people who will not get an electronic toll-paying device for their car for fear that they will someday get automatic speeding tickets; and the records of such devices can be used to establish how many days a year somebody spent in what state.

There is also anxiety about legal process as used to gain access to records. A company which had promised not to divulge records about its users went bankrupt, and the bankruptcy creditors wanted the user list as an asset of the company (they lost). Privacy policies in general will not prevent a litigant from obtaining records with a subpoena or discovery request, although the litigants will be restricted in what they can do with the records. The only sure answer is to destroy records that are not needed, a strange thing for a librarian or archivist to do, but now the policy of many library systems, at least with respect to book borrowing records. The New York Society Library, for example, still has the records detailing which books Herman Melville (the author of *Moby Dick*) borrowed in the nineteenth century; future literary scholars will be disappointed that they can't find the corresponding records for today's writers. If an author today is getting books from a public library, they'll probably discard the circulation records out of fear; if the author is getting them from a commercial site, they will be keeping the records as a trade secret.

Most recently, post-9/11, has come a fear of government access to more and more records. Acronyms like TIA ("total information awareness") have been used to describe systems that, hypothetically, would help law enforcement by gathering large amounts of information about everyone. The systems that flag people who should be scrutinized before they board flights are of course secret, but also raise fears among civil libertarians. People believe that there are systems with names like Echelon and Carnivore that enable the government to listen to phone calls and snoop on email (these may both be urban legends, of course). Many are happy when the NSA listens in to Osama bin Laden but fear they will do so to us. The individual databases that government agencies have are not well coordinated today, and there is a tension between privacy, law enforcement, and technological possibility in the steps taken to connect them.

Fundamentally, we have several hundred years of experience to guide us in our handling of traditional information. We expect our paper mail not to be opened, and we know police need warrants to search our houses. We have no such tradition for computer systems that were invented a few months ago, and we have a lack of understanding of what we would gain or lose by adopting one or another principle.

6.9 Summary

This chapter has reviewed ways in which information is transmitted. Physical distribution of information is dying out, while sending it over the computer networks that now pervade the world is growing. The Internet and the World Wide Web, in particular, provide a now widely-accepted standard for information access. The major problems posed by Web access are a lack of security and a lack of payment methodologies. Underlying technology exists to handle many of the security issues; there does not yet exist a standard way of paying for electronic delivery. The problem is not assembling the technology that would provide payment mechanisms; the problem is deciding what they should be and how they will be administered. This will be discussed later in Chapter 9.

Usability and Retrieval Evaluation

I n Chapter 5 we talked about finding the "Holy Grail" of knowledge representation. Making computers easy to use is the "Holy Grail" of the software industry. Frustration with computers is very common; we all know jokes like "To err is human, to really foul things up takes a computer." The SBT Accounting Group suggested that the average office worker wastes 5 hours a week because of computer problems, costing the US economy $100 billion a year (Gibbs, 1997; Shneiderman, 2000). In 2002 the National Institute of Standards and Technology (NIST) estimated that just software bugs were costing the economy $60 billion per year (see Tassey, 2002). Frustration and even "computer rage" are now common, often as a result of difficult interfaces. The BBC reported that three-quarters of users admitted to swearing at their computers (Welsh, 1999). Libraries accept a wide range of the public as their patrons and cannot force them to accept training. Users of Google and the other search engines are accustomed to just using them, with no training at all, and they are generally satisfied with the result. Library schools give a semester-long course in online searching. Yes, the trained people get better results and waste less time, but a lot of people enjoy searching and are happy with what happens. Nevertheless, some people are frustrated, and perhaps more important is the fact that many people could get better results than they do. Early experiments by Chris Borgman showed that a quarter of Stanford undergraduates had difficulty learning one of the commercial search systems. Searching is still often hit-or-miss; it is easy to find information on a person with an unusual name, say John Galsworthy, while if you are looking for information on the island of Java you will need to phrase the search carefully, perhaps looking for Java and Indonesia. A practical digital library has to build systems everyone can use. This chapter will emphasize the user and the considerations necessary to make systems effective, not just available.

7.1 General Human Factors Considerations

The general science of human factors is called *ergonomics* and it began with the study of physical tools and equipment, such as the shaping of handles and levers. Ergonomics is still referred to derisively as the "comfy chair" science. The basic principles of ergonomics come from cognitive psychology, and, as it happens, the research methods from that area are used in evaluating software as well. Two alternative technical solutions are implemented and tested on a group of subjects, traditionally, on undergraduates in elementary psychology courses.

Tests of this sort follow a traditional paradigm of scientific research. The subjects are divided into groups, each group using a different interface or trying a different task. For example, one group might be using an index language, while another is using a free-text search system. Statistical measures are used to decide whether there is a significant difference between the conditions. The measures may be based on the accuracy, speed, or preferences of the users. Preferences may be based either on some choice (e.g., the amount of time the users choose to spend on some condition), or on questionnaires given to the users. Time taken should always be recorded, as much good cognitive psychology data is based on human reaction times as a measure of how much processing is required in the brain.

Studies on human subjects need to be done with care. For example, it is always desirable to run some preliminary tests before the main experiments. Subjects will think of things the experimenter did not anticipate, and it may be necessary to revise the experiment in consequence. Subjects have to be balanced in terms of their computer expertise, experience with the subject matter of the experiment, and so on. Normally this is done by randomization: the subjects are assigned at random to two different conditions. If two computer systems are being compared, they need to be balanced as well. If one is on color screens and the other on black and white, unless that is the point of the experiment, the data are *confounded,* and it is likely to be difficult to learn anything from such an experiment. A critical point is response time of the systems, since people are relatively intolerant of slow response time and, again, unless this is the point of the comparison, response times should be balanced across experimental conditions. An even more serious issue is bugs in the software. All too often, an experiment produces confused results because the users hit new bugs in the process of testing which distort the results.

Often, an analysis of variance is done on the data to decide how much of the difference between the results can be assigned to different characteristics of the experiment. For example, an experiment might involve 16 students, 8 of whom had previous programming experience and 8 of whom did not. Half might be given one text editor, and half another. Thus, 4 students of each degree of experience would see each experimental condition. At the end, analysis of variance would indicate the relative importance of the programming experience versus the particular text editor. Such experiments are often discouraging, since the variance among individuals in many computer tasks is very high. Thus, the result of many programming comparisons has been to discover that some people are better programmers than others. Compared with individual skills and with the difficulty level of the particular task to be done, the programming language used is almost unimportant.

In fact, the history of experiments of this sort is that they have been valuable in developing the details of interfaces, but have not been as successful in generating new top-level paradigms. In the early days of computer, time-sharing attempts were made to do systematic comparisons of batch processing and time-sharing, and the results were inconclusive until time-sharing completely overran batch processing in the marketplace (to be pushed out in its turn by individual work-stations). Similarly, the number of truly appalling human interfaces which have been successful in the marketplace is testimony more to the ability of determined users to overcome obstacles in their path than to the success of human factors research in program design. Getting to the marketplace first and establishing some kind of standard is more important than having good research support for one's design.

Human factors research is going to become more important, however. The development of the computer interface is a major part of new software systems. More than half the code in many new software projects is running the interface, and the interface is often critical in someone's decision about which program to use (when there is a choice). However, the design of good interfaces is still as much art as science, since there is still insufficient experimental data and good models of how to build an interface.

One principle from studies is the speed-accuracy trade-off that sometimes exists. If people work more quickly, they may make more errors. This isn't true across the board; more experienced people often work both more quickly and more accurately. We all know that someone competent in a language can speak it both more rapidly and correctly than someone just beginning to learn it. For many tasks, however, there is some reasonable speed at which it can be done best. Asking people to read 2000 words per minute is not going to help them retain anything they are seeing.

A basic limitation in the design of many computer interfaces is the use of the display screen. Particularly for library information, there is often just not enough space to show everything that is wanted. This yields a set of trade-offs between packing the screen so tightly that the users are puzzled or intimidated by the amount of information, or having too many choices hidden behind multiple levels of menus. Using an 80-character by 24-line display is equivalent to looking at a newspaper through a 3×5-inch window and is likely to be frustrating for some users. A 640×480-pixel display is higher resolution than a TV screen, but it is not possible to read an ordinary printed page of text from a TV screen. Library projects using scanned images often have a particular need for large bitmap windows, and thought must be given to how to use the amount of space available.

Another principal human factors issue is whether the users or the system designers are in charge of placement of windows and screen displays. The system designers often wish to take over the screen and position all the necessary windows and the like. This avoids problems with users covering up or deleting some key information. But it makes it impossible for users to adjust the display to their individual preferences and for the particular task they are doing. This is a special case of the general problem of how adaptable programs should be. Greater adaptability is sometimes good, but other times means that users cannot cooperate (since the program is behaving differently for different people) and gives greater opportunity for people to become confused. In general, system design issues like this should be evaluated case by case.

Should computer programs be designed for expert users or novice users? This is another basic tension in system design. Often a system which has enough explanations and menu choices to help novices is annoying or slow for experts. There are two basic arguments, which go as follows:

1. Since most people who buy a program use it many times, they spend most of their time as expert users, and so the program should be designed for experts, perhaps with some aids for novices.
2. Since many buying decisions are made by people who look at a program in a store or a trade show for only a few minutes, programs should be designed for novices to increase sales.

Sometimes the decision is fairly obvious. Some programs by their nature are only run once in a while (e.g., a program that sets up vacation handling of electronic mail). Some programs by their nature are used mostly by people who use them a lot (e.g., programming language compilers). Other times it is clear that an organization has mostly permanent users or mostly transitory users. Libraries find themselves with many novice users. Relatively few people spend most of their working life in libraries. Many come in at the end of a semester or on rare occasions; the rule of thumb for university libraries is that you need one seat for every 4 students (to get through the exam-time crush).

Again, the question of how to train people to use programs that are only going to be used intermittently varies with the task. In practice, people rely heavily on those with slightly more expertise. Libraries can run training sessions, but this is very expensive. Asked once whether it was true that the introduction of computers into dormitory rooms was going to develop college students who spent all their time alone, hunched over their machines, a Columbia librarian replied that since they had introduced the online catalog, they had seen many more students in groups. They rarely, she said, had seen people working together at the old card catalog; everyone used it by themselves. But at the computer terminals, groups of two or three students were frequently together, one showing the other how to use it. So had they improved students' social skills by providing bad computer interfaces? Well, that was not the intent, but it was apparently what happened.

7.2 Text Displays: Fonts and Highlighting

Among the most important questions for digital libraries are those related to the willingness of people to read information from screens instead of from paper. Among the key studies done here were those by John Gould of IBM, who studied the reading speed of people from screens and from paper (Gould and Grischokowsky, 1984). He found that although people read from conventional "glass teletype" screens 25% more slowly than they did from paper, improving the screens to 91 dots/inch and using grayscale displays permitted people to read at about the same speed as they did from paper (Gould et al., 1987).

There are also principles derived from years of experience in the printing industry. People are used to reading, and prefer reading, lines not over 60 or 70 characters long. A 60-character line in 9-point type is about 4 inches long. This is why books are printed in sizes like 5 × 8 or 6 × 9 inches; it makes for a comfortable single-column size. Material printed on 8.5 × 11 inch paper should be double-column to avoid excessively long lines. Although line lengths vary with typefont design, the length of a line can usually be guessed by assuming that the average letter has a width one-half the type size, in points. Thus, in 9-point type the typical letter is 4.5 points wide, and at 72 points to the inch

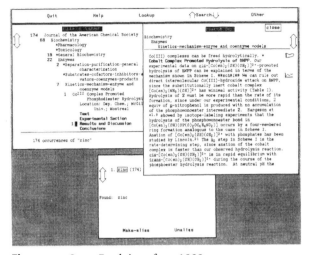

Figure 7.1 SuperBook interface, 1989.

64 characters would require 4 inches. In designing computer displays, 80-character lines are a little too long to be comfortable.

At Bellcore, the SuperBook project (Egan et al., 1989) experimented with careful design of an interface for text display, with combinations of prototypes and testing on users. The result was a multiwindow interface organized so that users would retain an orientation of where they were in the book they were reading. One window displays a hierarchical table of contents, with fish-eye expansion and a mark for current position; another displays a portion of the text; and other smaller windows show any searching and general controls. An example of the SuperBook interface is shown in Figure 7.1.

In this example, a search has been performed on the word *zinc* (see bottom window), and 174 hits were found. The distribution of these hits across the sections of the document collection is given by the numbers to the left of the section headings in the table of contents, which is shown in the large left window. Note that 22 of these hits are in the Enzymes section. The actual article is shown in the window on the right, along with an arrow to move forward or backward. The icons in the right margin of the text window point to a footnote and a figure.

In 1990, during the CORE project, a comparison was done between people reading from paper and people reading from screens. Two kinds of screen interface were used: the SuperBook system for ASCII display and an image system for page images. The experiment, done by Dennis Egan, used five kinds of tasks involving searching and reading chemical information (Egan et al., 1991). Thirty-six Cornell students were divided into three groups; 12 got the journals on paper, 12 got an image display interface, and 12 got the SuperBook interface.

Table 7.1 Comparison of search results.			
Format	Time (min)	Score	Gave up?
SuperBook	9.7	76%	8%
Image	11.3	72%	1%
Paper	19.5	23%	57%

The results, to oversimplify, showed that searching was much more effective with either computer system than with the paper journals and Chemical Abstracts on paper, while reading was the same speed on either system. Combining these into a realistic set of tasks suggests that the users would be much better off with electronic information.

For example, one of the tasks was to answer a simple question, something along the lines of, "What is the P-O distance in hydroxyphospine?" The answer was in one of 4000 pages of chemical journal text. Students had to locate the article with the answer and read enough of it to find the answer. Table 7.1 shows the results for the students using the SuperBook image display system and the traditional paper journals. Note that more than half the students with paper journals and paper Chemical Abstracts finally gave up after spending an average of almost 20 minutes looking for this.

For tasks which just involved reading text, rather than searching, the time was comparable whether the students were reading articles on paper, on a screen displaying an image of the article, or through the SuperBook interface. Consistently, the computer interfaces were much faster for searching and competitive in time for simple reading; combining both kinds of tasks, they were both preferred and they let the students get more done. This data explains why electronic libraries are not only effective, but recognized as such by the users and generally welcomed. In fact, we had one student ask to stay after the experiment so he could keep using the system to find out something he needed for his course work.

7.3   Image Displays and Compression Systems

When designing screen images, there is a conflict between what the eye can see and what can fit on the screen, as described earlier. The most accurate experiments on this subject were done by Michael Ester (1990) at the Getty. He found that people can see the differences in resolution quite clearly up to 1000×1000; above that resolution, the gains in perceptual quality are lower.

To judge this yourself, take a look at the sample images shown in Figures 7.2 and 7.3 (see Color Plates). The base picture shown in the first figure is a book illustration done in 1906 by N. C. Wyeth (and is from the book *Whispering Smith* by Frank Spearman). The resolution of the scan is 1075×1731 (300 dpi across the original book page). This has been reduced to half (537×865) and to quarter (268×432) resolution in Figure 7.3. Excerpts from the picture are shown at each resolution. Parts (a)–(c) show the man's face, and parts (d)–(f) show his foot with the saddlebelts. Look at the saddlebelts, for example. Notice that in the full resolution image you can see the holes both in the stirrup belt and the belt for the saddlebag; in the half resolution image, the holes in the stirrup belt can be counted, but not those in the saddlebag belt; and in the quarter resolution image neither set of holes is clear. Compare these images with the faces; note that the man's face survives the resolution loss better since we have a much better *a priori* idea of what a face looks like than we do of how many holes there ought to be in those saddlebelts. Also realize that even the worst of these resolutions is better than ordinary NTSC television.

We usually wish to reduce the space required by images, to save both disk space and transmission time. Many of the compression algorithms have been discussed already; see Chapter 4, Section 4.2. In general, compression algorithms operate by removing redundancy. If there is little redundancy in the original, compression will not save a lot of space. Images with large areas of a single color compress well, as do texts that contain many lines full of blanks. Conversely, if redundancy has been removed, there will be little compression possible. It never makes sense to encrypt first and then compress, for example; the encryption step should remove all the redundancy. If you ever find an encrypted file that gets noticeably smaller after compression, get a new encryption program. Conversely, compressing and then encrypting will produce a file that is extremely difficult for any cryptographer to decode, since there will be virtually no redundancy in the plaintext to use in breaking the cipher.

Text

The entropy of English, as shown by Shannon (1950), is about 1 bit per character. ASCII is normally stored at 8 bits per character. Often written text is so compact that there is little point in compressing it, but it is possible to compress it either by looking at pure statistics or at repeated strings. Letter frequency statistics, for example, are used in Huffman coding. Instead of the 7 bits that ASCII uses for each letter, a Huffman code assigns shorter codes to the frequent letters and longer codes to the rare ones (Sayood, 1996). Morse code is an example of a code of this form, but it is not optimized for compression. A typical Huffman code reduces English to about 3 to 4 bits per letter. A code that works with repeated sequences, such as the Lempel-Ziv algorithm, is more powerful. Such a code will also get to about 3 bits per letter on long enough texts.

Speech

The first step in compressing speech is to start with mu-law speech (8000 samples per second with 8 bits per sample) rather than CD-quality speech. Next, use the GSM algorithm from digital cellular phones. This algorithm is freely available and produces another factor of 5 compression, producing about 1600 bytes/second. Considerably better results can be achieved with a great deal more computing by using LPC (linear predictive coding). Fairly good intelligibility of speech at 300 or even 150 bytes/second is possible. Neural nets are also used, and there is considerable interest in these algorithms as a result of voice over IP telephony (see Besacier, 2001). Note that the most efficient speech compression algorithms will not handle sounds other than speech, whereas GSM can still compress music so that it is recognizable when decompressed. Of course, the best speech compression would be speech recognition followed by a program that resynthesized the original speech. A second of normal speech would have perhaps 2 words or 12 bytes. We do not know much about how to resynthesize the speech with the dialect, emphasis, and individual speech qualities of the speaker, however.

Images

Recall our discussion of image compression in Chapter 3, Section 3.4. In general, a book page consisting primarily of text will compress with Group IV fax compression to perhaps 30 KB; a very complex A4-sized journal page with small print, illustrations, and equations might take 100 KB. The DjVu system or JPEG2000, by separating background from text and compressing them separately, can do a factor of 3 to 5 better. Photographs can often be compressed to 10 KB with JPEG; although lossy, the loss is not perceived by users. We do not have good answers for very large detailed images such as maps; in particular, ways to search such images in the compressed format would be especially useful.

7.4   Web Page Graphics

The question of who controls the appearance of Web pages is a difficult one to resolve; should the readers or the creators decide on the bitmaps that are shown? Readers, on the one hand, have different screen sizes and different visual acuities, so they may want to choose how big the print on the screen is and perhaps which font it appears in. And those choices impact how words will be arranged into lines. Traditionally, publishers decided those issues and spent a great deal of effort choosing the appearance of their material, with particular attention to the style and visual impact of advertisements. The same issue comes up on Web pages; one even sees ordinary words being stored as images of their appearance to keep the users from resizing them or changing their appearance.

Matters have become worse as e-commerce has placed a premium on grabbing the users' attention. Methods include blinking text, pop-up and pop-under Web pages, and bright, colorful, and intrusive messages. With Java, one can program little bouncing balls, images moving about the Web page, and many other ways of trying to keep the user's attention.

Perhaps the most ambitious such efforts are plug-ins that display motion and can be used for movie trailers or TV-like advertisements. The best known such enhancements are Flash (from Macromedia) and Quicktime (from Apple). It's better to think of two different families, though: one called *web animation* aimed at low-bit-rate, animated objects; and the other called *streaming video* allowing higher bit rates in exchange for more realistic appearances. The animation programs best known are Flash and Shockwave; the streaming video players are Quicktime, RealMedia, and Windows Media Player (WMP).

In general, animation programs are used mostly for advertisements, and many users find they can do without them; one might well find that, on average, all they do is slow down the entrance to a site from which you hoped to get some useful information about a product. Of course, some sites will not let you access the content until you have looked at the ad; if your browser hasn't installed the relevant animation player, they block further access. It's not common to find Flash or Shockwave material with content; normally they are just attempts to seize attention, although the line between advertising and content is fuzzier on the Web than in traditional publications.

Streaming video, by contrast, often *is* the content. Bits of documentaries, news programs, and the like are presented in this form. Just as National Public Radio makes online versions of their radio news available through a Web broswer, PBS (Public Broadcasting System) allows users to watch selected news in video via RealMedia or WMP players. Streaming video can also be used for advertising, but suffers from the higher bit rate required; potential customers may give up, especially if on slow-speed connections, rather than wait through the video to get to whatever it is they really started looking for in the first place.

Sometimes, the advantages of animation are clear. Some kinds of Web animation are now considered art, and are likely to find themselves in museums in the future. The material being presented can be inherently visual, as with the PBS video news clips. Sometimes a few diagrams and animations can enormously simplify the process of explaining something. Consider, for example, the advantages to a bicycle repair site of showing an animation of the process of changing a wheel or fixing a flat. The videogame industry has branched out into educational applications, and some studies show games have educational benefit (BBC 2002).

Regrettably, much of the use of animation is merely advertising, as the process of grabbing for the user's attention is escalated. In addition to the general feeling that the Web is becoming unruly, there are those with more serious objections. Individuals with limited vision, for example, have trouble with displays that are visually driven, and it is particularly frustrating when such displays aren't even helpful. Those who fear viruses and worms dislike complex executables; it's too hard to assure yourself that downloading and executing something won't pose a problem. This has been aggravated by the discovery by virus writers that you can label an executable file as a picture, to entice users into clicking on it, thinking that they are only starting an image viewer; Windows will execute the attachment anyway.

Over time, the creation of video and animation will become steadily easier. We can anticipate creating video mail and animated sketches simply and easily, and we can hope that the inclusion of these materials in Web pages will be helpful. For digital libraries, this material poses the additional difficulty that it can't be searched as easily as text; even if cellphone cameras make it as easy to send a picture of your dog as to type *dog*, we can't search the picture.

7.5 Interface Controls: Menus and Keywords

When screen displays which were not limited to characters became feasible in the late 1970s, one of the most important steps forward was the invention of multiple-window interfaces. Window systems, once restricted to specialized machines and research systems, are now the standard on all workstations and PCs. Users are able to run different processes at once in the different windows and to look at one document while writing another.

Library systems today often still don't use window interfaces. Partly this reflects the fact that libraries were early adopters of networks for remote access; as users of the Gopher protocols, they did not have the opportunities to use pictures. Partly this reflects cost pressures both to use cheap terminals within libraries and to allow users with lower-cost computers to access the systems without feeling second-class. And partly it reflects the industry which supplies OPAC (online public access catalog) systems and retained text-display systems having operated from mainframe or midicomputers through the early stages of the PC/workstation boom.

To many researchers in computer interfaces, the most important advance in interfaces was the desktop metaphor invented at Xerox PARC and popularized by the Apple Macintosh. With the conversion of most PC architecture machines from MS-DOS to Windows, this metaphor is now the most common way to control machines. It replaced such methods as IBM JCL (job control language, dating from the 1960s) and the command line interfaces which characterized most other systems.

The key ingredients of the desktop metaphor are iconic representation, click to activate, drag-and-drop, and pull-down menus.

- Iconic representation means that each file or program is represented by an icon, which tries to show graphically what it is. On a Windows machine, for example, Netscape Navigator is represented by a small ship's wheel; solitaire is a deck of cards; and the deletion routine is an image of a wastebasket (labeled "recycle bin").
- Each file or program is selected by clicking on it once; to invoke it, the user clicks twice. Normally a bar listing some choices is either at the top or bottom of the screen, and after the item is selected, choices such as Rename or Copy can be invoked.
- Drag-and-drop lets the user apply a program to a file by dragging the file icon to the program (holding down the mouse) and letting go over it, as when files are deleted by dragging them to the recycle bin, for instance.
- Pull-down menus appear when the mouse button is held over a command, and a list of choices is produced which disappears when the mouse is released; if the mouse button is released while one of the choices is highlighted, that choice is invoked.

Other facilities are possible. For example, in many interfaces, moving a mouse around an image provides a panning capability for images too large to fit on the screen. Enlarging windows can be moved over images that are too small to view easily. Nevertheless, compared to command lines, this is an impoverished set of things the user can do. This makes life simpler; there are fewer choices. But it also means that complex arguments to commands must either be specified ahead of time or through pop-up forms.

There are strong advocates of interfaces based both on menus and upon command lines. The conventional wisdom is that keyword-type command line searches should be done by professional intermediaries (Krentz, 1978), while novice users should only be asked to choose from menus (Shneiderman, 1978). With time, however, more and more users are gaining interest in complex search systems; just as many people use desktop publishing systems to achieve page layouts once requiring professional typesetting, computer users are beginning to do Boolean searches and other kinds of searching once done in library settings.

One comparison done by Geller and myself (Geller and Lesk, 1983) looked at two different interfaces to a library catalog. The research was done in 1981, when essentially no one had any familiarity with online catalogs. One interface was a search interface based on command lines, searching for keywords. The other was based on tracking menus through the Dewey decimal system.

In the keyword system, the user could type any number of words; in the examples that follow, what the user types is shown in ***bold italics***. Thus, in the first example the user typed ***chocolate*** and responded with ***1*** to the prompt Which book?

```
chocolate
1 items
  (1/1)   1: Technology of chocolate.
Which book? 1
%T    Technology of chocolate.
%A    Kempf, N.W.
%I    Oak Park, Ill., Mfg. Confectioner
%D    1964.
%P    118p.
%#    663.92/K32
%S    Chocolate
%Z    Copies at: PR
```

The system, to minimize training, did not care whether words were title, author, or subject heading. Thus,

```
butter pecan
2 items (1/2)
 1: Peanut butter and jelly guide to computers.
 2: Neuropsychology; the study of brain and behavior.
Which book? 2
%T    Neuropsychology; the study of brain and behavior.
%A    Butter, C.M.
%I    Brooks-Cole.
%D    1968.
%P    211p.
%#    152/B98
%S    Nervous system
%S    Psychology, Physiological
%Z    Copies at: HO MH
```

Note that, failing to find ***pecan***, the system ignored it and found the one word that did appear in the catalog. Coordinate index-level searching was automatic. Thus,

```
salton kochen information retrieval
Postings: salton: 4; kochen: 6; information: 2237-C;
   retrieval: 347
6 items (3/4)
 1: Theory of indexing
```

```
2: Principles of information retrieval
3: SMART retrieval system: experiments in automatic d
4: Automatic information organization and retrieval.
5: Growth of knowledge; readings on organization and
6: Some problems in information science.
```

In the next case six books have three of the four terms, as indicated by the numbers in parentheses. The alternative menu system is based on the Dewey Decimal classification hierarchy. The first display is always

```
0   000     Generalities, Computing (280 groups)

1   100     Philosophy (87 groups)

2   200     Religion (5 groups)

3   300     Social sciences (306 groups)

4   400     Language and languages (71 groups)

5   500     Science (1063 groups)

6   600     Technology (Applied Science) (1175 groups)

7   700     Arts (64 groups)

8   800     Literature (8 groups)

9   900     History and Geography (69 groups)
```

and the user chooses down which branch of the hierarchy to continue the search. The focus of the Bell Laboratories library is obvious from the number of groups in each main heading. Suppose the user now types **5**:

```
1   510     Mathematics (242 groups)

2   520     Astronomy (68 groups)

3   530     Physics (248 groups)

4   540     Chemistry (354 groups)

5   550     Geology (72 groups)

7   570     Nature (38 groups)

8   580     Botany (7 groups)

9   591.1   Sense organs (13 groups)
```

The average book was five levels down in the menus, but in the worst case it took 10 decisions to get to

```
b 621.3815304 Transistor circuits (131 books)

1 621.381530401 Electronic circuits-Data processing (1 book)

2 621.381530402 Semiconductor circuits-Handbooks (2 books)

7 621.381530407 Transistor circuits-Programmed instruction
                (4 books)
```

Table 7.2 Percentage of keyword searches in sessions.

Was user looking for a particular book?	First Search	Later Sessions	All Sessions
Yes	75.7%	86.1%	82.2%
No	64.6%	82%	76.4%
All	71.3%	84.4%	79.8%

Users had considerable trouble learning some aspects of Dewey, for example, that psychology is neither science (500) nor social science (300), but is under philosophy (Dewey, of course, was working before William James, let alone Freud).

In seven weeks of trial, 900 people engaged in over 3000 sessions. Dropping all the sessions done by the library staff, people who did not identify themselves, and people who didn't do any searches at all, we had 1952 searches, of which keyword searches were 79% and menu searches 21%. After experience, even more were keyword searches: 71% of the first searches were keyword, and 84% of searches after that. Of 208 people who did at least one keyword search and one menu search, 84% chose keyword searches in their next sessions. Even among those who were "browsing" (i.e., not looking for a particular book), the decision was in favor of keyword searching. Table 7.2 shows the data.

The keyword searches worked better as well as being preferred by the users. Sixty-five percent of the known-item keyword searchers found their book, while only 30% of menu users found it (based on answers to questions they were asked at the end of each session). These results confirm the subjective answers summarized in the table: 24% of keyword users failed to look at any full citations (implying that they didn't find any promising titles), while 55% of the menu users read no citations.

We found users typing about 5 commands per minute (we counted even a carriage return to see the next item in a list as a command). Despite the single-keystroke menu, it was no faster to use. The queries were extremely short: the keyword searches averaged a word and a half, with 55% of the searches being only one word. Retrospectively, this justifies ignoring sophisticated term combination commands. The most common search terms are title words, followed by authors and then subject headings. Seventy-two percent of terms searched for are in the titles, 40% in the authors, and 36% in the subject headings. The users do not specify which field they want, and some words occur in all three kinds of fields, so the numbers do not add up to 100% (the catalog had items with author names like Department of Defense Joint Aircraft Design Committee, which is how the subject words get into the author fields).

We also asked the users to compare the computer system with the old paper catalog. Keyword users reported the computer as easier to use, more complete, and less time-consuming. There may be some wishful thinking here; the average session time is 4 minutes. Perhaps they are getting more done than they used to, but few people spent 4 minutes at the old catalog. The menu users thought the computer was easier and faster, but not as complete.

Most query languages are based on simple word matching. The standard technology in the library world for some decades was the Boolean query with truncation. Query processing proceeded by generating sets of documents and then combining them with Boolean operators: AND, OR, and NOT. The set retrieval is based on searches for words, possibly with truncation, and allowing searches for multiple words within some neighborhood. Searches can also involve *fielded* searching in which the search term must appear in a particular part of the document record, such as the author field.

Thus, to use DIALOG as a sample system, the search

```
S LESK
```

creates a set of all documents which contain the word or name LESK. This will retrieve, for example, full text documents which mention LESK. To retrieve only documents written by somebody named LESK, that is, with LESK in the author field, the query might be

```
S au=lesk, ?
```

where the ? character indicates truncation. This retrieves all authors with last name Lesk and any first name or spelling; thus, it would cover both initials and spelled-out first names. In some Dialog databases it would have to be written without the comma.

To find documents containing the phrase "white whale" the user would type

```
s white(w)whale
```

where the (w) indicates *word adjacency*. Neighborhoods can also be specified, as in

```
s character(5w)recognition
```

where the (5w) string means "within 5 words." Any of these searches yields a retrieved set of documents and its size. The user can then combine these sets with AND or OR or NOT and type them out.

This kind of interface is believed too complex for naive users, and many of the Internet search engines use simpler searching procedures. On Alta Vista, for example, word adjacency is handled just with quotes, so one types "*white whale*" for a phrase search. And there is minimal fielded searching, since most of the

Web pages indexed don't define fields. One can search for some fields, such as URLs, with prefixed strings:

```
url:lesk
```

This searches for *lesk* in an http string. There may be ways to specify "wild card" characters (typically the asterisk) and to specify "near" or some degree of fielded searching. In general, the search engine has an "advanced search" page with as many of these options as it supports.

Search engines conforming to the Boolean search rules are often implemented by using the standard protocol Z39.50, defined to permit clean separation of the client and server portions of a search system. In the Z39.50 protocol, a front-end system can send searches to a back-end retrieval engine, which would execute the searches, save up sets, and deliver values. Using this standard, it would be possible to buy a front end from one vendor and a back end from another. However, Z39.50 is definitely tied to the model of a Boolean search engine on a traditional document collection. It is not flexible enough to implement some other model of document retrieval.

The conventional wisdom on Boolean searches is that most users don't understand them. They confuse AND and OR, and they do not realize the effects of NOT. For example, suppose you live in New Jersey and are looking for plants which grow in the mid-Atlantic area and have red flowers. If you find that a search for "red flowers and mid-Atlantic" retrieves too many items which grow in Virginia but not further north, you should not just request "red flowers and mid-Atlantic NOT Virginia" since this will eliminate any plant which happens to grow in both Virginia and New Jersey. In addition to the confusion created in users, some of Salton's experiments indicated rather little advantage to Boolean queries over coordinate level matching (counting matching terms). As a result, although Boolean searches dominated early online systems, they are less common in the new Web search engines. The lack of operators does not matter much, since queries are short. AltaVista queries in the mid-1990s were only 1.2 words long, and even in 2004, Bar-Ilan reported an average query at 2.6 words.

Web search engines attempt to determine the relative importance of different words. A word used many times in a document is likely to be more reflective of the content than a word which is only used once. The exact details of assigning weights (importance) to terms by Web search engines is tricky to discuss. People sometimes attempt to "fool" the search engines so that their pages will come out at the top of search lists. Thus, they either put in words that they hope people will search for, or they add copies of the words hoping to make some term weighting function decide their page should be listed first. As a result, the search engines do not publicize their techniques. For example, many have taken to ignoring the meta field in HTML which is provided to let people insert keywords for searching. As discussed earlier in the text, the reality is that people were found putting the entire dictionary into such fields, hoping to be retrieved by all searches. With that route blocked, there are now people concealing words in their pages either by writing them in the same color as the background or putting them in 2-point type so they appear to be part of a wallpaper pattern. It does appear that many of the search engines respond to the number of hits in the files, but they do not publish the exact algorithm.

Clearly, we are moving towards systems in which people do their own searching. OPACs are now routine; text searching on the Internet is common; and more complex search systems are being learned. New library users may need to learn how to use the library itself, as well as search systems. Even traditional bookstores, after all, have people who can answer questions. Can this be done online? Will a Web page substitute for a person to provide training?

In fact, some companies justify their website on the grounds that it answers questions that would otherwise require the time of their help desk. And certainly users get a lot of help from each other. But librarians still find that there is an enormous demand for courses in the use of the Internet and for help with computer problems. In fact, the very lead that libraries have taken in providing the public with search systems has meant that they get more than their share of questions, being the first search systems many people have come into contact with. Various tools have been developed to help with user training.

An extremely useful online tool has been the FAQ list, with which most users are quite familiar. FAQ stands for "frequently asked questions" and FAQ lists are just that, lists of common questions with answers. There is a large archive of FAQs at MIT, and they have certainly been very useful for people with a reasonable amount of knowledge to find out more. There are rarely search systems for FAQ lists; they are each normally short enough to browse through.

One interesting experiment to try to improve help systems was the Answer Garden of Mark Ackerman (Ackerman and Malone, 1990). This system tried to help with questions about X-windows. The idea was that a user would be presented with a series of choices about the user's question, for example, "Is this a client side or server side problem?" The user would then answer these questions, one after the other, moving down a discrimination tree through the system's information. Eventually, the user either finds the question or reaches the end of the tree. In the first case, the answer is with the question. If the user reaches the end of the tree without finding the question, then it is a new question, and it goes to an X-windows consultant who answers the question and posts the answer in the tree at that place. In this way, each question should only have to be answered once.

The Answer Garden has been implemented at MIT. The first screen displayed the choices:

```
Are you having a problem with:
    Finding information about X
    Using an X application
    Programming with X
    Administering X
    Using Answer Garden
```

It has been tested on a group of 59 users at Harvard and MIT (Ackerman, 1994). It received consistent, if not overwhelming, use, and many users reported it of great value. Others, however, complained that the level of explanation was not right. It is difficult for an automated system to know whether the person confronting it is an expert or a novice and pitch its response appropriately; this is something people can do better. One advantage of the Answer Garden (and of any automated system) is that people perceive no loss of status in asking it questions, and so some people who might avoid asking for help from another person will feel free to consult the program. The reverse of this is that some contacts that might be made and might be useful are not made. It is likely that at least some training staff will be essential indefinitely.

7.6   Access Methods

Whether libraries in the future need to keep things or will just buy access to them is unclear. Many libraries may become "gateway libraries" which merely provide access to material stored elsewhere. This model has the great advantage that it postpones the work of dealing with any item until somebody wants it. Traditionally, libraries buy most of their content before anyone has actually seen it; and they commit to most of the cataloging and shelving cost before any user sees the book or journal. Thus, money may be spent on content which, in the end, no one uses. In a gateway library, until somebody tries to get at something the library has minimal cost for it.

Conversely, however, users are not likely to be pleasantly surprised to find that the library has something but that it has to be obtained in a slow or inconvenient way. Nearly all items will come from a search, and we do not know well how to browse in a remote library. Users will need help doing their searches and adjusting them to retrieve a reasonable quantity of results. Also, it will be important for many users that response be fast and that the material be available at all times. We are all familiar with the undergraduate who sets out to write a paper the evening before it is due. If the contents of the library are only available by remote delivery during business hours, as with many of the fax-on-demand services, this major segment of the user base is not served.

The uncertainty that may affect our willingness to use digital information is only heightened by a remote point of origin and a lack of cues as to the quality of the work. Librarians or faculty will have to help users learn how to research the background and context of works on the Web, as well as how to judge what weight to place on different retrieved documents.

Many users of traditional libraries are not searching, they are browsing. They do not have a particular document, or even a well-formulated query, in mind. For this purpose, the search engines provided on the Web, or in libraries, are often frustrating and inappropriate. Normal browsing is heavily dependent on visual scanning, going through fairly large numbers of items, looking at very little information in each, and picking out something to read. It is tolerable as a way of working only because it is usually done on some kind of classified collection, so that the general area is already selected.

Attempts to improve browsing have led to various innovative schemes other than searching. One plan which flourished in the 1980s was the idea of *spatial data management,* in which information is located by place rather than by key-word. It was modelled on the process by which people remember putting some document in this or that pile on a desk. Spatial data management was popularized by Malone (1985) and others, and persists for a few tasks, for example, in the way the Macintosh and Microsoft Windows interfaces allow the user to arrange the icons for files in any order. William Jones and Susan Dumais (1986) evaluated it and found that people are not very good at remembering where they have put anything. In fact, having two or three characters of a name is worth more than spatial organization. They evaluated both real spatial organization (asking people to put documents into piles on a table) and the computer metaphor for the same thing.

Another metaphor which has been tried is the idea of retrieval by criticism, explored by Michael Williams in his Rabbit system (Tou et al., 1982). In the Rabbit interface, database query operates by having the computer retrieve random records subject to constraints. At the beginning, the machine simply returns a random record. Imagine, as in Williams' example, that the problem is to find a restaurant. The system picks a random one, and the user says something like "too expensive" or "too far north." The system then makes another random choice subject to the constraint. If the database can be described as a set of independent dimensions, each of which has a reasonable range, this process will quickly converge on acceptable answers.

Although the Rabbit model is attractive, few databases lend themselves to this kind of partitioning. One can not see, for example, how to apply this to a

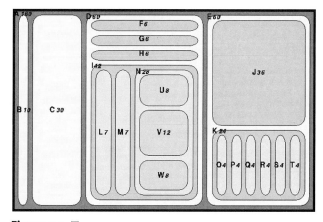

Figure 7.4 Treemap.

conventional text searching system; simply knowing a few words that you don't want does not restrict the search space much.

Although most library systems do not make much use of graphical screens, there are some interesting interfaces that do. For example, Ben Shneiderman has a treemap for hierarchial structures. In this model, moving down the tree one step changes the orientation of the diagram from horizontal to vertical and then back again (Johnson and Shneiderman, 1991; Shneiderman, 1992). For very complex structures, the treemap has the advantage of being able to show size relationships and categorization (via color). A simple treemap is shown in Figure 7.4.

A treemap can, for example, represent a file system. Each transition from vertical to horizontal packing is a step down in the directory hierarchy. Each set of items packed together is the contents of a directory. The relative size of the items in the diagram reflects their relative size in the file system. Color can indicate the kind of file (e.g., text, image, or program).

Some researchers are trying to indicate more than just a document-id in a retrieval presentation, instead of just a single list of documents. Marti Hearst has developed a display technique called Tilebars which represents another technique for visualizing the results of a search. Each document has a row of squares; each row represents a set of terms and each square is a portion of the document. The darkness of the square indicates the extent to which the terms are present. Thus, in Figure 7.5, document 1298 has matches at the beginning only, with a very dense match on *network* and/or *LAN*; while document 1300 has a well-distributed use of *network* and a single portion relating to *law*.

Ed Fox, on the Envision project, has an interface which also combines a great many attributes to describe a retrieval list. In Figure 7.6, documents are plotted

| Help | Search | Clear Query | TextDB | Toggle Color | Exit |

Term Set 1: law legal attorney lawsuit

Term Set 2: network lan

TileBars

1256	Regression testing handling hardware and softwa
1269	Toll fraud includes related article on MCI Commu
1270	In conversation Teleglobe Canada Inc Pres and (
1280	Deregulation indicates a healthy satellite services
1298	The last word letters to the editor letter to the edi
1300	What's wrong with network licensing includes rela
1302	Letters letter to the editor
1356	Protecting information now vital Law Viewpoint cc
1414	Letters O
1424	Loose LIPS sink ships logical inferences per seco
1433	Document management eases file control marke
1471	Connectivity O
1496	Document managers bring law and order Softwar
1571	When users write their own applications O
1640	Time lapse may scuttle Xerox claim includes relat
1690	Insider revisited AI Insider column
1758	Vendors offering more remedies for file buildup d
1762	Laser Lite Apple's new personal LaserWriters Ha
1766	Hacker's handicap Michael Colvin MP has won su
1779	No summer reruns artificial intelligence application
1781	How Seattle's biggest law firm put Windows 3 0 t

Figure 7.5 An example of Tilebars.

using the *x*-axis to display publication year, the *y*-axis to show index terms, and color (shown here in shades of gray) is used for degree of relevance. It is also possible to use shape and size to show yet another dimension.

These interfaces basically display lists of documents. Xia Lin has represented a document collection using a self-organizing system. A rectangular space, intended to cover all semantic meanings, is divided into nodes. At first, nodes are assigned random positions in a term vector space (used to represent the coordinates of a position). Documents are then picked and the closest node to each document adjusted so that the node will become even closer to the document. In this way, various nodes converge on the position values of different documents, and eventually each region of the space is associated with a group of related documents. The space is then tiled (divided into areas which do not overlap) and each area labeled with the corresponding documents (Lin and Soergel, 1991; Hearst 1999; Yang 2002, Borner 2003).

This process is known as the Kohonen map algorithm. Figure 7.7 shows a representation of documents in information technology, automatically organized into a concept space. Note that the largest areas are for the most common topics. This gives an overview of what topics matter and how they are related

Figure 7.6 — Envision retrieval list (screen capture):

File Edit Results
Best 100 Items Found

Find Icon	Icon Number: Est. Relevance ▼	Icon Size: Uniform ▼
	Icon Color: Relevance Rank ▼	Icon Shape: Uniform ▼

Y–Axis: Index Terms ▼

Estimated Rating — Least Relevant ... Most Relevant
User Rating — ☐ Not Useful ☒ Useful

	(3) 89	(5) 7	(6) 96	(7) 11	(7) 6
ALGORITHMS					●
DESIGN				63	59
DOCUMENTATION				41	
EXPERIMENTATION			46	66	
HUMAN FACTORS	20 / 25		44 / 45		
LANGUAGES			(2) 64		(2) 100
THEORY				67	
	1984	1985	1986	1987	1988

X–Axis: Pub. Year ▼

Figure 7.6 Envision retrieval list.

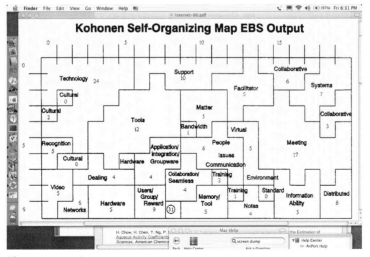

Figure 7.7 Kohonen map.

to each other. With interfaces of this sort, difficulties are likely to arise when extended to very large collections, where it will be hard to find some way to indicate the location of every document.

The basic difficulty is the problem of summarizing the kinds of books in one area or another. We might prefer that a query return not "Here are 200 books that matched the query," but rather "There were four basic topics, and fifty books in each, and here are what the basic topics are." How can this be done? One strategy is to use a library classification. Here is the result of a search for the word "screen" in a set of book titles with the number of hits in each part of the Library of Congress classification.

```
Type some kind of search query, one line:
   Query: screen
```

Occurrences	Subject	Title (No. Found = 194)
143	P/Language and literature	The face on the screen and other
99	R/Medicine	Toxicity screening procedures using
51	T/Technology	Environmental stress screening,
50	M/Music	Broadway to Hollywood/Can't help singing
30	L/Education	Finland: screen design strategies
21	H/Social Sciences	National ethnic survey, 1980. Mexican
17	N/Arts	The technique of screen and television
12	--/--	Alfalfa seed screenings as a feed
10	Z/Bibliography	Screen process printing photographic
8	Q/Science	NOS version 2 screen formatting
5	--/--	Screening inductees: An analysis
5	S/Agriculture	Climbing and screening plants

```
Which category should be expanded? (n for none)
```

This shows the two main blocks of usage: words related to screenplays and the cinema, and words related to screening via tests for various conditions. At the bottom of the list is another meaning: hedge plants. If the *S* category is expanded the result is

```
Type some kind of search query, one line:
   Query: screen
```

Occ.	Subject	Title
2	SB427/Climbing plants	Climbing and screening plants
1	SB437/Hedges	Hedges, screens and espaliers
1	SF961/Cattle--diseases	Blood protein screening in healthy
1	SH153/Fish-culture	Efficiency tests of the primary

With these category labels, a user interested in plants can now look through the categories SB427 and SB437, finding such titles as "Shelter effect: investigations into aerodynamics of shelter and its effects on climate and crops," which do not use the word *screen* but are clearly relevant.

So far, most library catalogs only provide textual representations, despite the attractiveness of some of the graphical systems shown here. Surprisingly, the rapid switch from the text-oriented gopher interfaces to the graphically oriented Web interfaces did not change this, and most online library catalogs still give only text-oriented interfaces.

What has changed is that full content of many publications is now available online. As a result, in some catalog-like databases one can move to the actual document from the bibliographic record. The most familiar example is the Amazon.com website, which now normally leads the customer to a sample of 20 or 30 pages from each book. More complete are sites like that of the National Academy Press, where every one of their currrent publications is online in full text.

Whether any of these more detailed access methods can substitute for running one's eyes over a set of shelves to find book titles that look interesting is not yet known. In principle, the cues used in shelf-hunting can be presented using one of the new graphics techniques, and the ability to organize books in response to each query should be helpful. Yet, not enough work has been done to ensure that adequate cues are given to compensate for the lack of immediate observation of the size of the book or the name recognition of a respectable publisher.

7.7   Retrieval Evaluation

User enthusiasm for a digital library depends on many things: the content of the collection, the cost of the system, the user interface, and so on. One aspect that can be systematically evaluated is the accuracy with which the system selects answers to questions. The standard methodology for this was defined by Cyril Cleverdon (Cleverdon et al., 1966) in the 1950s. He defined two measures, now known as *recall* and *precision*. The *recall* of a system is its ability to find as many relevant documents as possible. The *precision* of a system is its ability to select only relevant documents and reject the irrelevant ones. Thus, if we search for a query in a document collection, and there are 50 relevant documents in the collection, if the search returns 40 documents, of which 20 are relevant and 20 are not relevant, it has a recall of 40% (20 out of 50) and a precision of 50% (20 out of 40).

There is a trade-off between recall and precision. Suppose we have some way of tightening or loosening the search strategy. For example, if the user gave the system three terms and looked for any two of them, the strategy could be tightened by demanding that all three appear, or loosened by accepting documents with only one term. If the strategy were loosened, more documents would be retrieved. It is likely that some of the new retrieved documents would be relevant, thus increasing the recall. But it is also likely that the new strategy would also increase the number of nonrelevant documents found and would, in fact, decrease the precision (by introducing proportionally more nonrelevant documents than in the tighter search). In fact, one can always achieve 100% recall by retrieving every document in the collection; albeit the precision in this case will be close to zero. Conversely, if the system can retrieve a relevant document as its first response, by stopping there one can achieve 100% precision, but probably with very low recall. Many systems operate at around 50% recall and 50% precision; half of what is found is relevant, and half of what is relevant is found.

It has become customary to plot recall against precision to show this trade-off. Figure 7.8 shows one of the very earliest such plots, made by Cleverdon as part of the Aslib/Cranfield study of index languages. The care taken in this project to get good queries and relevance assessments was remarkable. The quality of the Cranfield work has not been equalled since; nor its economy (six staff years of effort for $28,000 on one project).

In practice, the parameter changing along the curve is the number of retrieved documents. As more documents are retrieved, the performance moves to higher recall and lower precision; as fewer documents are retrieved, the performance moves to higher precision, but lower recall. Ideal performance would be the top right corner, where everything retrieved is relevant (100% precision) and everything relevant is retrieved (100% recall). Conversely the lower left corner, where nothing useful has been retrieved, is the worst possible performance.

Retrieval algorithms are evaluated by running them against a set of test documents and queries. For each query, each algorithm being tested is executed, and for each result, the recall and precision are calculated. If the algorithm has variable parameters, it is often run with several values to produce different results (presumably moving along the recall-precision curves). All of the recall-precision results are then plotted and whichever algorithm has points closer to the top right corner is better. In practice, it is found that there is an enormous scatter among the results; some queries are much easier to answer than others, and the scatter across queries tends to be much larger than the differences between systems. The first lesson from these retrieval experiments is that the best thing to do for improved performance is to get the users to write better queries (or merely to get them to submit queries on easier topics).

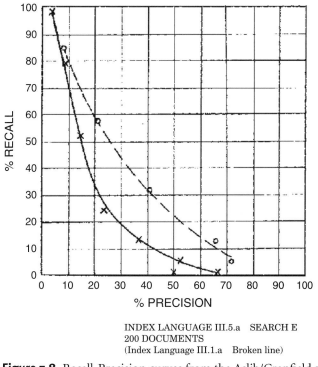

INDEX LANGUAGE III.5.a   SEARCH E
200 DOCUMENTS
(Index Language III.1.a   Broken line)

Figure 7.8 Recall-Precision curves from the Aslib/Cranfield study.

The difficult part of a recall-precision test is finding the relevant documents for the queries. Originally, Cleverdon tried to use seed documents, or use the reference lists in documents as data for these experiments, but he was criticized for this, and it became standard to have the relevant documents examined by people paid to do this. It is possible to examine only the retrieved documents, which is straightforward but gives only a good estimate of precision. If only the documents found in the course of the experiment are evaluated for relevance, there is no way to guess how many other relevant documents might be in the collection. This kind of evaluation was started in the 1960s, when it was difficult to process very large collections. With small collections, it was feasible to have every document examined for relevance to each query. Salton prepared several such collections for the SMART project, and they remained the basis of such studies for the next 20 years. The largest of them was a collection of 1400 abstracts of aeronautical literature that Cleverdon had gathered, and this remained one of the standard retrieval test collections into the 1990s.

Many felt that these collections were inadequate; that they were too small. In 1990 Donna Harman of NIST, one of Salton's students, began the first of the TREC experiments (Text Retrieval Evaluation Conference; see Harman, 1995; Voorhees and Buckland, 2003). Text retrieval researchers were presented with a gigabyte of text, half for training and half for experiments, and 100 queries. To estimate recall, the plan called for the first 200 documents retrieved by each system to be pooled and the entire set to be evaluated for relevance. The documents ranged from newswire stories to Department of Energy documents, and the queries were composed by professional analysts looking for information; consequently, the queries are particularly long and detailed. Fifty of the queries were imagined to be standing profiles so that it was acceptable to use the results on the first half of the collection to train or adapt the queries for the test on the second half. Fifty of the queries were imagined to be one-shot queries and no training could be done.

The TREC conference has been repeated each year, with new documents and queries. The document collection is now up to about 3 GB. Again, the scatter among systems exceeds the differences between them. Not only do the systems have widely different performance on different queries, but even two systems which may have about the same recall and precision on a query are likely to achieve it by retrieving entirely different documents. Some systems are also better able to deal with the entire set of queries. For example, some of the queries involve numerical comparisons ('companies with revenues above $100 M') but some of the purely text-oriented systems have no way of implementing this comparison.

There are multiple kinds of queries in the TREC experiment. Some queries are viewed as continuing (or, routing) and a set of documents that are known to be relevant is provided in advance; the queries are evaluated against a new set of documents. The other queries are new each time and called "ad hoc"; there are no relevant documents known in advance for such queries. Some systems do manual creation of queries for each ad hoc test; some do a fully automatic processing of whatever is presented to them. Many systems do the routing queries by ignoring the query and making a new query from the set of relevant documents (which, in aggregate size, is much larger than the query description).

As a result of the scatter in the results, it is not sensible to select a single 'winner' of the TREC competition and suggest that it be used for all queries. One leading system from City University, London, used term weighting, in which the weight placed on any term was roughly related to inverse document frequency (terms appearing in only a few documents are better content indicators). It also supplemented each query with a few dozen terms picked from the highest-rated documents, and it used passage retrieval (breaking long documents into shorter chunks for searching). Another high-performing system, the INQ101 system from Bruce Croft's group at the University of Massachusetts, also uses term weighting and query expansion using phrases detected in the collection.

Salton's group did well using term weighting and massive feedback expansion (up to 500 terms added from the top 30 retrieved documents). West Publishing relied on a system similar to Croft's system but with expansion based on manually made synonym groups. Queens College, CUNY, sent in a system which uses spreading activation on passages (a technique which, to oversimplify, creates links between words as they co-occur). ETH in Zurich combined three methods which include vector spaces, Markov models, and links from phrases. Note the importance of expanding the queries; nearly everyone found this useful in getting better performance. This models the reality that librarians do better if they can get their users to talk more about what they want. Too much of a conventional question is implied rather than explicit, and making it explicit helps.

The TREC conference series has been expanded to include multilingual retrieval, audio retrieval, and other areas. Researchers who participate feel that the ability to measure progress is extremely valuable in improving the state of the art in text retrieval, and researchers in other areas have looked wistfully at the process and wished they could have it in their own area (but have not been able to persuade NIST or someone else to fund the comparable activities).

7.8   Page Ranking and Google

The most important development in searching systems was the discovery by Sergei Brin and Larry Page (1998) at Stanford that one could use link counts to do a rating of the importance of different Web pages. As the Web grew, early Web search engines returned ever longer lists of items, and people regularly made fun of the thousands of undifferentiated documents. Finding a needle in a haystack seemed like an easy task compared to finding the useful documents in the middle of these lists. Attempts to judge the relevance of websites by counting words and using term weighting were not dramatically useful. Then the database group at Stanford, led by Hector Garcia-Molina, found that you could judge the utility of pages by the number of references to them. This was first called BackRub, but is now widely known as the basis of the page ranking algorithm in Google, the company founded by Brin and Page (Brin and Page, 1998).

The basic idea is, like that of collaborative filtering, to make use of the many decisions made by Web users every day as they create sites and hyperlinks. If there are a lot of hyperlinks to a site, that site is probably important and worth ranking as more valuable than other sites. Thus, among all 48 million sites with the word *sun* in them, the page for Sun Microsystems is retrieved first by Google, because lots of people link to it from other sites. This simple idea made short searches valuable again; Google can be used effectively to find leading pages on any topic, without the need to try to wade through thousands of obscure sites.

Google has exploited this idea, and other advantages such as very fast searching, to become the search engine that does more than half the searches on the Web.

Unfortunately, the people who try to "fool" search engines into listing them more highly have tried to deceive the ranking algorithm. Thus, the actual Google ranking system is more complex than just counting the number of links to each page. Google has to look for things like loops of a few pages, each referring to each other thousands of times, and discount such hyperlinks. It also organizes the list of search results to avoid repeating the same or slightly variant page; thus other high-ranking pages for *sun* are various newspapers with *Sun* in their name and a page about astronomy, even though Sun Microsystems has a large and impressive website. Google has a complex way of counting the rankings, so that a link pointing in from a high-rated page counts more than a link pointing from a low-ranking page. The data have proved to be reliable and stable over several years.

The same basic thought occurred to Jon Kleinberg of IBM and Cornell, and he has done other studies to organize and rate Web pages based on link counts. Kleinberg (1999) has looked at both link counts pointing at a page and those pointing from a page; some pages, such as gateways, mostly refer out, some are referred to, and some have many in and out links. He found that the Web has a large *core* of pages that link to each other, every page of which can be found by tracing hyperlinks within the core. It also has some *upstream* pages that point to the core but are not pointed to from it; some *downstream* pages that don't point back; and some *tendrils,* Web pages that can't reach the core or be reached by it. Similarly, for any single topic (such as the result of a search), Kleinberg's methods can identify a set of *authoritative* pages which are widely referenced and strongly linked. These are more likely to be useful to a reader than simply the page which uses a particular word the most times or earliest on the page.

Kleinberg points out, as Tom Landauer did earlier, that the best page for a topic may even be one that does not include the word sought. The site *www.honda.com,* he notes, does not contain the phrase "automobile manu-facturer" (and if it is rewritten to include it, it will be missing some synonym). His algorithms will retrieve pages such as this by using links from pages which do include that phrase.

It is also possible to use the link structure of the Web as anthropology, studying the way in which sites group into cliques. There is research to be done on the way that the links change over time and on the mathematical functions that model their distribution. Most of this research remains to be done as the Web is so new.

So far, all the measures discussed rely on static Web pages. It is also possible to try to gather information from the dynamic behavior of users. The Alexa portal, for example, tells you for each page "Other people on this page went to the following pages next . . ." as another kind of community guidance. Analysis of the current search stream can also tell you what is important and what people want to know. Google's Zeitgeist page shows current searches from different countries; similarly Yahoo's "buzz" feature lists the most popular 20 searches of the last week (as I write, both Britney Spears and Jennifer Lopez have been on this list for more than 2 years).

It is perhaps not remarkable that the combined activities of millions of Web users leads to a good way to rank pages and find the best ones; it is remarkable that nothing like this has ever been available before. The history of searching and retrieval has relied on experts for quality rating and has never been able to use masses of people as a substitute. The effectiveness of Google was completely unanticipated.

7.9   Summary

Again, this chapter describes a problem that has already been solved. We have retrieval systems that work well enough. We still have to think about accessibility for users with limited vision, inadequate computer displays, or no experience with keyboards and mice, but we have no basic difficulties building systems that work well enough to be effective.

Nevertheless, there are many difficulties with existing systems. Many tend to make inadequate use of graphical capabilities. Many offer inadequate guidance to users who have either retrieved nothing or have retrieved far too much. And many still suffer from the problems users have negotiating their way through very large information collections. Research projects such as those described in this chapter address some of these problems, and solutions need to make their way into practice.

Perhaps most interesting will be the problems of representing item quality. In a conventional library, most material purchased is evaluated for quality at the time someone decides to buy it (usually by selecting reliable publishers or journals). In a gateway library that only fetches things on demand, how will there be an instant reflection to the user about possible bias or unreliability in the material listed? For example, would one wish to have the only information about disk drives be the press releases of some manufacturer, just because they were available free? Certainly this information might be useful, but with even less contact between the librarians and the users, how will novice users learn about the relative importance and reliability of certain kinds of information?

In one conversation at a university, a faculty member argued that this was not a library's business; he felt that faculty should assign undergraduate reading and that graduate students were sophisticated enough to appreciate degrees of bias or distortion. Many librarians would disagree and point out that their purchasing decisions include quality and reliability considerations today. In the future, how can we ensure that an interface will reflect such considerations?

8 User Needs

D espite the widespread acceptance of digital content and digital searching in libraries today, the match to what users actually want and what they can do is very weak. Users are neither clear about what they want, able to operate the systems well, or doing much to get help. However, they're satisfied with the results. To the extent that we can tell, the acceptance of new systems is partly based on the inability of users to tell how badly things are actually working, and partly on the probability that older systems were also not being used very effectively. At least, we have opportunities for improvement, if we can pay enough attention to the users when designing the systems.

8.1 Overview

Despite jokes about librarians who think their job is to keep the books safe from the readers, libraries exist to provide information to people, today and in the future. Digital libraries also provide information and services to their users. How will those services change and what new things will be happening?

Traditional libraries provided services that extended from entertainment to advanced research, but did not cover as wide a range as that on the Web. For example, libraries often rented videotapes, but rarely encouraged patrons to use library television sets and VCRs to watch them on the premises. Libraries could feasibly provide daily newspapers for financial and weather information with 24-hour delay, but do not have current stock tickers or weather reports. On the other hand, as compared with the Web, libraries have librarians who can help users with their requests, and they provide a range of services to children (such as reading aloud to them) which are not realistic or practical online.

We have a model of the "information seeking" user in which the user has an "information need" of some kind, which is then expressed in some form of query, and then receives an answer in the form of a citation to some document. The user then reads the document and decides whether and how to rephrase the query. Once upon a time the user might have looked in some paper index, such as *Reader's Guide to Periodical Literature,* and found a list of traditional bibliographic citations; nowadays, the query goes to Google and the user gets a set of URLs, which are easier to turn into real documents. The user might also approach a reference librarian with the query, and the librarian might use a variety of sources, both print and digital, as well as personal memory and experience, to suggest a list of possible answers.

However, this model is oversimplified. Often, the result of seeing a possible list of answers is not just a change in the way the information need is expressed, but a change in the original need itself. That is, it's one thing to be unable to spell Alan Ayckbourn, but it's another kind of change to decide you really needed to look up Michael Frayn. In addition, many queries are really very vague and fuzzy. Although half the people in a research library enter with a particular item in mind that they want to find, the majority of the people who walk into a public branch library or browse the racks at an airport bookstall are just looking for something interesting to read; they have no particular book in mind.

Even to the extent that people can describe something that they want, often the description is not in a form that lends itself to description in keywords for either Google or a printed index. Qualities such as the language of the text or the place or date of publication are often in catalogs and may be supported by a search engine or OPAC (online public access catalog). Some additional qualities are imaginable as catalog contents: the user might want a short book, or a children's book, or an illustrated book, or a popularization as opposed to a book for experts. Often people say that they remember the color or shelf position of a book they want to find; regrettably, their memory is often wrong or at least insufficiently precise to be a useful search term (and of course shelf position can change over time, whether in a library, bookstore, or home).

But user wishes can be far less specific. The airport book buyer probably wants a book that is "exciting" or "absorbing." Christmas card publishers want landscape scenes that are "placid" and full of snow, while art catalogers write down the name of the place depicted and the painter's name. Allison Druin, who studies digital libraries for children, remembers one of her young patrons asking for a book "that will make me feel good" (Druin et al., 2003).

The process of retrieval is not just "turn a crank," but rather a negotiation between the user and the search agent, whether a person or a piece of software. The user is both elaborating and changing his or her needs; the system is responding to what it can deal with. How to deal with this dialog is more fundamental than screen color or font size.

8.2   User Services

The primary user service in the traditional library is access to books and journals, but most libraries also provide reference services, circulation, catalogs, photocopying, and simple study space. More elaborate services can include interlibrary loan, reading aloud to children, training classes, sound and video collecting, maintaining book reserves, running book sales, advice to tourists, running exhibitions, and more. The user population is usually defined in some way, whether residents of a particular town or students, faculty, and staff at some educational institution. However, enforcement of entry requirements is often minimal, the main reason for library cards being the need to keep track of those who borrow books. Typically, even in some large university libraries, anyone is allowed to walk in and browse (many state universities must, by law, admit every citizen for on-site services). Geography is enough to see that almost every user of a typical library will be somebody from the community which is paying for it.

Digital libraries have a corresponding but changed list of activities. Access can be larger and broader, with no need to limit collecting by shelf space. Circulation is unnecessary for Web access, since, in general, no physical copies of anything are being circulated. There are some services, such as Netlibrary, which do manage their materials on a simultaneous use basis. This kind of analogy to traditional borrowing lets each copy be read by only one user at a time; each user in turn gains access to the digital file for a time set by the library and then "returns" it so that some other reader may read it. The library can buy as many "copies" of each book as are needed to provide for simultaneous readers. The loaning of physical "e-books" may also involve a more traditional circulation.

More challenging problems are the provision of reference and help services. For those users in the library, it is much as before; but many of the users of a digital library service are not physically present and may be continents and hours away. Libraries offer telephone, email, and online chat alternatives; they even make arrangements with libraries around the world so that someone with a problem in the middle of the night in one place can try to get assistance from someplace in an appropriate time zone. For example, Global Librarian is a collaboration of libraries in the United Kingdom, Canada, and Australia; somewhere in this list, it is likely to be normal operating hours. However, it's impossible to provide the same degree of encouragement or service to those not on the premises.

Exhibitions in the digital world are, if anything, more straightforward than with paper. There are no issues of fragile materials that can't be exposed to light, of transporting loans from one place to another, or of removing materials from use while on exhibit. For many major libraries, their first activity in digitization of their own holdings (as opposed to purchase or access to the digital materials of others) involves the creation of Web-based exhibits.

8.3   Acceptance in the Past: Why Not Microfilm?

The Web, of course, is far from the first new technology to reach libraries. Some fifty years ago there was a great deal of hype about microfilm. H. G. Wells, Fred Kilgour, and Vannevar Bush all said that microfilm would be the basis of a revolution in information availability. To quote Wells' more colorful phrasing, a microfilmed encyclopedia would have "at once the concentration of a craniate animal and the diffused vitality of an amoeba . . . foreshadows a real intellectual unification of our race." Librarians were attracted to microfilm since a relatively cheap photographic process produced enormous space reductions and also a "user copy" that could be employed in place of fragile originals. Newspapers were particularly appropriate for film, since they were bulky, printed on volatile paper, and the combination of large size and weak paper meant that they were particularly likely to tear or be damaged by heavy use.

What went wrong with microfilm? Technically, it works just fine, but in every library microfilm readers sit idle while computer terminals have to have time limits. Let's take a look at the pluses and minuses of microfilm in contrast to the Web. We'll start with the downside. Disadvantages of microfilm include

1. Microfilm has no full-text search capability. A few things can be bar coded, but at most this usually gives you access to a frame number. Readers have the tedious job of paging through, frame by frame.
2. Microfilm requires visiting the library. You can't do it from your office or home.
3. Microfilm readers are often difficult to use, and in actual practice are often broken (partly because so many of the readers are unfamiliar with them and do not know how to use them), and sometimes produce either headache, eyestrain, or backache as a result of the chairs and lighting

conditions available. Film (or fiche), especially older photography, can be difficult to read.

4. Material on microfilm is usually not as up to date as even printed material, since normally it takes at least a few months from the time something is printed until the microfilm edition is shipped (if only because a number of issues of the journal or paper have to be collected). For those interested in timely information, microfilm won't do.

5. One microfilm can only be read by one person at a time; digital copies can be read simultaneously by many. This is rarely a problem, given the low use of most filmed publications; and of course what is listed here as an advantage of digital is considered a disadvantage by publishers.

Advantages of microfilm include

1. Microfilm contents are, in a way, twice-selected, at least for those micro-forms which are alternative versions of print publications (as opposed to films of original manuscripts or business records). This material was originally chosen for publication, and then it was selected for filming rather than just discarding. Thus, it's usually reliable and high-quality information.

2. Microfilm is known to be durable and accepted as a long-term preservation medium. This is more interesting to the librarians rather than the users.

Similarly, we could look at the CD-ROM versions of publications which flourished through the late 1980s and early 1990s. Like microfilm, CD-ROMs saved shelf space and avoided damage to paper originals. However, they share many of the disadvantages of microfilm. The user must go to the library to use them; a special machine is required; and often no search capability can be offered (since many early CD-ROMs were just page images of the printed version). Again, CD-ROMs are losing out to online digital.

8.4 Finding Library Materials

Perhaps most important among the problems we have discussed is that of search and access. Comparing the combination of card catalog and shelf browsing with the modern electronic full-text search, certainly we can find content more accurately, but not necessarily style or genre. The question of what kinds of queries users have, of course, varies not only with the users but also with the library system and the user experience. Users will learn to ask queries that they have found can be answered. Further, users choose which library to go to depending on what they want; there is little point in going to a research archive if you want a children's book or to a science library if you want literary commentary.

What do users actually do in libraries? This question depends, of course, on who the users are. For example, O'Hara and others collected diaries from 25 Ph.D. students at Cambridge University. They pointed to the amount of time people spend making notes and suggested that a handheld scanner would be a useful adjunct to library use. These students, of course, were doing long-term, serious academic work. By contrast, some years earlier Micheline Beaulieu looked at undergraduate students in City University and found they rushed from the catalog to the stacks as soon as they had found one book from which they could write a paper (typically due the next day).

What kinds of models do users have of a library's information system? If their model doesn't come close to reality, their ability to use the library will suffer (see Cool, 1996). Compared to the transparency of index cards and books on shelves, computer systems can be opaque. How many users understand the difference between ranking and Boolean retrieval? I remember once seeing a log of OPAC use in which someone had tried "Indians and magic," got no hits, and tried again with "Indians and magic and Arizona." Clearly, this user didn't understand the difference between logical AND and logical OR. At the other extreme, a nineteenth-century bowdlerizer once tried to clean up a poem that read "Oh, that my love were in my arms, and I in my bed again" by changing the "and" to an "or"; this shows a true faith in the readers' acceptance of Boolean logic.

Two famous papers on user models were written by Christine Borgman 10 years apart (1986 and 1996). She emphasized that users normally have a process in mind. They start with some kind of query, but then they change it as they do searches. System designers tend to think of isolated queries, each one to be answered and then forgotten. Designers assume that the users have read and understood the instructions so that they know whether or not the system does suffixing, whether they are searching a formal controlled vocabulary (e.g., LCSH, or Library of Congress Subject Headings) or ordinary words, and so on. In fact, users often do not know these things and often don't even know these issues exist, so they don't approach a librarian for help.

Ragnar Nordlie (1999) compared observations of users at OPAC terminals with users talking to reference librarians in Norwegian public libraries, using logs of the OPAC sessions and audiotapes of the reference interviews. He shows how far we have to go: basically some 2/3 of single requests and even 1/3 of all search objectives fail. Subject searches fail 70% of the time and, even after reformulation, 45% of the time. Nordlie's list of what goes wrong is depressing and includes "nearly 60% of the matching terms are in reality too general compared to the user's real needs"; "facilities for query refinement (Boolean combinations, truncation, . . .) are rarely used and almost never used correctly"; "help functions are almost totally ignored"; and "search experience seems to have very little influence on search behavior." The basic problem, Nordlie writes, is the inability of users to make clear what they are actually searching for.

By contrast, 90% of the searches done with reference librarians are successful, although again the users often start with a problem statement that is much too broad. The librarian, however, shows the user sample books, talks through the issues, and almost always comes up with a suitable problem statement and response. It doesn't matter as much exactly what the librarian asks, rather that the librarian shows interest and elicits additional information from the user.

8.5   Web Searching

If searching OPACS—something relatively well understood—poses such problems, what happens in more general Web searching? Again, people do not understand the possibilities and best use of the systems. Spink and coworkers (2001) looked at over a million queries and found that these queries are short, simple, and don't use a wide vocabulary. As they write, "Few queries incorporate advanced search features, and when they do half of them are mistakes." They conclude that "searching is a very low art."

Nor do people spend much time reading what they find. I looked at some Web logs in 1997 and found the data for the length of time somebody spent on one page before going to another, distinguishing search engine pages and other pages; these are summarized in Table 8.1.

These numbers suggest very fast skimming. If a typical URL is 12KB, or about 2000 words, reading through it at 400 wpm (fairly fast) would take 120 seconds. Our time per page on chemistry journals was about 90 seconds in the CORE experiment. Either the typical use of a Web page is browsing, not reading, or perhaps the effectiveness of actual searches is so poor that most pages presented are rejected immediately.

Are the queries given to the Web similar to the queries given to traditional libraries? I picked a few hundred queries at random from a list of a million

Table 8.1 Time spent per URL.

All Pages	Search Engine	Rating
52 sec	43 sec	Average
23 sec	23 sec	Median
5 sec	5 sec	Mode

queries sent to the Excite search engine and classified them into several groups. These groups are

1. Traditional reference queries of the sort you would expect people to ask school librarians or public librarians. Examples are "alexander graham bell," "australian business commerce," "apartments and virginia and manassas," "solar eclipse," or "plant + light + growth absorption." A few queries are suitable topics for traditional reference and I include them here, even though one might hesitate to actually type them into a search engine. An example was "making explosives pyrotechnics explosive propellants improvised detonation."

2. Queries about popular concerns that often are asked to traditional librarians, but which are so focussed on popular culture as to make them more frequently subjects of lunchtime conversation. However, they might well be answered better by librarians than by asking random friends. Examples of queries in this category were "kiss music concerts," "honda accord," and "celebrities addresses."

3. Queries about the Net and computers, such as "http://www.alc.co.jp./vle," "corel," "http://www.jpl.nasa.gov," and "office97." These queries make no sense in the absence of computers.

4. Sex-oriented queries, usually requests for pornography, such as "nudes sex pictures."

5. Queries I could not easily classify, such as "aunt peg," "apac," "sol," or "lh 4314." Typically, these queries are too short, or use abbreviations I didn't recognize, or I didn't feel comfortable guessing (e.g., LH 4314 might be a Lufthansa flight number, but who knows?).

Obviously, the results are sketchy; I only looked at a few more than 200 queries, and I might have made mistakes putting them in piles. Table 8.2 shows a sample of types of queries and their frequency.

Table 8.2 Frequency of visits by type of query.

Kind of Query	Frequency
Traditional reference	43%
Pop culture	13%
Sex	19%
Net and computers	12%
Unclear	12%

Color Plates

(a)

(c)

(b)

(d)

Figure 4.1 Color quantization: (a) 7 colors, (b) 20 colors, (c) 50 colors, (d) 256 colors.

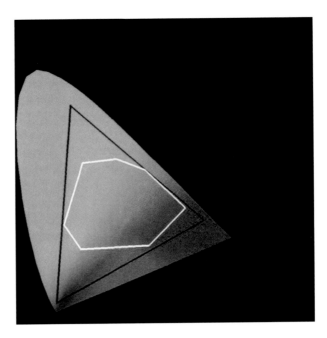

Figure 4.3 Gamut. The color space is the CIE representation of perceived colors, bounded by the spectrum. The black triangle is the limit of colors that can be displayed on a typical RGB monitor with three phosphors. The white polygon includes the colors that can be printed with a typical set of printing inks on an offset press.

Following the trail itself, Whispering Smith rode slowly.

Figure 7.2 Base picture.

(a)

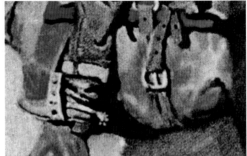
(b)

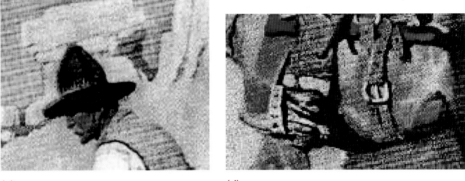
(c)   (d)

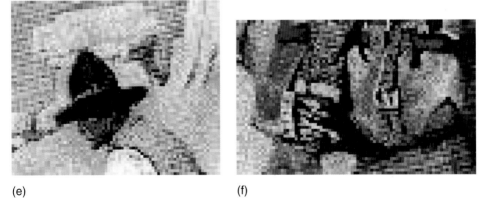
(e)   (f)

Figure 7.3 Color resolution examples: (a) & (b) 300 dpi, (c) & (d) 150 dpi, (e) & (f) 75 dpi.

The implication to me is heartening: more than half the questions asked are basically on the turf of traditional librarians, even if many of them would not have been asked of librarians were a physical trip to the library necessary. Looking at a longer list showed examples of a complete misunderstanding of what makes sense. For example, somebody typed a 1019 byte query: it was an entire movie plot summary, presumably as a search for the title. Single-letter queries also existed, as well as complete nonsense. The following sequence showed a triumph of persistence over spelling ability:

```
jakie onasis death

jackie onasis death

jackie onasis

jackie kenndy onasis

kackie kenndy

jackie onansis

jacklyn kennedy onansis

jackie onansis death

jacklyn kennedy onansis death

jacqueline kennedy onassis death
```

Analyzing logs is a difficult task. Privacy rules mean that one doesn't have the ability to track users over time, and one is often guessing what a query might be about. Is "Big Bertha" a query about a German gun, a NASA rocket, a golf club, or some kind of pornography? This came up in the Excite logs I studied; the context showed enough searches for secondhand golf equipment to draw a reasonable conclusion.

Users could also choose not to use search engines and to rely on other strategies for finding information. Three that make sense for online searching are (1) following hyperlinks, (2) using gateway pages, and (3) using some kind of classification system.

The hyperlink strategy would involve looking for links that are described in such a way that they would be believed to lead to better material. Hyperlinks, of course, were the method Vannevar Bush expected to be the primary information-seeking behavior on the Web. Certainly, once a relevant page is found, looking at hyperlinks is common. But as a way of finding information in general, chasing hyperlinks from arbitrary pages is not effective now that the Web is so big.

Starting with a gateway page, on the other hand, makes more sense. Gateway pages are created to point to a list of resources and are often created and managed by traditional libraries (Dempsey, 2000). For example, EEVL is a maintained guide to engineering information on the Internet, run by Heriot-Watt

University in Edinburgh. The United Kingdom has supported a variety of such pages, ranging from the BUBL page on information science to Vetgate on animal health. Certainly, these are extremely useful; for example, students often get their reference reading off a course gateway page for each of their classes (not necessarily given that name). Gateways have the advantage of giving quality information and often a little bit of context to help the user judge what the material is.

Unfortunately, gateways are expensive to maintain. It is more difficult to catalog a Web page than a book: the Web page doesn't come with a standard place where the author and title are given, and you don't have to check a book every so often to see if it has changed. At present, we have no economic solution to the maintenance of gateways. Nobody expects to pay for the use of such pages so, for example, an institutional library service runs into the objection that most of the users are not from the institution that is paying for the page. As a result, it's not clear how many of the formal gateways will continue.

Could there be an overall classification in which we put books in Dewey or LC categories? Certainly this is possible, but is it desirable? Users are not generally knowledgeable about navigating such systems. The older gopher system maintained an overall hierarchy, albeit by geography rather than subject. Yahoo started that way (see Chapter 5). Nowadays, full classifications are rarely used. Again, to do this for a billion Web pages would produce an unworkable and probably unfunded resource. On balance, people are likely to stick with search engines. Their speed and accuracy are remarkable and the quality of the results is good enough.

8.6 Performance Measurement

How well do retrieval systems work? Perhaps the most important result here is that of Blair and Maron (1985): systems don't work well but the users don't know it.

Blair and Maron studied the use of the IBM STAIRS system in a legal application, where full recall was expected to be of great importance. In fact, it was a stipulation of the system design that it achieve 75% recall. The lawyers were satisfied with the performance of the system and believed that it was meeting the 75% condition; in fact, the research showed that recall was actually 20%.

The kind of work done in this study is very expensive to repeat, and in general has not been done for large scale Web queries (but see Hawking 2001). The search engine companies do not find that their commercial success depends on winning recall-precision contests. Anecdotally, about 85% of Web search users report being satisfied with their results, regardless of what they are using (the groups interviewed covered a range of 100 in the number of web pages searched).

One reason that people are not sensitive to differences in the performance of information retrieval systems is that there is an enormous scatter in the results for different queries. Some queries are easy to answer and some are hard. People are not good at judging which are which; so they experience an enormous range of recall-precision results, and have no ability to know what they should expect. As a result, they are not disappointed by low recall: they don't know it has happened and they wouldn't expect anything else.

Talking to users about what they want is useful. In terms of subject searches, it draws them out and gets them to think of additional terms and therefore phrase the search more effectively. But talking to users about how searching should be done is not likely to be effective.

To contrast, consider two stories. In the 1970s, some friends of mine at Bell Laboratories were building services for the deaf community. We were very poor at guessing what services they would want. For example, we assumed they would want a list of the other deaf people with teletypes (and we were experienced at building phone books). In reality they wanted no such thing: they were afraid of burglars, being unable to hear someone breaking in, and didn't want any list compiled that might get into the hands of criminals. On the other hand, they wanted lists of foreign language movies, which we not only didn't predict but didn't understand until someone pointed out that those were the movies that were subtitled. It's hard to guess what people might want, and more effective to ask them.

On the other hand, random individuals don't know much about searching. One suggestion that comes up repeatedly is the use of spatial location as a way to classify documents; see, for example, Bolt 1979 or Robertson 2001. The idea, which sounds attractive, is to model physically placing a document in a particular place, say, into piles organized on a desk or notes put on a blackboard or corkboard. The user would remember things as "on the right" or "up top." Jones and Dumais (1986) tested this by putting people in an empty office, letting them put documents down wherever they wanted, and then measuring their ability to find things. The answer was that alphabetical labels were much more effective. This result so disturbed some referees, by the way, that they had to redo the experiment with a computer simulation of the table in the empty office; somebody hoped that perhaps virtual space would work better than real space. The overall message is that people are not good at guessing how a retrieval should work and that experiments do work.

The most well-known series of experiments on retrieval technology is the TREC series at the National Institute of Standards and Technology (NIST), run yearly by Donna Harmon. However, relatively few techniques from TREC have moved into actual digital library services, as pointed out by Tefko Saracevic. Why not? Part of the problem is that the TREC queries, modelled on the needs of intelligence analysts, are unusually long and detailed and not typical of short Web queries. Part of the problem is that the TREC winners may involve too much hand work or computer processing to be practical in a Web search environment. In fact, Web search algorithms actually do pretty well as it is; the performance gain from more complex methods is not large enough to be persuasive. And, finally, users are not that sensitive to details of recall and precision performance anyway.

What do the users want if they aren't crying out for higher recall? Well, fast response is clearly something that matters. Quality, meaning interest in the pages found, is another. For instance, Google achieves its success by getting "important" or "valuable" pages highly ranked. And response quality is certainly important; it's about how to find *good* material, not just more or less relevant material. For example, the third hit on "kennedy assassination" the day I tried it on Google was a conspiracy theory site arguing for additional gunmen firing from the grassy knoll (if you think this is ever going to go away, remember that we still don't know if Richard III killed the princes in the Tower). Will users want a way to find more reliable material? And if so, how will we achieve it?

8.7   Need for Quality

Is it better to have a few good books or a lot of them? Would you rather have a good response to a question that wasn't quite the one you asked, or a possibly bad response to exactly the right question? Historically, libraries have focused on collecting quality materials. When materials were expensive, it was important to choose well. Traditionally, you went to the library when the person in the next office couldn't answer your question; the library information was reliable but might not be on-point. Today we see most students doing all their research on the Web and using libraries as a last resort. The Internet is open all night long, provides full-text searching, and is bigger than all but the largest libraries.

So what is the future of the library collection as it goes online? Or the museum or archive, for that matter? As in the past, we will want "comprehensiveness." Oliver Wendell Holmes wrote, "Every library should try to be complete on something, if it were only the history of pinheads."

The Web is somewhere around 170 terabytes of text, with images probably four times as much, and the "deep Web" (databases found behind Web pages, often restricted in access) at perhaps 400 times more. The topics of interest to students are broader than they once were. History in United States colleges once focussed on European and American political and economic history. Today, universities routinely offer (and students enroll for) courses covering all areas of the world and extending across social history, the history of minority groups within countries, and other special topics. Students may find themselves writing papers on topics like sports history or food history. Santayana's remark that it doesn't matter what students read as long as they all read the same thing has vanished from the modern university (although the students have more TV programs in common than earlier generations had books in common).

Not only does the Web offer more complete coverage, particularly in areas that were of marginal interest to traditional collections, but the very informality of the Web and its content offers the chance of finding original source material in new areas. The modern equivalent of the letters and manuscripts that researchers sought in archives are perhaps the newsgroup postings and emails that one can find on the Web.

How bad off is an undergraduate doing all searches on the Web? I tried to look at a few sample searches to make comparisons with a traditional library collection to see whether the material found is reliable and useful. I ran a few queries on both Wilson's ArtAbstracts and on Google. Tables 8.3 and 8.4 show the first few results from comparative searches in the two sources, one of refereed and printed journals and one of the conventional Google search on the full Web.

Repeating the experiment in the topic area of computer science, trying half a dozen queries, it seems that the publications in the standard online search systems are very specialized. By contrast, the Google ranking tends to promote the more general and introductory items to the top of the list; more detail is available in the thousands of items further down. The Art Abstracts file does do better when the search terms spread outside of art; for example, looking

Table 8.3 Search results from ArtAbstracts and Google for "paleography."

Query: "paleography"	
Art Abstracts: 72 hits	Google: 21,100 hits
Cuneiform: The Evolution of a Multimedia Cuneiform Database	Manuscripts, paleography, codicology, introductory bibliography
Une Priere de Vengane sur une Tablette de Plomb a Delos	Ductus: an online course in Paleography
More help from Syria: introducing Emar to biblical study	BYZANTIUM: Byzantine Paleography
The Death of Niphururiya and its aftermath	Texts, Manuscripts, and Palaeography
Fruhe Schrift und Techniken der Wirtschaftsverwaltung im alten vorderen Orient	The medieval paleography tutorial has moved to . . .

Table 8.4 Search results from ArtAbstracts and Google for "Raphael, fresco."	
Query: "Raphael, fresco"	
Art Abstracts: 15 hits	Google: 8,950 hits
Sappho, Apollo, Neophythagorean theory, and numine afflatur in Raphael's fresco of the Parnassus	Raphael: The School of Athens
	WebMuseum: Raphael: the nymph Galatea
Accidentally before, deliberately after (Raphael's School of Athens)	OnArt Posterstore: Art Photography
Raphael's Disputa: medieval theology seen through the eyes of Pico della Mirandola and the possible inventor of the program, Tommaso Inghirami	Music Film Posters
	Raphael: Olga's Gallery
Raphael's use of shading revealed (restoration of the Parnassus in the Stanza Della Segnatura almost completed)	

for "St. Catherine" on Google retrieves information about various colleges and municipalities of that name (an experienced searcher could deal with this); other problems may be sites with too much advertising. For most of the queries I tried, an undergraduate looking for some introductory material would be better off with the Google results than the commercial abstracting and indexing services.

The greatest difficulties are not obscure research issues, but politically charged topics. Looking for words like "Kurdistan," "Tibet," or "Macedonia" often yields pages posted by political organizations with a clear agenda; similarly, a search for "Creationism" retrieves many one-sided Web pages. A naive reader might need some help sorting out what to believe. But on average, it is better to have a very large collection than a carefully selected small collection, since few queries are going to be directed at exactly the right documents.

The Internet is reversing a long trend to concentration in information providers: fewer radio stations than books published, fewer movies than plays, fewer TV networks than newspapers, and so on. On the Web, information comes from a hundred million hosts (literally); this is a fear for all dictatorships and a blessing for all scholars. We blame our predecessors for not saving things they didn't consider of sufficient value; Elizabethan drama or the literature of less developed regions come to mind. We should not make the same mistake, especially in an age of cheap technology. We need both the organizations that will save all of our creative work and a legal and economic framework to permit it.

8.8 Summary

Digital library services depend upon users; "write-only" storage is not very interesting. Users, unfortunately, aren't very good at saying what they want, and we haven't done very well at building systems to help extract this from them. I suspect, in fact, that compared to most automated help systems, we'd do better to put a friendly dog next to the workstation and tell the user to explain the search request to the dog; in the process of verbalizing it, the user would realize additional terms that needed to be specified. The systematic study of user needs is relatively little explored. Besides subject, we don't know what matters to most users—genre, length, illustration, date, country, or what? Fortunately, what we do know is that users are pretty easily satisfied. We have a real opportunity to try to do better.

Collections and Preservations

In a traditional library, the collections are the most important part. Libraries all have rules and policies for what they collect, even if they are Richard Brautigan's "Mayonnaise Library" that takes any book which publishers and other libraries have rejected. What should the collection rules be for digital libraries? What kinds of items should be acquired and retained? This chapter will focus on the split between those works that arrive in electronic form and those converted from older forms, and between those items a library holds itself and those it obtains from other sources when needed.

9.1 Traditional Paper Collections

As we have stressed throughout, the actual possession of books and other collections is less important than it has been in the past. Since digital items may be transmitted almost instantaneously across even international distances, what matters in the digital age is not what the library has but what it can get quickly. A few national libraries with preservation as their goal may need to have physical possession of objects (since they cannot ensure that other organizations will preserve and continue to make them available), but for most libraries the right to secure something for their patrons will be enough, and may be cheaper than the actual possession.

The traditional library acquired published material. Nonpublished materials went into archives, a related kind of institution. The fact that libraries acquired primarily published books and serials had several important consequences. Some degree of quality control could be taken for granted. A book which has been published by Harvard University Press or Morgan Kaufmann can be assumed to have some degree of integrity and accuracy. The library does not have to worry much about whether such books are plagiarized or fraudulent. As a consequence, most libraries do not have any procedure for examining the books they are buying to decide on their basic integrity. They may review their importance and significance for the library's users, but they rely on the publisher for some initial checking. In the digital world, where the "publisher" may be some fifteen-year-old clicking away at his terminal, somebody else is going to have to verify the quality of the material.

All printed books bought recently have been produced in multiple copies. The specific copy of any twentieth-century book held by a library was rarely of great importance (again, with an exception for national deposit libraries). Press runs may have been small, but it was unlikely that the copy in any one library was unique. In modern publishing, printing fewer than a few hundred copies is completely uneconomical, and is not done. In the digital world, this is no longer true. Unless there is coordination between libraries or between library and publisher, the library has no easy assurance that anyone else in the world has a copy of what it has. As a result, if it really cares about a particular item, it may have to think about how to keep it.

Published books are fairly static. Most books do not have a second edition, and if they do it is clearly marked on the copy. Those few books which are regularly changed (e.g., almanacs that appear yearly) are well recognized. And the appearance of a book does not change as it is read, unless it is falling apart. Again, in the digital world books may be much more dynamic. Each "reading" may be interactive and in some way change the book. The author or publisher may be revising constantly. The library has to think more carefully about which copy it has, and which version it wants. Traditional rules such as "the best edition for scholarship is the last version published in the author's lifetime" make less sense in a digital world. The library is going to have to think about whether it wants to capture some version of a changing item. Will the readers prefer to know that they are always reading the latest version, or will they expect that if they take the same book off the shelf twice, it will be the same? Can they reproduce the work (a principle of scientific investigation) if the data sources used have changed between the original publication and the time the work is repeated?

For all of these reasons, it is important for libraries in the digital world to augment their collections policies with an understanding of the new challenges of digital material.

In addition, of course, the original issues of collections policies continue. Few libraries can any longer afford what is called "comprehensive" collecting, meaning that every item of interest in a particular subject area is bought. Libraries must consider their audience. Are the patrons secondary school students needing introductory texts? Undergraduate students who need a variety of standard works? Or postgraduate students and scholars who want the most detailed material available? Vice President Gore was fond of suggesting that in the future a schoolgirl in Carthage, Tennessee, will connect to the Library of Congress. Any schoolchild might feel overwhelmed by the riches of that library; how will librarians provide some guidance, and will those librarians be in Tennessee or Washington DC?

Just collecting material that has been on paper is not enough. Digitally, we are now seeing online journals that are not and never were printed. Some of these are published by professional societies with the same kind of refereeing and editing that apply to the printed journals of those societies. Among the earliest known was *Psycoloquy*, published by the American Psychological Association, and *PostModern Culture* (University of Virginia). These are expected to be the equivalent of print publications in quality and deserve equal consideration in libraries. Now many commercial publishers also issue online-only journals.

For many items, a digital version will be a substitute for the original and will be all the user needs. For other areas, the digital version is only used to find items that the user will then look at in original form. Which items fall in which category? In general, the answer depends on whether the creator controlled the form of the work or not. For the typical printed book, in which the author wrote words but the book design and page layout were done by designers and compositors at the publisher or printer, it is not critical for the readers to see the original form. If digital versions can achieve the same readability and usability, the readers may switch to a digital format. For works such as paintings, drawings, and some poetry, the original author did control the actual appearance that the viewer sees. Scholars often demand to see the original of these works, especially those who study brushwork or other details of creation. With books, those few users who study typography, papermaking, or binding must view original copies, but they are a small fraction of library users. With time and better displays, computer surrogates are becoming more and more acceptable even for limited aspects of artwork or manuscript study, if only to select the items to be sought for examination. Even today, though, the overwhelming majority of library usage is from printed books for which digital substitutes can be used, and for which digital display is preferable to the alternative of microfilm for fragile items.

In the digital world, there are even more kinds of material of unclear status. Although some online journals are indeed edited to a standard equivalent to print publications, there are many mailing lists and other online files which have a variety of intermediate positions. They may be totally unrefereed, with content ranging down to the graffitti scratched into bathroom doors, moderated with more or less effectiveness, or actually selected and edited into high-quality digests of information. Some of these may be of great value to the library's users, perhaps only for a short time, but perhaps long-term. Libraries deciding what should be available to their patrons need to think about how to handle this material.

Today, relatively few libraries collect this more free-form material. After all, the users can normally get it for themselves, and it is often perceived as only marginally significant. We are beginning to understand the issues of digital archiving. Brewster Kahle has established the Internet Archive as an organization which sweeps and saves the Web regularly; several national libraries are also beginning to consider or implement saving Web material. More recently the National Archives of the UK (better known under the name of its largest part, the Public Record Office) have started a UK Web Archiving Consortium for UK government websites (see www.webarchive.org.uk), and a similar effort exists in Australia under the name Pandora. Libraries are likely to want to preserve digital information, but have not figured out how to coordinate this or how to pay for it.

A group of northern European national libraries has begun the job of collecting Web material, particularly in their national libraries. Hakala (2001) describes the efforts of the Royal Library in Stockholm, starting in 1996, to gather Web material in Swedish as part of their general collecting efforts. A consortium named NEDLIB has followed up and now includes harvesting of Web pages by the national libraries of Finland, Iceland, and the Netherlands. More recently a group of larger national libraries, including those of Britain, France, and Italy, has begun to explore Web archiving of their material. Such projects carry tension between the desire to select particularly interesting pages and the economy of just gathering everything, without manual selection. Sometimes they also raise fears that even a national library might need permission from the copyright holder to collect and save Web pages; in countries such as Denmark, Finland, and Norway the legislature has helped out by providing a deposit rule for electronic publication (see Lariviere 2000).

9.2 Traditional Preservation Problems: Acid Paper and Perfect Binding

What will survive of the contents of our libraries? We have only 7 of the more than 80 plays Aeschylus wrote. Of the books published by Cambridge University

Press in the eighteenth century, approximately 15% have no known surviving copies. Libraries must consider the users of tomorrow as well as today's patrons. Otherwise, what of today will be here tomorrow? Digital technology has completely changed the meaning of this question. With paper, this is a question about survival of the physical object. With digital technology, which can be copied without error, a copy is just as good as the original. The question is not whether the original object will last; it is whether the process of copying can be continued and whether the original bits can still be interpreted. The major issue for preservation is regular refreshing. Even if some objects are physically durable, they become obsolete. Today, one can hardly find a phonograph playing vinyl records or an 8 mm movie projector, and yet both technologies were once extremely common. Moving to new technologies is the only safe answer.

The technological inventions of 1800–1850 were not an unalloyed blessing for libraries. Books became much cheaper, but were made of paper that was less permanent. The use of chemical bleach, acid-process wood-pulp, and alum-rosin sizes all produced paper with a life in decades instead of centuries. Acidic paper is the major preservation issue facing libraries today. Most books printed between 1850 and 1950 were printed on this acid-process paper and have a much shorter expected life than earlier books. US research libraries have about 300 million total books, representing about 30 million different titles. Of these, perhaps about 80 million are acidic-paper books, covering perhaps 10 million titles. Considering books already reprinted, books already microfilmed, and some titles not to be preserved, there are probably about 3 million books that need some kind of treatment.

Other problems faced by libraries include the invention of perfect binding, the technique of gluing books together rather than sewing them. Early perfect-bound books tended to fall apart after use, in a way familiar from used paperbacks. This has not been a major problem in US libraries, which typically bought cloth-bound books; in France, where many books are only sold in less permanent bindings, it is more of a problem. And, of course, environmental problems have also increased in severity. Air pollution has become serious over the last century, and the advent of central heating in libraries without humidity control has not been beneficial. Figure 9.1 shows a sample document falling apart, not even a very old one; it is a 1958 railroad timetable, printed on newsprint.

Historically, the choices for a library with a deteriorating book were to simply put the loose, fragile pages in a box and ask the readers to be careful; or to photograph all the pages and bind the reproduction. Neither is really satisfactory; boxing still leaves the individual pages deteriorating, and replacing the book with a copy destroys the original copy. Some other alternatives, such as putting each page in a plastic sleeve, are practical only for items of great value. Each of these actions was a copy-by-copy solution. What became the

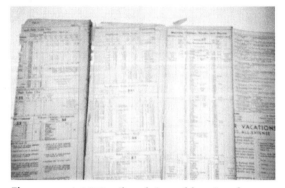

Figure 9.1 A 1958 railroad timetable printed on newsprint.

traditional proposals for a large-scale solution were mass deacidification and microfilming.

Deacidification has been done, on a small scale. Books were disbound and the pages soaked in buffering solutions such as sodium bicarbonate or sodium diphosphate. After the chemistry in the page fibers was stabilized, the book was rebound. This is again too expensive except for rare books. Even sprays that can be applied without removing the pages from the book, but must be applied page by page, are too expensive for general use. The hope is for a gas which could be applied to many books at once; the goal is to reduce the cost to about $5/book. The Library of Congress pioneered a process using diethyl zinc, but this compound is very dangerous and a fire destroyed the pilot plant in 1985. Akzo Chemicals, Inc. eventually did try a pilot commercial service, but demand from libraries was too low to support the work and it was abandoned in 1994. Progress in mass deacidifcation continued in Europe, and prices came down to some $15–20 per book (Pillette, 2003). Even bulk deacidification still has the problem that it treats one book at a time; it is of little use to the users of the New York Public Library that a copy of a deteriorating book at Harvard has been deacidified.

Microfilming is a more promising answer in many ways. Books are transferred to high-quality microfilm, a very durable medium. Typically, reductions of $10\times$ are used, with the book being photographed two pages per frame on 35 mm, high-contrast black and white film. The original filming is always to roll film, although the copies made for distribution to libraries are often on fiche, with about 100 frames on a 4×6 inch (105 mm by 148 mm) microfiche. Microfilming costs about $30/book for the filming, but it is easily copied once made (the costs of microfilming projects often run over $100 per book as a result of selection, cataloging, and overhead costs). Thus, once a book is filmed in one library, the next library whose copy of the same title is falling apart can purchase a copy of the film fairly cheaply. In fact, large runs of books are sold on film or fiche by publishers such as Chadwyck-Healey, at costs down to $1 per book, permitting libraries that never had good collections in some areas to improve them quickly. It is also a cheap way for libraries that want to reach some target, such as one million volumes, to close the gap. Microfilming thus helps distribute works more widely, while deacidification does not increase the availability of copies.

Unfortunately, microfilm is not particularly liked by users. The advantages it provides, namely durability and compactness, are of value to the librarian, not the reader. The reader sees that it is harder to get to a random page, you have to read from a screen, there is no ability to search, and in the early days of film you often had to read white on black. The low use of film also means that most readers are not familiar with the microfilm readers, have difficulty using them, and frequently find readers broken (or wind up breaking them as a result of their ignorance of proper use). Microfilm also suffers from politics. It is much simpler to scan a large number of books at a few institutions than to scan a small number of books in each of many libraries; thus, microfilming funds are more concentrated than, say, deacidification, leaving a lot of libraries who do not see enough local benefit to provide political support. Nonetheless, the United States has for some years had a major effort, funded by the National Endowment for the Humanities (NEH), to microfilm deteriorating books. About 600,000 books have been filmed under the NEH program; all are now more readily available and more likely to survive.

Some 60 million pages of newspapers have also been filmed by NEH; the poorer paper and inconvenient size of newspapers make them even more attractive candidates for filming. This program attracted a lot of attention in 2001 when Nicholson Baker published his book *Double Fold* attacking the practice of filming newspapers and then discarding them. Baker complained that filming lost us the variety of editions of papers, the occasional color illustration (typically comic strips), and the feel of the original. He claimed librarians were exaggerating the poor quality of the paper and that most of the originals could and should be saved. He specifically attacked the British Library for choosing to sell many of its old US newspaper sets, retaining the film copy.

Unfortunately, the paper used for most newspapers from the second half of the nineteenth century is badly acidic, and in worse shape than Baker suggests. Part of the problem is the expected behavior of the users, who may not treat these pages with the care needed to keep them from cracking. Baker embarrassed at least one library into buying a run of the *San Francisco Chronicle*, which they had passed up at the British Library sale; when they got it, this set whose condition he had extolled wound up labeled "one use only." More important, however, is that libraries do not have the funds to save everything, much less every copy of everything. Richard Cox (2001) wrote a reply to Baker emphasizing the constant need of librarians and archivists to choose what to keep and how much effort to spend on preserving it. Even a national library like the British Library has to select what it will keep and in what format. "Keep every copy of everything" is a noble goal, but it is not practical, nor has it ever been.

Libraries also have to worry about material which is not on paper. Today, many images, for example, are stored on photographic film. Black and white silver halide film is extremely durable, probably lasting for hundreds of years. Color films are more sensitive, and in fact some movie companies take their color negatives, make three black-and-white prints through different color filters, and store the result (interestingly, this is the original process for making color movies). Ektachrome is probably good for 25 years if stored properly, and Kodachrome for 50. Although Kodachrome is more durable than Ektachrome simply in terms of years, it does not stand up to repeated projection. If a slide is to be projected many times, Ektachrome will last longer. The failure, in either case, will be fading of colors. For movies, the film stock is more of a problem. Until the early 1950s, movies were made on nitrate-based stock, which is highly flammable. The newer "safety" film, which is acetate-based, is much better, but does suffer from slow creation of vinegar in the film stock. With luck, it will suffice until digital takes over. Early movies, by the way, were deposited with the Library of Congress as paper prints, and many survive only in that form and are now being reconverted to acetate-based movie film.

A somewhat more complex situation is the problem of preserving sound recordings. Libraries have saved scores for centuries, of course. But saving actual performances only began at the end of the nineteenth century with piano rolls, thousands of which survive in the Library of Congress and represent the primary storage medium for about two decades of piano playing. Technology soon changed to wax cylinders; the Library of Congress has some 25,000 of them. This exemplifies the problems with new technology. Both the piano rolls and the wax recordings are reasonably durable if not played, but there is almost no equipment left in the world that can play them. The Library of Congress is forced to preserve not just the recordings, but the machinery as well.

Of course, sound recording then moved on to vinyl and tape. These pose widely different kinds of preservation issues. Vinyl recordings, if not played, are quite durable, but they are very vulnerable to damage (scratching) when played. Magnetic tape, by contrast, is sensitive to temperature and humidity and is not very durable under the best circumstances. Yet it is very widely used for sound recording, not just by commercial cassette producers, but by libraries collecting oral histories and such material. The problems in the United States are aggravated by the lack of a legal deposit requirement for sound until the 1970s. As a result, many early recordings are not in the Library of Congress and need to be sought in other collections.

More recently, in turn, vinyl records have also become obsolete. The current technology is the audio CD. Audio CDs are durable and digital, almost an ideal solution from the standpoint of a library. However, given the history of sound recording, libraries must also worry about the future obsolescence of CDs. Also, as with the readers who wish to hang on to the smell and feel of paper, there are audiophiles who claim that analog sound has some quality that makes it better than digital.

CDs, like every other kind of storage that requires a playback machine, could in principle become unreadable while still appearing to be in good shape. The problem of knowing the state of a collection, previously only requiring visual inspection, for many kinds of material now requires some kind of sampling and playback. CDs, fortunately, are very durable. Short of idiots scratching labels into them with diamond markers, they are not likely to become unreadable.

They might, of course, be supplanted by some other kind of storage. Libraries somewhere have 8-track tape, wire recordings, and the visual format used on sound movies. Today, we have the DVD with 10 times the capacity of a CD and about the same production cost. Does this mean that the Library of Congress will need to have engineers repairing CD players in a hundred years?

It should not need to. CDs, unlike all the previous formats except player piano rolls, are digital. So a copy should sound exactly the same, and it should not matter whether a library keeps the original or migrates to a new format. And yet, one might think that vinyl records could be discarded when the same performance is available on CD, but there are people still attached to the vinyl. Will there be people in the future who develop an emotional attachment to the physical form of CDs?

9.3 Digitizing Special Collections and Archives

Libraries also house much material that is not in the form of traditional printed books and serials. Among the most common special collections in libraries are printed and recorded music (discussed in the last section), maps, manuscripts, rare books, drawings, advertisements, photographs, and slides. Newer kinds of special collections may include videotapes or oral histories; older kinds might be papyri, Inca quipu, and any other kind of material recorded on something other than paper. Figure 9.2 shows examples of different scanned items.

An important issue with special collections is that they may not be cataloged down to the individual item level. Collections of photographs, for example, may simply be placed in folders at the level of perhaps 100 photos per folder, and the entire folder given a catalog record. For example, the National Air and Space Museum (Smithsonian) issued a videodisk on the history of aviation which had

Figure 9.2 (a) Fifth design for the US Capitol, principal floor, by Stephen Hallet, 1793 (Library of Congress); (b) Letter from Thomas Jefferson to Charles William Frederic Dumas, Sept. 1, 1788 (Library of Congress); (c) Notebook page, draft of application to Carnegie Foundation by Charles Sanders Peirce, 1902 (Harvard University Library); (d) Gen. William Tecumseh Sherman, photograph by Matthew Brady, 1865 (Library of Congress).

(d)

Figure 9.2 Continued.

a few hundred pictures under the label *Amelia Earhart.* Some of these were photographs of her plane, her cockpit, her navigator, and so on. As a result, one cannot pick a photograph at random from this file and assume that it is a picture of Earhart herself. Collection-level cataloging makes it difficult for the user to decide whether there is an answer to a question in a particular folder. In traditional libraries this was dealt with by delivering the entire folder to the user and having the user flip through it. Digitally, browsing may be more tedious and complex and not serve the purpose.

To address this kind of material in the digital context raises two questions: first, can one digitize what one has now; and second, what new kinds of special collections will there be in a digital world? In terms of digitization, each kind of material must be discussed separately.

1. *Maps.* Although maps can be scanned, they pose a severe problem in terms of size and accuracy. Maps are printed on very large sheets and yet contain

small items that must be visible. A sample 1:25000 Ordnance Survey sheet measures 15 × 31 inches, and yet contains letters (in a blackletter font, no less) that measure 0.75 mm high. Even assuming that the Ordnance Survey would grant permission to scan this map, the scan resolution would have to be over 300 dpi, and given the sheet size it means that the full map would be 4500 × 9300, or 125 MB, of uncompressed data. The Library of Congress has a flatbed map scanner which scans 24 × 36 inches at 600 dpi, 24 bits per pixel; multiplying out, a single scan is nearly 900 MB. Some current maps can be obtained in digital form, but conversion of old maps will be expensive for some time to come.

2. *Music.* Sheet music can be scanned, but OCR for sheet music is not well developed, making it difficult to search the scanned music or arrange for a program to play it. There is an interesting possibility with recorded music: it is possible to produce a score from the sound, which may be more useful for searching. Recorded music was discussed in more detail in Section 9.2.

3. *Photographs, drawings, advertisements, slides, and other graphical items.* These again must be scanned. They pose severe cataloging problems, and it is hard to make flat recommendations for the kind of digitization that will be needed. Photographs of natural scenes, for example, will have wide color spaces to represent, while an artist's pencil drawing may have only gray values.

4. *Museum-type objects: papyri, scrolls, pot inscriptions, bone carvings, and the like.* We really do not know much about which kinds of digital images of these items can serve which functions. In practice, we can imagine photographing them and then scanning them, but individual evaluation is necessary to decide when (as with papyri) the digital image may be more useful than the original, and when the digital image is likely to be only a finding device. Recently three-dimensional scanning has become practical, and we can look forward to museums routinely providing the ability to look around all sides of an object.

Although this sounds pessimistic, there are many successful examples of digitizing special collections. In one early project, for example, Harvard has scanned and converted to PhotoCD some 250,000 posters and similar items from their Judaica collection. This was quite a cheap operation ($2/poster) done by a commercial firm. Again, however, note the particular circumstances. Posters are not made to be studied with a magnifying glass; they are expected to be read at a distance and are printed with large type. Nor do they usually contain subtle colorings. Thus, the resolution of PhotoCD is adequate for them. Posters are also flat and on paper, and, although large, can be handled easily enough if adequate space is available.

Special collections may sometimes be valued as artifacts, which poses additional problems in the digital realm. Unlike most book collections, they often contain unique items, and the items may be museum quality. As a result, the digitization must not destroy the original, and users are more likely to insist that a digitized version serve merely as a finding aid, rather than a substitute for the original. Nevertheless, perhaps more library digitization projects focus on special collections than on books and journals. The uniqueness of special collections also means that libraries don't have to worry about whether someone else is scanning the same thing. These collections are usually subject to access restrictions, and it is convenient to have a digital surrogate that anyone, even an elementary school student, can read without risk to the original. In many cases librarians have been pleasantly surprised by the increased usage of the material, once rarely removed from its safe storage and now readily available; JSTOR (the scholarly journal archive), for example, increased usage of older journals by more than a factor of 10 (Guthrie, 2000; Rader, 2000). Cloonan and Berger (1999) discuss some of the issues involved in digitizing special collections.

In the digital world, there will be new kinds of special collections entering libraries. Libraries do not really know what to do with videotape, let alone interactive computer programs. As scholars want to have access to these items, what will be required? Berkeley (the computer science department, not the library) set out some years ago to recover all the early versions of the Unix system, since the first one widely distributed was version 6. This required rebuilding some old drives to read such media as Dectape, which had become obsolete a decade earlier. Libraries cannot do this in general, but they are going to have to think about what new kinds of digital materials should be considered under the heading of special collections.

9.4   Preservation Through Sharing and Distribution

Libraries, for years, have been vexed by the lack of space for books. In 1902, the president of Harvard wrote an article recommending moving little-used books to an off-campus site (Eliot, 1978). Another option has been division of the burden of book purchasing. Libraries in the same geographic area have often shared collecting responsibilities. Harvard and MIT, CMU and the University of Pittsburgh, and other groups of universities have divided up the responsibility for subject areas. There are now nationwide cooperative agreements for collecting various kinds of foreign publications.

Collection sharing has been backed up historically by the interlibrary loan process. Almost any library is eligible to borrow books from this system.

Online Computer Library Center (OCLC) and RLG (Research Libraries Group) both operate a service using a union catalog to allow libraries to find a nearby holder of any particular book. The delays involved in mailing books from one place to another, however, have made this less than satisfactory for scholars. Furthermore, the book leaves the loaning library for a fairly long time, which may inconvenience the library's other patrons. As a result, in more recent years there has been a tendency to order photocopies or faxes of the particular pages needed.

Faxing copies of articles has been limited by the provisions of *fair use* in the copyright law. Fair use is an exception to copyright that was intended to support the relatively minor copying needed for scholarship and, in some sense, derives from the desire to let people make notes with pen and ink in libraries. For copying to qualify as fair use (and thus not require permission or payment), the law sets down four tests:

1. What is the purpose of the use? Educational uses are viewed more favorably than commercial ones.
2. What is the nature of the copyrighted work? Photographs and music (including song lyrics) are more protected than text.
3. What is the amount of the copying, both absolute and relative to the size of the original work? The more copied, the harder it is to argue fair use.
4. What is the effect of the copying on the market for the work? For example, copying out-of-print books is easier to justify than copying in-print books.

There are various guidelines circulated by libraries, although many users don't seem to adhere to them. The following are some typical limits:

1. Prose: 1000 words or 10% of a work, whichever is less (except that a whole article may be copied if less than 2500 words);
2. Poetry: up to 250 words;
3. Illustrations, cartoons, and the like: one per book or journal issue.

For libraries requesting photocopies from other libraries, the guidelines limit copying to five articles from the most recent five years of a journal. A library needing more articles than this from the particular journal should buy its own copies (or pay copying royalties). All of these guidelines are informal: the actual decision as to whether something is "fair use" remains a judgment call, and courts have the final say.

Dissatisfaction with the amount of photocopying led publishers to create the Copyright Clearance Center (CCC) to handle payments for photocopy royalties. Instead of trying to describe fair use, the publishers simply said that people could make copies if they paid a particular royalty, which is printed at the bottom of each article. Royalty payments (minus about one-third administrative fee) are forwarded from the CCC to the publishers. For large companies that do a great deal of photocopying, the CCC negotiates bulk arrangements and distributes the payments based on a sampling process.

Supplementing library photocopies are the commercial document delivery services. Several companies, such as the Information Store, will find and fax or mail a copy of any article on request. They pay the fees imposed by the CCC, and as a result charge perhaps $10 per article copied. Some libraries also operate extensive document delivery services; perhaps the best known is the Document Supply Centre of the British Library, located at Boston Spa, Yorkshire. However, libraries such as the John Crerar Library in Chicago also do considerable on-demand photocopying. Photocopying is not an answer to the budget problems of libraries, however (Hawkins, 1994); the United Engineering Library in New York was unable to support itself that way, despite a large journal collection.

In the digital world, shared collecting, like everything else, is going to become more complex. Since libraries will often be purchasing not just or not even a copy, but access rights to something that may or may not be on their premises, what rights will they have to redistribute it to other libraries? In CD-ROM sales, the library typically has no right to network for off-site use. Publishers will prefer to have no off-site use, of course. Under these circumstances, can libraries share collecting at all? Remember that shared collecting is not just a way of saving money on purchasing books; it is also a way of saving money on deciding what to purchase and on cataloging. Even if publishers offer libraries pay-by-the-use arrangements that promise low cost for access to a rarely used publication, this will not reduce the library's cost in deciding whether it needs this publication or whether it is worth cataloging.

Sharing for preservation is an attractive solution for digital materials. Digital copies are just as good as originals, so it really does not matter which copy survives as long as one copy does. If the copies are widely distributed organizationally, geographically, and in terms of technology, there can be great resistance to loss, whether the threat is failure of a disk drive, an earthquake or other physical damage to a building, or the economic failure of a library organization. If the material is in heavy and wide use, it is even possible to use multiple copies as a way of providing service.

Several groups are developing software to make it easy for libraries to share files as a way of providing backup. The common thread of these projects is that they keep track of which files are stored in which place, run checksums to verify that they are the same, and, if a file is found missing, replace it with a copy brought from somewhere else. Such systems can be designed so that when a library upgrades a computer, they can simply throw away the old disk and plug in a new one; the system will automatically realize that this machine is missing some files it is supposed to have and replenish them.

Perhaps the most interesting such project is the LOCKSS project at Stanford and Sun, run by Vicky Reich and David Rosenthal (2001). LOCKSS considers the problem of one of the participants to a library consortium behaving maliciously and answers it in a surprising way: by running more slowly.

LOCKSS considers the danger that a library, in the process of sharing files, will try to destroy some item (imagine, for example, the National Library in Teheran wishing to get rid of all the works of Salman Rushdie). Could it do so by sending out repetitive notices that it has a newer and better version of some file, and replacing the ones everywhere else with something erroneous? Or just by using the system to find each location where a copy of the Rushdie works are stored, and destroying those computer centers? LOCKSS deals with this by using a complex and slow voting system (deliberately slow, not inherently slow). In LOCKSS, it is fast to find a single copy of something; it is slow to find every copy. If somebody is trying to find every copy of something and destroy them, it will take long enough (weeks) that human beings can recognize what is going on and intervene.

The system also employs a kind of peer-rated voting system. A newcomer can't just log in and start replacing files. When a discrepancy is found among different files, the system tries to do a slow, weighted vote in which it polls different sites and sees what they think the correct version is. No particular site can guarantee that it will be chosen to vote on the issue or that its version will be accepted; in fact, until it has a long history of voting with the majority on "what is the correct version of file X," its votes will not be worth much. Thus again, it will take a long time, and a lot of effort, to build up enough respectability to be able to suggest that a file be destroyed, and a single site won't be able to do that in any case.

This strategy has even been generalized as a trust model for computer networks. In an environment where you can't identify a single system as the absolutely reliable master system, but must have a set of systems, all of which have the same nominal status and access to the code, this voting strategy is a way of preventing anyone from introducing viruses or other problems.

LOCKSS has participants on every inhabited continent, and in the spring of 2004 it moved from a research and development project to an ongoing service. More than 100 libraries are now participating in the system, along with dozens of publishers.

9.5 New Materials and Their Durability

Libraries can expect to receive many new kinds of digital material in terms of both format and content. There will be Web pages, created by individuals and corresponding neither to journal articles (not refereed), nor book manuscripts (much shorter), nor most letters (addressed to the world at large, not a single individual). There will be interactive software, including mutimedia CD-ROMs, which is generally akin to published material but is very hard to evaluate for content. All of these objects will have the property that they cannot be evaluated without some kind of machine; and the interactive software may require particular kinds of equipment. Will every library have to collect all kinds of hardware to be able to check whether the material on their shelves is still in working order?

A library with potential patrons who wish to learn a foreign language already has the choice of buying books, CD-ROMs, videotapes, and audiotapes. Shortly, it will have more ambitious multimedia programs on offer: Web pages, downloadable shareware, and priced software. Which are most important? What are the rules for using these materials? Which of these works correspond to textbooks and which to advanced study materials? All of that may depend on the kind of interaction with a user: we can easily imagine programs that watch the responses of their users and adjust from secondary school to postgraduate courses in some subjects. Admittedly, each of these materials could be studied to decide whether a library should buy it, but no library has the time to do so. A CD-ROM is already much harder to inspect than a book; a Web page will be even worse.

Again, each of these kinds of material may have different legal restrictions on what can be done with it. The library may be faced with material that cannot be lent out, but only used on the premises. Some material will become worthless quickly once the technology to run it becomes obsolete. This will pose a hard purchase decision, no matter how valuable the material is right now.

And, of course, the ability to combine new and old material will be vitally important. Just as an example, Figure 9.3 shows an overlay of a map of New England from 1771 with a modern view of where the boundaries are today. The old map was scanned; the newer map is a vector representation, provided by the US Government.

Libraries will have to come to some agreement on the appropriate acquisition policies for digital material. There is already shared cataloging; there may have to be shared evaluation of some of the more ephemeral material. Key questions will be

1. Is anyone else proposing to maintain copies of this? If the material is coming from a commercial publisher, is it likely that the libraries (again excepting national libraries with a preservation mission) can normally expect the publisher to do what is necessary to keep it into the future? Do libraries have a legal right to try to maintain a copy?
2. Has this been peer-reviewed or in any other way checked and reviewed? If not, the default action may be not to spend effort trying to save it.

Map of New England, 1771

Figure 9.3 Current New England state boundaries superimposed over New England in 1771.

3. Are there scholarly references to this material? If so, how are those going to be fulfilled in the future?
4. Can a library obtain legal permission to do what needs to be done to make this available to library patrons? Can it share the material with other libraries?

Many have suggested that libraries should be *gateways* more than repositories for digital material. But what they do not recognize is that in the future, it may be just as expensive to be a gateway as to be a repository, given the conflicting needs of users, publishers, and copyright law.

One enormous advantage of digital information is that much of it can be saved with very little difficulty. Pure ASCII text can be stored very compactly and indexed automatically. Thus, a library could decide (aside from some copyright issues) to preserve the entire contents of NetNews and incur relatively little cost.

In fact, such services are given away on the Internet today (by, for example, Google and the Internet Archive) with, at most, the hope of advertising revenue to maintain them. So we might find that the modern version of an archive (stored, not evaluated, not cataloged in detail) was an electronic pile of free-text indexed messages or Web pages with only an overall disclaimer; while elsewhere in the digital library there would still be serious publications maintained to traditional standards. Gaining prestige would involve moving one's writings from the archive pile to the library pile. The Cambridge University Library, for example, has two catalogs, one for material they select and one for material they receive via legal deposit and consider of less value.

Bill Arms, a Cornell professor with a long history of leadership in digital libraries, looking at the increasingly small cost of storage and the increasingly high cost of selection and processing, has suggested that in the future we may divide material into three piles: one of stuff so obviously valuable that we'll find the money to preserve it carefully, one of stuff clearly worthless that we'll toss, and one of the stuff in between that we'll just keep in its original form and hope that our successors have better tools to analyze it automatically. The last category, he hinted, might be 90% or more of the whole.

Libraries in the future are likely to have both material that has been converted from older formats and material that is new, just as they do today. Depending on the need, either may be better. Figure 9.4 is part of a fire insurance map of Orange, New Jersey, dating from the early 1900s, and Figure 9.5 is from the TIGER map file of Orange. There is a great deal of information in the old map that simply is not in the modern database, and just knowing that I-280 has been built across the area is not compensation. But remember that the TIGER file is automatically searchable, whereas there is no way to find a street in the old map except to look for it by eye. And the scanned old map is more than 100 times as large as the TIGER map. The last century devoted effort to both beauty and detail that we have traded for functionality and efficiency. Libraries are going to have to keep both kinds of data: the new and the old.

Magnetic disks are the standard online storage medium, as noted earlier. They are very sensitive to dust, but the most common current form, the Winchester technology, comes completely sealed. The usual warranty on a disk now runs five years. Again, however, regular copying is likely to be worthwhile. Each generation of computer disks is sufficiently smaller in size and larger in capacity that conversion often makes sense for economic reasons. Figure 9.6 shows different generations of obsolete diskettes.

Until recently, people tended to have online storage, off-line storage, and "near-line" storage. Off-line meant tapes to be mounted by operators, often with significant delay; online meant disks; and "near-line" meant tapes in robot tape handlers. Sometimes optical memory or magneto-optical memories were

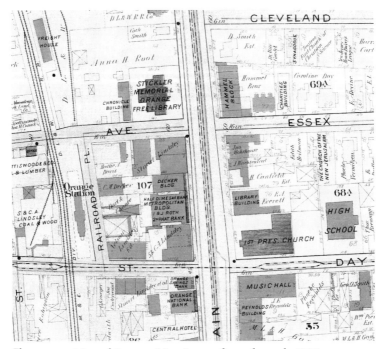

Figure 9.4 Map of Orange, New Jersey, from the early 1900s.

Figure 9.5 Vector map of Orange, New Jersey, from the TIGER map file.

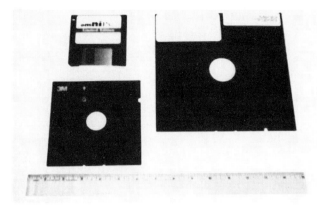

Figure 9.6 Diskettes (8-inch, 5.25-inch, and 3.5-inch).

used as alternatives to tapes. With time, however, all the alternative storage media are losing ground to disk drives. Even a blank CD-R at 30 cents or so is only slightly cheaper than a disk drive; the CD has a price per gigabyte of 60 cents and disks are now at 70 cents. Soon, disks will be cheaper. DVD-R is more expensive per byte, and even tapes are now more expensive (with 20 GB tape cartridges selling for $30).

As we cited earlier in the text, a book such as *Pride and Prejudice* is about 0.5 MB. If we had most of our literature available in ASCII, we could store it more cheaply online than on paper. Although write-only storage is available, such as CD-Rs, many years of attempts to make other forms of optical storage practical and competitive seem to have failed. DVD-R, once a single format is standardized, is the only likely successor to CD-R. Although durable, it can still be lost or destroyed in a fire, however, so some kind of second copy is always needed.

Magnetic tape is the oldest important digital storage medium that still matters to libraries and archives. Magnetic tape is a film of iron oxide on a substrate, originally steel but now mylar; samples of obsolete tape formats are shown in Figure 9.7. How long will it last? Digitally, this is the wrong question. Even tape, which is relatively fragile by the standards of many other computer media, is more vulnerable to technological obsolescence than to physical deterioration. I no longer know where I could find a 7-track drive or an 800-bpi tape drive. Even the newer 6250-bpi drives have disappeared as the world switches to 8 mm or 4 mm cartridges.

As another example of obsolescence, punched cards (Figure 9.8) were made from quite strong paper. Waste paper dealers would pay two to three times the price of newsprint for it. Stored under reasonable humidity, it would certainly

Figure 9.7 Magnetic tape formats.

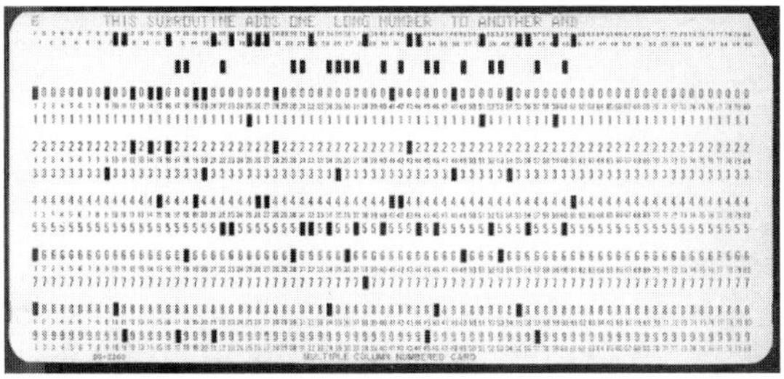

Figure 9.8 Punch card.

last for decades. But today you would only find a card reader in the Smithsonian or companies specializing in rescuing old data. Linear recording, half-inch magnetic tape, since 1964, has been through 7-track and 9-track widths and at least the following densities: 200, 556, 800, 1600, 6250, and 31,250 bpi. Readers for any of the early densities would be very hard to find.

The lifetime of magnetic tape depends enormously on storage conditions. It also depends on the quality and type of the original tape. Helical-scan tape, for example, is less durable than linear recording tape. And tape intended for the consumer video market is thinner and likely to be less durable than tape intended for the data applications. In fact, consumer videotape is probably the worst problem for libraries. It will neither last for many years nor stand many playings, and as video material it is hard to digitize. A frequently advertised service is to take people's 35 mm slides and convert them to videotape. One hopes that the

Table 9.1 Expected media lifetime.

Media	Lifetime (years)
9-track tape	1–2
8 mm tape	5–10
4 mm tape	10
3480 IBM cartridges	15
DLT (digital linear tape)	20
Magneto-optical	30
WORM	100

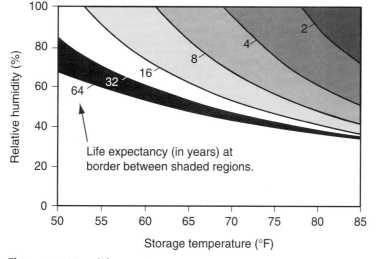

Figure 9.9 Tape life expectancy.

people using such a service know that while the slides are good for decades, the videotape will probably be gone in 5–10 years.

In general, few people rely on magnetic tape for decades. However, if stored properly, computer storage tape will last longer than most tape used for home entertainment. Table 9.1 shows lifetime estimates from Ken Bates of DEC. Perhaps most notable about this table is that virtually every medium shown in it is technologically obsolete or about to become so.

The key to long life is storage at low humidity and low temperature. Ideally, you would keep your tapes in a dry freezer (but be sure to defrost before use under circumstances that would prevent condensation!). Figures 9.9 and 9.10

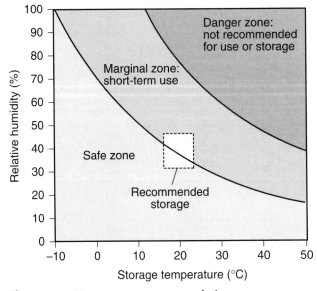

Figure 9.10 Tape storage recommendations.

show expected tape life and advice for the best storage conditions (Van Bogart, 1995).

Perhaps the most important thing to remember about durability of digital information is that permanence depends on copying. The devices used to store digital information become obsolete quickly. Where today is a paper-tape reader, a punched-card reader, a reader for 8-inch floppies, or a DEC tape drive? Libraries must expect to have to copy material in a few years whether or not the physical media are durable.

Here are some of the hardware formats that have existed over the life of computers:

- floppy disks in 8-inch, 5.25-inch, and 3.5-inch size
- digital linear-recording mylar-based magnetic tape, 1/2 inch, in densities of 200, 556, 800, 1600, and 6250 bpi
- punched paper cards (rectangular hole and round-hole) and punched paper tape
- digital helical-scan, mylar-based magnetic tape in 4 mm and 8 mm
- various linear tape cartridges such as 3480, QIC (quarter-inch cartridge), and DLT
- magnetic tape and disk jukeboxes (IBM datacell, digital video jukeboxes)
- removable cartridges for various kinds of large magnetic disks (IBM 2314, DEC RK05, RP05)

- magneto-optical cartridges (mostly 5.25 inch but some 8.5 inch and 3.5 inch), in several styles
- WORM optical storage, some 12-inch, some 5.25 inch
- CD-ROM and CD-R media
- DVD writeables in several incompatible formats

Hardware lifetimes seem to be typically 5 to 10 years. Even if the medium you have is not completely obsolete, it may still pay to abandon it. Why should a library store 1600-bpi, 1/2-inch reels which hold 46 MB in 140 cubic inches, when it can store 8 mm cartridges which hold 5 GB in 5.5 cubic inches? Instead of 1/2 GB per cubic foot, the library can hold 1000 GB per cubic foot. It is not the shelf space that matters so much, but the lower handling costs. The new cartridges are also easier and faster to load, as well as taking less time to get off the shelf. Maintenance costs are also higher for old rather than new equipment and may rise as the old stuff goes off the market. And even if a library wishes to try to keep old equipment running, eventually the lack of spare parts will do it in.

What is even worse than the variety of hardware formats is the plethora of software formats. There are many more software formats than there are hardware manufacturers, and they have flourished for even shorter times. Table 9.2 shows the word processing programs advertised in a 1985 issue of *Byte*, compared with those advertised in 1995, and those reviewed in 2004. Now in 2004, Microsoft Word is almost totally dominant, with some 90% of the office tools market belonging to Microsoft Office and its subprograms (Worthington, 2004).

Dealing with old software is even worse than dealing with old hardware. There are many more software formats, and they come and go much more rapidly than do hardware formats. Software formats may be extremely complex, even

Table 9.2 Word processing software advertised.

For Sale in 1985		For Sale in 1995		Available 2004	
Wordstar	PFS:write	Microsoft Word	Clearlook	Microsoft Word	OpenOffice Writer
Leading Edge	Samna	Lotus Word Pro	Wordperfect	Wordperfect	Appleworks
Multimate	Wordperfect	DeScribe	Accent Professional	Lotus Wordpro	
Microsoft Word	Xywrite	Nota Bene	Xywrite	Abiword	

deliberately so (to keep people from switching to competitors' products). They might be kept running by simulation on modern machines, and some work of this sort has been done. A full emulation for the PDP-10 exists, for example, to rescue the old software for it (including nearly everything done in AI research in the 1970s, for example). But in general, we will need to convert old formats to new formats, preferably standard ones (Born, 1995; Frey, 2000). This may not be easy. For example, Microsoft Word 6.0 would not read a Microsoft Word 1.0 document. Word 3.0 would, however, and Word 6.0 was able to read Word 3.0, so if the library had saved the intermediate program, the conversion could have been done.

The image world is actually in better shape than the ASCII world, however, since there are more accepted standards for images. In text representation, not only are the older formats obsolete, but they may have different capabilities than newer software. For example, the EBCDIC and ASCII character sets have different characters in them: EBCDIC has no curly braces ({}), and ASCII does not have the hook character for "logical not" (¬). The collating sequences changed so that putting a file in order means something slightly different. More recent word processor languages have introduced still more capabilities. Suppose a library has a catalog prepared in the 1960s. It is unlikely to have accent marks indicated for foreign titles. Should those now be inserted? The amount of work required to do that will far exceed any other costs in preserving the old title list, and may in fact be more work than redoing the entire job.

The worst situation of all is in databases. Commercial database systems change even more than image or text languages, and there is less context from which to decide what something means without the program or the database schema. A document with the formatting commands garbled may still be worth something. A table of numbers without the labels is essentially worthless. And the job of editing a database to move it to standard relational format can be immense; again, depending on what was in the original database, there may be undecidable issues requiring reference to some other source of information.

The message, of course, is to use standard formats. Refreshingly, SGML is likely to be straightforward by comparison with Wordperfect. Similarly, JPEG is going to be readable in the future. Since these formats are described in public sources, at a minimum you could always write your own program to read them. This may not be true of proprietary formats. We may find ourselves with a new kind of professional, a "digital paleographer," who specializes in understanding the formats used by bankrupt software vendors.

Fortunately, the costs of copying are decreasing rapidly. If we assume a 50% decrease in cost every five years, then any long-term cost for data migration is small compared with the cost of the first copy. The key to survival of digital information is systematic and regular copying, not air conditioning.

9.6 **Emulation as a Preservation Technique**

Emulation has recently come back as a technique for preserving old files. Among its advantages are

- There are relatively few hardware platforms to emulate, compared with the number of software programs and software formats.
- Commercial secrecy is making it difficult to find out the formats of many programs so that they can be converted.
- Program behavior can be very hard to understand and imitate; running the old code is easier.
- When you improve the emulator for a device, every piece of software you are trying to save on it improves at once.

Emulation, in fact, links well with the strategy of "Just save the bits and hope our successors can do something with them." The great disadvantage of emulation was the difficulty of actually making a faithful copy of an old machine. The reason it is becoming more attractive is the demonstration, by Jeff Rothenberg (1998) and others, that it can be done.

This demonstration was done on a particularly embarrasing example of technological obsolescence. In 1985, in honor of the 900th anniversary of Domesday Book, the BBC decided to make a modern version. Domesday Book was a survey of England undertaken by William the Conqueror to see what it was that he had conquered and help in its administration; it is a more detailed census than was done again for centuries. The BBC decided to recruit secondary school students from all over the United Kingdom to record the facts about their home villages and towns, but then it put the results on a 12-inch video disc. This format became obsolete almost immediately and hardly anyone was able to see the results of their work. Cynics noted that the original book, written with pen and ink on parchment, was still readable in the Public Record Office 900 years later; this computer version had become unusable in only a few years. The BBC decided to try and recover the computer Domesday (Finney 1996). The problem was not so much to copy the information to another medium; the problem was that the entire access system was written for a BBC computer that was no longer made. A team from the CAMILEON project (Mellor 2003) had to both copy the laser disks and write software to imitate the behavior of the microcomputer. They found laserdisk players that worked well enough to recover the information and write it on conventional disk drives (this only has to be done once). They also were able, remarkably, to write a Windows program that emulates the behavior of the 1980s microcomputer and thus can run the software that originally controlled the disk.

Unfortunately, as is true so often in this book, legal problems now arose. The BBC finds itself with a working computer system that displays the content of the new book, but it can't distribute it or post it on the Web, since nobody could have predicted what would happen and secured the correct copyright transfers and permissions in advance. It appears that only those who possess a copy of the original, technically useless disk will be able to use the new system.

9.7 Summary

We do not yet have collection principles for a digital library. There are no published lists of recommended holdings or details of what a library has to have for university accreditation. Furthermore, a digital library is more dynamic than a paper library; items will come and go more rapidly. This gives digital librarians an opportunity to look more carefully at what is used and what is useful, and to design collections which follow the needs of users more quickly than was possible in the past. The switch to access instead of purchase should leave us with better future collections, not just larger ones.

The problems of editing older formats to create current documents are harder. If the old format has some property which it is hard to convert to the newer format, how much effort should be spent trying to imitate or emulate it? Is it better to preserve the actual appearance of the older format, or its spirit? These issues resemble some of the preservation issues we have always faced in other areas. What should be saved under the heading "Beethoven's Ninth Symphony"? The score? A studio recording? Or a live performance with audience reaction? We can go to a church that existed in Bach's day and perform one of his keyboard works on the organ using seventeenth-century performance techniques. The result will be sound waves almost the same as those Bach's listeners would have heard. But the impression will be different. To our ears, the organ is not the standard keyboard instrument, and it will always sound old compared to the piano and the keyboard synthesizer. And Bach is no longer the most recent composer; we have heard Beethoven, Brahms, and the Beatles. Many of the same issues will arise in digital preservation: are we trying to produce the best possible copy of the old object or something that will serve the same function to a modern reader or audience? Homer is certainly valuable in ancient Greek, but may be more useful in a translation. At times we may not be able to do anything satisfactory. We do not know what a David Garrick stage performance was really like, nor an oration by Cicero. And what should we do to preserve the work of Julia Child or Jacques Pepin? Print their recipes? Videotape their cooking? Freeze-dry the food? Or take a gas chromatograph trace of the smell?

10 Economics

We still haven't figured out how to pay for supplying information to digital libraries. Steve Harnad writes that "making the refereed journal literature in all disciplines on-line and free for all, with no financial firewalls, is the optimal and inevitable solution for science and scholarship." By contrast, Floyd Bloom, while editor of *Science*, wrote that "neither the public nor the scientific community benefits from the potentially no-holds-barred electronic dissemination provided by today's internet tools. Much information on the Internet may be free, but quality information worthy of appreciation requires more effort than most scientists could muster, even if able." Is free information good or not? If, like traditional library services, digital libraries should be free, how will the money be found to pay for at least the transition, even if the eventual digital-only service becomes cheaper than what we do today? This chapter will review the ideas and experiments for supporting online digital information.

Economic justification for libraries has been hard to achieve. The economies of scale in publishing and in libraries make it hard to come up with suitable prices; cutbacks in subscriptions lead to higher prices and then more cutbacks in an unstable spiral. Libraries have rarely been able to use cost-recovery pricing, partly because it is difficult to find fair prices when a university library may have some users who are students on meagre budgets, while other users have ample research grants. Over the years, publishing has increased its economies of scale significantly, and digital publishing is making those economies even larger. Many of the publications shelved contain scholarly articles written by authors who are not paid in money, and often the referees and editors are also volunteers; this creates resistance to the expense of the publications and a tendency to cast commercial publishers as scapegoats. University presses, however, also have to charge high prices and are usually not making a profit even then. Some hope that digital information distribution will make everything cheap enough that the problem goes away, but it isn't happening yet. This chapter discusses how digital libraries can be paid for, beyond the simple issue of whether they can simply be cheaper than the paper libraries we have had until now. This is not really about libraries; it is about the sale of digital information in general, not just to and by libraries.

Harnad and his friends argue that digital information is so cheap that information distribution should not be a problem. For example, looking at the Association of Research Libraries (ARL) statistics for large libraries, their cost per book-year is in the range of $3–8, and they have 7000–20,000 books per staff position. By contrast, a large data center has a cost per megabyte-year (something vaguely comparable to a book-year) under a penny, and it has terabytes per staffer (millions of books). Yes, storage is cheap, but it is in libraries as well. A simple book depository has perhaps 20% of the cost of a typical library. If storage were all that mattered to libraries, we'd have gone to microfilm decades ago.

To confuse matters, the job of libraries is expanding. Once upon a time, library patrons were always physically present in the building where the books were held. Now libraries provide remote access across the campus and across the world. They do fax delivery, electronic displays, and other methods of information access. They provide sound recordings, videos, multimedia, and computer files. They have a tradition of providing access to books for no charge. Should that tradition also apply to these new services and these new users? Some of the new services appear to be filling needs previously filled by bookstores, journal subscriptions, and other paid-for activities. Some might be quite expensive to continue operating, for example, levels of computer support adequate to deal with much modern software. Does that mean that libraries should charge for these services, and, if so, on what basis?

The ability of users from around the world to access a digital library aggravates discussions about funding. The British service named BUBL (once meaning bulletin board for libraries) has only 15% of its users from inside the United Kingdom. Many university administrators ask why their money is being used to pay for services when most of the people using those services are not from that university.

Digital libraries are going to need a new model for funding. Among the possibilities are

- Institutional support, as most of them now have
- Charging users for unusual services, perhaps including assistance

- Charging users for everything
- Finding support from advertisers
- Finding some other mechanism for support, such as pledge breaks on the Internet (i.e., public appeals for donations)

Libraries will also have to realize that there are many other organizations hoping to be the supplier of digital information for a fee; these include publishers, bookstores, computer centers, and other libraries. Can libraries extend their reach into areas these organizations now serve? Or will these organizations extend their influence, cutting back the use made of libraries? The model of a library is that it provides information free, reducing costs by sharing those costs among a community of users. Will that model survive in the digital world?

10.1 Library Benefits

Libraries suffer to some extent because few of their transactions are monetized. Thus, people have little feeling for what the library costs and also have great trouble assigning a value to it. José-Marie Griffiths and Don King have done many studies on the perceived value of libraries (King et al., 1994, 2003). For example, they surveyed libraries in corporate organizations (Griffiths and King, 1993). The typical corporate research organization spends a range of $400–1000 per year per professional employee; a private law library, by contrast, was costing $1500–2000 in 2002 (Rataic-Lang et al., 2002; original numbers in Canadian dollars, corrected to US dollars). If the cost of libraries is compared with what it would cost to replace the library with other sources of information, they report numbers showing a 3:1 return on investment. Table 10.1 compares the cost of

Table 10.1 Cost comparison of company library to no company library.

Cost/Year	With Library
$515	Library subscription cost
$95	Library
$840	Professionals finding cost
$4100	Professionals reading cost
	No Library
$3290	Getting document
$840	Professionals finding cost
$4100	Professionals reading cost

Item	Cost to Acquire	Savings Reported	
Journal article	$37	$310	
Book	$83	$650	
Technical report	$77	$1090	

Table 10.2 Cost comparison of acquisition of item with savings from having it.

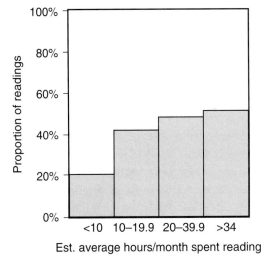

Figure 10.1 Proportion of readings that achieve savings vs. time spent reading.

documents from inside and outside a company (per professional staff member per year).

Based on the numbers shown in the table, they argue, the cost per professional per year would be $3290 to obtain the same documents outside, compared to $610 in a library, or a savings of $2680 per employee per year, greatly outweighing the $800 or so that might be spent on the library. And the information found in libraries does generally benefit the people that use it. Table 10.2, again from King and Griffiths, compares the cost to find different items against the savings claimed from having found it.

Similarly, in 2002 the Minnesota Department of Transportation library computed a table of the cost savings provided by their library, in which they found savings of $191,000 on delivery of 4500 items, counting both the cost of external document purchase and the cost of the reader's time saved; see Baldwin (2002).

King's data (Figure 10.1) also show that those who read more are the more productive employees; and the more people use the library, the more likely they

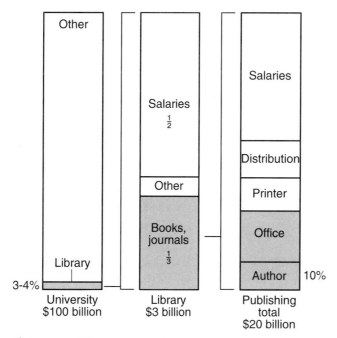

Figure 10.2 Library economics.

are to make savings by doing so. It is commonplace to talk about information exchange as a circle in which scholars write articles which are published, stored in libraries, and then read by scholars. Figure 10.2 summarizes very roughly a financial view of libraries.

The average US university spends about 3% of its budget on its library, with the university establishment as a whole spending $100B per year; this means that about $3B a year goes to libraries. Of what the library receives, about 1/3 goes to buy books, with half going on staff and the rest on computers and supplies (the typical US university does not monetize building costs, which would probably be about 1/3 of the current budget if they were calculated). Finally, of the money spent buying books from publishers, only about 10% goes back to the authors. Thus, viewing the university as a system designed to move information from inside one head to inside another head, there are many inefficiencies in the system. This has been viewed by digital futurists as a great opportunity, but so far neither librarians nor anyone else have been able to improve the system.

The ease with which online information can be found, and the tendency of libraries to provide desktop access to online journals, seem to be eating away at traditional paper subscriptions. King and Tenopir (2001) show that article reading by scientists is growing slightly, but the typical scientist in 1975 subscribed to 5.8 journals, and this is down to 2.8. As a result, the median circulation of a journal has decreased from 2900 to 1900. The average title is read in a library 137 times, while online articles from the online physics preprint server are read 140 times per article each year (it's hard to aggregate these articles into equivalent journal titles).

10.2   Traditional Economics and Economies of Scale

The mantra of the traditional economist is, "Price equals incremental cost," based on supply and demand curves. These curves show the changes in price as more or less of some commodity is needed in the marketplace. As drawn by economists, these curves look something like the chart in Figure 10.3. The "demand" line says that as the price of something goes up, the quantity that people are asking for at that price goes down. The "supply" curve here suggests that as the quantity needed of something goes up, the cost to provide it also goes up. Where the curves cross, transactions take place. As an example of a real demand curve, Figure 10.4 is a plot of Don King's (King and Tenopir, 2001) showing the number of times a week that a corporate researcher will visit a library, plotted against the time it takes to get there (i.e., time is money).

In a supply and demand plot, the price at the crossing point is the cost at which one more unit can be produced, that is, the *incremental cost*. Thus, the economic rule is that price will equal incremental cost. The shaded area is the *surplus value,* or the amount of money the producer left on the table—people would have paid more than the price at the crossing point for goods. If the seller is able to charge a

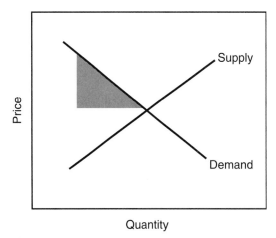

Figure 10.3 Supply and demand curves.

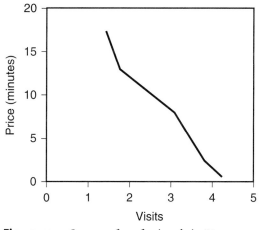

Figure 10.4 Survey of professionals in 21 organizations (N = 73,303; n = 7366).

different price for each purchaser, and can know which purchasers will pay how much, the seller can capture this money. The most familiar example of this is in the sale of airline tickets; airlines use nontransferability of tickets to keep people from buying tickets from each other, and they use rules like advance purchase or Saturday night stay requirements to separate the business travelers, willing to pay more, from the leisure travelers.

All this assumes, of course, that as more and more of some product is demanded, the cost of producing it goes up. This assumption is reasonable for the eighteenth-century Cornish tin mines which Adam Smith was thinking about; as you need more tin, the miners must either dig deeper or dig up less rich ores, and in either case their cost per pound of tin increases. However, this has nothing to do with modern publishing and even less with digital technology. In many new technologies today, we have economies of scale; it costs *less per item* to produce many items than to produce fewer.

With digital technology, the problem is even worse. Digitally, the incremental cost to view something is very close to zero. Even the few staffing expenses that might increase with the number of users in a paper library are hardly there digitally. Worse yet, the ease with which electronic information can be copied and transmitted raises expectations in the minds of users that copies will be free or cheap. This then frightens the publishers who still need a way to cover their average costs if they are to be able to produce material.

In printing journals or books, the costs of editorial, typesetting, and press make-ready dominate. The American Chemical Society estimates 75% of its costs are start-up, and other journal publishers agree. In 1996 HMSO (Her Majesty's

Stationery Office, then the official British government publisher) priced Hansard (the Parliamentary proceedings) at £12 per day, expecting to break even on sales of 5600 copies. The *incremental* cost of a copy was £1.07, so that 91% of the cost was start-up. Similarly, Sosteric et al. (2001) say that a journal with fewer than 1000 subscribers incurs 90% of its costs in composition and editing, with only 10% for the later expenses. If start-up costs are divided among more and more copies, the cost per copy decreases. Conversely, if press runs start to get shorter, the price per copy will have to go up if the publisher is to break even on the book or journal. With electronic information, there is the further difficulty of a low barrier to entry. People can go into the business easily; it doesn't cost a lot to set up a website (e.g., compared with buying a newspaper printing plant). The combination of low entry barrier and low incremental costs often leads to price wars alternating with monopolies; the airline industry is the most familiar example, and US railroads behaved similarly in the late nineteenth century.

10.3 Scholarly Publishing Today

Libraries are finding it increasingly difficult to buy books and journals. The steady increase in the cost of publications as well as the steady increase in the number of publications is outrunning the financial resources of libraries. Since libraries respond to this by cutting the number of books they buy, publishers print fewer copies of books intended mostly for sale to libraries. And that means that the prices have to go up again, putting even more financial pressure on the libraries. Figure 10.5 shows the number of books purchased by United States research libraries, compared with the number of books published (Cummings et al., 1992). The decline of book purchasing has continued: Kyrillidou and Young (2003) write that a typical ARL library in 1986 bought 32,425 monographs for 16,684 students, while in 2002 it bought 30,752 monographs for 19,911 students.

Consider, as an example of the problems caused by the economics of current printing, the cost of *Chemical Abstracts* (*CA*). In the 1950s, the preprocess costs of *CA* were paid by a group of chemical companies; *CA* cost dozens of dollars per year; and individual chemists subscribed to it. Today, it costs $24,800 per year, and even large libraries have trouble finding the money to subscribe. The number of subscriptions drops regularly, as library after library cuts back; and, despite the best efforts *CA* can make to mechanize and become more efficient, the cost of the publication goes up (of course, its size also increases, as the amount of published chemistry continues to increase). Fortunately, many *CA* users are now online, gaining access from institutions that no longer subscribe on paper.

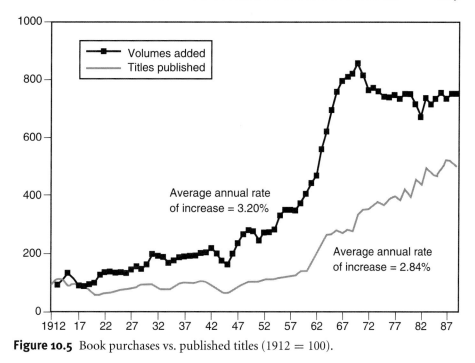

Figure 10.5 Book purchases vs. published titles (1912 = 100).

Figure 10.6 shows the change in journal prices compared with the general cost per issue (CPI). Routinely, journal prices increase faster than the CPI, even in a year when a rapid appreciation of the dollar held down the increase in journal prices from Europe. Library budgets, on the other hand, tend to track general university budgets at best and cannot keep up with steadily increasing journal costs.

Why do these increases occur? Many librarians blame the commercial publishers. Elsevier, which publishes 15 of the 20 highest-price journals (as of 2003), comes in for the greatest criticism. Initiatives like SPARC (Scholarly Publishing and Academic Resources Coalition) try to return more journals to nonprofit status. But that's not the whole answer. The number of journals is increasing faster than the number of subscribers, shrinking subscription lists. Figure 10.7 shows the number of "Transactions" published by the Association for Computing Machinery (ACM) compared with the number of members over the last few decades. Note that membership has been stable, but the number of journals is going up steadily. As a result, each journal circulates in fewer copies, and this is in a field which is booming. The situation for scholarly publication in general is even worse: the typical sales of a university press monograph have declined from 1500 to 200 in the last 20 years. Modern printing technology has enormous economies

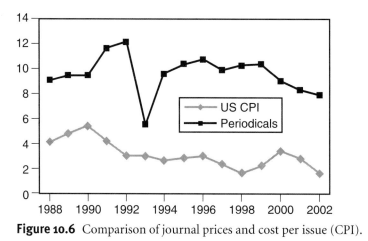

Figure 10.6 Comparison of journal prices and cost per issue (CPI).

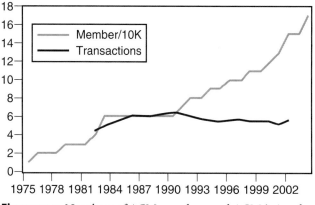

Figure 10.7 Numbers of ACM members and ACM journals.

of scale; to print only a few hundred copies of something is very inefficient compared to longer press runs. Even in the sciences, the number of pages published per scientist have increased 70%, while the number of subscriptions per scientist is declining (Tenopir and King, 1997; Tenopir et al., 2003). This is a recipe for economic failure: more pages to print but fewer subscribers paying to read them.

The number of scholarly periodicals continues to increase, as do their subscription prices. And libraries, faced with increasing expenditures for new equipment, have ever greater difficulties keeping up with the costs of publications. Libraries spend about one-third of their budgets on materials purchases, and few get budget increases comparable to the journal price inflation. As a result, libraries increasingly have less material directly available and get more of it from remote sources. About the only option for a paper-based library faced with price increases that it cannot pay is to stop buying material and obtain it on demand instead.

10.4   Models for Library Funding

Why should there be libraries at all? Harold Varian has described libraries as "buying clubs" in which different individuals, who would like to have some resource but who cannot each afford to buy it, pool their money to buy one copy which is shared. Computers used to be bought like this. Is this an adequate model in the digital world?

Consider one of Varian's examples which tries to take into account both economies of scale and different users placing different values on the same item. Traditional economic pricing may not work out in such a case. Suppose it costs $7 to make the first copy of some object and the second copy is then free. Suppose there are two customers, Smith and Jones.

If Smith will pay $6 and Jones will pay $3:

1. At a price of $3, the manufacturer gets only $6 and cannot stay in business.
2. At a price of $6, the manufacturer gets only $6 and cannot stay in business.

There is a total of $9 available, more than the cost of production of two items, but no single price which is acceptable.

Some other assumptions seem equally frustrating. If Smith will pay $8 and Jones will pay $3, then the item can be produced but Jones will not get one. Perhaps the most counterintuitive is the case where Smith will pay $20 and Jones will pay $8. The most lucrative choice for the manufacturer is to charge a price of $20. Smith pays it and Jones, even though willing to pay more than the entire cost of production, doesn't get a copy. But no lower price than $20 will bring the publisher more money.

Varian discusses two solutions to this paradox: price discrimination and bundling.

1. Some industries with this kind of problem move to different prices for different users. This may take the form of defining different services in a way that leaves the public with a perception that different values are being delivered but still lets the manufacturer gain economies of scale. For example, airlines put people paying widely different fares on the same airplane, and the same Postal Service letter carriers deliver different kinds of mail.

In the publishing business, a traditional separation has been hardcover versus paperback editions. In the context of digital libraries, sites differentiate between local users and remote users, or between authorized and anonymous users, and then limit either the number of connections or the number of requests that can be made by the less preferred users. Other possibilities include restrictions on bandwidth, time of day, currency of information, or amount of information.

2. Another answer, and one historically relevant to libraries, is bundling. Modifying the first case, where Smith was willing to pay $6 and Jones to pay $3 but the production cost was $7 for both of them, suppose there are two such publications. Suppose, then, that for the second publication Smith will pay $3 and Jones will pay $6. Then they can each pay $8 for both publications together, and the publisher can recover the $14 cost. This is what libraries do: they let people who place different values on different items get together to buy them. And, in this set of assumptions, the publishers are better off because the "buying club" is there.

Unfortunately, buying clubs do not always help the publisher. Take the preceding example: since the price was set at $8 for both or $4 for each publication, there is an item for which Smith was willing to pay $6, but gets it for $4. Could the publisher get that extra $2 from Smith? Perhaps the price for the publications could be raised to $9 for both. But what if there is also a Robinson, and Robinson will only pay $4 for each publication? Then $4 is still the best bundled price; it is not worth forfeiting the $8 from Robinson to get $2 more from Smith and Jones. The publisher can wistfully think that if it were possible to sell specific copies to specific purchasers at known prices, then each of Smith, Jones, and Robinson could be charged the maximum they are willing to pay. In terms of the supply and demand diagram (see Figure 10.3), the entire surplus value could be captured by the manufacturer.

In our discussion, we have assumed that each of the buyers is going to get a copy of the publication. Of course, with libraries the number of copies bought is generally less than the number of patrons interested, since they are sharing the copies by borrowing them. Public libraries started as a commercial business in the United Kingdom in the second quarter of the eighteenth century, as a way of loaning copies of such books as *Pamela* and other novels. Eighty percent of the rentals then were fiction, and 76% are fiction today. Partly this reflects the public desire for entertainment (documentaries do not typically outnumber features at the cineplex); partly it reflects the unlikelihood that mystery novels will be reread. The smaller the chance that a reader will want to go through the book more than once, the less the advantage of owning rather than renting or borrowing a copy. Even if the library is providing copies at no incremental charge, the cost of traveling to it will still discourage its use for books that will be needed frequently.

The idea that public libraries should be paid for by taxes rather than by their users is a US invention transferred back to Europe. Private lending libraries survived on a fairly large scale in the United Kingdom until a few decades ago (Boots, the chemists, were well known for their lending services). A few examples of subscription libraries still survive (the London Library in the United Kingdom and the New York Society Library in the United States). These, however, charge by the year rather than by the book borrowed, so they are a different economic model. Many university libraries charge nonaffiliated users, although the charge is often more to limit the demand on the library than it is a way of raising revenue.

The private rental library familiar to most of us is, of course, the video store. Prerecorded videotapes started out around 1979 at prices of $90, and some stores started renting them for $5. By 1988, the purchase price was down to $50 and the rental price down to $2. From the standpoint of the movie studios, this was a lot of money slipping through their fingers: people who might have bought a movie were choosing to rent instead. Although the studios tried to discriminate, with different prices for tapes to be rented rather than tapes to be retained by a consumer, they ran afoul of the "right of first sale" doctrine. This rule basically says that when you buy something, you can then do what you want with the physical object. It prevented the movie companies from selling a videotape and then claiming to control whether or not it could be rented. So, in 1988 Disney decided to start selling some of its tapes cheaply ($15–25) to see if they could get more money than they were getting in rentals and changed the market completely.

Again, items that will be viewed more than once are a better candidate for purchase than rental. It is not an accident that Disney is the studio that started selling tapes; they make children's movies, and children are the most likely customers to watch the same video over and over again. Among movies intended for adults, people are more likely to watch a comedy than a drama twice. Hal Varian gave as an example in one of his talks that Hollywood took *Fatal Attraction* and produced 500,000 copies to sell at $89.95 each, while the "press run" for *Good Morning Vietnam* was 2,000,000 copies to sell at $29.95 each. Clearly, the first was expected to be a rental title, while the second was a sale title. Documentaries, even more likely to be watched more than once, are typically sold; when was the last time you saw an ad to *rent* the Time-Life history of anything? As time goes on, the ease of home copying is destroying the rental/sales dichotomy, and video publishing is moving to DVD for sale rather than tape for rental, with the video stores following suit by renting DVDs as well as selling them.

The movie studios also try price discrimination in those areas where they can. Although once tapes are publicly sold, people can do what they want with them (except copy them), there is a carefully staged delivery of the movie. First, it is placed in theaters at $10/viewing; then it goes on pay-per-view at $5/viewing; then to video rentals at $2/rental; and finally to cable TV and then broadcast TV. Intermixed in all of this are hotel and airline viewings, plus sequential delivery around the world. The goal is to find the people who are desperately anxious to see this particular movie and get them to pay the higher price, while still getting some money from those who don't care much which movie they see.

Which model is likely to appeal to the operator of a digital library? Private rental libraries for books are no longer viable, but video stores certainly are. Why? The answer is the incredible concentration of video rentals: 80% of the rentals each week are the top 20 films. Thus, there is a predictable demand for a few films and the sharing of cost works well. By contrast, book sales are distributed over an enormously larger number of titles. In 2000, the United States produced 683 movies and published 96,080 new books. The large number of new books makes it difficult to concentrate demand.

Although the Web has certainly enticed many publishers to think of electronic distribution, few are willing to publish there: "We don't think there is safe commerce on the information superhighway . . . . Until we can be assured of copyright protection and until we can be assured authors and Simon and Schuster will be paid for our work, we are reluctant to post copy on the Internet," according to Simon and Schuster's Andrew Giangola.

There are a great many ways in which publishers might choose to charge for digital material. Donald Hawkins published a review of information pricing in 1989 which listed, among other charging mechanisms, connect time, CPU usage, fee per search, fee per hit, and download fees. All of these have one or another kind of problem: the users may not understand them; the charges may be unpredictable; or they may encourage unreasonable behavior. Vendors normally wish to charge for smaller and smaller units of activity, following traditional economic advice to allocate costs as well as can be done. This minimizes the risk that somehow the publisher will suffer from some kind of gaming behavior in which someone finds a hole in the charging method that allows them to get a great deal of service for less money than had been anticipated. Also, charging many small amounts for small transactions imposes high administrative costs.

In fact, some publishers do prefer simpler systems. Journal publishers, for example, are accustomed to subscriptions. Subscriptions give them many advantages, such as predictability of revenue, a six-month advance on the average payment (for yearly subscriptions), and no problem with bad checks and debt collection. Thus, they would often like to keep the prepaid subscription model in the digital world. The certainty and simplicity are worth something to them. Librarians often prefer these pricing models as well.

The other side is represented by some computer scientists proposing models involving micropayments in which each tiny use of anything would be paid for separately. Nelson (1996), who coined the word *hypertext,* has now proposed the name *transclusion* to describe the process by which people include quotations from other documents. In the future, instead of quoting his words, authors would provide a pointer to them. The act of following this pointer would incur a charge, paid by the reader. As Nelson wrote, "Every document will contain a built-in 'cash register' . . . but the system only works if the price is low. If the price is high then different users will [use and] hand each other dated [paper] copies." In the future, in his view, this sentence would not not appear in this text; only a reference to the file would be included, and as someone read this page, they would pay a small amount to him if they chose to access that sentence. He believes this would change the way we transmit information, or to quote his words, "Open transmedia—unique in power to aid understanding and to solve the copyright issue—represents a vital singularity in the great family of media cosmologies" (Nelson, 1996, 1982).

Ted Nelson was followed in his desire for micropayments by Corporation for National Research Initiatives (or CNRI, founded by Vint Cerf and Bob Kahn), and also by such groups as Marvin Sirbu's NetBill project at CMU (Sirbu and Tygar, 1995), Tenenbaum's CommerceNet (Tenenbaum et al., 1995), and start-ups such as FirstVirtual or Digicash. All believed that a detailed, byte-by-byte charging algorithm is both fair and implementable but failed in the marketplace (Reuters, 1998). A temporary revival with new companies such as Peppercoin also seems to be unsuccessful (Odlyzko, 2003), despite the interesting idea at Peppercoin of processing only one of each 100 transactions, at 100 times the value, as a way of reducing the overhead involved in many small transfers. More serious is the question, discussed by Odlyzko, of whether users want to have micropayments in any form, even if they can be handled economically. Many librarians feel that per-use charging is basically a bad idea, since it will discourage use of the library. There is an old saying, "A month in the lab can save you an hour in the library," but if people are charged for setting foot in the library and not for the time they spend in their own labs, scientists and engineers are likely to hesitate to use the library. Micropayments have also run afoul of a risk-averse set of users; neither the librarians, nor the publishers, nor their readers, seem to want to run the risks of unpredictable payments.

Among the models followed by commercial publishers (Krasilovsky, 1995; Budd, 2000) are

1. Monthly or yearly subscription fees. *The Wall Street Journal* charges $79 for a year's online subscription, for example (much less if you also buy the paper version). This is the most common model, with extensive collections

of scientific journals available from Elsevier, Wiley, Kluwer, and other publishers.

2. Per-minute fees. Once upon a time, services such as America Online would remit 10–20% of the money they collected per minute from their subscribers (when they charged a few dollars/hour) to the online information provider whose information was being browsed. However, this only yielded a few cents per minute, or perhaps $1/hr. By comparison, online services such as Lexis or Dialog are charging over $100 per hour, and in any case this kind of fee from an ISP has died out with the free content on the Web.

3. Bounties for signing up new users. Again once upon a time, the online services, trying hard to grow, paid publishers whose content attracted new customers. In fact, during 1994 Time, Inc. received $448 K from AOL as bounties and only $118 K as per-minute reading fees. This has died out at the ISP level but you now see Amazon, for example, paying a bounty to anyone who refers a book purchaser to their site.

4. Transaction fees for downloading. Publishers selling magazine articles, for example, can charge each time an article is downloaded. Mead Data Central, for example, using Open Market Systems software, sells articles to small businesses for prices ranging from $1–5 per article. NewBank sells back-issue articles from newspapers at prices like $2.95 per article.

5. Advertising. Many websites have tried to survive on advertising; it has proved difficult after the dot-com crash. Most advertising is now concentrated on a few portal and search engine sites.

6. Page charges. The Florida Entomological Society, for example, charges authors ($100 in 2001) to recover the costs of posting their articles online.

7. Cost avoidance. Online information can replace some calls that used to be made to customer service, although this is perhaps less important in publishing. In the computer industry, helpline costs are significant and reductions can easily justify a website (one manufacturer informally claims savings of $4 M/year).

On balance, a great many articles are available online today for free, particularly scientific papers, and a great many more are available for a price. Full-text books are still rarely available online except for out-of copyright works, although there is considerable access to reference works through the paid services.

There have been some suggestions that online availability of information, even free, would stimulate the sale of paper books. John Ousterhout's book *Tcl and the Tk Toolkit* (1994) was available online, and it appears that online readers then often went out and bought the paper copy. The same strategy worked more recently for Eric Raymond's *The Cathedral and the Bazaar* (2001). Similarly, the National Academy Press puts full copies of each of its publications on the Web, and results show that their printed copy sales have increased; the Brookings Institution, and (to a lesser extent) MIT Press and Columbia University Press have followed this idea (Jensen, 2001). On the other hand, the *New Republic* used to put its entire text online free via the Electronic Newstand but gave up doing that, feeling that it was cutting into sales. Perhaps for relatively obscure titles, the online availability helps and for common ones, it hurts; we still don't know.

All of the simple payment schemes run into difficulties providing off-site access to the library material. Obviously, the library would like to do this. In fact, on many campuses which have been wired, the library was often the first general information source for the students and faculty, with the online catalog for the library preceding the online phone book and course directory. But use from student rooms poses increased possibilities for abuse and increased difficulties charging for some users and not for others. Some libraries must, in addition, deal with either traditional or legal rights of alumni or the general public to use their collections; typically, publishers insist that this only applies to those who physically appear at the library building.

A possible model as a solution to this problem is the simultaneous-use site license concept from software. Many software programs are now sold to large organizations on the basis of "*n* people at once may use this program," and the purchasing organization pays proportional to the number of simultaneous users. This allows them to let everyone use a program without perceiving an enormous cost for a program that people only use once in a while; yet for those programs that are so important that a hundred people at once may be using them, the vendor gets a fair payment. Since use within the organization is fairly open (usually enough licenses are bought to cover even busy times), there is little incentive for anyone to cheat (Blyskal, 1983).

The serious question is whether there is enough financial support for the information on the Web. Traditional scholarly magazines are not advertiser-supported. What will pay for the material libraries want? Will a tradition of editorial independence develop on the Internet, or will ads only appear on Web pages that plug those products?

At present, the economic balance is as follows:

1. Connectivity is a business, dominated by AOL, but the people in it see no need to pay any of what they get for content.
2. Content sales to consumers are rare; *The Wall Street Journal* and *Consumer Reports* are the main success stories.
3. Sales of goods are now large but are not providing a useful model for the sale of information.
4. Advertising is dropping off and is limited to a few search engines.

We're still looking for an answer.

10.5 Access vs. Ownership

The speed with which digital information can be transmitted makes it relatively unimportant whether the information is stored in a particular library, so long as that library has the ability to get it when someone needs it. Our earlier coverage of library cooperation discussed shared collecting. In principle, a library in a digital world hardly needs any collections of its own at all; it only needs the data communications resources and legal permissions to access the material its patrons need.

This model also fits well with the desires of publishers to retain control of the material they provide. If libraries do not own material outright, but have only bought the right to access it as needed, then the rules under which they can deliver it to their patrons are specified by the contract between the library and the publisher. For example, the publisher can try to limit the ability of the library to loan or deliver the items off its premises, or to allow use by people unconnected with the school. Just as the libraries see opportunities to expand their "markets" by directly delivering information which had previously been obtained from bookstores, the publishers see ways to bypass the libraries and sell information directly to students and faculty.

The likelihood that libraries will not own information outright raises future dangers. At present, when a library cancels its subscription to a journal, it at least retains ownership of the issues it has already bought. In the future, if all the library has is a license to access the material, when the subscription is cancelled, the library will lose the rights to the material it had previously provided to users. This may not matter much, since the subscriptions that are cancelled are likely to represent material that was not much used. The reverse problem may also arise. When something goes "out of print," will this mean that the publisher no longer supports access to it? If the library does not own a copy, does this mean that there is no longer *any* way for the users to read it?

The idea of the public domain is also in danger in the long term. The law today provides that works go into the public domain 70 years after the death of the author, but no publisher is under an obligation to help this process along. If the only copies of a work are encrypted and the publisher doesn't care to help provide the keys to libraries, then the work is inaccessible, even if it is theoretically available free.

Professor Larry Lessig of the Stanford Law School, leading an organization named the Creative Commons, has argued for the value of a public domain to provide material that can be reused and inspire others (2004). Since items no longer become public by default, the Creative Commons has written some sample legal licenses that will let people permit others to use their work if they wish.

Similarly, the question of legal deposit for electronic-only publications is not straightforward. Many software publishers insist that what they do is not "publishing" and the transaction with the user is not a "sale." They claim that they are only licensing the right to use the software and that the user may not, for example, sell the copy to somebody else when it is no longer needed. And, in addition, if they are not "publishing," then they have no requirement to provide copies to the Library of Congress under the rules of legal deposit. Publishers are anxious to avoid providing these copies, since the Library would not be called upon to sign the usual contract, and thus the publishers would lose control of the copies provided.

Even the temporary contract raises issues libraries will have to face. Most libraries have not historically charged their users, nor kept track of what they did with the books they borrowed. Publishers may also wish to approve of users (for example, an educational discount for student use of a law resource may only apply to students enrolled in the law school, not to other students). And the collection-sharing that libraries have begun to rely upon to control costs may be forbidden by the license agreement.

Licensed access may require per-minute or per-byte charging, which in turn could require a degree of recordkeeping that is against traditional library ethics and which may offend some readers. The publishers are likely to want to have the most detailed possible recordkeeping and pricing, since it will be part of their marketing methods. They will argue, with some justice, that per-unit pricing will make it possible for libraries to acquire rights to access material that they could not afford if they needed unlimited use rights. But the libraries are not anxious to get into the chargeback problems and would rather have the security of budgeting provided by unlimited use licenses.

10.6 Administrative Costs

Economic studies, to be valid, must consider administrative costs. The fear of piracy has introduced enormous problems into the operation of network publishing. John Garrett (Garrett and Waters, 1996) reports that when IBM produced a CD-ROM to commemorate the 500th anniversary of the Columbus voyage, they spent over $1 M in clearing rights, of which only about $10 K was paid to the rights holders; all the rest went into administrative costs.

Many holders of intellectual property insist on maintaining very close control over their work. Irving Berlin was known for choosing which theatrical company would be allowed to perform which of his works. The copyright holder may wish to get as much money as possible, or may want artistic control, or may wish to prevent further reproduction of something now believed to be erroneous or embarrassing (Stowe, 1995). As a recent example, playwright Sam Shepard forced the closure of a production of his play *True West* because he disapproved of the director's decision to cast women in the roles of two brothers (Zinoman, 2004).

Or, even more frustrating, the copyright holder may be hard to find, too busy to answer mail, or refuse to sell any kind of license out of fear of making some kind of mistake with new technology. A class of my students assigned to write letters to intellectual property owners asking for permission to digitize something and put it on a Web page, and offering to pay, only got six answers from 18 letters after two months. And only two of the six actually offered a license. As guidance towards what is actually being charged, in their replies to these letters *The New York Times* asked for $100/month to put an article on a website, and *Sports Illustrated* wanted $250 for a picture. Picture Network International advertises rates of $30 for an image to be used on a Web page.

Unfortunately, the laws are being changed to make the administrative costs ever higher, partly at the request of copyright holders wishing to have even more power relative to users and partly as a result of the United States' bringing its laws into agreement with the Berne convention. Until 1976, published materials in the United States had to carry a copyright notice which included a date and the name of the copyright holder, and the material had to be registered with the Copyright Office. When the United States ratified the Berne convention, it became unnecessary to place a notice on works, and with the next revision of the law it is probable that there will be virtually no advantage to registering a work with the Copyright Office. As a result, a future reader may be faced with documents that show no date and no author and are not registered in any central office. How is the user expected to determine whether the work is still in copyright or to find the appropriate rights owner from whom to buy permission?

In other intellectual property areas, clearinghouses have been used to reduce administrative costs. The best known examples are probably those in the recorded music area. ASCAP (the American Society of Composers, Authors, and Publishers), BMI (Broadcast Music, Inc.), and SESAC (the Society of European Stage Authors and Composers) license large numbers of works for a blanket fee. For example, radio stations pay about 2.5% of their gross income for a blanket license to play all the music they want. Few musical works are licensed on a one-time basis. ASCAP overhead is about 20%.

Similarly, for traditional photocopying of journals, the blanket license organization is the Copyright Clearance Center of Salem, Massachusetts. Although its procedures provide for very detailed per-copy pricing, in practice it is moving to blanket licenses as well, with sampling techniques to decide on the fee. There is now an additional Author's Registry trying to provide low-overhead licensing payments to authors.

In photography, there are large photo agencies that can provide millions of photographs upon request. Among the best known are Picture Network International (owned by the *Chicago Tribune*), Hulton-Deutsch (which owns or has rights to the BBC, Fox, and Reuters archives), the Bridgeman Art Library, SIGMA, the Image Bank, and Black Star. Corbis, which is owned by Bill Gates, has been buying digital rights to many pictures (including the Bettmann Archive and the works of Ansel Adams).

Historically, individual photographers tended to sell one-time rights to their pictures. Thus, magazines sometimes cannot put their full content online because they do not have the right to do anything with the illustrations other than print them once. This has already made difficulties in building online systems for some current popular magazines.

All of these organizations have problems with intellectual property protection that predate computers. For example, the musical organizations regularly inspect bars and restaurants to see if they are playing recorded music without a license. Nevertheless, they seem in better shape than those areas where no standard contracts exist. Furthermore, those areas that have compulsory licensing do not seem to be particularly troubled. Playwrights in the United States, for example, can and do decide which theater companies they wish to let perform their works. Songwriters must allow any singer to record a copy of any song (that has been recorded once); a standard royalty is paid via the Harry Fox Agency. The compulsory license does not seem to be a disaster for songwriters.

In some countries, government-imposed charges attempt to compensate authors for the use of intellectual property in or from libraries. In the United Kingdom, for example, there is a "public lending right" which pays about 4 pence to authors when their books are borrowed from libraries. A similar scheme operates in Canada and paid C\$9.65 M to 13,269 authors in 2002, an average payment of over \$700. More interesting is the tax on blank audiotape which is imposed in Germany, with the proceeds paid to composers. This tax (of €0.0614 per hour of recording tape) yielded about 20 million euros in 2002, only a small part of the total royalties on music, but nevertheless an attractive method for recovering some money for composers and artists (see Kreile, 2002). The United States has a similar tax on DAT (digital audio tape) media of 3%, but not on other devices. Some countries, such as Canada and the Netherlands, tax CD-Rs, with different rates for "audio" and "data" disks; for example, the Netherlands collects €0.042 on each "audio CD-R" but only €0.014 on a "data CD-R," although computers are quite happy to write audio signals onto "data" CD-Rs.

Electronic distribution has moved from FTP sites through newsgroups (and mailing lists) to the Web. Most of these systems allow anyone to send out anything, leading to names like "netnoise" (for netnews) and to Eugene Spafford's likening of Usenet to a herd of elephants with diarrhea. However, the appeal of electronically distributed preprints is obvious: speed, total author control of format, and no hassle sending out paper. Online distribution also provides for the availability of machine-readable data tables. In some areas, such as biotechnology, this is essential, and so that field now depends upon electronic information distribution. Preprint distribution has no refereeing. However, since refereeing generally serves not to reject papers altogether but to route them to a more suitable place (most rejected papers appear eventually, just in another journal), some see this as a minor problem.

And certainly preprint distribution is popular. High-energy physics now depends entirely on a bulletin board at Cornell (until recently at Los Alamos National Laboratory) run by Paul Ginsparg. It has 20,000 users and gets 35,000 hits per day. There are 50 hits on each paper, on average (this does not mean that each paper is read 50 times; some other servers routinely connect and download each paper, meeting some criteria). When, even 10 years ago, Ginsparg felt overwhelmed by the clerical work involved in maintaining the physics preprint service and proposed giving it up, the outcry from physicists around the world was sufficient to persuade his management to give him an assistant (Taubes, 1993). When Ginsparg eventually moved to Cornell in 2001, Cornell boasted that they were acquiring the archive (Steele, 2001).

A problem with such an unrefereed and unevaluated bulletin board is that people do not know what to read. In the old days physicists could rely on *Physical Review Letters* to select important papers for consideration. Now, without refereeing, people tend to read only papers written by someone whose name they recognize. Thus, the use of electronic distribution has had the side effect of making it harder for a new physics researcher to gain public attention.

For academics and university libraries, scholarly journals and monographs are an important part of publishing. These publications usually do not pay significant royalties to their authors; in fact, they may charge them. The authors publish to get tenure or reputation. And the publications are much more driven by authors than by readers; in fact, many are hardly read at all. So many are trying to publish that the number of papers is enormous, most of them inaccessible except to specialists. Figure 10.8 shows the fractions of papers published in 1984 that were not cited in the next 10 years; clearly, much publication is going only into a wastebasket. Harvard subscribes to 96,000 journals and has 2000 faculty members; does anyone believe that the average faculty member is reading 50 journals? Françoise Boursin (1995) reports a 1993 study claiming that 90% of primary journal articles are read by nobody at all; and Brooks (2002) reported a claim that 98% of arts and humanities articles are never cited.

These numbers are, however, contradicted by Don King and his associates (King, 1998; Tenopir and King, 2000) who find much higher numbers of readers for the typical paper. His surveys show the average scientist reading more than

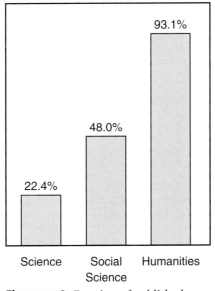

Figure 10.8 Fraction of published papers not cited in 10 years (for papers originally published in 1984).

100 articles per year and an estimate that the average article is read 900 times. This may reflect a particularly low readership in mathematics compared to other sciences. Few other researchers report readership rather than citation; for example, Rudener et al. (2002) find that articles in four educational measurement journals were cited 1.2 to 2.5 times on average.

Hal Varian (1997) also mentions a librarian who cancels subscriptions for any journal for which the cost per article read exceeds $50. Theodore Bergstrom (2001) suggests a rule that librarians should cancel any journal that costs more than $300/yr and more than $1/citation and recommends an aggressive boycott of journals in economics that cost more than $750 (e.g., suggest that the faculty not submit papers to such journals).

We are about to get large amounts of data on actual reading from online publications, and Holmstrom (2004) has suggested that libraries rate journals by cost per reading. He points out that an extremely expensive journal with 1777 readings per article is cheaper by this measure than a cheap journal with only 6 uses per article. Drexel University averaged $3.04 per article reading; Institute of Physics Publishing subscribers averaged $6.11 per reading. Even though the increasing university and scholarly population may be reading more articles, each individual reader can still feel overwhelmed by the amount of material presented.

Andrew Odlyzko (1995, 2001) of Bell Laboratories has written eloquently on the problems facing scholarly publishing, and mathematics publishing in particular. Although there were only 840 research papers in mathematics published in 1870, Odlyzko estimates there are now 50,000 papers each year. A good mathematics library now spends $100 K per year on journal subscriptions, plus twice as much more on staff and equipment. The cost of all the journals added up is $200 M/yr, 35% of which is spent in the United States. This means that the United States spends as much money buying mathematics journals as the National Science Foundation spends on doing mathematics research. It means that the average university mathematics department, if it gave up its library, could have another faculty member. If, as Odlyzko estimates, fewer than 20 people read the average published paper, the cost per reader is about $200. This means that any kind of pay-per-view is out of the question; nobody expects that a mathematician would pay $200 to read a typical paper.

In an effort to deal with increasing costs, some journals began to institute page charges in the 1960s. This places some costs on the authors and, furthermore, helps the journals to balance their costs. Suppose that a journal were able to raise enough money from page charges to cover the initial costs of composition and make-ready; and only charged the subscribers the printing, binding, and mailing cost (the incremental costs). This would leave the journal in an admirable situation: it would not matter if either the number of articles submitted or the number of readers changed. Since the authors were paying the costs proportional to the number of pages and the readers the costs proportional to the number of copies printed, either could fluctuate with no effect on the other. In reality, no journal can raise that much money from page charges, and so the number of pages must always be limited by the amount of money raised from the readers.

Page charges would have another enormous advantage, namely, that they would decrease the incentive for theft. If we imagine a publication system in which the readers paid only the real incremental cost of copying the pages they received, they would be unable to gain anything by cheating (if they can really copy them for a lower cost than the publisher can reproduce them, they shouldn't be wasting their time reading journals, they should be competing in the printing business). Any significant contribution by page charges to the journal cost brings the subscription price closer to incremental cost and decreases the cheating incentive.

Finally, page charges would reflect the realities of the situation. Few scholars are going around complaining that there is not enough to read. But they are trying to publish ever more papers, as tenure becomes ever harder to get. Page charges would reflect the true vanity press situation and put some degree of pressure on people to publish less.

Despite these arguments, page charges are dying out. The problem is that the subscription costs are paid by libraries and the page charges are paid by the authors or their departments. Thus, by publishing in a journal with no page charges, the author can shift costs away from a personal research grant (or department funds) and over to the library. And there is little the library can do about it.

One major effort that is being tried is to create a journal with so much prestige that even with page charges, authors will want to use it. The Public Library of Science (PLoS) journals are an effort to create online, freely available, high-quality journals in biology and medicine that can compete with such paper journals as *Nature* or *Science*. Starting with a grant of $9 M from the Gordon and Betty Moore Foundation, PLoS plans to be self-sustaining by charging $1500 for each article published, to be paid out of author research grants. The Howard Hughes Medical Institute and the Wellcome Foundation, both of which support many medical research projects, have already agreed to pay these fees for their authors, and the government funding agencies have traditionally allowed page charges as costs against grants, although the money competes with other uses of the funds for research. PLoS intends to find ways to support authors who cannot find support for their publications within their institutions, so that the refereeing decision does not depend on whether or not the page charges are covered.

The editorial board of PLoS is very impressive, including, for example, the Nobel Prize winner Harold Varmus. Not only is online access free, but non-technical summaries of the articles are available for the general reader. Paper subscriptions are available for $160/yr, which is intended only to cover the distribution costs. The traditional publishers have replied that $1500 is not enough to cover the article preparation costs; it remains to be seen if PLoS can do an acceptable job for that sum. The first issue of *PLoS Biology* appeared in late 2003, with the first issue of *PLoS Medicine* expected in 2004.

What is not clear is why much of scholarly publication needs to be on paper at all. This is a system entirely under the control of the university; if people could get tenure for online files, they would not need to get their university to pay publishers to chop down forests to distribute their words. Stevan Harnad has led the charge for replacing the entire scholarly journal system (Okerson and O'Donnell, 1994; Harnad, 2001; Walker, 2001) with an all-electronic system. He is the editor of an online journal, *Psycoloquy*. Harnad estimates that the cost to the American Psychological Association of providing journals like his is perhaps 25 cents per member per year, that is, too cheap to bill. Online journals are appearing everywhere, but as yet do not have the prestige of the good paper journals. And, as a result, they do not attract the best papers. In 1993, the Royal Society took a survey and found that authors would not put their best papers in online journals, for fear that they would not get proper credit for them. Similarly, when the Online Computer Library Center (OCLC) and the American Association for the Advancement of Science (AAAS) began printing the *Online Journal of Current Clinical Trials*, in the first year they got relatively few submissions, and little of what they did get was about clinical trials (most of the submissions were self-congratulatory letters about electronic publishing); eventually the journal was sold to Chapman and Hall (now Kluwer) and folded into their product line. Even in 2000, a survey of faculty and administrators at several Florida universities showed 18% of respondents saying that electronic publishing weakened academic rigor and 23% that electronic publications should not be counted for tenure and promotion (Sweeny, 2000). This lack of prestige is frustrating, since the system is entirely under the control of the universities; it is not the publishers forcing people to print things that few want to read.

However, more and more electronic journals are appearing and their prestige is growing. In the United Kingdom, the official research assessment process values online publication as equal to paper publication. When Harvard or Stanford gives someone tenure for an online publication, the balance will tip. Harnad guesses that in around 2010, 80% of the journals in the world will have stopped paper publication.

10.7 Electronic Commerce

How will we pay for information in general, let alone library publications? Starting in 1995, the Internet changed from a research tool to a hive of business activity. Looking at the spam and advertising of today, it is hard to remember that the Arpanet once had an "acceptable use policy" prohibiting commercial use. The dot-com boom of the late 1990s died out, but we still have thriving businesses in online travel, auctions, and the like. But there is still no clear model of how to get rich. Some companies sell access, some sell advertising, some sell stuff which is delivered in the mail and some sell online content. There are well-known failures, like pets.com; and there are success stories such as Amazon and e-bay, and others overseas. In Korea, for example, more money is spent on music downloads than on buying CDs. But we are still seeing a multiplicity of business models.

There are some conflicts between these different goals, since each would like the other services to be free. Those who sell access, for example, would be best off if the content was provided free after users had connected. Those who sell content would obviously prefer access to be cheap. And those who sell ads need the content available in such a way that the ads can be tied to it; the Dilbert comic strip, for example, introduced random names for its files to keep people from accessing the comics without getting the ads along with them. Nowadays people who provide links directly to content without the ads get sued.

Just running a website does not guarantee riches; Time Warner is said to have lost $8 M even back in 1995 running its website (Hill and Baker, 1996). The *Economist* (1996) pointed to arguments about whether sales tax should be charged on goods sold on the Web, and said that it knew the Internet had arrived when it was used for tax avoidance. In 1995, about $300 M was sold on the Web, and in 1996 it was about $500 M (Knecht, 1996). By 2002, the Department of Commerce had estimated "e-tail" at $45B, comparable to catalog shopping.

The largest category of information sold is airline tickets, but all sorts of other goods are sold. The rise of online shopping has, predictably, produced the shopping robot (although some of you may think you already know someone who deserves this label). Andersen Consulting (now Accenture) prepared a program, BargainFinder, which checks around the CD stores on the Net looking for the lowest price on the items you want. Not surprisingly, many of the stores block robots; they want a chance to impress the buyers with their service or stock and not be rejected by a price-shopping program. Shopping robots, however, are common in some areas; electronics stores in particular seem to be more cooperative with them.

Selling connections to the Web is presently more lucrative than online shopping sites. The number of US people accessing the Net has grown from about 30 million in 1996 to about 170 million today; world-wide the number of Net users is about 600 million. Nicholas Negroponte predicted a billion users by the year 2000; that didn't happen, but we might well reach a billion in 2004 or 2005.

Vast amounts of information are available on and distributed from the Web. The Web, as of April 1996, contained about 10–20 TB of text content, comparable to a library of 10–20 million volumes. By 2003, this had reached some 150 TB, larger than any paper library in the world (there is perhaps 10 times as much online material behind search engines and commercial sites, the so-called dark Web). Almost all of this material is still available free. Much of it is posted to raise the reputation of either individuals or corporations. Some of it is provided as an alternative to helplines or customer service.

Some of the more popular content is advertiser-supported. Rates for Internet advertising have dropped steadily; starting at about 10 cents per exposure, they were under 2 cents by the end of 1996 and are now a tenth of that number. Nevertheless, some $10 M per month is being spent on Web advertising, mostly at a few very popular sites. Most library publications, of course, have never been advertiser-supported in the past, and it seems unlikely that they will be soon. Advertising is also not likely to distinguish material on the basis of quality as opposed to readership. Furthermore, the total amount of Web advertising is no longer growing. Web advertising by year flattened off after 2000, as shown in Figure 10.9 in a comparison of predictions to reality.

Subscription sales of serious publications online to the general public are still few and far between. The two poster children for selling information to the

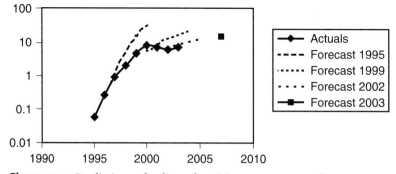

Figure 10.9 Predictions of online advertising revenue vs. reality.

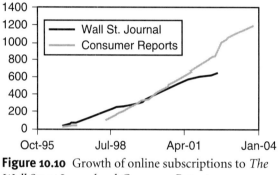

Figure 10.10 Growth of online subscriptions to *The Wall Street Journal* and *Consumer Reports.*

public are *The Wall Street Journal* and *Consumer Reports.* Their sales are shown in Figure 10.10. Each now delivers more than half a million copies, with the online *Wall Street Journal* charging $79/year and *Consumer Reports* $24 (discounts are available).

Although they are selling a large number of copies, it's not clear that either publication is breaking even yet; there's a major problem doing cost allocation between the online and paper publication.

To summarize:

1. Libraries are selling information to each other.
2. A few things get sold to the public, but not much.
3. Nobody has figured out an alternative source of money now that advertising online has dried up.

We're still looking for the answer to our economic questions.

10.8   The "dot-com" Boom and Bust

At the end of the 1990s, a large number of new start-ups attempted to exploit the Internet. For a brief period of time, it seemed possible to raise enormous amounts of money for almost any idea. Companies with no profit and minimal sales were, according to their market capitalization, worth more than long-established industrial giants. Some companies, like Pets.com, raised tens of millions of dollars and disappeared almost immediately. Some of the larger ones, however, are still around. Table 10.3 shows the market values of several companies in October 1999 as compared to April 2003.

And to balance the well-publicized demise of Pets.com during the dot-com bust, Bethlehem Steel, despite having 17,000 employees, $4.5B of sales in 1999, and shipping more than 8 million tons of steel a year, was worth $915 M in 1999 and is now worthless, having gone bankrupt.

Several companies, of course, tried to exploit the idea of selling online information. Among them were netLibrary, ebrary, and Questia. Each had a slightly different business model. Questia had the most books, some 50,000, and tried to sell subscriptions to individual students at $20/month. NetLibrary had about 28,000 books and sold subscriptions to libraries, allowing one person to read each book at a time. Ebrary had 20,000 books and charged per page for printing or downloading (10–50 cents per page, at publisher option). None of these were wildly successful; netLibrary now belongs to OCLC, and ebrary is still in business.

For the amount of money raised by these start-ups (more than $200 M total), we could probably have digitized every book ever printed.

10.9   The Future of Quality Information

When I was learning elementary probability, I was told that if a million monkeys sat at a million typewriters, they would eventually write all the

Table 10.3 Market value in October 1999 and April 2003.		
Company	October 1999	April 2003
Yahoo	$46.5B	$14.9B
Amazon	$27.5B	$11.3B
AOL	$131.4B	$59B (now AOL-Times Warner)
The New York Times Co.	$6.8B	$6.8B
Barnes and Noble	$1.5B	$1.2B
Borders	$1.0B	$1.2B

works of Shakespeare. The Internet has shown that this is not true (Here, I adapt an oft-quoted remark made by Blair Houghton of Intel).

More fundamentally, does the switch from paper to electronics mean a loss of quality? In an interview with *Publisher's Weekly* (Milliot, 1996), Ian Irvine, the chairman of Elsevier, said that the publisher was seeing no drop in submissions to its journals, that it rejected 80% of those submissions, and that the rejected manuscripts are "what's being put out over the Internet," also saying "information you get for nothing (over the Net) is worth nothing." Similarly, Gerry McGovern wrote an article entitled "Quality publishing is about saying no" in 2004, arguing that often the people who have less to say are the ones writing Web pages. And the low quality of the typical netnews group is certainly familiar to most.

The physical quality of electronic materials is no longer at issue. Some years ago, online distribution was associated with ASCII-only formats that could not support equations, images, or even reasonable type fonts. In those days paper journals had a clear advantage in display quality; this has now reversed. Online material can include not only all the usual typography and illustrations, but also color pictures, sound excerpts, and animation. All of these are hard for any paper journal to include at reasonable cost. In addition, online material can be searched and reformatted by the user. The gap in physical quality is now in favor of the online material.

Harnad (2001) and Odlyzko (1995) argue that the intellectual quality of printed journals is maintained by the refereeing process, not by the fact that subscription prices are so high. They believe that electronic journals could have quality equal to or better than paper by maintaining refereeing standards and procedures, and in fact Harnad does this with the electronic journal that he edits, *Psycoloquy.*

What must be recognized is that the refereeing process introduces some delay. Those who like the immediacy of writing a paper this afternoon and having it read in India an hour later cannot have this along with no refereeing. Thus, the fast-reaction bulletin boards are likely to be low-quality. In this context, at least, we cannot have both fast and good information. The difficulty this introduces on the bulletin boards, as mentioned, is that people read only those papers written by somebody whose name they recognize, making it harder for new scientists to break into the circle of those who get attention.

Other changes are likely to result from the fact that online journals do not have page limits. This may mean that editors may become less careful about asking authors to limit what they write. More important, it is likely to mean that prestigious journals, which get far more submissions today than they can print, will expand at the expense of marginal journals. If this shrinks the total number of journals, it might make it easier to deal with the literature, although the prestige value of the best journals will shrink somewhat. Again, we will be relying more on searching and less on editors to find what we want. This is not, however, inherent in electronics; there is no reason why an electronic journal editor could not impose size limits and quality standards, accepting the resulting need to hassle the authors. It just can't be blamed on the printer, the way it is today.

The reverse problem may also appear. There is no reason why electronic journals with low overhead might not accept shorter articles. There are undoubtedly those who imagine that if there had been electronic journals 90 years ago, Einstein could just have sent in the six-character message $E = mc^2$. Then, too, some of them may think their own most recent one-liner is worth sending to a journal; few of them will be right. Fortunately, the editorial overhead in handling very short submissions is likely to discourage this.

As an alternative to refereeing, we might decide to try to rely on the behavior of individuals reading papers, as in the community-rated movie experiment described earlier in the book. If a system permitted it, for example, a reasonable way to select references on electronic libraries might be to read anything Bill Arms or Ed Fox (two leaders of the field, respectively at Cornell University and Virginia Tech) had spent at least an hour with. Whether they would like having people know that much about what they were doing is less likely; in corporate research, it would clearly be viewed as a danger. Whether a technique could be found for anonymously recommending articles that could not be manipulated by people looking for attention is not clear.

What this means is that we can have high quality in electronic journals, but we are going to have to fight for it. So far, there is no automatic refereeing software. In fact, the advent of spell checkers has probably made the serious job of editors a little bit harder, since there is less correlation than there used to be between those authors who have bothered to correct their errors in spelling and grammar and those who have bothered to get their equations right. Achieving decent quality online is going to require the same refereeing and high-level editorial work that is required for paper. Since most of that work is unpaid, it does not follow that online journals have to be expensive. But if the work is not done, we will be back to the "great graffiti board in the sky."

10.10 Summary

Economics is emphatically not a solved problem. Many earlier chapters ended with my facile assurance that we could build workable systems. And certainly the Web has been a very successful way of distributing free information: library catalogs, computer parts lists, or CD titles for sale. But we do not have a way to support the creators of information who need a way to be paid. Nor do they even know what would be best for them. Jack Valenti, in 1982, made an oft-quoted remark that the VCR was as threatening to movies as the Boston Strangler to a woman walking alone; today, movie studios get about twice as much revenue from video rentals as they do from box office receipts. This chapter has reviewed the economic methods used by online publishers today and the hopes for funding the Web in the future. It has not, however, found a clean, acceptable answer.

Economic problems interact with many issues of library collections and quality. Will we find students using cheaper but less accurate information? The cost of printing books placed some kind of floor under the quality of what was printed; a Penguin paperback might not have the durability of a hardbound book, but it would still provide a reliable text. Online, there is nothing to stop random people from presenting totally corrupted texts as accurate, whether through incompetence or maliciousness. And if there is no economic incentive to provide quality material, we may find bad material driving out good.

Similarly, the ability of libraries to gather material from remote sites encourages cutbacks in actual holdings. Will libraries coordinate what is saved and what is abandoned? How do we see to it that the present structure by which libraries share collecting responsibilities and preserve at least one US copy of important works remains? The incentives on university administrations, and thus on libraries, may be to cut back to frequently used material only, and hope that someone else will keep the rare material. I am told that when the Ayatollah Khomeni came to power in Iran, there was not a single copy in the United States of any of his writings, all of which had been published overseas. How can we avoid this in the future, if economic pressures encourage libraries not to acquire books until needed? What kind of pricing will see that both common and rare materials can be created and purchased by libraries?

Finally, economic problems also interact greatly with intellectual property rights issues. What can be charged for is strongly related to the legal rights of the owners of the works. And whether the legal framework is well matched to the economic framework is a major question, to be discussed in the next chapter.

Intellectual Property Rights

Legal issues, arising from intellectual property law, are the most serious problems facing digital libraries. The problem is not that libraries or users aren't willing to pay for intellectual property as much as it is a problem of finding an administratively workable and fair way of doing it. An increasing set of intellectual property issues interacts with our growing technology and bogs down the entire field. This chapter tries to summarize the legal issues and explain what our choices might be.

As the early chapters have discussed, we have a wide choice of technological solutions related to issues of intellectual property law. But we cannot solve the economic problems that arise from intellectual property law. Publishers are too familiar with the destruction of the software game industry in the early 1980s by illegal copying, with the amount of piracy facing the recording and software industries today in some foreign countries, and with the amount of music downloading even within the United States.

A complete range of opinions is available on the Net. Here's one extreme posting from 1996:

```
RHONDA announces its existence in CyberSpace promising to rob
books from the rich and give them to the poor.
```

```
RHONDA stands for Robin Hood -- Online Network Distribution
Anarchy. Like Robin Hood in Sherwood Forest RHONDA robs from
the rich and gives to the poor. Specifically RHONDA intends
to provide the poor with electronic books including classic
literature and textbooks and revolutionary manuscripts and
all manner of text that will help educate the poor and lift us
from our poverty. We will make these works available via the
Internet ... We refuse to recognize any copyright claimed on
any text. "PropertyIsTheft!" We claim the right of eminent
domain on text on behalf of society. Books come from the minds
and mouths of the People so books rightfully belong to
the People.
```

This group appears to have vanished, but large amounts of copyrighted music are downloaded, and the record industry is using both technology and lawsuits to try to stop it. Publishers do not yet see adequate technology to protect their information, nor do they have policies for dealing with it if they did have the technology.

It is normally accepted that protection of intellectual property is necessary to encourage people to create it. How much protection this requires, however, is not clear. The market does not always work smoothly. For example, early in the history of aviation, the Wright brothers had many of the most important patents while Glenn Curtiss, another aviation pioneer, held others. Neither would license the other, so no one in the United States could build a state-of-the-art airplane. This standoff lasted until World War I, at which point the military services realized that American pilots would be shot down and killed if the best planes couldn't be built and forced cross-licensing on the patent holders.

Typefont design offers another interesting example that appears to disprove the common wisdom. In Europe, the shapes of letters can be protected, but not in the United States (although US companies can trademark the font name and copyright a particular digital representation of the shapes). One would think, if the lawyers and economists were right about protection encouraging creation, that all typefont advances would take place in Europe. In fact, they currently happen in the United States (since they are largely tied to laser printer factors).

One thing that most digital library proponents do agree on completely is that creators of intellectual property should be paid for it. The problem is one of administrative costs (see Chapter 10, Section 10.5); that is, we need practical ways of regulating such compensation. History does not show that relying on the owners of intellectual property produces fair and smoothly operating schemes, nor those necessarily in the best interest of the owners themselves. For example, some years ago in a famous case, *Sony v. Universal*, two major movie studios sued to block the sale of videocassette recorders in the United States. They lost. As a result of losing, the movie industry now makes almost twice as much money from videotapes as from box office receipts (in 2002, 46% of theater revenues came from videos, 24% from the box office). How can we arrange the rules and procedures for selling information in digital form to be fair to creators, users, and the intermediaries?

11.1   History of Copyright Law

There are three basic forms of intellectual property protection. These are copyright, patent, and trade secrecy. Trade secrecy (i.e., restricting access to your company's information and making any employee who has the information sign agreements to keep it private) is not of great relevance to libraries. Copyright laws, on the other hand, are of primary concern to digital libraries.

The first copyright law dates from 1709 and was designed to offer authors and publishers protection against pirated editions of books. Traditionally, developed countries have always wanted protection for their work, and undeveloped countries have argued lack of foreign currency, general poverty, and other reasons why they should be permitted to avoid paying for it. In the eighteenth century, Ireland was known for pirated editions of English books. In the nineteenth century, the United States was a major pirating country. And now Asian and eastern European countries are perceived as the main villains.

The United States did not pay royalties to foreign authors until 1891. It started paying them not because Congress responded to the pleas of foreign authors, but because US authors complained that American publishers were ignoring them in favor of foreign writers to save on royalties. This exact scenario has recently been replayed in Europe, where the software companies in eastern Europe argue for enforcement of copyright and anti-dumping laws because they have enough trouble competing with Microsoft at its prices in hard currency, let alone having to compete with pirates.

What has changed from the last century is that it is much easier to export intellectual property. When, in the 1950s, the Soviet Union reprinted *Chemical Abstracts* (*CA*) without permission, they cost *CA* its sales in the Communist bloc, but not its sales in other countries. Now, the Chinese appear not only to produce pirate copies for internal consumption but are exporting to other Asian countries, including places (such as Hong Kong) where substantial progress had been made reducing local piracy. Figure 11.1 shows trends for software piracy around the world, according to the Business Software Alliance (2003). Trends for dollar value of software piracy don't look as good, since the downward trend in percentage of piracy is outweighed by the rapidly growing size of the industry. Table 11.1 gives the estimates for the dollar value of pirate software, measured at retail price.

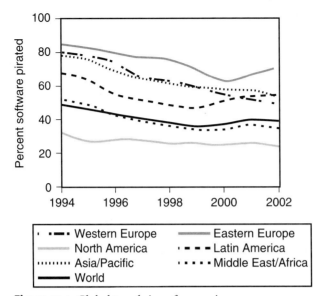

Figure 11.1 Global trends in software piracy.

Table 11.1 Costs of software piracy.

Software Piracy Worldwide (at retail prices)

Year	Value ($B)
1994	12.346
1995	13.332
1996	11.306
1997	11.440
1998	10.976
1999	12.163
2000	11.750
2001	10.975
2002	13.075

Similarly, piracy of music is widespread in many countries. Here, unlike software, the main location of illegal copying is in the developed world, with many students using personal machines for music downloading, as will be discussed in Section 11.5.

Copyright is a technique to protect a form of expression. Its goal is to encourage authors, and it is (in the United States) based in the Constitution: Art. I, sect. 8, lets Congress "Promote the Progress of Science and useful Arts, by securing for limited Times to Authors and Inventors the exclusive Right to their respective Writings and Discoveries." Copyright does *not* protect useful objects. In fact, if something is useful, that would be a legal argument for not granting copyright protection. Nor does it protect ideas, as opposed to the way they are expressed. Copyright prevents other people from making copies of your work, providing a public performance of it, or creating derivative works (translations, movie versions, and so on).

The length of time that a copyright is valid has been getting longer. Under the original 1709 British law, it lasted 14 years. The US law until 1976 provided for a 28-year term with an extension valid for another 28 years, or 56 years total. In 1976, the United States changed its law to provide for a 75-year term on an interim basis; starting with 1988 copyrights, terms here were to match the Berne convention, life of author plus 50 years. Various details in the process for extending the copyright law meant that any work that was up for renewal in 1964 or later would be treated as if the copyright had been renewed. Then, in 1998, copyright was extended for another 20 years by the Copyright Term Extension Act.

In summary, in the United States, any work published before or during 1922 is out of copyright. Those which were published between 1923 and 1963 and not renewed have lapsed and are also in the public domain, as are works published since 1922 that were not copyrighted for some reason. The reason for a lack of copyright may be deliberate; for example, all US government works are in the public domain. You may freely photocopy (or scan) a US Geological Survey map, for instance. Lack of copyright may be an accident; in the past, books published without proper notice, or which were not registered in the Copyright Office, became public domain. Anything created after 1988, in general, is in copyright and will be so until 70 years after the author dies.

In the United States, the flat term (historically, 56 years maximum) meant that only a few creators lived to see valuable compositions pass into the public domain (Irving Berlin and *Alexander's Ragtime Band* comes to mind as a notable exception). This was not true in Berne countries, which already had a life + 50 rule. So, for example, the stories of Conan Doyle were, under that law, public domain in the United Kingdom in 1980 (since Doyle died in 1930), but only those works published before 1923 were public domain in the United States. Conversely, *Caesar and Cleopatra* (written in 1899) is public domain here but is still under copyright in the UK, since Shaw died in 1950. When the United States joined the Berne convention in 1988, it joined with Europe in counting from the author's death rather than the date of publication.

The extension act of 1988 meant that, instead of another year's worth of books becoming public domain each year, the threshold for possible copyright would stay at 1923 for two more decades. The copyright rule becomes 95 years from date of publication, and the eventual rule, aligning with Berne, will be life of author plus 70 years. Pamela Samuelson has pointed out that not even Congress would believe a more generous copyright law would encourage authors who have been dead for 50 years to produce more works. At least in the United States, books already in the public domain stay there. In the United Kingdom, the corresponding law was applied even to works already public, so that Conan Doyle's writings were *again* copyrighted in the UK (although they are now public domain again).

The US proposed law revision also contains several other changes to the advantage of the copyright holders. The need to provide notice on a publication is gone, and virtually all incentives to register the copyright will disappear. The publishers are trying to arrange digital distribution so that it is *not* called "publication," since that will incur the obligation to deposit copies in the Library of Congress and the allowance of fair use rights. If digital distribution is called either "performance" or something new, neither of these burdens will be placed on the publishers.

There was a major court challenge to the copyright extension as it referred to old books, in the case of *Eldred v. Ashcroft.* Eldred, an Internet republisher of public domain books, sued to invalidate the copyright extension. Larry Lessig of Stanford Law School argued for him that the extension with respect to retroactive works could not possibly encourage more creativity or publishing in 1925 and thus did not fulfill the constitutional mandate that the purpose of copyrights and patents is to encourage authors and inventors. The Supreme Court felt that Congress had the discretion to do this; an argument that seemed to weigh heavily with them was that by Lessig's logic, even the 1976 extension of copyright would have been unconstitutional.

More important to digital libraries is the relation of the new law to digital transmission. The law defines any digital transmission as copying so that, for example, a purchaser of an electronic copy of a text is not allowed to pass it on to somebody else (unless this is done by handing them a physical object). Compared to the current rights available under the "first sale" doctrine, this will be very restrictive. There will also be no digital fair use. Thus, viewing a Web page will be the same as making a copy, and the copyright holder will have the right to refuse to let you do that (Samuelson, 1995).

The law revision did give libraries the right to do digital copying for preservation purposes. Under the previous law, libraries could only make analog copies (photocopies, microfilm, fax) to replace deteriorating books; now they can make digital copies (assuming that they cannot find a replacement copy on the market). However, even for books long out of print and of no commercial value, there is still no easy way to legally copy them for other libraries. Professor Larry Lessig of Stanford has suggested that we return to the idea of renewing copyrights, with a potentially long series of renewals covering a long enough span of years to satisfy the publishers, but with some action needed every few years so that material of no economic importance would go into the public domain. Unfortunately, he has little support in the publishing or entertainment businesses.

A major change that did go in the direction of loosening copyright control came from the Supreme Court in 1991. Historically, copyright was viewed as a way of protecting creative work. In addition, however, a tradition had arisen of protecting intellectual work in general, even if it was not creative. This was called the "sweat of the brow" standard; if somebody did enough work, they were entitled to protection for it. However, nothing in the laws as passed by Congress enabled protection for noncreative effort, and in 1991 the Supreme Court (*Feist Publications, Inc. v. Rural Telephone Service Co.*, 111 S.Ct. 1282) held that, sympathetic as they were to somebody who spent a lot of effort piling up some data, if there was no creativity involved, it was not protectable. The *Feist* case involved white pages telephone directories, and the Supreme Court felt that alphabetizing names was not creative enough. As a result, telephone books in the United States became fair game, and there are now websites with full name and address listings for the United States.

The courts seem to have felt that they were being unfair in letting people copy significant amounts of work, and so the threshold for calling something creative has been set fairly low. In two 1991 cases (*Bellsouth Advertising and Publishing Corp. v. Donnelley Information Publishing, Inc.*, 933 F.2d 952; 11th Cir., and *Key Publications v. Chinatown Today*, 945 F.2d 509, 514; 2d Cir.) the courts have held that yellow pages phone directories are creative and may be protected. Baseball box scores are now officially creative (*Kregos v. Associated Press*, 937 F.2d 700, 705; 2d Cir. 1991), but horse racing charts (*Victor Lalli Enterprises v. Big Red Apple*, 936 F.2d 671, 673–74; 2d Cir. 1991) and radiator parts catalogs (*Cooling Sys. & Flexibles, Inc. v. Stuart Radiator*, 777 F.2d 485, 491; 9th Cir. 1985) are not.

More interesting for digital libraries, in at least part of the United States, a photograph of an artwork is not copyrightable if the photograph was routinely taken just to depict the artwork (*Bridgeman Art Library, Ltd. v. Corel Corp.*, 36 F. Supp. 2D 191, Southern District NY). In other countries this kind of problem is compromised. The United Kingdom has a special 25-year protection for "typographic arrangement" which will protect merely the particular typeset version of a book which is out of copyright so that, in the United Kingdom, you cannot just photograph an Oxford version of Dickens, say, and reprint it. The phone book issue is dealt with in the EU with a special "data compilation copyright" that lasts for 10 years. A late 1996 World Intellectual Property Organization proposal for database protection proposed to create a new right in data compilations. This proposal attracted much debate for its lack of a fair use exemption and is still pending. In the United States, a bill introduced into the

House of Representatives in late 2003 would provide a new right of protection for data compilations, but a similar bill failed a few years ago, and it is unclear whether this one will succeed. It does contain an exemption for research activities, but both the degree of protection in general and the research exemption are vaguely worded and will require court interpretation.

New laws may also introduce the concept of "moral rights" to the United States. Moral rights are separate from copyright and derive from a French tradition. They give the creator of a work the right to be identified as the creator and the right to prohibit destruction or degradation of the work. For example, moral rights would have allowed Noguchi to object when a sculpture of his was cut into pieces in 1980 by a landlord trying to get it out of a building which had doors installed after the sculpture had been installed, and that were too small to accommodate it. The Visual Artists Rights Act of 1990 now provides such protection for public art. Moral rights cannot be sold. For example, I can transfer the copyright in this book (and will have to do so to get it published), but I cannot sell somebody else the right to be named as the author. Moral rights can be waived, however, and in moral rights countries, contracts will frequently have to provide for such waivers. The introduction of this right into the United States, with no history of getting such waivers, is likely to create chaos, especially as the courts start to interpret it. For example, in Canada, the Eaton's department store in Toronto has a sculpture depicting some flying geese. For Christmas one year, they tied red ribbons around the necks of the geese. The sculptor protested and won; he felt the ribbons diminished his work.

Finally, a small note for those of us who treasure one small exemption in the copyright law. Recognizing that if you needed the permission of a copyright holder to parody his work, few parodies would ever get written, the courts have allowed an exception for satire. Berkeley Software sold a famous screen saver named *After Dark* which showed toasters flying across the screen. Delrina attempted to market a screen saver which showed Opus the Penguin (licensed from Berk Breathed) shooting down toasters. Berkeley sued for copyright enforcement. Delrina defended, claiming protection as a satire. The list of participants in the case was remarkable; Mark Russell showed up on the side of Delrina and the Irving Berlin estate on the side of Berkeley. In *Delrina v. Berkeley Software*, Judge Eugene Lynch shot down Delrina, saying (a) that this was commerce and not literature, and (b) that the toasters were too similar in design. Although Opus eventually resumed shooting down toasters, but with propellers instead of wings, the precedent is set that you cannot legally parody a computer program. All of this ignores the fact that toasters with wings were originally drawn for a Jefferson Airplane album by artist Bruce Steinberg in 1973. Jefferson Airplane sued too, but lost for failure to register the copyright in the album cover as required under the law at time of publication.

11.2   **History of Patent Law**

The other intellectual property protection most relevant to digital libraries is the patent law. Patents are to protect devices or processes. Patents must cover something useful, new, and not obvious. Since copyrights cover things that must not be useful while patents must be useful, it would seem that nothing could be both copyrighted and patented, but that's not true. A computer program can be covered both ways: the idea or algorithm underneath can be patented, while the text of the program, the form of expression, can be copyrighted.

For software, copyrights protect against someone who simply copies the code and attempts to resell it. Patents stop someone who would rewrite the code, so long as the underlying algorithm is reused. However, software is not what the original patent law had in mind, and sometimes it is a pretty rough fit from software to patents.

Patents are much shorter-term than copyrights. Traditionally, in the United States, they lasted 17 years from date of issue. Now they last 20 years from date of application; since most patents issue in under 18 months, this is usually a slightly longer term. From the standpoint of computer software, either number is still so long as to be comparable with the life of the field. There is also a special kind of patent called a design patent, which can be used to protect industrial designs such as bottle shapes; they have a different life but have not been used much for software.

For many years, the question was whether software should be patentable at all. Traditionally, methods of business are not patentable. In a famous 1876 case named *Baker v. Selden,* a set of accounting forms was held not patentable. The best precedent for computer programs seemed to be player piano rolls, which were copyrighted, not patented. This did not satisfy some software companies or authors, who did not like the fact that copyrighting a program only keeps someone from using your text; they can legally reimplement the same solution in their own code. Patents give an absolute monopoly on the method; even someone who independently reinvents the idea cannot use it.

Early in the days of software, in fact, the solution to software patenting was to convert the program into a circuit diagram and patent the circuit. This could be used to stop somebody from using the same process in a different program. But it was clear that this was unsatisfactory, and the patent lawyers kept trying to patent the actual software algorithm directly. The Patent Office tried to fend this off.

The first step in the legal process was *Gottschalk v. Benson* (1972), in which Bell Laboratories tried to patent a binary-to-decimal conversion algorithm. The algorithm was very simple and might have been known to Euclid, but both sides agreed not to raise the novelty issue. They thought that this was a good test case as the algorithm was so simple that the judges could understand it, often not the case with computer programs. Unfortunately for the patent applicants, the Supreme Court justices not only understood the algorithm but realized they could do it in their head. As a result this looked to them like a constraint on how you could think, and they rejected the patent, saying that any process which consisted entirely of "mental steps" was not patentable.

So the next case was *Diamond v. Diehr* (1981) about a patent application for a rubber curing plant control system that was certainly so complicated that nobody was going to do it in their head, and, in fact, was inherently linked to a nonmental process (the rubber plant). The Supreme Court now agreed that software patents were legal, and the Patent Office began to issue them. There are now over 1000 software patents issued per year. Since software is a relatively new field, it is often hard to establish what should be considered obvious in terms of "prior art," and many patents issue that some consider obvious. The League of Programming Freedom attacks software patents regularly. And Bernard Galler (at U. of Michigan) founded the Software Patent Institute in an effort to assist the patent office by creating a database of prior art and helping train patent examiners.

It also does not appear that major software companies rely on patents the way hardware companies do. Leading hardware companies in the past got far more patents than software companies; the gap is closing, but it still seems that patents are not closely linked to industrial success in software (Table 11.2). There are some famous hardware patents which led to large industries: Alexander Graham Bell and the telephone, Chester Carlson and the photocopier (Xerox), and Edwin Land and instant photography (Polaroid). There are no such stories for software.

Table 11.2 Patents applied for by hardware and software companies.

Company	Patents 1994	Patents 2002
IBM	1362	3288
Hitachi	1192	1602
Canon		1893
Micron		1833
GE	993	1416
Microsoft	27	511
Borland	3	
Lotus	0	
Novell		22

The difficulty that the patent office has evaluating software patents also means that some of them have taken a very long time to issue. This has raised the issue of "submarine patents," patents which no one knows about but suddenly appear to disrupt an industry. It is perfectly possible for someone to invent something, develop a program, start selling it, and only later discover that a previously written patent has just issued and controls the process (a time-bomb patent). The best known example is probably the Pardo patent (US 4,398,249), which looks like an invention of the spreadsheet. The application was received in 1970 but the patent did not issue until 1983; under the law at that time, it did not expire until 2000. The Pardo patent had no effect on the early development of the spreadsheet industry (which was carried on by Visicalc and Lotus). Nevertheless, litigation about it affected the industry. A submarine patent affecting the JPEG compression algorithm, which was carefully built to avoid patent issues after problems with GIF, has arisen in the last few years. There are even patents which have taken more than 20 years to issue; at least one has taken 40. Under the new law, patents of this sort are much less important since the term of 20 years from filing would mean, for example, that the Pardo patent would have expired in 1990. Patent applications also become public after 18 months.

Some legal problems arise from the use of old materials in new ways. For example, in the early 1950s, Disney hired Peggy Lee to sing in *Lady and the Tramp*, for which she was paid $3200. Some 40 years later Disney released the video version and Peggy Lee sued, claiming Disney did not own the video rights to her voice and song. She was awarded more than $3.2 million in damages for copyright infringement. Similarly, in the case of *New York Times v. Tasini*, the courts found that the *Times* did not have the right to put articles written by freelancers on its website without permission. Thus, libraries may have to worry about whether, when something is converted, all the necessary rights were obtained originally from the creators or performers.

Traditionally, in the case of libel, the law distinguished between authors and publishers, who were responsible for what they wrote and distributed, and organizations like the Post Office or printing plants, who were viewed as providing general services and were not responsible for knowing the detailed content of what they transmitted or produced. Libraries, bookstores, and magazine stands, as well, were historically immune from libel suits; no one really believes that a bookstore owner reads all the books in the store and is ready to stand behind their content. There is, however, a case in the United Kingdom in which the then Prime Minister, John Major, sued and won a libel action against not only *Scallywag* and the *New Statesman*, the magazines which had published the libel, but against the printers and distributors (W. H. Smith and John Menzies). So far, this is not the law in the United States.

Where does an online service provider or a website manager stand in this rule? Are they responsible for what they transmit, or not? Stratton Oakmont, a suburban New York brokerage company, objected to something said about them on a Prodigy bulletin board. Although they had paid a $2.5 M penalty for securities law violation, they objected to a description of their behavior as "fraud" and "criminal." They sued Prodigy and won. Prodigy had been advertising itself as the "family friendly" online service and employed people to read and approve messages for its chat groups, with the intent of keeping out obscenity. The court held that this turned Prodigy into a publisher and found it responsible for libelous statements posted by their users. Congress was so distressed by this result that it reversed it in the Telecommunications Reform Act of 1996. Actions taken to limit obscenity can no longer incur legal liability. More generally, Internet service providers are no longer liable for online content if they respond in a specified way to requests to remove the offending page.

Would a library be responsible? Not, one expects, if all it does is put books on a shelf in the traditional way. But the many suggestions that libraries should provide more services, including recommending specific items, selecting particular bits of Web pages, and so on, all move closer to what has traditionally been publishing. And to the extent that libraries try to gain the advantages of publishing (e.g., being able to claim that information they are passing along has a better than usual chance of being valid), the more they incur the risks of a publisher as well.

Trademark law has also started to appear on the Internet. The problem here has been that, traditionally, two different companies may use the same trademark as long as they are in well-separated businesses. HP hot sauce and HP electronics (Hewlett-Packard) coexist, as do Sun Oil (Sunoco) and Sun Microsystems. On the Web, however, there can only be one *www.sun.com*, and it belongs today to Sun Microsystems. As between legitimate trademark holders, the rule is first come, first serve. Originally, domain name authority was held by Network Solutions Inc., of Herndon, Virginia, via an NSF contract to operate the InterNIC registration service. Now there are multiple registries and they compete; the price of a domain name has dropped from $50/year to perhaps $20.

The worst problems arise as international business on the Web grows. TBS, for example, may well be Turner Broadcasting to an American, but it is Tokyo Broadcasting to a Japanese. Right now the Web encourages foreign companies to use national domains, thus for example, *tbs.co.jp* for Tokyo Broadcasting. Not surprisingly, other countries do not think the United States should have special rights for *.com*, and it is not clear how this will be handled. Similar problems arose with toll-free 800 numbers. This has been partially alleviated by deciding that the international toll-free 0800 code will be followed by eight digits rather than seven, meaning that few national toll-free numbers can move without a change to the new space and that, given a sufficiently larger number space, congestion may be less important. The Internet has turned the namespace problem over to a new group called ICANN (Internet Corporation for Assigned Names and Numbers), but a series of squabbles has left the situation confused.

Perhaps the most serious legal problem eventually will be strict liability, raised by Pamela Samuelson. Traditionally, in the United States, the warranty on a book merely said that the paper and binding would hold together. The content was not warrantied. If you read a book on investment strategy and go broke trying to follow its advice, the publisher is not responsible. The rules are different for stockbrokers; if they give sufficiently bad financial advice, they are liable for discipline and damages. What about an electronic program which gives financial advice? As yet, we do not know.

It seems likely that in the not-too-distant future, somebody will sue an online provider for sending out bad information and win. The questions again, as with libel, will be whether liability only attaches to the Web page owner or to other people in the transmission chain. Again, given the number of Web page owners who are young and without financial resources, the tort lawyers will be very anxious to be able to sue somebody large, like a phone company. Will libraries also be held liable? Again, the more they position themselves as "information providers" and claim to be reviewing, editing, or improving the Web pages or whatever else they take in, the more chance that they too may have to take responsibility for the consequences. Realistically, we can expect an insurance industry to arise to deal with the potential liability issues, and libraries may have to buy insurance against these problems.

11.3 Access Regulation and Control

The Internet, as well as being useful to educators and businesses, carries with it risks when used by bad guys. At the moment, the "four horsemen of the Web" are drug dealers, foreign espionage agents, terrorists, and child pornographers. For the 1990s the greatest danger, at least in Congress, was child pornographers; after 9/11 it changed to terrorists.

The result of the focus on pornography was the Communications Decency Act, joining existing state laws that prohibited certain kinds of pornography on the Net. The act ran into legal trouble, since it was insufficiently precise about defining the prohibited material. The question of what kind of indecency restrictions should exist on the Net is still a public policy issue. The use of programs which attempt to scan the Net for dirty words is being circumvented by pornography vendors, who instead of giving their sites names like XXX Super Hot call them Barney and Sesame Street. In turn, the programs which protect against pornography have gotten smarter. Reconciling the right of free speech with the desire to keep people from pushing pornography at children remains difficult.

Unfortunately, we haven't learned how to use the Net to stop terrorism. After 9/11 rumors circulated, for example, that Al-Qaeda was using *steganography* to hide messages in pornographic pictures as a way of communicating. However, the Internet is now recognized as so important that nobody has suggested stopping it as a way of preventing terrorism. What has happened is that some sites with details of public infrastructure, such as reports about nuclear power plants, have been taken off the Web. (We will discuss steganography and digital watermarking later in the chapter.)

There is also danger from traditional distribution methods, of course. Studios typically release movies six months earlier in the United States than in Europe, and they wish to stop Europeans from buying DVD disks in the United States and carrying them across the Atlantic. In fact, we have incompatible DVD formats in the two countries so that US disks won't work in European players. The concept of deliberately introducing incompatibility may seem ridiculous, but it appealed to the studios, at least until the advent of digital transmission to theaters. By thus removing the need to make multiple prints of movies, the reason for not distributing movies simultaneously around the world was essentially eliminated. In 2003, as a result of pirate production of DVDs, the studios finally began releasing some movies simultaneously around the globe.

Perhaps the most important issue in the copyright law revision is the question of responsibility for enforcing copyright law violations. Suppose a website contains an illegally copied work. Whose problem is this? The Internet community would like it to be only the problem of the site creator; the publisher should attack the site owner directly. Publishers would like to be able to place the responsibility for enforcement on the company which is hosting the site (and on anyone else as well). Their position is that suing the site owner, who may well be a 14-year-old with no financial resources, is unproductive. If the responsibility is placed on the Internet service providers, they hope, they can both collect damages and have a workable enforcement mechanism.

The Digital Millenium Copyright Act gave a special protection to ISPs. The publisher notifies the Internet service provider, and the provider then must block access to the site. By doing so, the ISP escapes liability. The ISP then notifies the person whose site is blocked, and that person may claim that there is no copyright infringement. Should a court case result, access to the site can be unblocked until it is settled. Some copyright holders are also asking the search engines to remove references to sites they would like to have off-line, in cases where the site is in a foreign country and it's not possible to get it blocked. The website chillingeffects.org has a discussion of these issues.

As mentioned before, US cryptographic technology export laws are also a major issue. The US government is trying to retain the ability to wiretap with court order for law enforcement purposes, and has proposed that encryption devices contain hidden keys kept by the government and available with a warrant. This proposal, the so-called Clipper chip, has not met with much welcome from other countries or many private organizations. A replacement proposal for commercial key escrow organizations does not seem to be catching on either. Private corporations will have to think about alternate administrative processes. With modern cryptography, if all my files are encrypted with a password that nobody else knows and I am suddenly taken ill, no one else will be able to salvage them for my employer.

Anonymity on the Internet is also a major issue. At present, people visiting websites have their originating computer net address, but not their individual user name, reported to the site. Electronic mail is normally delivered with an electronic user identification. However, people often use pseudonyms for their email, so this is less useful than it might be. Nevertheless, on request systems administrators can be asked which actual user has any particular name. Those requiring still more security have sometimes gone through an anonymous remailer or proxy server. Anonymous remailers are machines which take any message and pass it on with a new, anonymous address. The remailer keeps enough records to permit replies to the message, however. Proxy servers still exist to let users access websites without getting cookies or otherwise letting their identity be traceable (e.g., google-watch.org allows you to use Google without cookies).

During 2003, the amount of unsolicited advertising email, known as "spam," exploded, and various laws are being considered to help stop it. One of the major issues is anonymity: it's hard to find or block the email because of mislabelling of its origin. Some of the "spammers" have resorted to planting viruses in unsuspecting computers merely to be able to send out email from computers that are not associated with them.

Somehow, the Internet community has to decide whether anonymity is a good thing or not. Each side can point to its favorite cases: the democratic political dissident in a dictatorship or the terrorist planning a bombing. The practical politics of the situation, however, is that a continued defense of anonymous email leads to an increased prospect of government regulation on a stricter scale.

11.4 Technology for Intellectual Property Protection

The hope of the publishers is that some technology will arise that protects their intellectual property effectively. At the moment, there is a substantial fear of theft. The United States balance of payments in intellectual property is positive by $46B, but it is believed that another $15–17B is being lost to piracy.

What are the techniques used today to keep people from stealing online intellectual property? Here is a list of current and proposed technologies for this purpose:

1. Fractional access
2. Control of interface
3. Hardware locks (dongles)
4. Repositories
5. Steganography
6. Crytolopes
7. Economic approaches
8. Flickering
9. Special hardware

Fractional Access

Mead Data Central has many terabytes online. You can steal a few hundred bytes, but not find somebody else who wants those bytes enough to pay for them. For a large enough database which is doled out in small units, it is not practical to do small-scale cheating. Large-scale copying, with advertising of the result, will come to the attention of the copyright holder and can be shut down legally. Most of the large online journal services, for example, monitor for "systematic downloading" and cut off any customer who is doing that.

This is not, however, an answer for textbooks; the entire book is often of use to the reader, and the typical user knows who else is in the class and would want a copy of the book. In general, sales of individual, self-contained items can't just rely on providing access to only small parts of the material.

Control of the Interface

If people can only access material through a proprietary interface, they may have trouble back-translating it to something easily redistributed. Imagine, for example, reverse engineering one of the complex screen displays of a modern browser. This was relied on by many CD-ROM vendors; the format on the CD-ROM was private and the software to access it was on the CD-ROM. It is hard to try to arrange any other access to the material. Again, if someone does this and tries to market the result they will come to public attention, and it is too hard to do on a small scale. But now everything is supposed to be on the Web, and there are many browsers, so this method has dropped from favor.

Figure 11.2 Examples of hardware locks.

Hardware Locks (Dongles)

If some part of information access can be made to depend on a piece of hardware, then nobody without that hardware can use a copy. In a typical case, part of the access program (e.g., the decryption key) is kept out in the hardware, which must be on the machine. In the extreme case, an entire special purpose machine is designed only to run the vendor's programs; video games are the practical example.

Usually, the special-purpose hardware looks like a parallel or serial port (a plug on the back of the computer used to connect printers or other devices), which normally acts like a cable and just transmits through whatever it gets, but which traps and responds to a few special commands. An example is shown in Figure 11.2. These devices, however, met considerable consumer resistance and also cost enough that they can only be used to protect fairly expensive products (they cost perhaps $20 apiece). Effectively, they have failed in the marketplace.

Repositories

The idea behind repositories is that if there was a copy of everything copyrighted in one place, unauthorized copies could be found mechanically. Stanford, for example, explored a case of Net plagiarism by comparing papers from a specific source with the online database of technical reports. Such a repository could either rely on copyright signature codes included in a document, or it could generate its own signatures and do searching.

Among groups trying to build a repository are InterTrust (previously known as EPR), and CNRI, the Corporation for National Research Initiatives, which is working with the Copyright Office. The European Union has Imprimatur

(Intellectual Multimedia Property Rights Model and Terminology for Universal Reference). There is also a consortium called the Electronic Rights Management Group, as well as the Electronic Licensing and Security Initiative. There is now so much information online, however, that the thought of keeping track of all of it, even by using a hash code, is impracticable.

Steganography

The word steganography describes hidden messages. Originally, it meant the kind of cipher in which the first letter of each word spelled out a secret message. Sherlock Holmes solved such a cipher in *The Adventure of the Gloria Scott.* Steganography has been extended into the idea of *digital watermarks* which are hidden in digital materials. Secret codes are hidden in each copy sold, and then any illegally detected copies can be tracked to the original purchaser and legal remedies pursued (Komatsu and Tominaga, 1990; Langelaar et al., 2000; Cox et al., 2001). The idea is that each copy sold would be labelled with a different identification number, and illegal copies could thus be tracked back to the original purchaser so that legal remedies could be sought against that purchaser. These codes have the difficulty that they may be easily removed, and they may be hard to insert. It is easier, for example, to find spare places to put extra bits in a picture (where low-order detail can be adjusted with little notice) than in text or in software (Matsui and Tanaka, 1994; Blue Spike, 2004).

There are many research efforts on digital watermarking now, and a variety of commercial products from companies such as Digimarc, MediaSec, and Alpha Tec. Normally, the goal is to have a mark which is not noticeable to the user and yet is hard to remove. Many of the most trivial suggestions, which would involve manipulating the low-order bits of an image, would be removed by any kind of lossy compression and decompression, or even just by low-pass spatial Fourier transforms. More complex and robust processes might involve, as at MIT, adjusting overall gray densities in different parts of the picture. The eye is not very sensitive to absolute levels, so this kind of coding passes unnoticed. Because it is not in low-level bits, it survives JPEG or other compressions.

Placing digital watermarks in text, as opposed to pictures, is harder. There is no spare space in ASCII text to hide anything. L. O'Gorman and others at Bell Laboratories came up with a scheme that manipulates the spaces between letters or words, or the exact shapes of letters, as shown in Figures 11.3 (Berghel and O'Gorman, 1996; Brassil et al., 1994). Huang and Yan (2001) followed with a method that used both interword and interline spaces to achieve greater robustness.

Again, as with any scheme that depends on detecting pirates and then suing them, legal procedures against many small infringers with limited financial

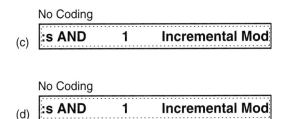

(a)

(b)

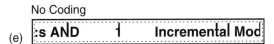

(c)

(d)

(e)

Figure 11.3 Bell Labs document marking. Examples (a) and (b) show word-shift coding. In (a) the top text line has the same spacing after the "for." In (b) these same text lines are shown again without the vertical lines to demonstrate that either spacing appears natural. Examples (c)–(e) show feature coding performed on a portion of text from a journal table of contents. In (c) no coding has been applied. In (d) feature coding has been applied to select characters. In (e) the feature coding has been exaggerated to show feature alterations.

resources are not effective. Watermarking is on the rise in many situations, for example, the movie studios have found that many of the pirate versions of their movies originate from the promotional copies they distribute, and marking these promotional copies helps them find the original recipients who have resold or passed on their copies.

Cryptolopes

This heading covers the general technology of supplying information in encrypted form, with software that decrypts it under rules provided by the copyright holder. *Cryptolope* is a word referring to a particular system of this sort which once existed at IBM. Information is distributed only in encrypted form, and the access software controls the ability to print or download. The idea is that the user can do what they want with the encrypted version; in fact, redistributing it might even help the copyright holder. But when the user asks to view the material or print the report, some kind of financial transaction may be started.

The idea of these "envelopes" is that they could implement a wide variety of policies for selling information. The information owner can choose to allow or forbid viewing, downloading, copying, printing, or whatever. So long as the user stays within the limits of the program, the policies are secure. As with other techniques, the user, having got a screenful of information, may be able to capture it with screendumps or some such system, and then abuse it. Although IBM has abandoned cryptolopes, similar rights management technology is sold by EPR (Electronic Publishing Resources), which has Digiboxes and NetTrust, or by Release Software Corp with its AutoPay. Some users might not appreciate one fact about AutoPay, that it can scan the user's hard drive looking for competing products and adjust the price accordingly.

A long-term worry that has been raised by Clifford Lynch of the University of California is what happens to encrypted material in the long run. If libraries only buy access to material and at any given instant it is only encrypted, how does it become generally accessible 70 years after the author has died? Publishers are under no affirmative obligation to assist books into the public domain, and perhaps when the current sales are no longer lucrative, they will simply forget about the book. With no library having an unencrypted copy, it will be gone. It may be desirable to require that at least one clean, unencrypted copy be deposited with the Library of Congress. As it happens, though, all of the cryptographic envelope systems seem to be failing in the marketplace, so this may not be a worry.

Economic Approaches

It would be ideal, of course, if some pricing strategy could remove or alleviate the piracy problem. The existing pricing strategies are often very frustrating. For example, CD-ROMs use a technology designed to stamp out millions of pop records. Yet the price of some library CD-ROMs is so high as to encourage the library to do networked delivery as a way of sharing the resource, prompting fears that the networked access would in some way produce abuse. Few publishers, however, have arranged for libraries to get multiple copies of CD-ROMs on the same site, with the extra copies at the site being very cheap.

Among possible economic solutions for scholarly journals, page charges might make it possible to reduce the per-issue price to the point where copying just did not carry sufficient economic incentive, as discussed earlier. More generally, site licenses at least remove the issue of cheating within an organization. Many university libraries are likely to pursue this route for acquiring material so that they have no policing requirement within their university. Institutional sponsorship of publications, although going out of favor, would also mean that piracy was less relevant. And, of course, advertiser-supported publications do not care if people copy them. Aside from site licenses, it seems unlikely that any of these suggestions would cover most library material. Perhaps someday we will have pledge breaks on the Internet.

Flickering

Is there a way to let people see something and read it but not capture it by screen dumping? This would seem contradictory, but a proposed solution relies on retinal persistence, the ability of the human eye to average rapidly changing images. Movies and television work because a human eye presented with images changing 24 or 30 times per second tries to average the result, rather than perceive the separately changing images (as it would if the images changed every second or every two seconds). Computer screen dumps, on the other hand, capture an instantaneous appearance. They don't do any time-averaging over the screen appearance.

Thus, imagine taking a text to be displayed and adding random bits to the background. Do this twice, producing two bitmaps which contain all the bits in the letters, plus perhaps 50% of the remaining bits turned on at random. Then rapidly alternate between these bitmaps. The human eye will perceive the steady letters as letters; it will take the irregular flickering bits in the background as equivalent to a 50% gray background. After all, this kind of display is how dithering is used to represent a 50% gray rectangle so that the eye will perceive steady letters on a gray background. Any screen dump, however, will capture the background bits and the resulting screen image is almost useless.

Figure 11.4 shows this process. The top two bitmaps, if merged together, produce the appearance of the lower image (the text is from the prolog to *Henry V*). In a static paper, it is not possible to show the flickering, so the lower image is 100% black letters on a flat 50% gray background. However, if read on a screen with about 30 repeats per second, this is roughly the appearance that results. An even higher flicker rate would be desirable; rates as low as 15 repeats per second cause the changing background to appear as an annoying moiré-like pattern, rather than as a steady gray level. The separated bitmaps, although barely readable by the human eye, have been tried on OCR programs, with no useful output. The eye is of course much better than an OCR program at deciding what represents a possible letter and what is random noise.

The density of the background can be adjusted. Clearly, moving to a lighter background (fewer dark bits) produces a more readable image, at the expense of making it easier to imagine an OCR program that can deal with the separated bitmaps. Tests suggest, however, that even 10–20% of random bits added to a

Figure 11.4 Flickering for protection.

Figure 11.5 Flickering, lower density.

bitmap will make OCR ineffective. Note, however, that this assumes a normal letter size; if the letters are greatly enlarged relative to the dots, the noise is easier to remove.

The flickering is annoying, but the text is readable. A screen dump of the window gives one of the two bitmaps with the obscured data. Even with only a 25% dark bit-density level, these can only be read with considerable annoyance by the human eye, and certainly not by an OCR program.

There are various choices in this system. The random bitmaps can have any gray level. In particular, if the background gray level is about 10%, you get a very easy-to-read onscreen display, though a reader can just as readily make out the cluttered images when isolated (but OCR programs still fail). If the background level is 50%, the display is now a fairly dark background, but still quite readable when flickered. The individual cluttered images are then not easily recognizable even as text by eye, let alone readable(Figure 11.5).

Another choice is to have the background as flat white and flicker between two images of the text, each of which has half the bits from the letters. This produces a different impression: instead of seeing good letters against a flickering gray background, flickering letters appear against a clean background. The half-images are recognizable as text but not easy to read, and again won't make it through OCR (Figure 11.6).

```
Piece out our i   Piece out our i        Piece out our i
with your thoug   with your thoug        with your thoug
into a thousand   into a thousand        into a thousand
divide one man.   divide one man.        divide one man.
```

Figure 11.6 Flickering letters.

Note that it may not be desirable to have too many background bitmaps. If a method of attack is to capture both images and try to logically "AND" them to uncover the letters, the more random backgrounds that are used, the more likely it is that the letters will be apparent. It is also possible to combine the idea of flickering backgrounds and flickering letters, with perhaps a 25% background and a 75% letter density.

Another feature in this program is to "wobble" the text up and down the screen slowly. This doesn't bother the reader as much as the flickering, and it defeats a pirate who might try taking 100 screen dumps in succession and averaging the result. With the text wandering up and down the screen, the averaging will be destroyed. This idea does not work as well with displays of pictures as opposed to text. Without the familiar letter-shapes to guide the eye, the addition of noise to a photograph of a real scene makes it considerably noisier, rather than being an apparent "background." However, the digital watermarking techniques are applicable to exactly such pictorial images. Thus, the flickering technique is applicable exactly when the watermarking techniques are not and fills a slot in copyright defense technology.

This technology hasn't succeeded in the marketplace (to my disappointment, since it's my only patent), but in 2003 a movie company proposed using something similar to protect against camcorders in movie theaters.

Special Hardware

What may turn out to be the solution is special hardware for digital rights management. For example, an audio card could include a digital-to-analog converter that included a decryption chip, possibly with a unique key for this particular chip. To download music, the user would provide the ID of that particular audio board decryption chip; it could be used to make a special password that would be used to encrypt the music so that it could only be decrypted by that particular chip. Copies would be useless to anyone else. Similar technology could be in video cards, laser printers, and other devices.

More likely is a general solution currently proposed by Microsoft and Intel, with the tentative name Palladium. This system involves a special coprocessor not under the user's control. Information routed to it could not be copied or written to files except as the codes in that processor allowed. All information entering the computer would go first to this processor, which would pick off the material that was under digital rights management and only give the rest to the programs the user wanted to run.

These systems are called *digital rights management* (DRM) systems and they try to maintain quite elaborate rules about who can do what with content. For example, normally I can buy a CD for cash and not leave my name with the store; most DRM systems are going to require user identification. Sometimes this is useful (e.g., it may let me move a purchased item from one computer to another), but other times it may subject me to a barrage of marketing I would rather have avoided. Also, DRM systems are not required to enable fair use rights or first sale rights. They can, for example, prohibit transferability or quotation for review. Mulligan et al. (2003) have described the mismatch between what users think they should be able to do with purchased music and what the DRM systems are likely to permit.

Again, the major issues here are likely to be market issues. If such a system means that only Microsoft can deliver content, there are few constraints on what they can charge. The studios, of course, would like to have a choice of delivery systems, so that they can bid them against each other. Nobody so far has an open solution to the digital rights management issues.

11.5   Peer to Peer Systems

In the late 1990s, we actually saw the development of widespread music distribution systems, via what are known as *peer-to-peer* systems. Instead of centralized servers, individual users placed digital music recordings on the disks of their home machines and offered to let others copy them. Most of these recordings, of course, were illegal copies. The recording companies tried to shut down all such systems but have found it frustrating.

In the context of digital libraries, note that the process did work. Lots of information was online—hundreds of thousands of music tracks delivered by Napster to some 20 million users. It turned out to be a highly reliable service, thanks to the multiple copies of most files, and the main technological problem was that it overloaded the bandwidth in many university dormitories. Institutions had to go to bandwidth rationing to keep some level of service operating.

The recording companies are known for their aggressiveness in protecting their copyrights. Once, for example, ASCAP tried to claim royalties from a group of Girl Scouts singing songs at a campfire. The record companies experimented with CD formats that could not be played on computers, but only on the traditional audio CD players. These CDs were not compatible with the official definition of a CD and provoked considerable annoyance among the customers.

Labelling them has not been a successful answer, and the record companies have moved on.

The recording companies sued Napster, which was a central server holding a large database where all the music was stored. Napster attempted to comply by asking for a list of infringing files, which it would then delete or block. A flurry of unproductive activity followed as the file-sharers renamed their files in some trivial way, perhaps Beetles instead of Beatles, so that there would be no match with the files coming from the recording companies. The recording companies, for their part, started distributing incorrect files, sometimes just noise, labelled as music, with the intent of frustrating the users. Eventually the courts ruled that Napster was part of the infringement and closed down the general file-sharing system. Bertelsmann bought Napster, in the hope of building some kind of commercial service out of it, but was not successful. In a final legal effort, the recording companies have now sued the venture capital firms that funded Napster.

The peer-to-peer advocates moved on to technologies without a central database (Morpheus, Kazaa, and others). In these systems, requests for music are broadcast until somebody pops up and offers a file to download. There is no single place to be shut down in these systems. They now have more users total than Napster did; Kazaa claims more than 200 million people have downloaded its software. More important, given the lack of a central database, these systems do not know what files are being shared. They thus claim that they are not part of the infringement and point to the other uses of their technology that are not illegal. They thus hope to avoid Napster's fate, insisting that any violations of copyright are the responsibility of their users, and not theirs (see for example Landau, 2003). Of course, the lack of any central service or registry makes it hard to imagine what kind of business plan they could have.

CD sales have dropped in both 2001 and 2002, all around the world. The recording companies have blamed piracy, pointing to the immense number of CD-R disks sold. Worldwide, about 5 billion recorded CD disks are sold and about 5 billion blank CD-Rs are sold; but the amount of recorded music CD disks is slipping slightly, while the number of blank CD-R disks made is jumping. Critics argue that many other products are slipping in a worldwide recession and also that there are no big new stars in the music field. DVD music sales are still going up.

These disputes are not new (see Lesk, 2003). Music sales have dropped after other new technologies came along, starting with the radio in 1922, and the industry has attacked these technologies with equal determination. The statements made about radio, called the "murderer of music," were just as angry as those made about downloading. In fact, measured by fraction of the GNP devoted to buying recorded music, the industry has never quite gotten back to

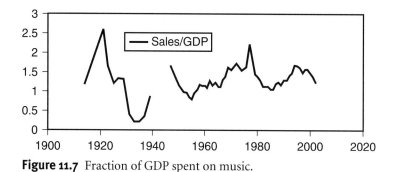

Figure 11.7 Fraction of GDP spent on music.

its high point of 1921. Figure 11.7 shows the fraction of GDP (in thousandths) spent on music, with a correction before 1976 to compensate for a change in the way statistics were gathered (see Lesk, 2003).

The recording companies continue to try legal methods to attack the peer-to-peer networks. They sued the software companies that distribute peer-to-peer software, but lost; the court held that the software was useful for legitimate copying and it was the users who were infringing. There are many bands who allow their music to be distributed free, hoping that getting public attention will let them sell concert tickets, get club gigs, or otherwise gain more success. Thus, the court considered the distribution of the software to be legitimate. We can expect an appeal. Legal remedies are also confused by the relocation of some companies out of the United States; Kazaa, for example, is claiming to be located in Tuvalu.

The companies also tried suing some users. The Recording Industry Association of America (RIAA) sued four college students, one at Princeton, one at Michigan Technological University, and two at Rensselaer Polytechnic Institute, whom they claimed were storing many songs online, and asked for damages of up to $150,000 per song, which could come to $97 billion total. This certainly frightened many of the file-sharing sites offline; RIAA quickly settled for numbers in the $10,000–15,000 range, a large amount for an undergraduate.

Perhaps it is more promising to note that at the same time, restrictions on the for-pay downloadable music services were slackened. It is now possible to subscribe to services that allow legal download, storage, and burning to CD. In the long run, the goal should be to develop a legitimate industry, not simply try to stop progress with lawsuits. In November 2003, for example, Penn State signed a university-wide license for music so that downloading from the Napster site would be legal and paid for (Associated Press, 2003).

Digital librarians should note the extreme reliability of the peer-to-peer sharing system; despite enormous efforts to wipe out these files, they persist.

Certainly such sharing systems are safe against any inadvertent mistake or natural disaster.

11.6   Summary and Future Research

This chapter has described another unsolved problem. Many of the most important future issues of digital libraries involve legal questions. Should the United States extend or limit protection in these new digital areas? Will greater protection encourage the creation of digital information, or will it bog us down in rights negotiations? Perhaps the most important problem will be to reduce administrative costs, perhaps with some kind of compulsory licensing scheme. Although print publishers have argued against compulsory licensing, it seems to work in the songwriting business. Perhaps a voluntary clearinghouse will be acceptable; the Copyright Clearance Center, for example, has most important publishers as members.

We also need ways of authenticating publishers and users. There is nothing in an electronic message which can be inspected to convey age or authorship. Cryptography does provide solutions to this, but the complexities of US export regulations and the lack of agreement on implementation means that we do not have routine, commonly agreed-upon authentication procedures, and we will need them to build economically reliable systems.

There are many details of legal procedures which are going to make great differences to libraries. Should collected facts be eligible for protection, and, if so, should the protection be as long-lived as creative works? Should a document converted from one form to another acquire some kind of protection, and, if so, what? How much responsibility do libraries, communications carriers, and others have for stamping out undesirable uses of their services? How much privacy are readers entitled to?

Perhaps the hardest choice to make is when laws should be used and when contracts and technology should be used. If there are no laws protecting a given kind of information, we are likely to see elaborate contracts and complicated technological protection devices, raising administrative costs. Imagine what it would mean to book sales if every purchase meant reading and approving a contract, and every reading meant going through some kind of verification procedure. It's much easier if the standard legal framework is something both sides accept as reasonable and find straightforward to implement. A legal framework for information economics, however, is likely to be slow to enact and change, and this is a rapidly changing area. And finally, the international nature of the Web makes it harder for either United States law or United States contracts to operate in isolation from the rest of the world.

 # A World Tour of Digital Libraries

The previous chapters have focussed more on the potential of digital libraries for the future: how to store information, how to pay for it, how to protect it. There is actually a great deal of current activity in this field, in which things are being accomplished every day. This chapter looks at many of the existing digital library projects and some of the more interesting work to date. The Web, as we've emphasized, is now a "wrapper" for every digital library project, and the contributions to it are expanding in media, quantity, and location. Perhaps the model we should look to is that of the Perseus project of Greg Crane and Elli Mylonas, which took the conversion of ancient Greek literature into digital form (the Thesaurus Linguae Gracae) and added dictionaries, maps, and other material to enhance it for teaching; this project, first on CD-ROM and now on the Web, has had a major impact on the teaching of classics in colleges and universities.

12.1 Information Policy, Not Industrial Policy

The Web is worldwide, and digital library research exists in many countries. Many countries have identified information technology as some kind of national goal, as in Singapore, which has declared its intent to become the "intelligent island." After memory chips and software, content in digital form may be another industry which countries target as a way of gaining international advantage. As noted earlier in the book, the digital format has enormous economies of scale and sufficiently low entry costs that even small countries can try it.

Many nations have major digital library initiatives underway. One point of variance is whether these programs are focussed around libraries or around computer science research departments. The United States is at one extreme: the digital library effort has been run by the National Science Foundation (NSF), and it focusses on computer science research, building new tools, and new methods of access. The collections involved per se are of less significance. Japan is at the other extreme: the major digital library effort is run by the National Diet Library and the focus is on collections. European countries are directing their efforts in a mixed mode, less towards either end of the balance.

Another contrast is the difference between some projects that are very international and some that are trying to exploit particular resources at hand. In some nations, the culture supports working on the nation's own history and library collections; in other nations, the culture supports access to international information. Countries also may have specific skills that they can exploit: Singapore has many people who are expert in both English and Chinese; Switzerland has people skilled in several European languages; and Japan has expertise in devices, displays, and the like.

The degree to which the publishing community is involved and is working with the digital library effort differs from country to country. In the United States, publishers are involved in many of the digital library projects and work frequently with universities. This is less common in some other countries, particularly if the digital library project is defined merely as "save the national heritage" and doesn't work on anything modern.

Information delivery, viewed in retrospect, is an American success story of government stimulation of a new industry. Beginning in the 1950s, the NSF and other government agencies funded research in information retrieval. Today, information retrieval is an enormous industry and is dominated by the United States, which consequently has an enormous positive balance of trade in database and information services, as shown in Figure 12.1. Even with Japan, in 1999 the United States sold $94 M of exported services against $20 M of imports; with China the United States sold $20 M and imported $4 M.

Everyone recognizes that this industry began with Federal funding. The *Encyclopedia of American Industries* (Hillstrom, 1994) says: "Government investment in the 1960s initiated many of the private information retrieval services that dominated the market in the 1980s and early 1990s." For instance, the well-known online search system DIALOG sprung from a 1964 proposal of the

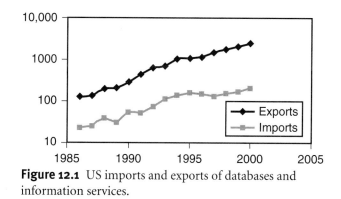

Figure 12.1 US imports and exports of databases and information services.

National Aeronautics and Space Administration (NASA) to create an online search system, named Project RECON, and developed by Lockheed first as a contractor, and later as the DIALOG commercial service. Similarly, ORBIT Online, now owned by Questel, came from work System Development Corporation performed for the National Library of Medicine. Even Mead Data Central, predecessor of what is now Elsevier's Lexis-Nexis online service, started with US Air Force contracts. Bibliographic Retrieval Services (BRS), now part of the OVID online system belonging to Walters Kluwer, began with work done for the CIA (Central Intelligence Agency) and the National Library of Medicine.

The NSF, in particular, started the text search industry, which relies heavily on techniques developed in programs funded originally by the Office of Science Information Services more than 30 years ago and which the NSF has continued funding. Text search today as software is a $500 M/year business. However, the largest use of text search is, of course, in web searching, led by Google, whose 2004 revenues are estimated at $1.6 B (Sullivan, 2004).

Retrieval systems hold out promise in entirely new areas. For example, clothing manufacturers report that 27% of clothing costs are avoidable with better information (e.g., excessive inventory or lack of product) and that only 10% of the costs are wages. Thus, clothing manufacturers can gain more by introducing better information systems than by paying their workers zero.

US government funding is still stimulating new efforts in retrieval. The NSF funded Bruce Croft at the University of Massachusetts, and his software is the base of the Thomas system at the Library of Congress, which has put congressional information online for everyone. Mosaic began at the National Center for Supercomputing Applications at the University of Illinois, funded under the High Performance Computing Clusters (HPCC) program, and turned into Netscape. Google began with two graduate students in Stanford University's database program.

12.2 Multilingual Issues

Of course, any effort to work across countries involves the problems of materials in many languages. For example, the Indian partners in the Million Book project are scanning material in languages of the Indian subcontinent, such as Tamil, Telugu, Kanade, and Marathi.

Some national libraries have as their goal the preservation of material in particular languages, such as those in Wales and Sweden. Sweden's library, for example, tries to collect all Web pages in Swedish. Digital libraries can be used to preserve languages from smaller communities, counteracting the trend of the broadcast media to be dominated by the major world languages. The Web can enable Welsh speakers in Australia or Canada to link up with those in Wales and provide a mechanism to distribute publications whose small readership would make print publication uneconomical.

The Web can also serve as a source of information for machine translation projects, as we discussed earlier in the book (see for example chapter 5.6). The collection of information in new languages will assist in the creation of machine translation software for them. It is possible to mine large amounts of information in multiple languages and also to locate translated texts, for example, by looking for the same book in multiple languages on literature sites. Here, for instance, is the beginning of Jules Verne's *Le Tour de Monde en Quatre-Vingts Jours*" in French:

DANS LEQUEL PHILEAS FOGG ET PASSEPARTOUT S'ACCEPTENT RÉCIPROQUE-MENT L'UN COMME MAÎTRE, L'AUTRE COMME DOMESTIQUE

En l'année 1872, la maison portant le numéro 7 de Saville-row, Burlington Gardens – maison dans laquelle Sheridan mourut en 1814 –, était habitée par Phileas Fogg, esq., l'un des membres les plus singuliers et les plus remarqués du Reform-Club de Londres, bien qu'il semblât prendre à tâche de ne rien faire qui pût attirer l'attention.

A l'un des plus grands orateurs qui honorent l'Angleterre, succédait donc ce Phileas Fogg, personnage énigmatique, dont on ne savait rien, sinon que c'était un fort galant homme et l'un des plus beaux gentlemen de la haute société anglaise.

On disait qu'il ressemblait à Byron – par la tête, car il était irréprochable quant aux pieds –, mais un Byron à moustaches et à favoris, un Byron impassible, qui aurait vécu mille ans sans vieillir.

And this is the English version from Project Gutenberg:

IN WHICH PHILEAS FOGG AND PASSEPARTOUT ACCEPT EACH OTHER, THE ONE AS MASTER, THE OTHER AS MAN

> Mr. Phileas Fogg lived, in 1872, at No. 7, Saville Row, Burlington Gardens, the house in which Sheridan died in 1814. He was one of the most noticeable members of the Reform Club, though he seemed always to avoid attracting attention; an enigmatical personage, about whom little was known, except that he was a polished man of the world. People said that he resembled Byron—at least that his head was Byronic; but he was a bearded, tranquil Byron, who might live on a thousand years without growing old.

To give the reader an idea of how much remains to be done in machine translation, here is the result of the SYSTRAN system running on the French paragraph. Despite the dysfluencies, if you don't know French, this is still probably better than having only the original.

> IN WHICH PHILEAS FOGG AND PASSEPARTOUT ACCEPT One AS MASTER RECIPROCALLY, the OTHER AS SERVANT
>
> In the year 1872, the house carrying number 7 of Saville-row, Burlington Gardens – house in which Sheridan died in 1814 –, was inhabited by Phileas Fogg, esq., one of the most noticed members most singular and Reform-Club of London, although it seemed to take with task anything to make which could draw the attention. With one of the largest speakers who honour England, thus succeeded this Phileas Fogg, character enigmatic, of which one knew nothing, if not which it was a fort gentleman and one of the most beautiful gentlemen of the English high society. It was said that it resembled Byron – by the head, because it was irreproachable as for feet –, but Byron with moustache and favourites, impassive Byron, which would have lived thousand years without aging.

For some time two parallel threads have been operating in machine translation research: (1) using expertise and working in the major world languages, and (2) using parallel corpora and working in less important languages.

The European Union, in particular, has an enormous demand for translation services among their languages. Thus, they have funded considerable research, making use of the large number of multilingual speakers in Europe and their expertise in language teaching. A great deal of this work has been to support human translators and involves workstation design to facilitate their work and the creation of online lexicons. European companies have also built systems that try to combine a very rough machine translation with manual postediting. It's also possible to build systems that attack particular subject areas, such as patents. Newer work is looking at the problems of translating spoken language, an extremely difficult problem.

There are also machine translation projects involving expertise in major languages in the United States, and a rise in systems to help access information in obscure languages. Sudden needs, resulting from international crises, for more competence in languages like Somali, Rwandan, Croatian, and Pashto have stimulated additional work on example-based machine translation. The goals of this research are to minimize the amount of bilingual text needed, to produce fluent translations, and to build the systems very quickly. Researchers such as Jaime Carbonell of Carnegie Mellon University and Fred Jelinek of Johns Hopkins have led efforts to build statistically based machine translation software which does not depend on elaborate grammars.

Most recently there is again a confluence of these efforts. The expansion of the European Union has increased the number of languages and encouraged European research in example-based translation, at the same time as additional research has appeared in the United States on dictionary creation. Japan also has research efforts in speech translation and online lexicons. One large project, for example, combines ATR (the Advanced Telecommunications Research Institute) in Japan, Carnegie Mellon in the United States, and the University of Karlsruhe in Germany in research on translation of spoken Japanese, German, and English.

Of course, the dot-com bust has affected translation research as well. In 1998, William Meisel, speaking for the KPR group, predicted that 1999 speech technology sales would be $2 B, and in 2003 they would be $36 B. A more realistic number for 2003 is probably about $1 B (which is what Meisel said it was in 1998). Machine translation software sales are estimated by IDC as $378 M in 2003.

An area which has not been adequately explored is the use of computers in language learning. There are some 60 million people every year trying to learn to speak English, for example. Some aspects of language learning seem well-tailored to computers. For example, there are times when one would like a large amount of text written in a small number of words and with a small number of grammar rules. It's expensive to get people to write such text; computers might be very good at it. There are some interesting research projects in aspects of computer-assisted language learning; for example, Ron Cole and other researchers at Oregon and Colorado have built an animated head, "Baldi," which they use to help deaf children learn and understand how to speak.

12.3 Multicultural Issues

As libraries convert to digital information, everything becomes available worldwide. What, then, should a library focus upon? How should libraries strike a balance between looking inward and looking outward? On the one hand, part of the mission of a library is to offer its patrons the information available throughout the world and to give patrons the opportunity to read material from many sources and with many viewpoints. On the other hand, if a library in a particular place does not look after the heritage of that place, who will? Each library must strike its own balance.

I am reminded of a wonderful story, which I haven't chased down for fear that it will turn out to be apocryphal. Allegedly, in the early days of Harvard College, some local Congregationalist ministers visited and went to the President to complain that there were too many books by Anglicans on the library shelves. He responded by telling them that they had, of course, many more books of which the ministers would approve but that those books were all out, being read by the students. Would that it were always so easy for libraries to satisfy the critics of their collections.

An interesting example of a worldwide project is the International Children's Digital Library (Figure 12.2). This project, run by the University of Maryland and the Internet Archive, is planning to digitize and provide online 100 children's books from each of 100 cultures. It is also building new interfaces to help children deal with books. For example, conventional cataloging is not always the way children want to find books to read; they ask for books in unusual ways, such as, "I want a book that will make me feel good." Different cultures have responded in different ways to requests to allow digitizing of a particular book. In the main, the larger publishers have resisted requests to digitize the most popular books, as one might expect. Authors or publishers in small countries have often given permission more easily; they know they have no real chance of large sales in the United States, and they are prouder of being selected for an international effort.

Many libraries focus on their heritage in choosing the first things to be digitized, often selecting special collections and objects which are attractive

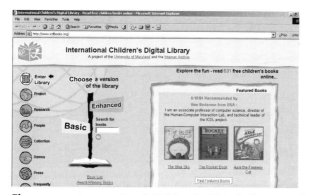

Figure 12.2 International Children's Digital Library Web page.

when scanned. Special collections are generally unique, so there is no overlap with digitization elsewhere, and they often reflect the particular interests of the institution. Thus, the University of Mississippi library online exhibit deals with the history of the state and its literature, including their special material relating to William Faulkner. Objections to digitizing special collections may arise from their fragility, from problems with copyright status, or from faculty hoping to keep others from knowing about unusual research resources (fortunately, a rare objection).

A more serious problem, in my opinion, is the high cost of digitizing valuable materials; not only must they be handled with extreme care, but people feel compelled to digitize them at extreme quality levels, to minimize the chance that they will need to be handled again. As a result, it is often possible only to digitize a small amount of material. And these projects cannot be shared with other libraries. If libraries focussed their digitization on shared material, of lower artifactual value but perhaps greater intellectual utility, we might get much more done. JSTOR, the scholarly journal archive, is an example of a project which could be done at a large scale because of the number of institutions involved.

An extreme example of local heritage is anthropological information, such as oral histories. Many libraries have fascinating collections of such material for many cultures. But how available should such information be? Will the people who narrated their stories be pleased or angry if those stories are made available to everyone in the world? Museums face similar issues with some kinds of objects; the United States has a long-term plan under which many objects of religious or cultural importance to Native American groups are to be returned to them. May the museum retain a digital copy? That may depend on the particular role the object plays in its original culture.

Another form of restriction to material arises when the completely free expression typical of the Web doesn't appeal to some cultures or to some political regimes. Best known are the limits imposed on Web access in China, which controls Internet access and limits access to many sites. Some of these are pornography; many Western corporations similarly limit what their employees can access from computers at work. Others are political; the Chinese are best known for limiting access to Web sites dealing with internal Chinese political issues. Singapore has also, at times, limited access to particular sites; both of these countries have also at times interfered with traditional print publications.

12.4   Text-oriented Projects

A great many digital library projects revolve around books and journals; these are, after all, the basic holdings of most libraries. What has changed from the early tentative digitizations is the large scale of some of the current projects. We now see several projects which have tens of thousands of volumes and some reaching beyond that level. Among the more ambitious are:

- Gallica, an effort of the Bibliothèque Nationale de France (BnF), which has scanned about 100,000 French books focussed on the history, culture, and literature of France and related topics. About half these books are in copyright and are only available at the BnF site; the others are on the Web. This is, as far as I know, the largest completed scanning effort by a major library.
- The Making of America, a joint effort of Michigan and Cornell (but inviting others to join), which is scanning material related to the nineteenth century. It has scanned over ten thousand volumes. This project has carefully designed its digitization practices, has published them, and has influenced practices throughout the field.
- JSTOR, previously mentioned for its importance as an economic experiment, which has placed online about 12 million pages, the equivalent of 4000–5000 volumes.
- Project Gutenberg, a volunteer effort led by Michael Hart, which has now digitized more than 10,000 books, primarily of English and American literature.
- The Electronic Text Center at the University of Virginia (and also their Institute for Advanced Technology in the Humanities) which distributes public domain e-books, at present about 1800 in number; the total resources of the Center are about 70,000 books, many of which were obtained under commercial license and can't be redistributed. The Internet Public Library at the University of Michigan has over 20,000 public domain books, many obtained from Project Gutenberg.
- The Networked Digital Library of Theses and Dissertations, created by Ed Fox, with a goal of placing as many dissertations online as possible. His university, Virginia Tech, now requires electronic theses. Few have joined in that, although a great many universities now encourage the practice. There are about 17,000 dissertations in the system, from all over the world.

It is also worth noting some of the commercial projects, such as English Books Online, by University Microfilms, which is providing online copies of the 60,000 books in the Short-Title Catalog of books published before 1640. Each of Elsevier, Wiley, and Springer sell hundreds of journals in electronic form. The Association for Computing Machinery not only provides its current journals electronically, but is retrospectively converting the entire backfile so that most of the history of American computing research will be available online. There are also large government projects: the entire backfile of US patents has been scanned.

And, as mentioned earlier in the chapter, the largest text digitization project is the Million Book Project of Professor Raj Reddy (Carnegie Mellon University) and Professor N. Balakrishnan (Indian Institute of Sciences); this project plans to scan one million books, at approximately 25 scanning centers within India, over two or three years.

In addition, it's worth mentioning some text-oriented projects that are working with much more unusual materials.

- A US/UK project deserving special mention is the Electronic Beowulf project of Professors Kevin Kiernan (University of Kentucky) and Paul Sharmak (SUNY), which is working with the British Library to scan the *Beowulf* manuscript. The *Beowulf* manuscript was damaged by a fire in the eighteenth century and portions of it have become much more difficult to read. By scanning under different light conditions (including UV), it is possible to obtain scanned images that display more than an ordinary reader could see by eye. Thus, in addition to providing access to a fragile and unique manuscript to scholars at a distance, it can even provide better access than the original (Kiernan, 1995). A sample page is shown in Figure 12.3.
- Another international example is the project led by Keio University to digitize as many copies as possible of the Gutenberg Bible. This sheds light on early printing techniques by letting scholars do comparisons they could not otherwise do without extensive travel. A sample page is shown in Figure 12.4.
- In Japan, the digital library effort includes the preparation of a national union catalog and also a set of experiments on primary material at the National Diet Library. These experiments are testing and demonstrating digitization over a range of different kinds of library materials. Figure 12.5 is a sample of a children's book (entitled *Yatsu Yagi*, or "Eight Goats"). The work in Japan explores not only many different holdings but also different kinds of digitization techniques (National Diet Library, 1995).

Among the materials being digitized in Japan are:

- 7100 sheets of especially valuable rare materials, of which 1236 sheets are national treasures or important cultural properties, including woodblock prints, scrolls, and old maps. These will be digitized (via photographic film) in color, at high resolution (5000×4000 pixels).
- 21,000 books in the social sciences published during the Meiji (1868–1912) period. These are to be scanned in monochrome from microfilm.

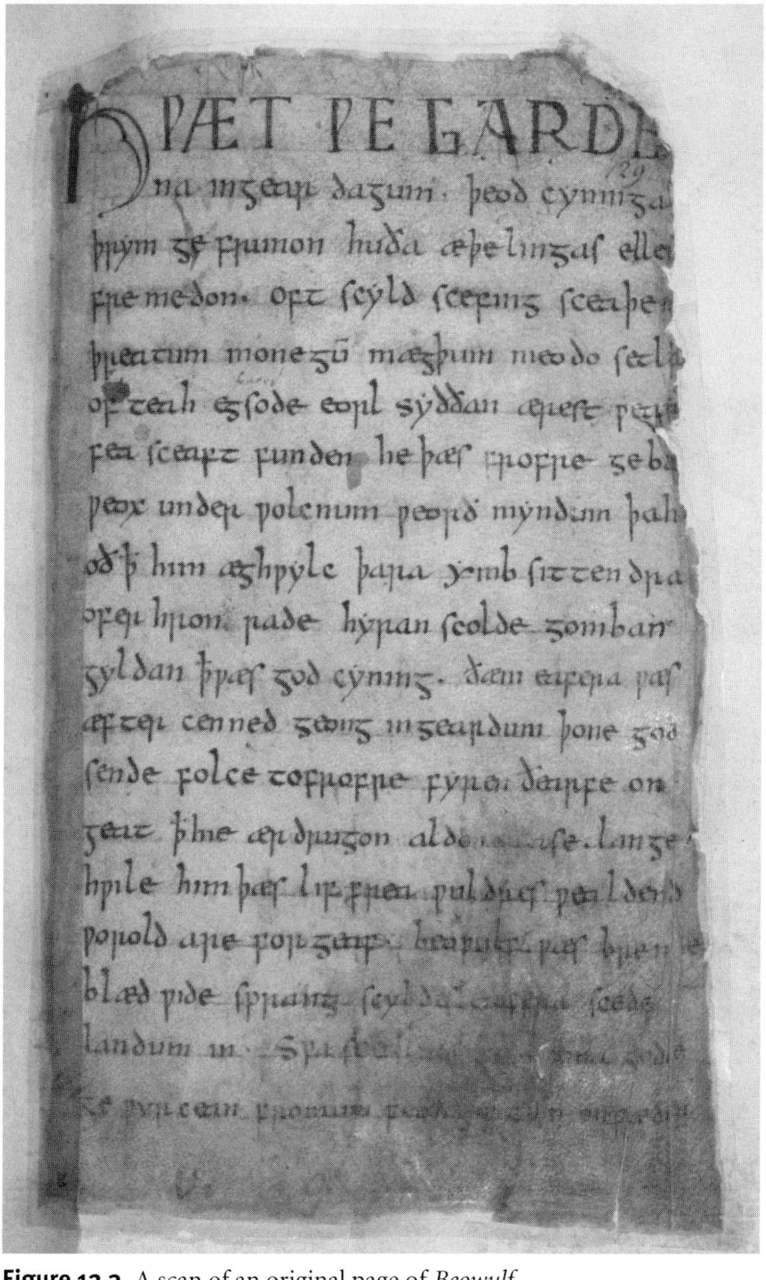

Figure 12.3 A scan of an original page of *Beowulf*.

Figure 12.4 A scan of an original page of a Gutenberg Bible.

- 3000 books published during World War II on poor-quality paper which are both deteriorating badly and present in few copies. Again, these will be scanned from microfilm.
- 20 serial titles, totalling 800,000 pages, to be scanned directly with sheet feeders.
- 260 volumes of Diet (Parliamentary) research materials, amounting to about 6000 pages, to be both scanned and processed by an OCR program which can recognize kanji.
- 7000 documents in political history related to Michitsune Mishima, comprising 340,000 frames of microfilm.
- 1,600,000 pages of material, largely Diet proceedings, to be scanned directly from paper.

Figure 12.5 Scanned pages from *Yatsu Yagi*, or "Eight Goats," a
Japanese children's book.

Figure 12.6 Storage of the wooden printing blocks of
Tripitaka Koreana.

In Korea, there is a fascinating project to digitize the wood carvings at the
Haeinsa monastery, which contains 81,258 wooden printing blocks with the oldest known copy of the Buddhist canon in Chinese, the Tripitaka Koreana. The
risk of mold damage to these thirteenth-century printing blocks (Figures 12.6
and 12.7), plus the desire to make them accessible to more people, prompted

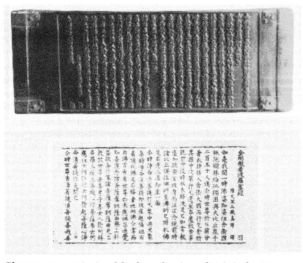

Figure 12.7 Printing block and print of Tripitaka Koreana.

a digitization project plus work on the preservation of the actual wood—although the fifteenth-century buildings with clay floors turned out to be excellent storehouses.

A number of US digital library research projects have worked on trying to simplify the process of generating online books. For example, the University of Illinois worked with publishers on the problems of creating both online and paper versions of the same material and doing the format conversions efficiently. The University of Michigan worked on catalog management and techniques for finding books in an online world. We still don't have good agreement on the ways of doing the conversion. Although research remains to be done to determine the best practices, the following is a summary of the necessary steps involved.

- *Scanning.* The first step is scanning, and the library community has argued for a standard quality of 600 dpi, one bit per pixel. This matches well with the demands of laser printing for reproducing the books, but it's not really best for readability. It would be faster to scan at 400 dpi, 2 bits per pixel, which would also produce smaller output files and more readable screen displays. This isn't done, however, partly because too many postprocessing steps would immediately throw away the grayscale information and leave a lower-quality image behind.

- *Encoding.* Next comes encoding, for which Tiff Group IV, a lossless compression system, is favored. However, the most efficient encoding comes from a style in which the background and foreground are separated, with different compression techniques for the two. The background is most efficiently handled by a JPEG-like or wavelet compression method; the foreground is best handled with some kind of dictionary or other technique using the fact that letter shapes are repeated so often. The DjVu compression algorithm of AT&T uses this kind of separation, as does the JPEG2000 standard.

- *Searching.* Some kind of searching system is needed. This can rely on cataloging, or on manual keying of all or part of the material; for example, when *The New York Times* microfilm was scanned for the ProQuest Historical Newspaper file, the beginnings of each story were keyed to avoid the problems incurred with OCR for some low-quality images. More often, OCR is used; as of early 2003, the favored OCR software is Abbyy Finereader, but there are competitors; AT&T's DjVu includes its own OCR, and for some historical material Olive Software sells a package of search and OCR bundled together, with the search software understanding the typical mistakes made by the OCR and trying to compensate.

- *Display.* Finally, some way of displaying the result to the user is needed. Should the user be allowed to see the OCR or only the image? Should the focus be on reprinting to paper, on distribution to handheld e-books, or on-screen display over the Internet? As yet, we haven't got a standard answer.

The costs of digitization are extremely variable, depending on quality demands. Commercial vendors will quote as low as 4 or 5 cents per page if they can take the book apart and use mechanical sheet feeders. Many libraries are paying up to a few dollars a page, using careful handling and nondestructive scanning.

In summary, there are a lot of large text-oriented digital library projects. We're making progress at these, but we still don't have a completely cut and dried answer. Nor can we make a complete list of these projects. The National Library of China wishes to scan Sung and Yuan dynasty books, from 960–1368 (Jishi, 1992). IBM scanned 9 million pages of the Seville archives between 1987 and 1992, as part of the celebration of the 500th anniversary of the Columbus voyage (Mintzer et al., 1995a, 1995b). This kind of note could be extended indefinitely. It's not just a problem that no book can include a permanent list of machine-readable texts; it's so difficult to find out whether a book has been scanned that some books are undoubtedly being scanned twice or more (as an example, Prescott's *History of the Conquest of Peru* has been done both by Gutenberg and by the Million Book Project). OCLC has recently announced a "Digital Registry" as a way of keeping track of conversion efforts.

These are, however, the problems of success. We know how to digitize books; we even see ways of getting some of the money; we're stuck on copyright issues and user access, not the technology. But we are still getting so much digitizing done that we get to complain about the lack of coordination.

12.5 Images

As we discussed in Chapter 3, the importance placed on special collections and the attractiveness of pictures for Web displays have led to a lot of digitizing of images. Most important is the new research being done on techniques for searching and classifying images. This is perhaps the most active research area in digital libraries at present.

As with text, much digitizing is focussed on items of great local importance; the British have scanned *Magna Carta*, the *Lindsifarne Gospels*, and *Canterbury Tales*. Some digitization is both important and attractive. Figure 12.8 is a map from the French national collection, and Figure 12.9 is an Aztec manuscript from the Vatican library.

Large photographic scanning projects can be of great interest to researchers. The State Library of Victoria, for example, has converted 107,000 of its 650,000 historical photographs to digital form, averaging 35 K for the JPEG file for each picture. An item-level catalog was prepared for each picture. The picture in Figure 12.10, for example, is from the portrait file and shows four aboriginal men at Corranderrk.

Other projects being undertaken in Australia are the digitization of important early Australian literary works, through the Ferguson 1840–1845 project, after the major bibliographer of Australian publishing. This project will scan (at 400 dpi, 8 bits of gray-level) 150,000 images representing 75 serial titles

Figure 12.8 Map from the French national collection.

Figure 12.9 Aztec manuscript from the Vatican library.

Figure 12.10 Historical photograph from the
State Library of Victoria.

and 4 novels. There is also digitization of aboriginal language recordings,
scanning of the journals of Sir Joseph Banks, creation of a computer file of biographies of Australian scientists, and the conversion of Australian war photographs
to electronic form.

The Library of Congress, as part of its American Memory project, has
scanned millions of photographs. Again, this kind of work provides access

to researchers; often it goes with recataloging of the images to improve access; and it also protects the originals from handling. Unfortunately, it tends to be very expensive; conversion tends to run from $2–10 per item, and sometimes higher. The cost of conversion depends on the care needed in handling and the amount of special photographic processing, such as a need to adjust the color of each picture. These costs may be dwarfed, however, by the recataloging; it is not uncommon for cataloging a picture to cost $25.

Many organizations are scanning art works or slides of art works. Some years ago, the Getty funded an experiment in the use of digitized art works in university education, and Carnegie Mellon is now building ARTSTOR, on the model of JSTOR, to provide about a quarter of a million digitized art images. They are beginning with the collection at UC San Diego.

Among the most interesting projects are those that involve research on image analysis in addition to image conversion and access. For example, researchers at Xerox PARC and the University of Massachusetts are looking at what can be done with handwritten documents. One can, for example, find bitmaps of words and then search for similar bitmaps. Figure 12.11 is a sample of such work, from Professor Manmatha in Massachusetts, showing a letter written by George Washington.

Aerial and satellite observation of the earth is producing a very large number of images and data. The University of California at Santa Barbara, in a project led by Terry Smith, is working on maps, aerial photographs, and other "spatially-indexed" information in their 'Alexandria' library. They cooperate not only with the other Digital Library Initiative projects, but also with a group of NASA-funded efforts to make earth observation data more readily accessible.

- *Spatial indexing and retrieval.* UCSB tries to determine, for each query and library item, the "footprint" on the earth, which may be a precise point or area or may be fuzzy. Geographic names or coordinates are mapped to the footprint, which can then be used for spatial retrieval. Given the size of the images, UCSB is also researching technologies for rapid response to image data, including multiresolution image storage and display.
- *Image processing.* A key question is partitioning: dividing the image into areas, which can then be characterized by texture, color, and location. This can be used to find particular kinds of land use in aerial photographs. Their edge location algorithms are doing very well, holding out hope for queries such as "find a photograph of Ventura County in the 1950s showing orchards." Figure 12.12 is a sample of the partitioning algorithm from their website.

Some important image analysis work involves medicine. Figure 12.13 is a chest image from UCLA. The goal, of course, is to suggest possible diagnoses;

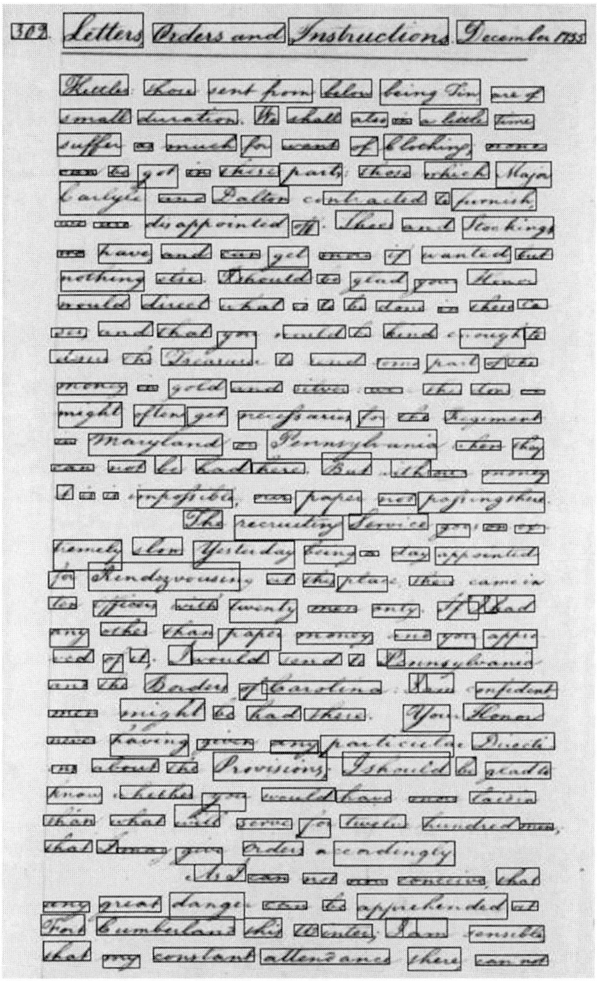

Figure 12.11 Bitmap of a letter written by George Washington.

the software to do this is now gaining competitiveness with radiologists. Similar work is proceeding in other places. One odd twist on medical image research at Stanford has been driven by the need to protect the privacy of medical records. To ensure that nothing is ever attributed to the wrong patient, as one group introduces automatic labelling of radiographs with patient numbers, another group looks at how to remove this information so that the records can be displayed without identifying information when desirable.

Another project is a digital library of marine mammals, done by Kelly Debure at Eckerd College in Florida. Each dolphin on the east coast of the US can be

Figure 12.12 Partitioning of aerial photography into areas of similar land use.

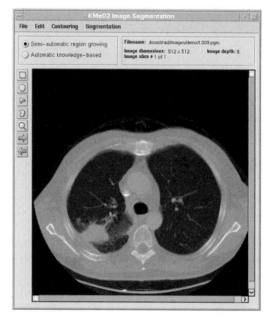

Figure 12.13 Chest radiograph from UCLA.

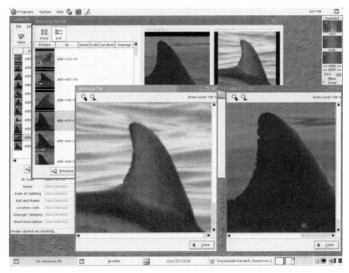

Figure 12.14 Images from a dolphin fin digital library at Eckerd College.

identified by its markings; they have built a database to display them. Users can sketch a fin, or compare with the existing database, as a way of identifying a particular animal. The interface screen is shown in Figure 12.14.

Face recognition has been a particularly active topic in image processing for decades. The rise of international security concerns has focussed new attention on it; some companies claim that given a set of photographs of faces, they can spot those individuals walking down an airport corridor past their camera. Similarly, the British police announced at one point that they had connected the security cameras around a south London housing development to a computer system that watched for the faces of a hundred known criminals from the area. Whether or not this was a bluff, it cut burglary in the area by a third. Software methods to find the nose, ears, or corners of the mouth on a picture are now routine; if the faces to be compared are oriented the same way, they can be scaled and then compared in a straightforward way. The research problems revolve around the need to detect people who are not quite facing the same way as when the picture was taken.

Some images pose a particular problem: whether Figure 12.15 should be considered text or image may be doubtful. This is another international cooperative project, on papyri. It allows scholars to compare bits of papyri in different places to see if they can be lined up; thus, manuscripts separated long ago may potentially be reassembled (Bagnall, 1995).

General image retrieval is still an extremely difficult problem. Perhaps the leading work is that at Berkeley, where David Forsyth and Jitendra Malik

Figure 12.15 Papyrus.

(Forsyth and Malik, 1996) are experimenting with automatic labelling of pictures. Given a large collection of pictures that have alphabetic labels, they partition the pictures and try to identify which shapes and colors go with which words. Then, given an unlabelled picture, they can try to see if they can correctly label parts of it. An example was shown earlier in Chapter 4 (see Figure 4.6 in Section 4.4).

12.6 Sound and Music

Another active area of research has been the use of digital libraries to store sound and music collections. A major difficulty has been that virtually all sound recordings are under copyright. In the United States, even the sound recordings that you would think would be in the public domain, because of their age and the unlikelihood that their copyright would have been renewed, turn out to be protected as a result of the way the laws were amended to include sound recordings. Obtaining permission to use resources may thus be extremely difficult. Nevertheless, some very interesting projects exist.

One of the larger digital library research efforts in the United States is the National Gallery of the Spoken Word. Run by Mark Kornbluh at Michigan State University, this collection includes such resources as the Vincent Voice Library, historic sound recordings including every President back to Grover Cleveland, and the collected radio interviews of Studs Terkel. Searching and accessing such a collection is complex, because speech recognition software doesn't work that effectively on the old, historic sound recordings. Just as the early days of OCR saw some projects look at how accurately one could do retrieval if only some fraction of the words were correctly recognized, the same is now happening with speech resources. Speech recognition programs that only recognize an occasional word may still be useful for some kind of rough classification of recordings.

The BBC has a major effort to digitize much of its history, representing many millions of pounds over at least five years. They are able to exploit this in making new broadcasts; much of the material broadcast on their new radio channels is repurposed material digitized from older broadcasts of their existing channels. Valuable as this collection is, the digital material is not readily available to outside researchers.

There is an effort at music OCR at Johns Hopkins University, based on digitizing of their collection of sheet music songs; Sayeed Choudhury is leading the project. A sample of the collection is shown in Figure 12.16. Even more ambitious is the work of Bill Birmingham (1995) to parse and search music. He attempts to find themes in music and then search for them by pattern. In Figure 12.17, the left side shows the attempt to distinguish theme from harmony and the right side shows the program recognizing the particular melody so that it can search for it elsewhere. Other music searching programs exist at the University of Massachusetts and elsewhere.

12.7   Video

Of course, if we can do both images and sounds, we should be able to have digital video libraries, and these now exist. The rise of digital broadcasting and digital film production has meant that lots of companies and devices exist to convert moving image material to digital form; the difficulty is usually going to be getting permission, since again virtually all movies and video are under copyright protection.

Some collections have particularly interesting historical material and would be worth digitizing. Vanderbilt University, for example, has a set of recordings of TV news broadcasts back to 1968 (before the TV networks were routinely saving their evening news broadcasts). They are in the process of trying to turn this into a digital file; the copyright law makes special allowance for news broadcasts recorded by educational institutions (thanks to Senator Howard Baker of Tennessee). UCLA has a set of newsreel material originally used by the Hearst Corporation and covering 1928–1968; fortunately they got the

Figure 12.16 Score from Aida in Johns Hopkins University music library project.

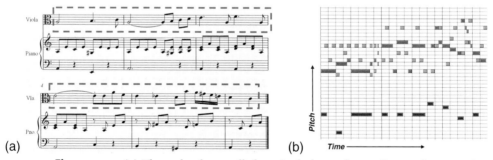

(a)   (b)

Figure 12.17 (a) Theme has been called out in dark grey boxes. Sonata for arpeggione and piano in a minor, D. 821, i. Allegro moderato, Franz Schubert (1797-1828). (b) The theme is again shown in dark grey, this time in piano-roll notation, where its significance is less obvious.

collection with the copyright but have not yet identified funding to convert it to digital form.

In terms of retrieval from video, one of the earliest projects, and still a leading one, is the Informedia project at Carnegie Mellon University (CMU), led by Howard Wactlar. Informedia works with a collection of video from CNN and from the Discovery Channel, and brings together multiple techniques to do retrieval, including image and voice recognition. Video is partitioned into scenes, and different techniques are applied to the scene and the accompanying soundtrack.

1. *Image analysis.* Images from the video are partitioned, and then image features are found and categorized for search. Users can pick particular frames and then look for others that are similar. Research is underway on classifying frames (meetings, real events, speeches, and so on).

2. *Speech recognition.* Although some of the video is closed-captioned and thus comes with a reasonably accurate transcript, CMU is using automatic speech recognition to handle uncaptioned material, to align the captioning with the spoken words, and to allow spoken questions. This work builds on a long history of speech recognition research at CMU (e.g., the Sphinx system).

3. *Face recognition.* CMU software looks for faces in the video and attempts to match them with names in the voice transcript. Again, this is preliminary, but there is moderate success at this. Color values and shapes are used to find faces, and then a face similarity algorithm attempts to match them up.

4. *Natural language understanding (NLP).* Given the transcript, to assign names to faces it is still necessary to find personal names in the transcript. CMU again has a long history of work in NLP and is applying it to analysis of the transcripts. Some semantic problems can be quite difficult: if the announcer says, "Sinn Fein announced today that…" and the screen shows a picture of Gerry Adams, it is difficult to realize that Sinn Fein is not somebody's name.

The CMU project went on to look at display techniques and interfaces to assist access. One option for still images that is not so easy for video is to make use of the ability people have to scan pictures very quickly. CMU tries to exploit this by using *key-frames* from each scene and putting up menus of these frames. A sample of the interface is shown in Figure 12.18. In this case, the user has searched for "bin laden couriers" and a menu of frames was shown, along with geographic information about the locations of the stories in the hits, a transcript of part of one video clip, and the top right window showing the clip itself. Smeaton (2004) has reviewed recent video search and retrieval projects.

Another very difficult video-based retrieval project is the effort by the Visual History Foundation to automatically index their database. The Visual History Foundation has digital video recordings of more than 50,000 Holocaust survivors and needs to index them; a typical recording is more than 2 hours long. Indexing has proved to take longer and be more difficult than the original recording; listening to the recordings is so disturbing that few indexers can stick with the job for a

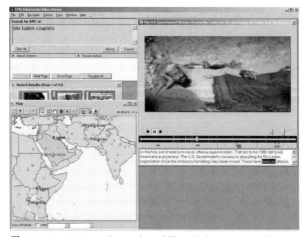

Figure 12.18 Search results of "bin laden couriers" in CMU's video digital library.

long time. In principle, one could make a transcript by speech recognition. The speakers here, however, are frequently not speaking their native language (about half the interviews are in English, but virtually no Holocaust victims had English as their first language). They are usually very emotional, and their narration involves geographic names of places in Europe and personal names in various languages. An effort is being made to see how speech recognition software can be improved to deal with problems like this; if it can be successful, there are many applications for automatic recognition of accented or emotional speech.

None of the collections mentioned so far is available to outside researchers, and one problem with video retrieval has been the difficulty of finding material with which to experiment. Gary Marchionini has been working on the Open Video project, collecting copyright-free material such as NASA video. Another source is the work of the Internet Archive with Rick Prelinger, who has been willing to make over a thousand hours of film publicly available (see the Archive website). These films were typically industrial or educational films, but retain a great deal of interest.

12.8 3-D Images

The research frontier as of 2003 appears to be in the collection and searching of 3-D material. It is now possible to scan in 3-D, normally using one of two methods:

- If multiple cameras observe the same object, it is possible by combining their images and triangulating to determine the position of each visible point in 3-D space.

Figure 12.19 Three-dimensional cuneiform tablet from UCLA's 3-D digital library project.

■ By spinning a laser rangefinder around an object, thus measuring the distance to each point the laser can spot, a slice can be positioned in 3-D space; by moving the object systematically, each point can be measured.

As an example of simple use of 3-D techniques, Figure 12.19 shows a cuneiform tablet (from the work of Robert Englund at UCLA). Often, these tablets are very worn and hard to read; by using a 3-D scan and then artificially deepening the scratches, they can be made more readable. The Digital Hammurabi project at Johns Hopkins is also scanning cuneiform.

A much more ambitious use of 3-D imaging has been the Digital Michaelangelo project of Marc Levoy at Stanford. Using laser rangefinding, the David statue in Florence has been scanned to an accuracy of 1/4 mm; it is possible to tell which chisel was used on which part of the work. As an example of what this made possible, it turns out the weight of the statue has been reported incorrectly for centuries. It was also possible to compute the balance of the statue and confirm that a block of stone behind one lower leg is really necessary; without that block, the statue wouldn't stand up.

Professor Levoy has also been using 3-D scanning in a fascinating project to reassemble the world's largest map. In classical Rome, the census office had a map of the city chiseled into a marble wall, 60 feet long. It showed not just every building, but the rooms on the ground floor of each building. Years ago the wall fell down, and what we have is more than a thousand blocks of stone in a museum basement; this is the world's largest jigsaw puzzle. The typical block, regretfully,

Figure 12.20 One side of a 3-D scan of a piece of chiseled stone originally belonging to an ancient Roman map chiseled in marble.

Figure 12.21 Digital representation of Beauvais Cathedral.

doesn't have much detail on it; see an example in Figure 12.20. They've all now been scanned in 3-D, meaning that instead of just trying to fit them together based on their front surfaces, it's possible to try out possible fits of the blocks based on their side and rear surfaces as well.

Laser scanning can even be used on whole buildings. Figure 12.21 is an image of Beauvais Cathedral, calculated as a result of scanning done by researchers from Columbia University. This cathedral has fallen down several times in the past and is threatening to fall down again; the idea is to make a digital representation which can be used with civil engineering software to do calculations of how best to repair the situation.

Even more ambitious is the attempt to create models of historical buildings that no longer exist. Figure 12.22 shows a photograph of the synagogue in Wiesbaden before its destruction by the Nazis in 1938, and then an image from a computer visualization of a 3-D model of the synagogue made by students at the University of Wiesbaden. Creating the model involved study of surviving photographs and plans and interviews with people who remembered details of the design (e.g., the colors painted in areas where no color photographs had survived).

Sometimes one can even make a model of the inside of something. Tim Rowe at the University of Texas is building a digital library of fossil vertebrates, doing CT (computer tomography) scans of the bones. This allows students to see inside the fossil, without cutting it open. They can see how birds developed hollow bones, or look inside eggs. With 3-D "printing" techniques, fossils can be reproduced so students can handle them, and they can be made bigger or smaller to reach a convenient size. Figure 12.23 is an example of some crocodile skulls. Perhaps the best-known result of this project was the discovery that a recently ballyhooed fossil of Archeoptryx (auctioned for $80,000) had been made by gluing together two unrelated sets of bones.

Another very complex representation problem in three dimensions is that of human motion. Professor Jezekiel Ben-Arie of the University of Illinois (Chicago) has been analyzing videos of people and classifying their activities into walking, standing, sitting, and so on. He identifies the skeletal positions and then studies how they change from image to image (Figure 12.24). Patterns of changes are identified with one of the standard actions.

The advent of 3-D databases, of course, implies that we need 3-D searching techniques. These are enormously important economically if we can learn how to do searches on the shapes of protein molecules, with the aim of designing new drugs for instance. However, research projects in 3-D searching are just beginning. A sample of the work of Tom Funkhouser at Princeton is shown in Figure 12.25, showing searching for different kinds of chairs. Queries in this work may be sketches, 3-D tracings using a spaceball or dataglove, or the result of pointing to existing objects.

12.9 Scholarship in Digital Libraries

A great many important digital libraries have been built of data from the special collections of university libraries, many with the intent of helping teaching and education in different areas. Only a few of the many important ones can be

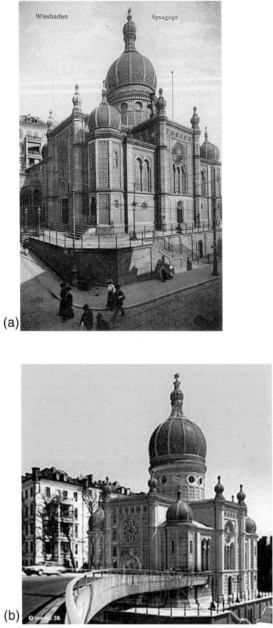

Figure 12.22 (a) Historic photograph of the synagogue in Wiesbaden; (b) Computer visualization of a 3-D model of the synagogue.

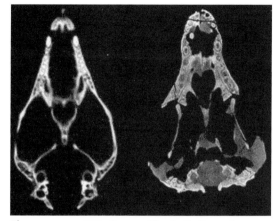

Figure 12.23 CT of crocodile skulls from the University of Texas digital library of fossil vertebrates.

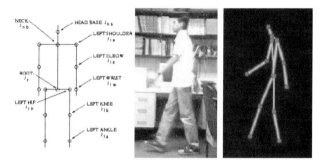

Figure 12.24 Analysis of human movement.

touched on here. There are, for example, many sites devoted to the works of particular authors: Cervantes at Texas A&M, Blake at Virginia, Horace Walpole at Yale, Chopin at Chicago, Chaucer at Harvard, and so on. There are also cooperative projects such as the Making of America (Cornell and Michigan) and a great many efforts tailored to the interests of specific libraries. Alaska has digitized information about the Inuit, while Florida has scanned images of plants from the state's herbaria. Nonuniversity libraries also have wide-ranging digital collections, such as the American Numismatic Association's site on coins and money, or oceanography at the website of northern California's Monterey Bay Aquarium.

Ed Ayers and coworkers at the University of Virginia have built a website called The Valley of the Shadow about two communities in the Shenandoah Valley at the time of the Civil War. It includes diaries, newspapers, drawings,

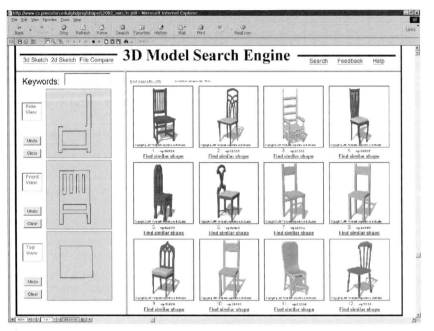

Figure 12.25 Searching an experimental 3-D digital library for chairs.

maps, and other information about one town at each end of the valley. This site demonstrates how important—but rarely accessible—historical information can be brought out on the Web so that students and scholars everywhere can use it. It also shows the value of good content and professional editing and commentary. Unlike many sites, it is not just scanned books, but contains a great deal of organization and commentary provided by the specialists at Virginia.

It's hard to exaggerate the breadth of digital library collections. The works of British women poets from the romantic period are at UC Davis, vegetable diseases are tracked online at Cornell, the origins of ragtime can be found at a private site operated by "Perfessor" Bill Edwards, and children's art at a private foundation (Papaink). What does characterize them in general is an avoidance of copyright disputes, by choosing older material or scientific material, and a true enthusiasm for their contents. Collectors can now share their passions with the world. Looking at *D-Lib Magazine's* featured site of the month, as I did to write this paragraph, turns up a steady sequence of remarkable websites.

Again, most of these sites are more than just scanned books or pictures. Many of the literature sites are devoted to comparisons of different editions (e.g., the Cervantes site), to attempts to create new scholarly editions, or to bringing together disparate collections. What this also means is that the cost of most of them is not primarily scanning but scholarly and editorial time (perhaps not charged for in the project proposal). They are comparable, in many cases, to a scholarly monograph, although universities haven't yet agreed to value them similarly for tenure.

Digital library sites, however, don't read like scholarly monographs. They are far more likely to involve images, are broken up into short sections, and are usually designed to be accessible to the nonspecialist. Thus, they are finding use in education even down to elementary school level. Original documents that a schoolchild would never have been allowed to handle can be given to children on the Web. Even if the published edition of George Washington's diary is easier to search and contains helpful reference notes, it's still remarkable to see his original handwriting and see how clear it is. Figure 12.26 is from the American Memory site of the Library of Congress.

The Perseus site, mentioned at the start of the chapter, has led in the application of digital libraries to education; it is widely used in the teaching of classical Greek throughout the country and even the world. It provides in one easy place a full library of Greek texts, translations, dictionaries and glossaries, atlases, and illustrations of Greek culture. An equivalent textbook would be a series of books taking many feet of shelf space and without the ability to quickly link from text to dictionary or text to atlas. Similarly, the National Science Foundation is encouraging the development of sites with scientific and engineering content through the NSDL program. A great deal of material is being placed online, and courseware is being built to support the use of this material in colleges and universities.

We don't yet know whether digital libraries will actually be effective in education. We know that people are enthusiastic, but education has a long history of failed experiments to introduce computers into classrooms. Pedagogical techniques will have to be revised to deal with the wealth of online material, and this is a hard task in an educational establishment that has still not quite come to grips with the existence of pocket calculators. Nor, despite the recent emphasis on measurement of student performance, have we agreed on ways to do such testing. At the college level, however, we can clearly see the adoption of many of these sites, including the commercial ones, in research projects and class reference throughout many disciplines.

12.10 Scientific Data

Another form of digital library that will become increasingly more important is the library of scientific data. Historically, science has progressed through the paradigm of

1. Make an hypothesis.
2. Design an experiment to test it.

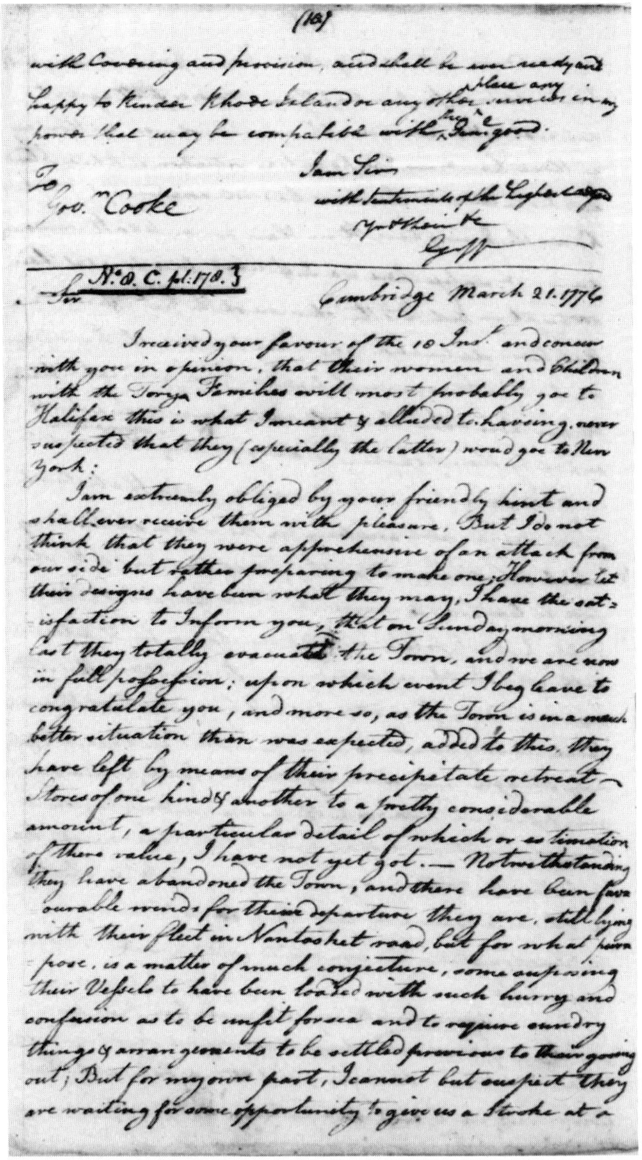

Figure 12.26 Page from George Washington's diary from the American Memory site.

3. Run the experiment and gather the data.
4. Decide whether the hypothesis is true and then repeat.

It is now possible in some situations to avoid running the experiment, because there is so much data online that one can just look up the answer. The first area where this became true was molecular biology, thanks to a practice in the field that you cannot publish a paper announcing that you've measured the structure of a protein molecule unless you deposit the data in the Protein Data Bank. Similarly, the various genome data banks have collected and published the many gene sequences. An entire discipline of computational biology has grown up to exploit this data, and in many cases lab work has been replaced with database lookup. The growth of the Protein Data Bank is shown in Figure 12.27

The next field to make this transition was astronomy. The Sloan Digital Sky Survey has provided an image of the sky which can be used as needed by astronomers; efforts are now underway to extend it (in wavelength and by time), and the astronomy community is learning how to exploit this resource. For example, a brown dwarf has been discovered by analysis of the Sloan survey and the 2 MASS (Two Micron All Sky Survey) data. The images from the Sloan survey are very detailed and can be quite beautiful (Figure 12.28).

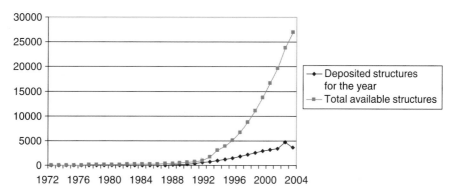

Figure 12.27 Growth of the Protein Data Bank.

Figure 12.28 Image from the Sloan Digital Sky Survey.

Data can also be produced by or used with simulations; in different situations, it may be better to calculate or to look up the answer. In chess, for example, the computers typically play the opening and the endgame by looking the position up in a database and only compute during the middle game. Both methods of using computers complement each other; either one is likely to be much faster than experiments.

Note, however, the simplicity of solutions by data lookup: often they require less analysis or knowledge. Consider two ways of predicting tomorrow's weather. Strategy 1: measure the weather today, take a set of equations which model the hydrodynamics of the atmosphere, and run them forward 24 hours. This is what we actually do today. Strategy 2: measure the weather today, and look through a big file of all past weather to find the day in the past that is the best match to today. Then take the next day's weather from the past file and give it as today's prediction. At the moment, the weather is too variable and too dependent on small changes for strategy 2 to work as well as strategy 1. Strategy 2 would be a lot easier, however, since we wouldn't need any equations, nor the need to understand atmospheric physics at all.

Many projects are gathering large amounts of scientific data. Chemical structures, engineering design data, spectroscopic measurements, and the like are all pouring on to disk drives. Figure 12.29 is, for example, a chart from the IRIS consortium's seismic database, showing earthquakes around the world.

There are also massive databases in the social sciences from sources such as public opinion polls and elections, as well from national census organizations. The ICPSR (Inter-university Consortium for Political and Social Research) in Ann Arbor, Michigan, is a major holder of such information, along with the UK Data Archive at the University of Essex.

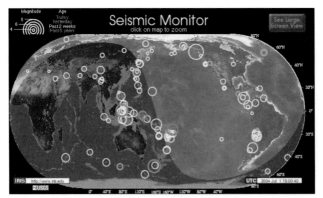

Figure 12.29 Earthquakes around the world from the IRIS consortium's seismic database.

We do not know how to effectively search and use these databases. The San Diego SuperComputer Center is collecting many of them and studying techniques for metadata and analysis of such data. But it is distressingly true that as one moves from text to image to data, the programs to deal with the material become ever more limited, and the amount of specialized knowledge required of the user is ever greater. Although you would think we understood numerical data better than we can understand language, somehow we have general tools to search any text collection, but we do not have the same kind of access to collections of numbers.

12.11 Access and Infrastructure

In fact, many digital library projects do focus on access to data and interfaces to help users. As with the content-based projects, there are too many to mention exhaustively, and it is only possible to skim and mention a few of them.

Professor Robert Wilensky at Berkeley has pushed the idea of *multivalent documents*, meaning that you can get different views of different forms of a document. You can, for example, overlay a vector street map on an aerial photograph. Users can search or view any representation. For example, if some documents were translated into Spanish, users could choose to view that form, even if they had searched in English. Processing of the multiple representations is also supported, for example, cut and paste works with images as well as with text.

The University of Michigan has used earth and space sciences as a subject domain and includes journal articles, books, and video and audio recordings of scientists discussing research questions in the collection. Among the related projects is the Space Physics and Aeronomy Research Collaboratory, an attempt to provide communication among scientists studying the upper atmosphere and space. Researchers such as Elliot Soloway and Dan Atkins have explored the best way to use the collaboratory idea in education. This collaboratory has been going on for many years; it's not entirely clear why it's been so successful when (for example) a collaboratory about nematodes seems to have withered.

The University of Washington has been studying the way experts use a document collection to see if users can benefit from following their methods and experiences. Similarly, Columbia University has a project in generating explanations for medical patients. Both of these products are looking at the problems of communication with users and understanding how they can best use the information they find.

The Library of Congress under James Billington raised $60 M to digitize 5 million items from its collections. This follows earlier work in their American Memory Project, in which they digitized (and have now placed on the Web) such materials as Matthew Brady's Civil War photographs, documents from the Continental Congress, sound recordings of speeches from World War I, and early motion pictures (Library of Congress, 1995, 2002). There has been considerable use of the American Memory project in schools (see for example Flanagan and Fitch, 2002). The Library of Congress now envisages a $175 M project to further create a National Digital Library and is planning activities (and fundraising). And the Library also administered a series of awards from Ameritech that supported digitization projects in many smaller institutions around the country. The American Memory website (memory.loc.gov) has continued to expand and now contains a large variety of text, image, sound, and audiovisual resources.

There are several projects trying to establish some kind of networking infrastructure for the library community to support file sharing. The CEDARS project in the United Kingdom did this, for example, and one of the leaders in this area is the Stanford digital library project. Stanford, best known for creating Google (and by that act alone justifying the entire government investment in digital libraries), has also built an interoperability protocol for digital libraries and a model of digital preservation relying on multiple libraries storing copies of information.

12.12 Summary

To end this quick tour, consider two spectacular projects: the Internet Archive and the International Dunhuang Project.

The Internet Archive, the creation of Brewster Kahle, has an immediate goal of saving the Web so that we will not lose this new development in creativity the way we have lost large chunks of the movies created before 1950, most of live radio, and most Elizabethan drama. The Archive receives a sweep of the Web about every two months and squirrels it away; the service it offers is basically "give us a URL and we'll tell you what dates we have that page from and let you look at those older versions." As of early 2003, the Archive is about 100 terabytes, and grows 10 terabytes a month. There are two copies, one at the Library of Congress and one at the Biblioteca Alexandrina in Egypt, although neither is yet regularly updated. It is remarkable for the tiny size of the staff (six or so people maintain the archiving operation) compared with the enormous amount of information stored; 100 terabytes is several times the content of the books in the Library of Congress.

The International Dunhuang Project, supported by the Andrew W. Mellon Foundation, is an example of digital technology applied to international cooperation. This project deals with material from the caves near Dunhuang in the

Figure 12.30 Cave paintings from Dunhuang, China, as digitized by the International Dunhuang Project.

western deserts of China. It tries, by digitization, to bring together the paintings still on the walls of those caves with the manuscripts, many more than 1000 years old, now in libraries in London, Paris, Berlin, and St. Petersburg. The project makes use of virtual reality technology to represent a three-dimensional cave, and allows the user to "walk around" the cave as well as compare the cave paintings with the manuscripts once in the same place. Figure 12.30 shows some of the digitized cave paintings.

It has been possible in this chapter, long as it is, only to touch on a few of the many digital library projects now going on. Perhaps the most important lesson to take away from such a survey is the need to give serious consideration to these projects, both in terms of their current impact and how it could be improved. Much of the library material being digitized in these projects is from special collections, preservation material, or other content not heavily used in traditional libraries. It is understandable that libraries are avoiding copyright problems in their choice of collections to digitize, but it does run the risk that their material will seem less important to users. It would be of the greatest value to libraries if early digital library projects included materials heavily used by their patrons to reinforce the idea that digital information is easy to use and valuable. Not only would this build up public support for and familiarity with digital libraries, but it would help us learn more about the relative value of various digital formats to the user.

The international nature of the Internet revolutionizes our ability to move information around the world. US undergraduates can be assigned papers with topics requiring data from worldwide sources, and they can find it with less effort than was traditionally required. If we can continue the library tradition of open cooperation and access, in which scholars from any country are welcome at any library, we can increase the flow of transnational information and compensate for the growing number of libraries which lack the funds to maintain their purchases of foreign journals and books.

Internationalism interacts with the previous issues of economics and intellectual property rights. Will there be a single place where most online information is collected, or will files, like books, be distributed around the world? Will there be the equivalent of "flags of convenience" in shipping as digital publishers or libraries try to locate in places whose legal system is perceived to be more generous? We are already seeing "offshore" gambling on the Internet. Fortunately, libraries have a history of cooperation, extending around the world for decades. The British Library reorganized the reference shelves in its reading room into the Dewey classification. And the British Library's Document Supply Centre returns the favor by sending the United States copies of UK publications and doctoral theses. Libraries must continue to work together and help each other deal with the economic problems of the digital world as they have done in the analog world.

Scope of Digital Libraries

How far can digital libraries go? This chapter is about how many people will get how much information from digital libraries and how the flow will be handled. The Web will be how information is delivered; what will be collected and how? Looking at undergraduates, one hardly needs the future tense: the Web is where they get information, and they accept whatever is there. Our goals have to be to expand the community of online readers, extend the amount and kinds of information that are readily available, and improve the quality.

In this chapter we'll deal with the conventional information flow first: readers, authors, and whatever comes between them. Then we will look at some new kinds of information: courseware and scientific data. The overall message is "even more": more users, more information, and a greater role for online digital libraries in all forms of intellectual life. If we do this right, we should have a better educated and more productive society as a result.

13.1 Readers

Libraries, traditionally, are used by everyone. Children come to story hours even before they can read, students at all levels learn through libraries, adults borrow recreational reading, and the elderly can often enjoy the library when the sports arena is no longer relevant. What about digital libraries? They are perceived as difficult and complex by some, and the usage of online information varies by age, wealth, and geography. Most serious, we worry about the "digital divide." This phrase refers to the lack of access to modern technology among the poor. If one looks internationally, for example, the gap in Internet access between rich and poor countries is even greater than the basic gap in national income. Similarly, within the United States, the poor are less likely to use computers than the rich.

Given the history of libraries as a force for equality, it will be a shame if digital libraries cannot be made to serve the same role. Andrew Carnegie pushed us to provide free public libraries in essentially every town and city, and we then heard many stories of people who used these libraries to learn and advance themselves. For example, Chester Carlson, the inventor of the Xerox machine, did his research at no cost in the New York Public Library, still open to anyone. Must today's individual inventor find a way to afford a subscription to *ScienceDirect* at a cost of over a million dollars a year?

In fact, the United Kingdom adopted a policy a few years ago with the intent of making traditional libraries the place where ordinary citizens would gain access to online information. But in most places around the world, access is moving to the home. The highest rate of household broadband access is in South Korea and is over 50%. The Scandinavian countries are not far behind, and although the United States lags, the rate of broadband takeup is accelerating.

Certainly, in universities, you no longer find any students without computers and without Internet connections. All sorts of information now comes this way. All sorts of private organizations, from universities to corporations, used to publish organizational directories and telephone books on paper. Now they all rely on websites. All sorts of forms are now online, instead of being exhanged on paper. User manuals for all kinds of gadgets you might buy are available online. Don King and colleagues (2003) report that about 40% of faculty reading is now from electronic copies; this may be one reason why reading is accelerating. His data show a steady increase in the number of articles read by the typical scientist in a typical year (Figure 13.1).

Of course, what this means is that people without Internet connections are ever more disadvantaged. They will find branch offices closing as the functions they served move online, and then they will have to travel farther to find an equivalent place to do their business. Society, then, will need to push particularly hard to see that no one is left out, that everyone can gain access to the information systems on which we will depend.

In fact, usage of even rather obscure digital library materials can spread out to an entire community. Cherry and Duff (2002) reported that 62 of 159 users of Early Canadiana Online were using it for teaching and research; this means the

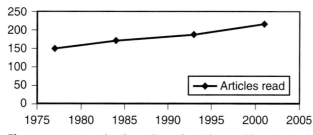

Figure 13.1 Growth of number of articles read by a typical scientist in a typical year.

majority of the users were doing something else (e.g., one recipient was using it as a source of knitting patterns).

In the United States, we have a fund to support communications services in rural areas and schools, based on a tax on long distance telephone calls (for political reasons, it's called a fee). We don't have a similar fund for inner cities, whose inhabitants also find phone service unaffordable at times. When I worked for the telephone company and we discussed bad debts, one comment made was that the electric company was worse off: everyone has electric service, but the very poorest, who had the most difficulty paying bills, didn't have phone service. They relied on neighbors and pay phones (and the rise of cellphones has caused a decline in the number of payphones). An ironic problem will arise if telephone service moves to the Internet and the result is that the Universal Service Fund no longer has a revenue source to support Internet access.

One answer may be wireless: the new kinds of wireless access have very low capital costs, and we may see methods of computer connection that become cheaper and cheaper and thus alleviate the "digital divide" problem. Already, for example, groups in downtown New York are providing free wireless connections in a variety of spots in lower Manhattan.

The demographics of digital library users also continue to expand. We may think of digital library users today as students or scholars associated with universities; that's changing, as well. Projects such as the International Children's Digital Library are building systems that even preschoolers can use, and we have services being built for private interests such as geneaology, tourism, and the like, as well as supporting governmental systems to deliver practical information to citizens. Much like our previous libraries, we will need digital libraries for everyone.

13.2 Authors

Traditionally, authors sent articles to publishers, who printed them on paper and then sent them to libraries. The academic community has gotten increasingly annoyed at the prices charged by publishers and is looking for other models. They focus on the possibility of self-publishing or using alternative, noncommercial publishers. Will this help?

Again, part of the problem has been a loss of access to modern information technology. Over the years, the number of articles being written grew faster than the number of people waiting to read them, or the size of library budgets able to buy them. If half as many scholarly journal articles or monographs were written, it would mean that libraries would only need to find a way to pay for half as many subscriptions. Those subscriptions would be cheaper, because each would have a longer press run, and greater economies of scale. But we can't just ask the academics to write fewer articles: they need them to get tenure. Remember the old line, "Deans can't read, they can only count." The true cynic has changed this to "Deans can't read or count, they can only weigh." But the impact is real: if we tried to cut back the number of journals, we would be forcing some number of researchers out of the system.

Digital libraries look like a way out of this. The visionary asks why we need the publishers at all: perhaps we can just post papers on the Web. Or perhaps the universities can do it for us. All of the systems are in place; we only need to persuade the authors that this is the way to go. High energy physics shows us one information system for scholars which does not involve conventional publishers. Professor Paul Ginsparg at Cornell (previously at Los Alamos National Laboratory) runs a preprint server for the physics community that accepts papers directly from authors and then lets readers download them. There's no charge and no refereeing. Anybody can send in a paper, and there is no delay while the paper is evaluated or while the post office delivers the eventual journal issue. Thus, the preprint server is faster than traditional publishing and preferred by authors fearful that somebody else is going to scoop their research, as well as by readers anxious to know the latest news.

Other authors can post information directly on their own website. The problem here is that prospective readers may not know where to look. There are some collections, such as the research sites of major companies, where readers may routinely look, but these are more likely to be sites representing a whole laboratory; it's too time-consuming for readers to be checking lots of personal sites.

You can get spiders to do this, though. In computer science, the Citeseer site, also called ResearchIndex, goes through the Web looking for research papers and tracking citations between them. Thus, if scientist A posts a paper, the Citeseer engine will find it and enable both free text search and citation tracing for locating it. Many of us find this site extremely effective for finding serious papers on a subject where a full Web search engine may turn up too many sales brochures or undergraduate essays.

What about those who do want their papers refereed, but would still like to avoid the standard paper publication route? If your purpose in publishing is tenure, rather than communication, is there a way that authors can use electronic publishing and libraries will not have to pay large subscription bills? Yes, there are several new organizations that publish online journals and run traditional peer-review systems, yet are less expensive than the commercial online journals. Among the earliest such journals (distributed free) are Psycoloquy and Postmodern Culture. As mentioned earlier, the Public Library of Science is making a major effort to create online, free-access journals with prestige as high as any paper journal, supported, not by reader fees, but by charging authors $1500 per article published.

13.3   Flow Control

Traditionally, one function of libraries is to be a "buying club" in the sense that the demands of everyone at a university are pooled so that the costs can be shared. If several of us want to read a specific book now and then, it is cheaper if we buy one copy than if all of us buy our own. Expanding on this function, university libraries have become the organization specialized to evaluate books, decide which should be purchased for the university's use, and then hold them and deliver them to the readers.

More and more, however, publishers in the digital world send information directly to the end user. The library may buy the subscription, but the information is on a publisher's server and the user connects directly to it. Particularly in the e-book area, we see publishers trying to sell directly to the end user. Will there still be intermediaries between the publishers and the reader? What about the library's role as selector of materials and advisor to the readers?

The same question exists at the other end. Authors send information to publishers who referee it, edit it, format it, and then package it and distribute it. But, as was mentioned in the last section, authors can post information directly or through new organizations such as preprint servers. In "amateur" research areas such as geneaology, lots of information flows directly from the websites of those collecting it to the eyes of the readers, directed only by search engines or with the help of individuals maintaining gateway pages. Do we need either the publishers or the libraries as intermediaries in the new world?

If we look at the various functions provided by these organizations, we still need some of them. For example,

- So long as universities award tenure and promotion based on peer-reviewed papers, we need some equivalent of the journal reviewing system. One could imagine completely different reviewing systems that did not end in publishing a paper, but there's no move to that visible in the universities.

- Students will still arrive at universities enthusiastic but inexperienced, and will still need some guidance in how to find useful information. Reference librarians of some sort are useful, although even today many students make much less use of them than they might, for a variety of social and practical reasons.

- To the extent that certain resources are needed for a university to teach and do research, how will they be chosen and gathered? The world of digital information seems to be encouraging each reader to find his or her own material, and particularly for students, this may mean that poorer sources are read for lack of knowledge of better ones. Can we still imagine a role for those who choose the information most appropriate for the university? Is this tangled with the issue of who pays for information?

- Information on a personal or even a project Web page can easily go away. How do we see that informally published material is kept around for the future?

Whether traditional publishers and libraries play these roles is hard to predict. Certainly we are moving to worlds where people do more and more for themselves; the self-service model is coming to libraries. To some extent, other groups encourage this: the e-book publishers would much rather sell a copy of each textbook to each student than share the sales among them by having the libraries buy fewer copies. Sometimes we'd rather have professionals doing the job, though. For example, in the digital world, with students doing their research in a dorm room at midnight rather than in the library during the working day, they are more likely to get help and advice from their equally inexperienced roommate than from a trained reference librarian.

Libraries are trying to deal with this by providing access through email and online chat, but we're still learning how to build these systems. For example, when users approach librarians face-to-face, the librarian can get some sense of how confident the user is from facial expression and general demeanor. The librarian can then judge whether to take the query presented at face value or try to explore alternatives, should the user seem in doubt about what he or she needs. This is harder to do in email, and thus the service will be less appropriate. So far, it doesn't look like video email would solve this problem (and text messaging makes it worse).

The role of libraries as the permanent repository is also unclear. Few university libraries today make a point of visiting the websites of research groups in the university and collecting the material posted. Few publishers will allow libraries to download for permanent storage every article in a journal to which the library has subscribed; they call this "systematic downloading" and forbid it. So where will this stuff remain? The Internet Archive will download the website if allowed, but it's only one organization, and it is unlikely that when the research group decides whether or not to turn on robot exclusion, it is thinking about the Archive. Government websites, for example, block the Archive at times out of fear of information misuse by terrorism, without real thought about what is dangerous and what is not (they say they cannot afford the time or staff to evaluate it). Libraries and archives have not yet arrived at a position in the digital world where they are funded to collect and save information, expected to do so, and used by the readers to find older websites.

As before, our technology is outrunning our organizations. We need more experiments to see how the different functions that libraries once performed will be done in the future; the question is not whether they will be done, but whether they will be done as well by whomever winds up with them. It would be better if the choice can be an informed one rather than a default.

13.4 Education

Computers in the classroom have been a promise for decades, mostly a disappointing one. Digital libraries seem an easier transition; they have been so successful in higher education that moving them into schools might seem easier. Once again, however, the changeover is not simple.

The flexibility of digital information allows the old "textbook" to be replaced by a multimedia extravaganza. This is happening, perhaps more than is desirable. To the extent that material for use in education has to be "exciting," it will have to be built by a committee and will be expensive. Given the lack of any evidence that bombarding students with Flash and Shockwave plug-ins helps them, it may be premature to be building such complex materials, but it's happening. More promising to education is the use of interaction, which does allow the students to do more; but it also makes the design of what is now called "courseware" more expensive and complex. We don't have a straightforward path for turning textbooks into "courseware": sometimes the publishers do this, sometimes groups of authors, sometimes university departments, and sometimes the government.

The National Science Foundation has been funding a program called the NSDL to help move digital libraries into education. The name is a recursive acronym: NSDL is the National SMETE Digital Library, where SMETE stands for Science, Mathematics, Engineering, and Technology Education. The program includes a few dozen projects, most attempting to develop courseware and resources in different areas. Among projects, for example, is the Columbia Earthscape program, which gathers information in the geography and geosciences areas and hopes to improve education by making this available in schools. So far, the NSDL projects have not finished (or even started) their evaluation process, so we don't yet know how well this will work.

There have also been large efforts by universities and publishers to build materials. Fathom, for example, was a combination of Columbia, LSE, and other universities to provide online information for education; it folded as another victim of the dot-com crash. Looking at examples like that, MIT has decided not to try to make a for-pay site and has instead announced "D-Space" as a place where teachers can share resources without a fee. How much will get posted is unclear; we still have no sense as to the extent to which faculty will be sharing their resources. Informal sharing is, of course, very common, with many sets of transparencies and class notes all over the Web, but the extent to which organized ways of doing this will take over is not clear.

In some areas the advantages of digital information are clear.

- Natural language technology should make it possible to have simple conversations in a foreign language limited to a specific set of grammar rules and vocabulary words, and then slowly increase the number of words and rules used. This should enable each student in a language class to improve at their own best pace.
- History students should be able to read newspapers and magazines from the period studied and feel truly immersed in the place and period. Modern digital libraries have made this much easier than in the past, when such efforts depended on microfilm.
- Simulations should help educate environmental students; much of this is being done today, but we need to take advantage of the large quantities of earth observation data to do it better.

All these approaches are used today; the question again is not the technology, but the organizational processes that will encourage their creation, distribution, preservation, and use.

13.5 Science

Science is about to have a paradigm shift provoked by online data. Traditionally, a scientist proposed some hypothesis, designed an experiment to test it, ran the experiment, and then studied the results. Now, sometimes, you can just look up the answer, because of the vast amounts of automatically collected online data. This happened first in molecular biology, thanks to the Protein Data Bank and the genome data banks, and now astronomy is going through the same transformation courtesy of the Sloan Digital Sky Survey and the National Virtual Observatory. Earth studies and environmental issues are probably next.

The use of data, in this way, as a replacement for experiments, is explained in Section 12.10. Data 're-use' by other researchers is a growing activity. Funding agencies are increasingly asking for data collected with their money to be made accessible and stored permanently, and even private pharmaceutical companies are feeling pressure to make their research study data public (and some are doing so).

Other large databases exist in seismology (IRIS data consortium) and in many other areas. Earth-sensing data is now measured in terabytes, but there are also databases of plant occurrences, people tracking dolphins and whales, databases of the properties of chemical substances, and many others.

Large database storage, like book storage, requires curating in addition to simple storage. In fact, a novice is usually less able to use data than to use an ordinary printed book; you have to know things like data schema, query languages, and enough about statistics to know what to request. Worse yet, you need to know something about the specific subject area. Strangely enough, without parsing English by machine nor understanding the meanings of words, we have been able to build pretty good search systems that work in any domain. Even though we can define data formally and have exact descriptions of the database, each data searching or visualization problem tends to be solved in a specific way for each area of knowledge.

The storage of data, as opposed to discussions of data, is a new area for libraries in general. The material is not in the same kinds of formats, instead involving databases, schemas, and other kinds of structures that need more technical knowledge to exploit. Typically, these sorts of data resources are stored in university organizations related to the subject areas they deal with, e.g. the biology department for the Protein Data Bank or the astronomy department for the virtual observatory. There are places where the libraries are taking the lead, such as the environmental sciences data at Rutgers University; and there are also inter-university organizations such as the ICSPR group in Ann Arbor, which stores information for social scientists. Perhaps most interesting is the move of the San Diego Supercomputer Center into data storage; its budget is larger than that of almost any library, and perhaps organizations like this will be performing the "digital library of data" service into the future.

13.6 Technology and Creativity

What effect will all this information have on new invention, as opposed to access to existing material? Berlioz once said that Saint-Saens "knows everything but lacks inexperience," suggesting that too much knowledge of a field interferes with new ideas. In contrast, the National Academy of Sciences produced a report on information technology and innovation which pointed to the way that new technology was being used to encourage creativity in the arts and humanities. Similarly, in the sciences most, commentators think that more information is helpful, not harmful, in coming up with innovative solutions.

The Internet lets everyone write, draw, compose, and distribute what they do. It thus serves as a counterbalance to the increasing dominance of large entertainment conglomerates. But it is unclear what this new "art form" might be. Will it be cut and paste from other Web pages, collages of digital images and sounds? Will it be animated programs? Blogs? Traditional drawings, photography, or writing? We don't know, and so we can't answer questions like, "Will strict enforcement of copyright laws increase creativity by forcing people to do new things, or block creativity by preventing the use of existing material as references?"

Ben Shneiderman (1999) has argued that having lots of information will improve creativity. In his model, creativity involves collecting existing information and then jumping off from that point; so the more effective the collection, the greater the opportunity for creativity. His model has four steps in creativity: collect, relate, create, and donate. Collecting is the first step, gathering the background; then these previous ideas and facts are related to the current problem or issue; and then the user tries to create something new. Eventually, the cycle closes when the user donates the new idea back to our common knowledge.

Similarly, Gerhard Fischer (2001) proposes that information resources are vital for improving group creativity. Any group will be lacking in some information, and the appropriate information systems can bring together the needs and the knowledge of the different group members. Certainly, many human advances are made by analogy: taking a solution that works in one area and trying it in another. Digital libraries, or any other way of improving information transfer, can assist in this process. They can also, of course, help avoid the embarrassment of suggesting something that is well known or has been tried before.

But then we don't know what is needed for creativity. I once had the honor of meeting James Houston, the man who first recognized that Inuit carvings were salable and encouraged the Inuit to develop both carving and printmaking. I asked him why such a small community, some 25,000 Inuit, had so many artists. The first words out of his mouth were "because they have no art schools."

Perhaps one of the most remarkable examples of the use of online information is the automatic discovery of new research. You may recall from Chapter 5 (Section 5.8) one very provocative example from the work of Don Swanson (1987, 1991, 1997, 2001) at Chicago. Some years ago, he observed that (a) Reynaud's disease is associated with some changes in blood chemistry; (b) related changes in blood chemistry are associated with fish oil in the diet; (c) there were no citations in the medical literature between the two areas. Thus, he hypothesized that this was a potential medical effect that nobody had studied. And, indeed, it turned out that fish oil was effective as a treatment for Reynaud's disease. Swanson then went on to find another example of two apparently related areas with few citations between them: magnesium and migraines. Again, he turned out to be right. However, neither he nor others have been able to mechanize this process and automatically detect areas justifying medical investigations.

Is this an example of a new strategy, in which computers will automatically suggest new research areas? Can we look for analogies at a high enough level to make this practical? We don't know yet. But in terms of the new roles for digital libraries, this would be the largest and most important increase in scope that we can imagine.

13.7 How Big Can They Get?

The University of California has recently surveyed the total amount of information produced in the world. They estimate a total of 5 exabytes (an exabyte is a million terabytes) being recorded, more than 90% of which is on magnetic disks, and another 18 exabytes being transmitted (e.g., phone calls). To get a sense of how big five exabytes is, it's perhaps 500,000 libraries the size of the Library of Congress. Or, it's about one 30-foot-long bookshelf for every person on earth (and remember, this is all new). Clearly, the average person is not writing that much stuff. Instead, what we have is a flood of automatically generated data, such as the scientific databases arising from remote sensing equipment. But we do have vast amounts of stuff that is being written: emails are almost half an exabyte. And the surface Web is 167 terabytes by their measure.

What this means for the digital librarian is that the amount of material that might potentially be available is enormous. We can barely imagine how a library is going to select from it; we can say that it's going to be automatic, not by hand. What is likely is that the digital library of the future contains some objects that have been picked, and many more that are accessible "at your own risk." This will mean relying on individuals to evaluate and use the material they find, rather than depending on the publication system to pick out what is best.

Some years ago the phrase "information overload" was common, reflecting the problems of somebody who has too much information. Historically we dealt with this by manual analysis: selection, routing, and summarization. Today, we have made enormous strides in the engineering of search systems, while selection and cataloging are still expensive. In the future, we're likely not to catalog many things, or evaluate them. As it gets cheaper and cheaper just to buy disk space, and to search for each query as it comes up, it becomes less and less attractive to be choosing what to save and what to discard, or to catalog it. For example, in a digital world, throwing away the text of a thick novel would save under a cent of disk space. It can't possibly be worth deciding whether it should be saved. Instead, we have to see how we can advise a user whether it is worth reading.

Similarly, the whole idea of cataloging and storage is going to be less and less attractive as time goes on. We can do searches on billions of items in a fraction of a second; why try to arrange things in order when we can produce an order suited to the individual user instantly?

So the digital library of the future is a place with a great deal of information, but much more of a self-service attitude. Yes, undergraduates will still be told what to read, but the researcher looking for something will have a much greater field to explore. Even the problem of quality judgment must be approached carefully. A genealogist, for example, may well want to read a thoroughly boring history, or an exaggerated and sensational newspaper article, if they mention a particular proper name.

Digital libraries thus become bigger and bigger. In the future the users of any library may range all over the world and include everyone from children to professional researchers to the retired. The material included will not just be "published" books, records, and videos but email blogs, scientific data, personal snapshots, and everything else that turns up. The problem won't be judging what to keep, but what to give the user.

The Indian professor Shiyali Ranganathan wrote "The Five Laws of Library Science," Madras Library Association (1931 and many later editions), which are

1. Books are for use.
2. Books are for all; every reader has his book.
3. Every book has its reader.
4. Save the time of the reader.
5. A library is a growing organism.

Item 3, at least, makes no sense in the digital context: the average piece of information is not going to get any attention from anyone. There are just too many of them. The job of the digital librarian is to help the user find something useful, as it is with all librarians, but without any expectation that everything will be useful to someone. We will deliver just-in-time information, acquired on a just-per-case basis.

13.8 Summary

We are still finding our way understanding how broad the field of digital libraries will be. It is certainly expanding very fast; unfortunately, it is expanding so fast that the practice and theory of the area have already diverged. There is an old line, "Theory and practice are the same in theory but not in practice." Tefko Saracevic

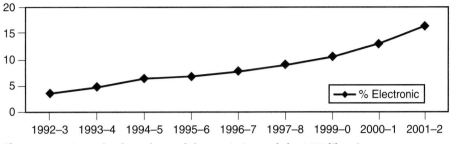

Figure 13.2 Growth of purchase of electronic journals by ARL libraries.

writes that "digital library research and digital library practice presently are conducted mostly independently of each other, minimally inform each other, and have slight, or no connection." Is the future digital library something that will be used by children, students, researchers, teachers, or the general public? Will it be used for scholarship, education, entertainment, or commerce? The answer is all of the above.

ARL statistics show that the large research libraries are now spending over $100 M on digital resources; the share of purchases which are electronic has grown to over 12% of acquisition costs (Figure 13.2). The Dana Medical Library of the University of Vermont had about 1300 paper journal subscriptions during the period 2000–2002, but went from 370 electronic journals to 814 in those three years. Corporate libraries often spend even larger fractions of their acquisitions on electronics, especially if one includes spending on interactive systems such as Dialog as well as electronic journals.

With time, the economic benefits of digital libraries will increase. Looking at the statistics of ARL libraries, the typical cost per book per year is in the range of $3–8, and the number of books per employee is in the range of 7,000–10,000. If one looks at a large data center, typical costs per megabyte-year are under a penny, and there are several terabytes (or million megabytes) per employee. Even without noting the advantages of searchability and remote access, economics will force the expansion of digital libraries.

Whether libraries of scientific data will be stored in the organizations now called libraries is less clear. Managing scientific data today requires a great deal of discipline and expertise, and the data tends to remain in the departments where research is being done. Unless we make real progress in more general database systems, this is not likely to change. It would be ironic if we learned to search through almost all the text in the world, but found ourselves swamped with vast amounts of data that we lacked the human resources to organize and the computer techniques to search. Digital libraries are growing, but the amount of information in the world is growing faster.

Future

Ubiquity, Diversity, Creativity, and Public Policy

So the dream of Vannevar Bush with whom we began our discussion is about to be realized. We will have whatever information we need at our fingertips. What will this mean for society? Is there something we should be changing about our laws or our institutions to deal with the coming digital library?

14.1 Dream to be Realized

In the future we expect that artifacts will be relatively less important. More and more, it will be the digital version that is used. Just as the reading of old newspapers moved from paper to microfilm, and music moved from performance to recordings, and the theatre stage to the cinema, we can expect a major shift towards digital reading. Just as in these other examples, the old will survive, but the new will be dominant.

Yogi Berra said that it's tough to make predictions, especially about the future. Harold Stassen wrote in 1955 that nuclear energy would create a world "in which there is no disease . . . where hunger is unknown . . . where food never rots and crops never spoil." And Douglas Hartree wrote in 1951, "We have a computer here in Cambridge; there is one in Manchester and one at the National Physical Laboratory; I suppose there ought to be one in Scotland, but that's about all" (Corn, 1986). And, there is no fanatic like a convert. The chief engineer of the British Post Office, Sir William Preece, wrote in 1879, "I fancy the descriptions we get of its [the telephone's] use in America are a little exaggerated, though there are conditions in America which necessitate the use of such instruments more than here. Here we have a superabundance of messengers, errand boys, and things of that kind." By 1898 he had switched sides and wrote, "If any of the planets be populated with beings like ourselves, then if they could oscillate immense stores of electrical energy to and fro in telegraphic order, it would be possible for us to hold commune by telephone with the people of Mars." Similarly, what should one make of a claim by International Data Corporation at the beginning of 1996 that within one year up to a fifth of large companies with websites will have closed or frozen them (see *The Times*, 1996)? Now that you have been warned, here are some predictions collected by *Wired Magazine* in 1995 on digital libraries.

	Half of the Library of Congress is Digitized	First Virtual Large Library	Free Net Access in Public Libraries	VR in Libraries
Ken Dowlin	2050	2020	2005	1997
Hector Garcia-Molina	2065	unlikely	2000	2010
Clifford Lynch	2020	2005	unlikely	1997
Ellen Poisson	2050	2030	2005	2020
Robert Zich	2030	2010	2005	2000
Average	2043	2016	2003	2005

The distinguished forecasters were:

Ken Dowlin: Librarian of the city of San Francisco

Hector Garcia-Molina: Stanford professor, principal investigator on the Stanford digital library project

Clifford Lynch: Executive Director of the Coalition of Networked Information (CNI).

Ellen Poisson: Assistant Director, New York Public Library, Science Industry and Business Library

Robert Zich: Director of Electronic Programs, Library of Congress

And what actually has happened so far? Net access in public libraries is already here and fairly common; the United Kingdom even adopted this as their strategy for providing general public access to information (although it is likely to be replaced there as broadband local service increases). The BnF Gallica project, with 100,000 digitized books, probably qualifies as the first virtual large library, and the Million Book Project should follow by 2006. As for virtual reality in libraries, I'm not quite sure what the *Wired* editors envisioned in this category. Digitizing half the Library of Congress is more a legal problem than a technical one; perhaps by 2020 we'll make some progress on the law.

If the electronic library comes to pass, there may be, as a result, a greater distance from the real world. People will study more, and do less. Simulation may replace experiment. Some of this is clearly good. Simulators can be used to teach airline pilots emergency maneuvers that would be too dangerous to try in a real airplane, for example. Simulation can let many students "visit" an ecological area which is too sensitive to stand much foot traffic or too expensive to travel to. Similarly, objects which are only in one place can be seen everywhere. Rare manuscripts, paintings, and photographs can be viewed. Material which is too bulky to be collected by many facilities may yet be made readily available.

Not everyone is as enthusiastic as I am about the future. Nicholson Baker's book *Double Fold* (2001) attacked the practice of microfilming old newspapers and discarding the originals; many of his arguments would also apply to digitizing them (especially since the digitization is likely to be done from the microfilm rather than the originals). Baker actually bought as many original sets of old newspapers as he could afford and is storing them in New Hampshire. He points to the occasional color comic, for example, while both microfilming and digitizing of newspapers is usually done in high-contrast black and white. A major newspaper appears in many editions. If one thinks of the *Los Angeles Times*, for example, it publishes four regional editions (Metropolitan, San Fernando Valley, Orange Country, and Ventura Country), plus it appears several times a day with variations as late news breaks, and there is split-run advertising which differs from copy to copy; there are dozens of somewhat different versions each day, and only one is normally preserved either through filming or digitizing. Thus, Baker argues for preserving the originals; unfortunately he has no way of generating the funding for doing that, let alone a substitute for the enormous convenience of online searching (if the cost of preserving the originals meant that we could not afford to also have the digital version).

What Baker omits in his discussion of the importance of the original is the enormous gain from the digital version. Full-text searching, availability in your home and office regardless of the location of the originals, and the potential for even more ambitious services like machine translation make digital versions more convenient and more useful. Students are losing touch with the traditional forms of information; they find websites faster and easier to deal with.

Yet there are also costs. Will we see buildings collapse when architects rely on simulation programs that they do not entirely understand? Will children lose even more touch with the physical world and other people as computers add to television as an artificially created distraction? Can we tell what the consequences will be? We don't seem to know much about the effects of television on society; how will we find out about the effects of computers?

14.2 Future Roles in Information Handling

In this new world, if everyone can contribute information, how will we know what is good and what is bad? Our supermarkets are already full of publications claiming that Elvis is still alive or that space aliens walk among us. How will we know what is true and what is false? We have various cues today; books from university presses, or whose authors have faculty appointments, are usually more dependable than paperbacks with lurid covers. What TV network newscasters say is more credible than what callers to talk radio say. In the world of the Net, many or most of these cues will be gone. What will replace them? How will we know what to believe? As mentioned earlier in the chapter, the replacement of a refereed letters journal by a preprint bulletin board has made it more difficult for people who are not well known to get attention in the research physics community. This is an example of an unexpected social effect from a technological change. What other effects will we have?

One possibility is that the job of evaluating and assessing information will become more important to everyone. Perhaps, at some point, it will be more lucrative to check information than to create it. Don King suggested that engineers typically spent about 1/5 as much time finding what to read as they did reading. Perhaps this will change, and we'll spend a higher fraction of our effort on selection. Certainly, most people I know have no more time to read additional items, but could use some help picking the right thing to read.

From what source will we get information? Today we have places we go to get things that we carry away at once: bookstores, newstands, and libraries. We get things through the mail, from publishers and from bookstores. We hear information on broadcast media, television and radio. Where does the Net fit? Information comes immediately, as from a library or bookstore, but no travel is involved. It can be generated simultaneously with our inquiry, but no broadcasting is done. Who should run such a service? It doesn't mesh with any of the existing organizations, and the field is still up for grabs.

Libraries will need to expand their cooperative activities. Today, most libraries are judged and budgeted on the basis of how many books they have. The *Association of Research Libraries* website (`www.arl.org`) publishes a regular table showing the ranks of libraries. In 2002, Stanford was ranked as 7th while Michigan was 8th, because Stanford had 7,698,099 books and Michigan had only 7,643,203. It cannot really matter, in evaluating a library or a university, what the third significant digit in the number of books owned might be. We should note once again that access to books may be more important than possession in the near future. Richard Atkinson (2003) has recently written on the counterproductive nature of counting books owned rather than books available. It discourages sharing collection policies and trying out innovative online access experiments. And the habit of valuing libraries by the size of their collections has meant that inadequate attention is paid to the assistance provided by staff to faculty and students. The services and training given by the librarians to the university community are the aspects of the library which an outside vendor will have the most difficulty providing. On many campuses the library building also doubles as a student center, or a study hall, or other functions. Libraries need to be valued for their functions beyond buying and shelving.

Similarly, we have in the past obtained information from a great variety of sources. Perhaps these will shrink. Partly this reflects the concentration in the publishing and media industries, as Viacom buys Paramount which had previously bought Simon & Schuster which had previously bought Prentice-Hall. Partly this reflects the low incremental cost of electronic publishing, meaning that to lengthen a press run will be much easier than putting out a new book. This will be particularly true if everything has to be a "multimedia production" with art, animation, video, and sound. Any such production requires a team of specialists, with expensive skills in each area.

Some years ago I was talking to an executive at Elsevier. He commented that Elsevier published a large number of introductory college physics textbooks. They were looking at producing a fancy multimedia physics textbook, but given the costs involved he feared they might only be able to finance one such CD-ROM. Now it may not matter if everyone in the United States learns first year college physics from the same book. But would we like a world in which everyone learned history or philosophy from the same book? Are there advantages to a local textbook which is tailored to the particular environment? Or to publishing different viewpoints on the same subject?

The danger to all of us is that much lightly-used research material may be bypassed in a rush to provide the heavily-used and commercially lucrative current textbooks and major reference material online, and that the broader mission of keeping our entire cultural heritage will be overlooked. Digitization should be a way of increasing memory and diversity, not a way of standardizing everything and abolishing university institutions.

And how individual can a website created by a committee really be? Would we expect the same level of individuality, even in physics, from a committee-produced object that we find in, say, Feynman's textbook? Secondary school texts are already committee productions, and few feel they demonstrate eloquence, creativity, or an individual spirit. Will we lose something if all texts and even all publications move towards committee work?

14.3   Effect of Digital Technology on Universities

If using a library merely means connecting to its computer from a dorm room, it doesn't matter where the library is. Earlier this was discussed as an advantage, letting libraries avoid the need for expensive central-campus buildings. But, like the Force, it also has a dark side. If someday Berkeley has digitized all or most of its library, and students everywhere can access it, why does a small college need a library? What will it have that is not easily accessible from a larger library? If the students in a university library cannot tell whether the books they are reading come from the local network or from a remote library, does it matter whether the university library actually owns any of its own books? Soon larger universities may approach smaller colleges and offer to provide library services for them at a lower cost than the small college could do for itself. And in the current university financial world, the small college president may jump at the chance.

But then, what about teaching? Stanford already sells all of its computer science courses on videotape. If the Berkeley library were online, why would a small college need a library? If all the Stanford courses were online, perhaps some college would question its need for a faculty.

Along with the dot-com crash, perhaps fortunately, went a crash in "distance learning." In the 1990s it was all the rage, and universities proposed that they would create campuses with no resident faculty, merely places where students can access remote information. If libraries can be merely nodes on the Net, what about universities? At one point California thought about creating a new state college campus with no library, and we also saw the creation of "Western Governor's University" as a distance learning operation, with the goal of bringing college and university education to people living in towns too small to support even a community college.

Neither of these ideas panned out. As we have seen, it may be technically possible to convert most of what is in a conventional library, but it hasn't been done yet. In some companies with a restricted span of research interests, we have seen libraries close in favor of online services; for the breadth needed by a university, it's not quite practical yet. Western Governor's University ran afoul of social needs; high school graduates in small towns go away to college partly to go away, and they're not necessarily interested in something that keeps them at home. Nevertheless, shared and distance learning are still likely to grow, if only as a way of letting small colleges supplement their course offerings.

Again, we often see small colleges going out of business, or large university systems absorbing them. The larger institutions can offer a wider array of courses, more famous faculty, and economies of scale. Does the variety and individuality of different colleges and universities have value? Is the ability of the students to ask questions, and the ability of the professor to adjust the lecture to the student reaction, worth something? Or would we rather have each student given a selected and preserved lecture by the best professor, even if that professor is on video or on the Web? What if the best professor has even been dead for years? Will students watching on the Web know or care?

14.4   Digital Libraries and Society

Perhaps it does not matter if universities are decimated. Once upon a time, there was a vaudeville theatre in most American towns. The radio and the movies did them in, and lots of vaudeville comedians lost their jobs. A few were able to go into politics, but most had to find other employment. So what? I once heard the argument that, after all, Jack Benny was funnier than all these individual comedians, so when he went on the radio and the individual theatres closed, the total amount of laughter in the United States increased. Perhaps; perhaps not. Perhaps the ability of the individual comics to make jokes about that particular town let them do better than Jack Benny, whose jokes had to cover the entire nation.

Is there value to the wide variety of universities, of books, of sources of information? Each year the United States publishes 50,000 books and produces 500 movies. There are 2000 legitimate stage productions, and there are about 85 network prime-time slots each week. Will there be an enormous variety of Web pages, as we now see, or will a few massive information providers send us everything?

Some of this depends on what we ask for. If we demand that each Web page we look at has to have animation, cartoons, music, and sound effects, then producing a Web page is going to take substantial capital resources, and there may not be many. Each would be made by committee, intended for a wide audience, and probably fairly bland as a consequence. If, in contrast, people are satisfied with a Web page that just contains somebody's poetry, we can have many more, and they can be much more specialized. Would Rembrandt have succeeded as a painter if he had to sing and dance as well? Just as a theatrical audience accepts that the car chases which characterize action films can't really be done on the stage, if we want variety in our information sources, we can't expect them all to be multimedia extravaganzas.

14.5 Digital Libraries, Society, and Creativity

Initial results suggest that the Internet is aggravating the difference between rich and poor; computers are even more available to the wealthy than cars or houses. But there are many aspects we do not understand. Why are poor people in the American West more likely to have computer access than poor people in the American South? Why do the Scandanavian countries have such particularly high rates of computer usage? These questions are likely to take care of themselves; as computers continue to get cheaper and bandwidth more available, we are likely to see everyone in the world gaining access to the Web as the world's digital library. What will this mean for them?

The benefits of libraries to society are enormous, if hard to quantify. Digital libraries can often improve them. For example, the National Library of Medicine has examples of people whose lives have been saved by Medline. An article by Mary Jo Dwyer (1998) offers a case in point. In this particular example, very fast response proved to be critical: she tells of one surgeon who called up in the middle of an operation with a question and needed an answer within twenty minutes. It is hard to imagine providing so fast a response without online information. Many people have done personal research or, indeed, have been educated in public libraries; the best known example is Chester Carlson's invention of the Xerox copier through his study of papers on photoconductivity in the New York Public Library.

It is also important to preserve the large-scale benefits of libraries. We understand "intelligence" in war, but fail to realize that libraries, whether in war or peace, can be similar sources of information. Two examples, one from war and one from peace, may help show how the kinds of information found in libraries can affect society in major and unexpected ways.

Many readers will have heard how, in the late nineteenth and early twentieth century, the Standard Oil monopoly was able to get preferential rates for moving oil on the railroads (the first large, long-distance pipelines were not started until 1942). A similar scandal erupted in Germany; the German response was to require that all rates for oil transport be published in the official railway newspaper. A refugee petroleum economist, Walter J. Levy, knew of this and realized that from the published rates he could figure out where new oil production facilities were being built. Throughout the war, an OSS agent went to a library in Switzerland and copied down new information about railway tariffs for petroleum shipments. When, for example, new rates showed up for moving oil from some town to major German cities, Levy (working first for British and then US intelligence) would know that a refinery had been built in that town and would pass the information to the 8th Air Force, which would then bomb the site; the Germans would then helpfully confirm the raid by publishing a suspension of the rates; and when they later published a reinstatement, Levy would know they had repaired the refinery and would send the bombers back.

An even more important story is the discovery of penicillin. Many have heard, again, of the mold that blew in the open window of Sir Alexander Fleming's laboratory at St. Mary's Hospital, Paddington, in 1928, and killed bacteria on a Petri dish left open on a bench (actually, it probably blew up the stairs from a different lab, not in from the street; Fleming left his door open but not his window). Few realize that there was a 10-year gap in following up the discovery, because Fleming was not trained as a chemist and was not able to persuade somebody to help him isolate the active ingredient secreted by the mold. Also, he had somehow persuaded himself that the substance would be metabolized before it could be effective; therefore, although he had tested it for toxicity by injecting it into a healthy rabbit, he did not try giving some to a sick animal. Fleming published a paper in the *British Journal of Experimental Pathology* in 1929 and largely ceased work on penicillin. Ten years later, two Oxford biochemists, Sir Ernst Chain and Sir Howard Florey, decided to stop basic research and work on something that would help with the war. They knew of the very large number of soldiers who had died of infected wounds in the first World War, and Chain went to the library to look for any paper about something that would kill bacteria. He found three, one of which was Fleming's; and fortunately a sample of the mold that Fleming had sent to Prof. George Dreyer at Oxford was still there. Chain and Florey were able to isolate the active chemical, injected it into a sick mouse, and then realized what they had. Without Fleming's journal article, the sequence of work that brought us antibiotics might never have happened.

Will we have, 50 years from now, equally impressive stories of the value of digital publication? Although there are fewer self-educated people than in the past, there are even more scientific researchers and even more material being published; so I am confident we will.

14.6 Public Policy Questions

There are many public policy issues related to the Web. How do we ensure universal access to the Web so that we do not have a country in which the amount of information available to the rich and the poor is even more distorted than it is today? How do we ensure access for writing, as well as reading? Some of the technological proposals (e.g., systems based on video-on-demand as the business driver) provide only one-way communications.

Do we want single large libraries, or library cooperatives, or many small ones? Small libraries might well go the way of the corner hardware store. Should libraries be linked to educational institutions, or businesses, or what? Perhaps the greatest difficulty here is that faced by librarians, who must simultaneously cope with budget difficulties, threats of commercial competition for some of their most valuable uses, and the need to educate an entire population of users.

There are many controversial questions about control of the Internet. Part of this arises from desires for censorship, or fears that the Internet will be used by terrorist or drug dealers, or concerns for privacy of individual citizens (would you like it, for example, if your electronic mail provider read your mail to decide which advertising to send you?) Even on a more mundane level, who should decide the format of works presented on your screen? Is this something publishers need to control, or will users wind up arranging books to suit their individual tastes, just as they once had custom binding of printed books?

International issues will also rise in importance. Today the Web largely originates in the United States, as mentioned earlier. Most of the new technological developments are also coming from the United States, but the Internet is international, and, just as new companies often lead new industries, new countries could lead Web business. Unlike manufacturing, there is little fixed capital investment that would stop people from suddenly accessing only pages in some new country. The Internet might, of course, reverse some current business imports. US libraries and scholars buy many books and journals from foreign-based publishers that contain mostly papers written by American faculty. If the current scholarly publishing system is largely overthrown, this might decrease that particular item in the balance of payments. But whether we should simply hope for it or try to do something about it has attracted no real political interest. Does it even matter where intellectual property leadership is found? Perhaps not, if we judge by the attention given to it in recent elections.

It is not just economics and technology that decide how many information creators we will have, or where they will be. Engineers tend to believe in technological determinism; if it can be built, it will be built. Bigger guns, bigger buildings, and bigger disk drives are all foreordained and unstoppable. But this is not true. Public concerns, law, or society can, in fact, stop a technology.

Centuries ago, Japan, having seen early European guns, decided they did not want them and resumed using swords instead of muskets and artillery (Perrin, 1980).

More recently, we have seen public concerns and liability lawsuits end such technologies as nuclear power or new research on birth control methods. Childhood vaccines are a particularly frightening example, since the risks seem easier to measure and less widespread than, for example, the possible dangers of nuclear power. Everyone agrees that childhood vaccination is good. And yet only one manufacturer of whooping cough vaccine survives in the United States, for fear of liability lawsuits. Whooping cough (pertussis) vaccine may carry a risk of encephalitis, which, if real, affects about one in 100,000 children who get the vaccine. Of course, before 1930 about one child in 80 *died* of whooping cough. Nevertheless, we can barely keep the vaccine on the market. Streptomycin, once a wonder drug for which Selman Waksman got the Nobel Prize, is no longer available in the United States. It is, in fact, possible for technology to be brought to a halt, and we have to think whether we want digital libraries and, if so, in what form.

The greatest benefit and the greatest risk of digital libraries are the same: we can foresee a world in which everyone can get any source of information at their fingertips. We have to remember that many earlier technologies had great promise for teaching; both the phonograph and television were first thought of as educational tools. Both turned almost entirely into entertainment. Perhaps that is acceptable as one use of these technologies. But with the capacity available in digital networks, and the wide variety of sources of information that might be available, it would be a shame if the only future pages on the Web were those for pop music videos and special-effects movies. Let us design our networks to support open access for everyone, our copyright laws to provide access for the small as well as the large, and our educational system to encourage diversity and local options.

President Clinton called in August 1996 for "every single library and classroom in America [to be] connected to the Information Superhighway by the year 2000 . . . every 12-year-old will be able to log in on the Internet . . . Americans will have the knowledge they need to cross that bridge to the twenty-first century." But if true diversity is our goal, it will require more than universal access to information—it will require the ability to create and distribute information as well.

14.7   Projections

Vannevar Bush's dream is going to be achieved, and in one lifetime. Bush wrote his far-reaching paper about technology and information access in 1945.

Now, less than 70 years later, it is clear that the early twenty-first century will see the equivalent of a major research library on the desk of every individual. And it will have searching capabilities beyond those Bush imagined. We can capture newly written documents; we can convert old documents; and we are rapidly figuring out how to provide access to pictures, sound recordings, and videos.

We still lack a clear picture of how we're going to pay for all of this, but the explosion of the Web cannot be turned back. Whatever combination of greed and fear winds up supporting millions of websites, we will find some solution. Most likely, someday each scholar will have subscriptions to a variety of online services, just as they own a computer and word processor program today. If we look at the cost of digitizing a book as not more than $10 given large enough press runs, and the total number of books as under 100 million, the $1 billion it would take to digitize everything is smaller than what is spent each year on academic libraries or computers, or what was wasted in the dot-com boom. There is enough money to pay for a switch from paper information to electronic information; we only lack the procedures and organization.

And what will come of librarians? Bush envisioned the profession of "trailblazer" to describe people who found and organized information. Perhaps the Web-page evaluators of Google and Yahoo are the next step toward this profession. As information becomes easier to use, we can expect those who help others to find information to become more important, just as accountants changed from people who were good at arithmetic to those who run corporations. Similarly, in the sea of information of the future, librarians will not be those who provide the water, but those who navigate the ship.

Shakespeare, in *As You Like It*, described seven ages of man. His ages correspond roughly to the development of this field. First there was the infant, the time until perhaps 1955 when only a few even thought about electronic information. Then the schoolboy, the period of initial experiments and research in the 1960s. Then the lover, the first flush of excitement about computers and word processors and our ability to do online information. The soldier followed on, working through the 1980s producing the technological development to make this all possible. The justice, probably about our state today, has to decide how the new technology will be used. And we look forward to the elderly character who can simply use it. And, finally, we hope not senility, but perhaps the movement of advanced research into new areas. The story will play out in one lifetime, and we will move from a world of paper information, decaying and hard to find, to a world of screens, with fast access to almost everything. Those born in 1945 will see the entire play, from the days when computers were strange new machines in science-fiction stories to the days when computers are our normal source of information.

References

Lee Kyong-Hee, Haeinsa Monks Computerize the Tripitaka Koreana, Website: www.nuri.net/ ~hederein/intro/korecult.htm (2000).

American National Standards Institute, *Information Retrieval Service and Protocol*, ANSI/NISO Z39.50-1992 (version 2), American National Standards Institute, NY (1992).

Gale Research, *The Encyclopedia of American Industries, Volume Two: Service and Non-Manufacturing Industries*, Gale Research, Detroit, Mich. (1994).

Wired Magazine (eds.), "The Future of Libraries," *Wired Magazine*, p. 68 (Dec. 1995).

The Times (London) (eds.), "Net outlook gloomy in 96," *The Times* (London) (January 24, 1996).

Economist (eds.), "Taxed in cyberspace," *Economist*, vol. 340, no. 7974, p. 67 (July 13, 1996).

Mark Ackerman and Tom Malone, "Answer Garden: A tool for growing organizational memory," *Proc. ACM Conf. on Office Information Systems*, pp. 31–39 (1990).

Mark Ackerman, "Augmenting the organizational memory: A field study of Answer Garden", *Proc. ACM Conf. on Computer Supported Cooperative Work* (CSCW), pp. 243–252 (1994).

Alfred Aho, Ravi Sethi, and Jeffrey Ullman, *Compilers, Principles, Techniques, and Tools*, Addison-Wesley, Reading, MA (1986).

Alfred V. Aho, Ravi Sethi, Jeffrey D. Ullman, and Monica Lam, *21st Century Compilers*, Addison-Wesley, Reading, MA (2004).

Alexandria Digital Library Project, Alexandria Digital Library. University of California, Santa Barbara (UCSB), Website: http://alexandria.sdc.ucsb.edu.

James F. Allen, Donna Byron, Myroslava Dzikovska, George Ferguson, Lucian Galescu, and Amanda Stent, "Towards conversational human-computer interaction," *AI Magazine*, vol. 22, no. 4, pp. 27–37 (2001).

R. C. Alston, *The Arrangement of Books in the British Museum Library*, British Library Humanities & Social Sciences, London (1986).

American Memory Project, Website: http://memory.loc.gov.

R. Amsler and D. Walker, "The Use of Machine-Readable Dictionaries in Sublanguage Analysis" in *Sublanguage Description and Processing*, R. Grishman and R. Kittredge (eds.), Lawrence Erlbaum., Hillsdale, N.J. (1985).

Apostolos Antonacopoulos, B. Gatos, and D. Karatzas, *ICDAR 2003 Page Segmentation Competition* (International Conference on Document Analysis and Recognition), p. 688 (2003).

ARL Supplementary Statistics, Association of Research Libraries (ARL) Website: www.arl.org.

ARTSTOR, The Digital Library, Website: http://www.artstor.org.

Research Library Trends, Association of Research Libraries (ARL) Website: www.arl.org/stats/arlstat/01pub/intro.html (2002).

Richard Atkinson, "A new world of scholarly communication," *Chronicle of Higher Education*, (Nov. 7, 2003).

Audio Engineering Society, *Recommendation for Recorded Music Projects*, Document AESTD1002.1.03-10, Website: www.aes.org/technical/documents/AESTD1002.1.03-10-1.pdf (2003).

Ed Ayers et al., The Valley of the Shadow, Two Communities in the American Civil War, Website: http://valley.vcdh.virginia.edu.

Roger S. Bagnall, *Digital Imaging of Papyri*, Commission on Preservation and Access, Washington, DC (September 1995), ISBN: 1-887334-44-0.

Henry S. Baird, "The Skew Angle of Printed Documents," *Proceedings SPSE 40th Conf. on Hybrid Imaging Systems*, pp. 21–24, (May 1987).

Nicholson Baker, *Double Fold*, Random House, New York (2001).

Jerry Baldwin, "Libraries reduce cost, add value," *Technology Exchange Newsletter*, Minnesota Department of Transportation, Website: www.cts.umn.edu/T2/TechExch/2002/ july-sept/librarytable.html (Summer 2002).

Judit Bar-Ilan, "The use of Web search engines in information science research," *Annual Review of Information Science and Technology*, vol. 38, pp. 231–288 (2004).

Serge Belongie, Jitendra Malik, and Jan Puzicha, "Shape matching and object recognition using shape contexts," *IEEE Trans. on Pattern Analysis and Machine Intelligence*, vol. 24, no. 4, pp. 509–522 (2002).

Hal Berghel and Lawrence O'Gorman, "Protecting ownership rights through digital watermarking," *IEEE Computer*, vol. 29, no. 7, pp. 101–103 (July 1996).

Michael K. Bergman, "The Deep Web: Surfacing hidden value," *J. of Electronic Publishing* (August 2001); also available as a white paper at www.brightplanet.com/ deepcontent/tutorials/DeepWeb/index.asp.

Theodore Bergstrom, "Free labor for costly journals," *Journal of Economic Perspectives* (Summer 2001); see also http://repositories.cdlib.org/ucsbecon/bergstrom/ 2001C.

UC Berkeley Digital Library Project, University of California at Berkeley, Website: http://elib.cs.berkeley.edu (1995).

T. Berners-Lee, R. Caillau, J. Groff, and B. Pollerman, "World-Wide Web: The information universe," *Electronic Networking: Research, Applications, Policy*, vol. 1, no. 2, pp. 52–58 (1992).

Tim Berners-Lee, James Hendler, and O. Lassila, "The Semantic Web," *Scientific American*, vol. 284, pp 35–43 (May 2001).

L. Besacier, C. Bergamini, D. Vaufreydaz, and E. Castelli, "The effect of speech and audio compression on speech recognition performance," *IEEE Mutlimedia Signal Processing Workshop*, (October 2001).

William Birmingham, University of Michigan Digital Library Project, Website: http://http2.sils.umich.edu/UMDL/HomePage.html (1995).

David C. Blair and M. E. Maron, "An evaluation of retrieval effectiveness for a full-text document retrieval system," *CACM*, vol. 28, no. 3, pp. 289–299 (1985).

Floyd Bloom, "The Rightness of Copyright," *Science*, vol. 281, p. 1451 (4 Sept. 1998).

Blue Spike.com (eds.), Digital Watermarking Frequently Asked Questions, Website: www.bluespike.com/watermarkingfaq (2004).

Jeff Blyskal, "Technology for technology's sake?" *Forbes*, vol. 131, p. 196 (May 9, 1983).

John Van Bogart, *Magnetic Tape Storage and Handling: A Guide for Libraries and Archives*, Commission on Preservation and Access, Washington, DC (June 1995).

R. A. Bolt, *Spatial Data Management*, Architecture Machine Group, Cambridge, MA (1979).

J. M. Bone, FRVT 2002: Overview and Summary, Website: www.frvt.org (March 2003).

J. S. Boreczky and L. A. Rowe, "Comparison of video shot boundary techniques," *Proc. IS&T/SPIE*, vol. 2670, pp. 170–179 (1996).

Christine Borgman, "Why are online catalogs hard to use?" *J. Amer. Soc. for Inf. Sci.*, vol. 37, no. 6, pp. 387–400 (1986).

Christine Borgman, "Why are online catalogs still hard to use?" *J. Amer. Soc. for Inf. Sci.*, vol. 47, no. 7, pp. 493–503 (July 1996).

Gunter Born, *The File Formats Handbook*, Van Nostrand Reinhold, New York (1995).

Katy Borner, Chaomei Chen, and Kevin Boyack, "Visualizing knowledge domains," *Annual Review of Information Science and Technology*, vol. 37, pp. 179–275 (2003).

L. Bottou, P. Haffner, P. G. Howard, P. Simard, Y. Bengio, and Y. LeCun, "High quality document image compression with DjVu," *Journal of Electronic Imaging*, vol. 7, no. 3, pp. 410–425 (July 1998).

L. Bottou, P. Haffner, and Y. LeCun, "Efficient conversion of digital documents to multilayer raster formats," *Sixth Int'l Conf. on Document Analysis and Recognition (ICDAR)*, (Sept. 2001).

Francoise Boursin, "Stemming the Flood of Paper," *Chemistry & Industry Magazine* (1995).

W. G. Bowen, JSTOR and the Economics of Scholarly Communication, Council on Library Resources, Washington, DC (September 18, 1995), Website: www-clr.stanford.edu/clr/econ/jstor.html.

J. T. Brassil, S. Low, N. Maxemchuk, and L. O'Gorman, "Marking of document images with codewords to deter illicit dissemination," *Proc. INFOCOM 94 Conference on Computer Communications*, pp. 1278–87 (1994).

Sergey Brin and Lawrence Page, "The anatomy of a large-scale hypertextual Web search engine," *Computer Networks and ISDN Systems*, vol. 30, pp. 107–117, available at http://www-db.stanford.edu/~backrub/google.html (1998).

Michael Broughton, "Measuring the accuracy of commercial automated speech recognition systems during conversational speech," *HF2002*, (Human Factors conference), (2002).

Neil Brooks, "*Canadian Tax Journal:* Fifty years of influence," *Canadian Tax Journal*, vol. 5, no. 6, pp. 2059–2094 (2002).

P. F. Broxis, "Syntactic and semantic relationships or: A review of PRECIS: A manual of concept analysis and subject indexing, D. Austin," *Indexer*, vol. 10, no. 2, pp. 54–59 (October 1976).

E. Brynjolfsson and L. Hitt, *New Evidence on the Returns to Information Systems*, MIT Press, Cambridge, MA (1993).

Erik Brynjolfsson, "The IT productivity gap," *Optimize*, no. 21 (July 2003).

Karen Budd, "The economics of electronic journals," *Online Journal of Issues in Nursing*, vol. 5, no. 1 (January 31, 2000); see also www.nursingworld.org/ojin/topic11/tpc11_3.htm.

Quentin Burrell, "A note on aging in a library circulation model," *J. Doc*, vol. 41, no. 2, pp. 100–115 (June 1985).

Business Software Alliance, *Trends in Software Piracy 1994–2002*, Eighth Annual BSA Global Software Piracy Study, Washington, DC (June 2003).

Luciano Canfora, *The Vanished Library: A Wonder of the Ancient World*, Martin Ryle (transl.), University of California Press, Berkeley, CA (1990).

Patty Carey and Linda Gould, "Per-Page Costs of Atmospheric Sciences Journal Titles at the University of Washington," Website: www.lib.washington.edu/subject/atmosphericsci/scholcom (2000).

Shih-Fu Chang and John R. Smith, "Extracting multi-dimensional signal features for content based visual query," SPIE Symposium on Visual Communications and Signal Processing, 2501, Pt 2, pp. 995–1006 (May 1995).

Ben Chamy, "VoIP providers face price war," CNET News.com, Website: http://news.com.com/2100-7352_3-5101663.html (Nov. 4, 2003).

Ronald Chepesiuk, "JSTOR and electronic archiving," *American Libraries*, vol. 31, no. 11, p. 46–48 (2000).

Joan Cherry and Wendy Duff, "Studying digital library users over time: A follow-up survey of Early Canadiana Online," *Information Research*, vol. 7, no. 2 (2002).

Vishal Chitkara and Mario Nascimento, "Color-based image retrieval using binary signatures," *Proc. ACM Symposium on Applied Computing*, pp. 687–692 (2002); see also Vishal Chitkaraand, (same title), University of Alberta Technical Report TR-01-08 (May 2001).

Y-Ming Chung, Qin He, Kevin Powell, and Bruce Schatz, "Semantic indexing for a complete subject discipline," *Proc. 4th ACM International Conference on Digital Libraries*, pp. 39–48 (1999).

Ken Church and L. Rau, "Commercial applications of natural language processing," *Comm. ACM*, pp. 71–79 (Nov. 1995).

Ken Church, "A stochastic parts program and noun phrase parser for unrestricted text," *Second Conference on Applied Natural Language Processing*, ACL, pp. 136–143, (1988).

C. W. Cleverdon, J. Mills, and E. M. Keen, *Factors Determining the Performance of Indexing Systems*, ASLIB Cranfield Research Project, Cranfield, UK (1966).

Michéle Cloonan and Sid Berger, "Present and future issues for special collections," *Rare Books and Manuscripts Librarianship*, vol. 13, no. 2, pp. 89–94 (1999).

Library of Congress, The National Digital Library Program—A Library for All Americans (February 1995); see also The American Memory Project, Website: http://lcweb2.loc.gov/amhome.html.

C. Cool, S. Park, N. Belkin, J. Koenemann, and K. B. Ng, "Information seeking behavior in new searching environment," *CoLIS 2*, pp 403–416 (1996).

M. D. Cooper, "Cost comparison of alternative book storage strategies," *Library Quarterly*, vol. 59, no. 3, pp. 239–260 (July 1989).

G. V. Cormack, R. N. Horspool, and M. Kaiserswerth, "Practical perfect hashing," *Computer Journal*, vol. 28, no. 1, pp. 54–58 (Feb. 1985).

Joseph Corn (ed.), *Imagining Tomorrow: History, Technology, and the American Future*, MIT Press, Cambridge, MA, pp. 58 and 190 (1986).

Ingemar Cox, Matthew Miller, and Jeffrey Bloom, *Digital Watermarking: Principles and Practice*, Morgan Kaufmann, San Francisco, CA (2001).

Richard Cox, *Don't Fold Up*, Society of American Archivists, Website: http://www.archivists.org/news/doublefold.asp, Chicago, IL, (April 2001).

Fabio Crestani, "Effects of word recognition errors in spoken query processing," *Proc. Conference on Advances in Digital Libraries*, pp. 39–47 (2000).

W. B. Croft, S. M. Harding, K. Taghva, and J. Borsack, "An evaluation of information retrieval accuracy with simulated OCR output," *Symposium on Document Analysis and Information Retrieval*, pp. 115–126 (1994).

Anthony M. Cummings, Marcia L. Witte, William G. Bowen, Laura O. Lazarus, and Richard H. Ekman, *University Libraries and Scholarly Communication: A Study Prepared for the Andrew W. Mellon Foundation*, Association of Research Libraries, Washington, DC (November 1992).

D-Lib Magazine, Website: www.dlib.org.

Jason Dedrick, Vijay Gurbaxani, and Kenneth L. Kraemer, "Information technology and economic performance: A critical review of the empirical evidence," *ACM Computing Surveys*, vol. 35, no. 1, pp 1–28 (2003).

Scott Deerwester, Sue Dumais, Tom Landauer, George Furnas, and Richard Harshman, "Indexing by latent semantic analysis," *J. American Society for Information Science*, vol. 41, no. 6, pp. 391–407 (Sept. 1990).

Hans Delfs and Helmut Knebl, *Introduction to Cryptography: Principles and Applications*, Springer-Verlag, New York, NY (2002).

Lorcan Dempsey, "The subject gateway," *Online Information Review*, vol. 24, no. 1, pp. 8–23 (2000).

Peter Drucker, *Post-Capitalist Society*, Butterworth-Heinemann, Oxford, UK (1993). [And a great many other of his publications.]

Allison Druin, B. Bederson, A. Weeks, A. Farber, J. Grosjean, M. Guha, J. Hourcade, J. Lee, S. Liao, K. Reuter, A. Rose, Y. Takayama, and L. Zhang, "The international children's digital library: description and analysis of first use," *First Monday*, vol. 8, no. 5 (2003).

Sue Dumais, "Latent semantic analysis," *Annual Review of Information Science and Technology*, vol. 38, pp. 189–230 (2004).

Mary Jo Dwyer, "Circuit riding in Texas: An update," Gratefully Yours, Website: http://www.nlm.nih.gov/archive/20040415/pubs/gyours/novdec98.html (Nov./Dec. 1998).

East Carolina University, Voice Services Business Plan, Office of the CIO, Website: http://voip.internet2.edu/meetings/slides/200310/ECU_VoIP_Business_Plan200303.doc (March 2003).

John Edwards, *University of Michigan Conference on Scholarly Publishing*, Website: www.cic.uiuc.edu/programs/CenterForLibraryInitiatives/Archive/ConferenceSummary/ScholarPubMay2001.pdf, p. 11 quoted from Conference Summary.

D. E. Egan, J. R. Remde, T. K. Landauer, C. C. Lochbaum, and L. M. Gomez, "Behavioral evaluation and analysis of a hypertext browser," *Proc. CHI '89, Human Factors in Computing Systems*, pp. 205–210 (1989).

D. E. Egan, M. E. Lesk, R. D. Ketchum, C. C. Lochbaum, J. R. Remde, M. Littman, and T. K. Landauer, "Hypertext for the electronic library? CORE sample results," *Proc. Hypertext '91*, pp. 299–312, (15–18 Dec. 1991).

Charles W. Eliot, "The division of a library into books in use, and books not in use, with different storage methods for the two classes of books," *Collection Management*, vol. 2, no. 1, pp. 73–82 (Spring 1978); reprint of original 1902 essay.

Michael Ester, "Image quality and viewer perception," *Leonardo*, SIGGRAPH 1990 (special issue, 1990).

David Ewalt, "Just how many Linux users are there?" *Information Week* (June 13, 2001).

Christiane Fellbaum and George Miller (Editors) *Wordnet: An Electronic Lexical Database*, MIT Press, Cambridge, MA (1998).

Matthew Finlay, *The CD-ROM Directory 1994*, TFPL Publishing, London (1993).

Andrew Finney, The Domesday Project, Website: www.atsf.co.uk/dottext/domesday.html (1996).

Gerhard Fischer, "Symmetry of ignorance, social creativity, and meta-design," *Knowledge Based Systems*, vol. 13, no. 7–8 (2001).

Charlie Flanagan and Nancy Fitch, "Using resources from American memory in U.S. history classes," *The Source*, Library of Congress, Washington DC (April 2002); see also http://memory.loc.gov/ammem/ndlpedu/community/am_newsletter/article.php?id=35&catname=teaching%20ideas.

Michael Flanders and Donald Swann, "A Song of Reproduction," *At the Drop of a Hat*, sound recording, re-released 1991 by EMI; original recordings from 1956–1960.

L. A. Fletcher and R. Kasturi, "Segmentation of binary images into text strings and graphics," *Proc. SPIE Conf. on Applications of Artificial Intelligence V*, vol. 786, pp. 533–540 (1987).

M. Flickner, H. Sawhney, W. Niblack, J. Ashley, Qian Huang, B. Dom, M. Gorkani, J. Hafner, D. Lee, D. Petkovic, D. Steele, and P. Yanker, "Query by image and video content: The QBIC system," *Computer*, vol. 28, no. 9, pp. 23–32 (September 1995).

R. Florian and D. Yarowsky, "Modeling consensus: Classifier combination for word sense disambiguation," *Proc. Conf. on Empirical Methods in Natural Language Processing (EMNLP02)*, pp. 25–32 (2002).

David Forsyth, Jitendra Malik, Margaret M. Fleck, Hayit Greenspan, Thomas K. Leung, Serge Belongie, Chad Carson, and Chris Bregler, "Finding pictures of objects in large collections of images," *Object Representation in Computer Vision*, vol. 1144, pp. 335–360 (1996).

David Forsyth, Jitendra Malik, and Robert Wilensky, "Searching for digital pictures," *Scientific American*, vol. 276, no. 6, pp 88–93 (June 1997).

Bette-Lee Fox, "These joints are jumpin'," *Library Journal*, (Dec. 15, 2003).

Marc Fresko, Sources of Digital Information, Report 6102, British Library R&D Department, London (1994).

Franziska Frey, File Formats for Digital Masters, Digital Library Federation, Website: www.rlg.ac.uk/visguides/visguide5.html (2000).

W. Gale, K. Church, and D. Yarowsky, "A method for disambiguating word senses in a large corpus," *Computers and the Humanities*, vol. 26, pp. 415–439 (1992).

John Garofolo, Cedric Auzanne, Ellen Voorhees, The TREC Spoken Document Retrieval Track: A Success Story, Website: www.nist.gov/speech/tests/sdr/sdr2000/papers/01plenary1.pdf (April 2000).

John Garrett and Donald Waters, *Preserving Digital Information*, Commission on Preservation and Access (Washington, DC) and Research Libraries Group joint publication, Mountain View, CA (1996).

R. Garside, G. Leech, and G. Sampson, *The Computational Analysis of English: A Corpus-Based Approach*, Longmans, London (1987).

B. Gatos, S. L. Mantzaris, and A. Antonacopoulos, "First international newspaper segmentation contest," *ICDAR 2001* (International Conference on Document Analysis and Recognition), p. 1190 (2001).

V. J. Geller and M. E. Lesk, "User interfaces to information systems: Choices vs. commands," *Proc. 6th Int. ACM SIGIR Conference*, pp. 130–135, Bethesda, MD (June 1983).

Malcolm Getz, "Evaluating digital strategies for storing and retrieving scholarly information," in *Economics of Digital Information: Collection, Storage and Delivery*, Sul H. Lee (ed.), Haworth Press, Binghamton, NY (1997).

W. Wayt Gibbs, "Taking computers to task," *Scientific American*, pp 82–89 (July 1997).

Sallie Gordon, Jill Gustavel, Jana Moore, and Jon Hankey, "The effects of hypertext on reader knowledge representation," *Proceedings of the Human Factors Society—32nd Annual Meeting*, pp. 296–300 (1988).

J. D. Gould and N. Grischokowsky, "Doing the same work with hard copy and with cathode-ray tube (CRT) computer terminals," *Human Factors*, vol. 26, no. 3, pp. 323–337 (1984).

J. D. Gould, L. Alfaro, R. Fonn, R. Haupt, A. Minuto, and J. Salaun, "Why reading was slower from CRT displays than from paper," *Proc. ACM CHI+GI 87*, pp. 7–11, (April 1987).

Jim Gray and P. S. Shemoy, "Rules of thumb in data engineering", *Proc. ICDE 2000*, pp. 3–12, (April 2000).

Albert N Greco, "The general university market for university press books in the United States 1990–9," *Journal of Scholarly Publishing*, vol. 32, no. 2, pp. 61–86 (2001).

José-Marie Griffiths and Donald W. King, *Special Libraries: Increasing the Information Edge*, Special Libraries Association, Washington DC (1993).

Chris Gulker, "Global IT firm predicts Linux will have 20% desktop market share by 2008," *Newsforge* (August 14, 2003).

Kevin M. Guthrie, "Revitalizing older published literature: Preliminary lessons from the use of JSTOR," *The Economics and Usage of Digital Library Collections*, University of Michigan, Ann Arbor, MI (March 2000).

Kevin M. Guthrie, "Archiving in the digital age: There's a will, but is there a way?" *EDUCAUSE Review*, vol. 36, no. 6, pp. 56–65 (Nov./Dec. 2001); also available at www.educause.edu/ir/library/pdf/erm0164.pdf.

R. Haigh, G. Sampson, and E. Atwell, "Project APRIL—A progress report," *Proc. 26th Annual Meeting of the Association for Computational Linguistics*, pp. 104–112, (June 1988).

Juha Hakala, "Collecting and preserving the Web: Developing and testing the NEDLIB Harvester," *RLG Diginews* (April 2001).

Don Hammann, "Computers in physics: An overview," *Physics Today*, vol. 36, no. 5, pp. 25–33 (1983).

Donna Harman, *Overview of the Third Text Retrieval Conference (TREC-3)*, NIST Publication 500-225, National Institute of Standards and Technology (NIST), Gaithersburg, MD (April 1995).

Stevan Harnad, For Whom the Gate Tolls? How and Why to Free the Refereed Research Literature Online Through Author/Institution Self-Archiving Now, Website: www.ecs.soton.ac.uk/~harnad/Tp/resolution.htm (2001).

Alexander G. Hauptmann, Rong Jin, and Tobun D. Ng, "Video retrieval using speech and image information," *Electronic Imaging Conference (EI'03), Storage Retrieval for Multimedia Databases*, (January 20–24, 2003).

Alexander G. Hauptmann and M. Witbrock, "Story segmentation and detection of commercials in broadcast news video," *Advances in Digital Libraries Conference ADL 98* (1998).

David Hawking, Nick Craswell, and Peter Bailey, "Measuring Search Engine Quality," *CSIRO Mathematical and Information Sciences*, TR01/45, 2001 WWW-10 Poster Proceedings (2001).

Brian L. Hawkins, "Planning for the National Electronic Library," *EDUCOM Review*, vol. 29, no. 3, pp. 19–29 (May/June 1994).

Donald T. Hawkins, "Electronic books: Reports of their death have been exaggerated," *Online*, vol. 26 (July/August 2002).

Donald T. Hawkins, "In search of ideal information pricing," *Online*, (March 1989).

Michael Hawley, "Structure out of Sound," Ph.D. diss., MIT, Cambridge, MA (1993).

Marti Hearst, "User interfaces and visualization," in *Modern Information Retrieval*, Ricard Baeza-Yates and Berthier Ribeiro-Neto (eds.), Addison-Wesley, Reading, MA, and ACM Press, ch. 10 (1999).

G. Christian Hill and Molly Baker, "Companies remain in the dark about size of on-line markets," *The Wall Street Journal*, Interactive Edition (June 17, 1996).

Will Hill, Larry Stead, Mark Rosenstein, and George Furnas, "Recommending and evaluating choices in a virtual community of use," *Proc. CHI Conference on Human Factors in Computing Systems*, pp. 194–201 (1995).

Kevin Hillstrom, *Encyclopedia of American Industries*, Gale Group, Detroit (1994).

Oliver Wendell Holmes, Sr., *Poet at the Breakfast Table*, VIII. Houghton Mifflin, Boston, Mass. (1892); quoted from the online Project Gutenberg edition, Website: www.gutenberg.net.

Jonas Holmstrom, "The cost per article reading of open access articles," *D-Lib Magazine*, vol. 10, no. 1 (January 2004).

Roger Hough, "Future Data Traffic Volume," *IEEE Computer*, vol. 3, no. 5, p. 6 (Sept/Oct 1970).

Ding Huang and Hong Yan, "Interword distance changes represented by sine waves for watermarking text images," *IEEE Transactions on Circuits and Systems for Video Technology*, vol. 11, no. 12, pp. 1237–1245 (Dec. 2001).

David A. Hull, "Stemming algorithms: a case study for detailed evaluation," *J. American Society for Information Science*, vol. 47, no. 1, pp 70–84 (January 1996).

Susanne Humphrey, "A knowledge-based expert system for computer assisted indexing," *IEEE Expert*, vol. 4, no. 3, pp. 25–38 (1989).

Susanne Humphrey, "Indexing biomedical documents: From thesaural to knowledge-based retrieval systems," *Artificial Intelligence in Medicine*, vol. 4, pp. 343–371 (1992).

International DunHuang Project, Website: http://idp.bl.uk.

Internet Domain Survey, Website: www.isc.org/ds/www-200301/index.html (January 2003).

Sherille Ismail and Irene Wu, "Broadband Internet access in OECD countries: A comparative analysis," *Office of Strategic Planning and Policy Analysis*, FCC (October 2003).

Alejandro Jaimes and S.-F. Chang, "Automatic selection of visual features and classifiers," *Storage and Retrieval for Media Databases 2000, IS&T/SPIE* (January 2000).

J. Jeon, V. Lavrenko, and R. Manmatha, "Automatic image annotation and retrieval using cross media relevance models," *SIGIR 2003*, pp. 119–126, Toronto, Ontario (2003).

Michael Jensen, "Academic press gives away its secret of success," *Chronicle of Higher Education*, vol. 48, no. 3, p. B24 (Sept. 14, 2001).

Rong Jin, Rong Yan, and Alexander Hauptmann, "Image classification using a bigram model," *AAAI Spring Symposium Series on Intelligent Multimedia*, pp. 83–86, AAAI Press Publication SS-03-08, Menlo Park, CA (2003).

Rong Jin, "Learning to identify video shots with people based on face detection," *Proc. IEEE Int'l Conference on Multimedia*, paper MD-P3.8, Baltimore, MD (2003).

Bao Jishi, "Optical disk document storage and retrieval system of the National Library of China," *Library in the 90's: Int'l Symposium on the Latest Developments in Technologies of Library Service*, pp. F6-1–F6-8 (September 7–11, 1992).

Brian Johnson and Ben Shneiderman, "Treemaps: A space-filling approach to the visualization of hierarchial information structures," *Proc. 2nd Int'l. IEEE Visualization Conference*, pp. 284–291 (Oct. 1991).

William Jones and Susan Dumais, "The spatial metaphor for user interfaces: Experimental tests of reference by location versus name," *ACM Trans. Office Information Systems*, vol. 4, no. 1, pp. 42–63 (January 1986).

Dale Jorgensen, *Economic Growth in the Information Age*, MIT Press, Cambridge, Mass. (2002).

Brewster Kahle, Rick Prelinger, and Mary Jackson, "Public access to digital material," *D-Lib Magazine*, Website: www.dlib.org/dlib/october01/kahle/10kahle.html (October 2001).

Ashish Kapoor, "Automatic Facial Action Analysis," Master's thesis, MIT, Cambridge, Mass. (2002); see www.whitechapel.media.mit.edu/pub/tech-reports/TR-552.pdf.

Anne Kenney and L. Personius, *Joint Study in Digital Preservation*, Commission on Preservation and Access, Washington, DC (1992). ISBN 1-887334-17-3.

K. Kiernan, "The Electronic Beowulf," *Computers in Libraries*, pp. 14–15 (February 1995); see also www.uky.edu/~kiernan.

Donald W. King, Jane Castro, and Heather Jones, *Communication by Engineers: A Literature Review of Engineers' Information Needs, Seeking Processes and Use*, Council on Library Resources, Washington DC (1994).

Donald W. King and Carol Tenopir, "Scholarly journal and digital database pricing: Threat or opportunity?" *PEAK Conference* (March 2000).

Donald W. King and Carol Tenopir, "Using and reading scholarly literature," *Annual Review of Information Science and Technology*, Martha Williams (ed.), vol. 34, pp. 423–477 (2001).

Don King, Carol Tenopir, Carol Hansen Montgomery, and Sarah Aerni, "Patterns of journal use by faculty at three diverse universities," *D-Lib Magazine*, vol. 9, no. 10 (October 2003).

Bruce Kingma, "The costs of print, fiche and digital access: The Early Canadiana Online Project," *D-Lib Magazine*, vol. 6, no. 7 (February 2000).

Jon Kleinberg, "Authoritative sources in a hyperlinked environment," *J. ACM*, vol. 46, no. 5, pp. 604–632 (1999).

Rob Kling and Ewa Callahan, "Electronic journals, the Internet, and scholarly communication," *Annual Review of Information Science and Technology*, vol. 37, pp 127–177 (2002).

G. Bruce Knecht, "How Wall Street whiz found a niche selling books on the Internet," *The Wall Street Journal*, p. 1 (May 16, 1996).

Eastman Kodak Company, *Comparing Kodak Picture CD and Kodak Photo CD Discs*, Technical Information Bulletin 164, Website: www.kodak.com/global/en/service/professional/tib/tib4164.jhtml (April 2003).

Heidi Koester, "User performance with speech recognition systems," *Proc. RESNA Annual Meeting*, pp. 112–114 (2002); see also http://sitemaker.umich.edu/speechrecognition/files/resna2002-speechperf.pdf.

N. Komatsu and H. Tominaga, "A proposal on digital watermarks in document image communication and its application to realizing a signature," *Electronics and Communications in Japan, Part 1 (Communications)*, vol. 73, no. 5, pp. 22–23 (1990).

Ronald Kostoff, "The practice and malpractice of stemming," *J. American Society for Information Science*, vol. 54, no. 10, pp. 984–985 (August 2003).

Peter Krasilovsky, "Into the black," *American Demographics: Marketing Tools Supplement*, pp. 22–25 (July/Aug. 1995); see also www.marketingtools.com/mt_current/MT285.html.

Reinhold Kreile, "Revenue from and distribution of the statutory levy on hardware and blank tapes used for private copying in Germany: A system proves its worth," *GEMA Yearbook 2001/2002*, Website: www.gema.de/engl/communication/yearbook/jahr_01_02/themadesjahres.shtml (2002).

D. M. Krentz, "On-line searching: specialist required," *J. Chem. Inf. Comp. Sci.*, vol. 18, no. 1, pp. 4–9 (1978).

Martha Kryllidou, "Journal costs: Current trends and future scenarios for 2020," *ARL Bimonthly Report*, no. 210 (June 2000).

Martha Kyrillidou and Mark Young, "ARL statistics 2001–02: Research library trends," Association of Research Libraries, Website: www.arl.org/state/arlstat/02pub/intro02.html (2003).

Lori Lamel and Jean-Luc Gauvain, "Automatic processing of broadcast audio in multiple languages," *XI European Signal Processing Conference*, Paper 702, (2002).

F. Wilfred Lancaster, *Towards Paperless Information Systems*, Academic Press, New York (1978).

Michael Landau, "Why Grokster does Not Infringe Copyright and Napster Does," Website: www.gigalaw.com (August 2003).

T. K. Landauer and M. L. Littman, "Fully automatic cross-language document retrieval using latent semantic indexing," in *Proceedings of the Sixth Annual Conference of the UW Center for the New Oxford English Dictionary and Text Research*, pp. 31–38, Waterloo, Ontario, October 1990.

Tom Landauer, *The Trouble with Computers*, MIT Press, Cambridge, MA (1995).

Gerhard C. Langelaar, Iwan Setyawan, and Reginald L. Lagendijk, "Watermarking digital image and video data: A state-of-the-art overview," *IEEE Signal Processing Magazine*, vol. 17, no. 5, pp 20–26 (2000).

Jules Lariviere, *Guidelines for Legal Deposit Legislation*, UNESCO, Paris (2000); see also IFLANET at www.ifla.org/VII/s1/gnl/legaldep1.htm.

Steven Leach, "The growth rate of major academic libraries: Rider and Purdue reviewed," *College and Research Libraries*, vol. 37, pp. 531–542 (Nov. 1976).

D. S. Le, G. R. Thoma, and H. Weschler, "Automated page orientation and skew angle detection for binary document images," *Pattern Recognition*, vol. 27, no. 10, pp. 1325–1344 (1994).

William Lemberg, "A Life-Cycle Cost Analysis for the Creation, Storage and Dissemination of a Digitized Document Collection," Ph.D. diss., University of California at Berkeley (1995).

Douglas Lenat and R. V. Guha, *Building Large Knowledge-based Systems: Representation and Inference in the CYC Project*, Addison-Wesley, Reading, MA (1990).

M. E. Lesk, "Automatic sense disambiguation using machine readable dictionaries: How to tell a pine cone from an ice cream cone," *Proc. SIGDOC Conference*, pp. 24–26 (June 1986).

M. E. Lesk, "Television libraries for workstations: An all digital storage transmission and display system for low rate video in multimedia information," *Proceedings of the Second International Information Research Conference*, Mary Feeney and Shirley Day (eds.), pp. 187–194 (July 1991).

Michael Lesk, "Chicken Little and the recorded music crisis," *IEEE Security and Privacy*, vol. 1, no. 5, pp 73–75 (2003a).

Michael Lesk, "The price of digitization: New cost models for cultural and educational institutions," *NINCH Symposium* (April 2003b); see also www.ninch.org/forum/price.lesk.report.html.

Lawrence Lessig, *The Future of Ideas*, Random House, New York, NY (2001).

Lawrence Lessig, *Free Culture*, Penguin (2004).

Lawrence Lessig and Associates, Creative Commons, Website: www.creativecommons.org.

Library of Congress, "Report to the digital library federation," *DLF Newsletter*, Website: www.diglib.org/pubs/news03_01/lc.htm (Jan 30, 2002).

N. Liolios, N. Fakotakis, and G. Kokkinakis, "Improved document skew detection based on text line connected-component clustering," *IEEE Int'l Conf. on Image Processing 01*, pp. I: 1098–1101 (2001).

Peter Lyman and Hal Varian, "How Much Information 2003?" Website: www.sims.berkeley.edu/research/projects/how-much-info-2003/.

Xia Lin and Dagobert Soergel, "A self-organizing semantic map for information retrieval," *Proc. 14th Int'l SIGIR Conference*, pp. 262–269 (October 1991).

J. B. Lovins, "Development of a stemming algorithm," *Mechanical Translation and Computational Linguistics*, vol. 11, no. 2, pp. 22–31 (1968).

Yue Lu and Chew Lim Tan, "Improved nearest-neighbor based approach to accurate document skew estimation," *Proc. Int'l Conf. on Document Analysis and Recognition (ICDAR03)*, pp 503–507 (2003).

F. Machlup, *The Production and Distribution of Knowledge in the United States*, Princeton University Press, Princeton, NJ (1962).

T. W. Malone, "How do people organise their desks? Implications for the design of office information systems," *ACM Transactions on Office Information Systems*, 1, pp. 99–112 (1985).

Gerry McGovern, "Quality Publishing is About Saying No," Website: www.gerrymcgovern.com/nt/2003/nt_2003_08_04_no.htm (August 4, 2003).

S. McIlraith, T. Son, and H. Zeng, "Semantic web services," *IEEE Intelligent Systems*, vol. 16, no. 2, pp. 46–53 (Mar./April 2001).

Martha McKay, "VoIP's growth is loud and clear: Net phoning is wave of future," *The Record* (Feb. 4, 2004); see also www.vonage.com/corporate/press_news.php?PR=2004_02_04_3.

The Making of America, Website: www.hti.umich.edu/m/moagrp/.

Jennifer Mankoff, Scott E. Hudson, and Gregory D. Abowd, "Interaction techniques for ambiguity resolution in recognition-based interfaces," *Proc. UIST Conference*, pp. 11–20 (2000).

K. E. Marks, S. P. Nielsen, H. Craig Petersen, and P. E. Wagner, "Longitudinal study of scientific journal prices in a research library," *College and Research Libraries*, vol. 52, no. 2, pp. 125–138 (March 1991).

K. Matsui and K. Tanaka, "Video-steganography: How to secretly embed a signature in a picture," *Technological Strategies for Protecting Intellectual Property in the Networked Multimedia Environment*, vol. 1, issue 1, pp. 187–206 (Jan. 1994).

H. Maurer, A. Holzinger, A. Pichler, and W. Almer, "TRIANGLE: A multi-media testbed for examining incidental learning, motivation, and the Tamagotchi-Effect within a Game-Show like Computer Based Learning Module," *Proceedings of ED-MEDIA 2001*, pp. 766–771 (2001).

L. McKnight, A. Dillon, and J. Richardson, "A comparison of linear and hypertext formats in information retrieval," *HYPERTEXT: State of the Art*, R. Macaleese and C. Green (eds.), Intellect, Oxford, United Kingdom (1991).

Jack Meadows, "Too much of a good thing?" *The International Serials Industry*, Hazel Woodward and Stella Pilling (eds.), Gower Publishing, Aldershot, Hampshire, pp. 23–43 (1993).

Jack (A. J.) Meadows, *Communicating Research*, Academic Press, San Diego, CA (1998).

Phil Mellor, "CAMILEON: Emulation and BBC Domesday," *RLG Diginews*, vol. 7, no. 2 (April 2003).

Jason Meserve, "NFL, IBM kick off content management deal," *Network World Fusion* (July 23, 2003).

Sheldon Meyer and Leslie Phillabaum, *What is a University Press*, Website: http://aaup.princeton.edu/central/press.html (1996).

Artem Mikheev, Luc Vincent, Mike Hawrylycz, and Leon Bottou, "Electronic document publishing using DjVu," *Proc. IAPR Int'l Workshop on Document Analysis (DAS'02)* (Aug. 2002).

Jim Milliot, "Publishers still searching for profits in new media," *Publishers Weekly*, vol. 243, no. 1, p. 22 (Jan. 1996).

Marvin Minsky, "A framework for representing knowledge," in *The Psychology of Computer Vision*, P. H. Winston (ed.), McGraw-Hill, New York (1975).

F. C. Mintzer, A. Cazes, F. Giordano, J. Lee, K. Mager-lein, and F. Schiattarela, "Capturing and preparing images of Vatican library manuscripts for access via Internet," *Proc. 48th Annual Conf. Society for Imaging Science and Technology: Imaging on the Information Superhighway*, pp. 74–77 (May 1995a).

F. C. Mintzer, L. E. Boyle, A. N. Cazes, B. S. Christian, S. C. Cox, F. P. Giordano, H. M. Gladney, J. C. Lee, M. L. Kelmanson, A. C. Lirani, K. A. Magerlein, A. M. B. Pavini, and F. Schiattarella, "Toward online, worldwide access to Vatican Library materials," *IBM J. of Research and Development*, vol. 40, no. 2, pp. 139–162 (1995b).

William Mitchell, Alan Inouye, and Marjorie Blumenthal, *Beyond Productivity: Information Technology, Innovation and Creativity*, NAS report, National Academic Press, Washington, DC (2003).

R. Morris, "Scatter storage techniques," *Comm. of the ACM*, vol. 11, pp. 38–43 (1968).

Deirdre Mulligan, John Han, and Aaron Burstein, "How DRM-based content delivery systems disrupt expectations of personal use," *DRM-03 Conference*, pp. 77–89 (October 2003).

Brad Myers, Juan Casares, Scott Stevens, Laura Dabbish, Dan Yocum, and Albert Corbett, "A multi-view intelligent editor for digital video libraries," *ACM/IEEE JCDL* (Joint Conference on Digital Libraries), pp. 106–115 (2001).

Marc Najork and Janet Wiener, "Breadth-first search crawling yields high quality pages," *Proc. of the 10th Int'l World Wide Web Conference*, pp. 114–118 (May 2001).

Lisa Napoli, "Frequent search engine users, Google is watching and counting," *The New York Times*, p. c3 (Oct. 6, 2003).

National Diet Library (eds), *NDL Newsletter*, National Diet Library, Tokyo, vol. 96, pp. 2–5 (1995).

Theodor H. Nelson, *Literary Machines*, Mindful Press, Sausalito, CA (1990).

Theodor H. Nelson, "Rants and raves," (letters column) *Wired Magazine* (March 1996).

Wayne Niblack, Xiaoming Zhu, James L. Hafner, Tom Breuel, Dulce B. Ponceleon, Dragutin Petkovic, Myron Flickner, Eli Upfal, Sigfredo I. Nin, Sanghoon Sull, Byron Dom, Boon-Lock Yeo, Savitha Srinivasan, Dan Zivkovic, and Mike Penner,

"Updates to the QBIC System," *Storage and Retrieval for Image and Video Databases SPIE*, pp. 150–161, San Jose, CA (January 1998).

Jakob Nielsen, "Evaluating hypertext usability in designing hypermedia for learning," *Proceedings of the NATO Advanced Research Workshop*, D. H. Jonassen and H. Mandl (eds.), pp. 147–68 (1990).

Jakob Nielsen, V. L. Phillips, and Susan Dumais, Information Retrieval of Imperfectly Recognized Handwriting, Website: www.useit.com/papers/handwriting_retrieval.html (1993).

Michael Noll, "Voice vs. data: An estimate of broadband traffic," *IEEE Communications*, vol. 29, no. 6, pp. 22, 24, 29, 78 (June 1991).

Ragnar Nordlie, "User revealment—a comparison of initial queries and ensuing question development in online searching and in human reference interactions," *Proc. SIGIR Conference*, pp 11–18 (1999).

Andrew Odlyzko, "Tragic loss or good riddance: The impending demise of traditional scholarly journals," *International Journal of Human-Computer Studies*, vol. 42, no. 1, pp. 71–122 (1995).

Andrew Odlyzko, "The Public Library of Science and the ongoing revolution in scholarly communication" (web forum: Future E-Access to the Primary Literature), *Nature* (Sept. 18, 2001).

Andrew Odlyzko, "The Case Against Micropayments," Website: www.dtc.umn.edu/7Eodlyzko/doc/case.against.micropayments.txt (April 13, 2003).

V. E. Ogle and M. Stonebraker, "Chabot: retrieval from a relational database of images," *Computer*, vol. 28, no. 9, pp. 40–48 (Sept. 1995).

Kenton O'Hara, Fiona Smith, William Newman, and Abigail Sellen, "Student readers' use of library documents," *Proc. ACM SIGCHI 1998*, pp. 233–240 (1998).

Ann Okerson and Kendon Stubbs, "ARL annual statistics 1990-91: Remembrance of things past, present . . . and future?" *Publishers Weekly*, vol. 239, no. 34, p. 22 (July 27, 1992).

Ann Okerson and James O'Donnell, *Scholarly Journals at the Crossroads: A Subversive Proposal for Electronic Publishing*, Association of Research Libraries, Washington, DC (1994).

Steven Oliner and Dan Sichel, *The Resurgence of Growth in the Late 1990s: Is Information Technology the Story?* Federal Reserve Board, Washington DC (2000).

Stefanie Olsen and Robert Lemos, Can Face Recognition Keep Airports Safe? CNET News.com, Website: http://news.com.com/2100-1023-275313.html?legacy=cnet (Nov. 1, 2002).

G. M. Olson, D. Atkins, R. Clauer, T. Weymouth, A. Prakash, T. Finholt, F. Jahanian, and C. Rasmussen, "Technology to support distributed team science," *Coordination Theory and Collaboration Technology*, pp. 761–783, Lawrence Erlbaum, Hillsdale, NJ (2001).

"Text retrieval: The next steps," *Online & CD-ROM Review*, vol. 20, no. 3, pp. 150–152 (1996).

John Ousterhout, *Tcl and the Tk toolkit*, Addison-Wesley, Reading, MA (1994).

Thomas Pack, "Preserving our digital history," *Information Today* (December 15, 2002).

Massimo Pagotto and Augusto Celentano, "Matching XML DTDs to relational database views," *SEBD 2000*, pp. 183–195 (2000).

Chris Paice, "Another stemmer," *ACM SIGIR Forum*, vol. 24, pp. 56–61 (1990).

Aliasgar Pardawala and Hatim Kantawalla, OCR Software: How They Fared? Website: www.zdnetindia.com/reviews/software/applications/stories/65498.html.

R. D. Peacocke and D. H. Graf, "Introduction to speech and speaker recognition," *IEEE Computer*, vol. 23, no. 8, pp. 26–33 (1990).

Claudia Pearce and Charles Nicholas, "TELLTALE: experiments in a dynamic hypertext environment for degraded and multilingual data," *J. Amer. Soc. for Inf. Sci.*, vol. 47, no. 4, pp. 263–75 (April 1996).

Alex Pentland, "Smart Rooms," *Scientific American* (international edition), vol. 274, no. 4, pp. 54–62 (April 1996).

Associated Press (eds.), "Penn State, Napster in harmony," *Associated Press* (Nov. 7, 2003).

Noel Perrin, *Giving Up the Gun*, Random House, New York, NY (1980).

Michael P. Perrone, Gregory F. Russell, and Aiman Zig, "Machine learning in a multimedia document retrieval framework," *IBM Systems Journal*, vol. 41, no. 3, pp 494–503 (2002).

P. J. Phillips, P. Grother, R. J. Micheals, D. M. Blackburn, E. Tabassi, and J. M. Bone, "FRVT 2002: Overview and Summary," *Face Recognition Vendor Test 2002*, Website: http://www.frvt.org/FRVT2002, NIST, Gaithersburg, MD (March 2003).

Jeremy Pickens and W. Bruce Croft, "An exploratory analysis of phrases in text retrieval," *RIAO Conference*, Paris, France (April 2000).

Roberta Pillette, "Mass deacidification: A preservation option for libraries," *69th IFLA General Conference* (August 2003).

M. F. Porter, "An algorithm for suffix stripping," *Program*, vol. 14, pp. 130–137 (1980).

Gerasimos Potamianos, Chalapthy Neti, Giridharan Iyengar, and Eric Helmuth, "Large-vocabulary audio-visual speech recognition machines and humans," *Proc. EUROSPEECH* (Sept. 3–7, 2001).

Derek de la Solla Price, *Little Science, Big Science—and Beyond*, Columbia University Press, Columbia, NY (1986).

Protein Data Bank, Website: //www.rcsb.org/pdb/.

Mark Przybocki and Alvin Martin, "NIST's Assessment of Text Independent Speaker Recognition Performance," *The Advent of Biometrics on the Internet, A COST 275 Workshop* (Nov. 7–8, 2002); see also www.nist.gov/speech/publications/papersrc/cost275.pdf.

Public Library of Science, Website: www.plos.org.

Publishing Trends (eds.), "Changing course: With academic sales dwindling, university presses target the trade market," *Publishing Trends* (December 2003); see also www.publishingtrends.com/copy/03/0312/0312upresses.html.

Steven Puglia, "The costs of digital imaging projects," *RLG Diginews* (March 1999).

Yanjun Qi, Alexander Hauptmann, and Ting Liu, "Supervised classification for video shot segmentation," *IEEE Conference on Multimedia* (July 2003).

Hannelore Rader, "The impact of digital collections," *The Economics and Usage of Digital Library Collections*, University of Michigan, Ann Arbor, Mich. (March 2000).

M. V. Ramakrishna and Justin Zobel, "Performance in practice of string hashing functions," *Proc. Fifth International Conference on Database Systems for Advanced Applications*, pp. 215–224 (1997).

Katherine Ramsland, The Origin of Voiceprints, Court TV's Crime Library, Website: www.crimelibrary.com/criminal_mind/forensics/voiceprints/1.html (2004).

Joan Rataic-Lang, Anna Holeton, and Lynne Mogenson, 2002 Private Law Library/ Corporate Law Library SIG Operations Survey, Website: www.callacbd.ca/imags/PLL_CLL_ops_survey_2002.pdf.

Vicky Reich and David Rosenthal, "LOCKSS: A permanent web publishing and access system," *Serials*, vol. 14, no. 3, pp. 239–244 (2001).

Daniel Renoult, "The digitizing program of the French National Library," *International Symposium on Digital Libraries 1995*, pp. 87–90 (August 22–25, 1995); see also www.bnf.fr/enluminures/aaccueil.shtm.

Philip Resnik and David Yarowsky, "Distinguishing systems and distinguishing senses: New evaluation methods for word sense disambiguation," *Natural Language Engineering*, vol. 5, no. 2, pp. 113–133 (1999).

Reuters, The Bankrupt Promise of Micropayments, Wired News, Website: www.wired.com/news/business/0,1367,11704,00.html.

Stephen Rice, Frank Jenkins, and Thomas Nartker, *Fifth Annual Test of OCR Accuracy*, TR-96-01, Information Science Research Institute, University of Nevada, Las Vegas, NV (April 1996).

Fremont Rider, *The Scholar and the Future of the Research Library*, Hadham Press, N.Y. (1944).

S. S. Roach, "Services Under Siege: The Restructuring Imperative," *Harvard Business Review*, pp. 82–91 (1991).

George Robertson, Mary Czerwinski, Kevin Larson, Daniel Robbins, David Thiel, and Maarten van Dantzich, "Data mountain: Using spatial memory for document management," *ACM UIST Symposium on User Interface Software & Technology*, 11th UIST Symposium, p. 153–162, San Francisco, CA (1998).

Peter Robinson, *Digitization of Primary Textual Sources (Office for Humanities Communication Publications)*, Oxford University Computing Services, Oxford, United Kingdom (1993).

Barbara Rosario and Marti Hearst, "Classifying the semantic relations in noun compounds via a domain-specific lexical hierarchy," *Proc. 2001 Conference on Empirical Methods in Natural Language Processing* (2001).

Philip Ross and Nikhil Hutheesing, "Along came the spiders," *Forbes*, vol. 156, no. 10, pp. 210–217 (Oct. 23, 1995).

Jeff Rothenberg, *Avoiding Technological Quicksand: Finding a Viable Technical Foundation for Digital Preservation*, CLIR report, Washington, DC (January 1998).

Tony Rothman, *New Republic*, vol. 206, p. 14 (February 3, 1992).

Lawrence Rudener, Marie Miller-Whitehead, and Jennifer Gellman, "Who is reading on-line education journals? Why, and what are they reading?" *D-Lib Magazine*, vol. 8, no. 12 (Dec. 2002).

Alexander Rudnicky, Alexander Hauptmann, and Kai-Fu Lee, "Survey of current speech technology," *Comm. ACM*, vol. 37, no. 3, pp. 52–57 (March 1994).

Hans Rutimann, The International Project 1992 Update, Commission on Preservation and Access, Website: http://palimpsest.stanford.edu/cpa/reports/intern92.html.

Gloriana St. Clair, "Million book project," *Proc. CNI Conference*, Coalition for Networked Information, Website: http://www.cni.org/tfms/2002b.fall/abstracts/PB-MillionBooks-StClair.htm (Dec. 2002).

G. A. Salton, "Automatic processing of foreign language documents," *J. Amer. Soc. for Inf. Sci.*, vol. 21, no. 3, pp. 187–194 (May 1970).

G. A. Salton and C. Buckley, "Automatic text structuring and retrieval: Experiments in automatic encyclopedia searching," *Proc. 14th SIGIR Conference*, pp. 21–30 (October 1991).

G. Sampson, R. Haigh, and E. Atwell, "Natural language analysis by stochastic optimization: A progress report on Project APRIL," *Journal of Experimental and Theoretical Artificial Intelligence*, vol. 1, no. 4, pp. 271–287 (1989).

A. L. Samuel, "The banishment of paperwork," *New Scientist*, vol. 21, no. 380, pp. 529–530 (27 February 1964).

Pamela Samuelson, "Copyright's fair use doctrine and digital data," *Publishing Research Quarterly*, vol. 11, no. 1, pp. 27–39 (Spring 1995).

Roland Sanguino, CSC Evaluation of CYC, Website: www.csc.com/aboutus/lef/mds67_off/uploads/sanguino_eval_cyc.pdf (March 2001).

T. Saracevic and M. Dalbello, Digital Library Research and Digital Library Practice, Website: http://www.scils.rutgers.edu/~tefko/Saracevic-Dalabello_DLib-02.doc, (2003).

S. Satoh, Y. Nakamura, and T. Kanade, "Name-it: Naming and detecting faces in news videos," *IEEE Multimedia*, vol. 6, no. 1, pp. 22–35 (Jan./Mar. 1999).

Jacques Savoy, "Statistical behavior of fast hashing of variable length text strings," *ACM SIGIR Forum*, vol. 24, no. 3, pp. 62–71 (1990).

Khalid Sayood, *Introduction to Data Compression*, 2nd ed., Morgan Kaufmann, San Francisco, CA (1996).

F. Schaffalitzy and A. Zisserman, "Multi-view matching for unordered image sets, or 'How do I organize my holiday snaps?'" *Proceedings of the 7th European Conference on Computer Vision*, p. 414–431 (2002); see also www.robots.ox.ac.uk/~vgg/publications/html/index.html.

Bruce Schatz, "Building the Interspace: Digital Library Infrastructure for a University Engineering Community," Website: http://surya.grainger.uiuc.edu/dli/ (1995).

Seybold Publications, "Kodak enhances Photo CD," *Seybold Report on Desktop Publishing*, vol. 10, no. 10, p. 25 (June 10, 1996).

Urvi Shah, Tim Finin, and James Mayfield, "Information retrieval on the Semantic Web," *10th Int'l Conference on Information and Knowledge Management* (November 2002).

Claude Shannon, "Prediction and entropy of printed English," *Bell System Technical Journal*, vol. 3, pp. 50–64 (1950).

Carl Shapiro and Hal Varian, *Information Rules*, Harvard Business School Press, Boston, Mass. (1998).

Upendra Shardanand and Pattie Maes, "Social information filtering: Algorithms for automating 'word of mouth,'" *Proc. CHI Conference on Human Factors in Computing Systems*, pp. 210–217 (1995).

Ben Shneiderman, "Improving the human factors aspect of database interactions," *ACM Trans. on Database Systems*, vol. 3, no. 4, pp. 417–439 (Dec. 1978).

Ben Shneiderman, "User interface design and evaluation for an electronic encyclopedia," *Cognitive Engineering in the Design of Human-Computer Interaction and Expert Systems*, G. Salvendy (ed.), Elsevier, Burlington, Mass. pp. 207–223 (1987).

Ben Shneiderman, "Tree visualization with Tree-maps: A 2-D space-filling approach," *ACM Transactions on Graphics*, vol. 11, no. 1, pp. 92–99 (1992).

Ben Shneiderman, "Supporting creativity with advanced information-abundant user interfaces," in *Human-Centered Computing: Online Communities and Virtual Environments*, pp. 469–480, Springer-Verlag, London (2001).

Ben Shneiderman, Leonardo's Laptop: Human Needs and the New Computing Technologies, MIT Press, Cambridge, MA, Website: www.cs.umd.edu/hcil/pubs/presentations/LeonardoLaptop/LeonardoLaptop.ppt (2002).

Daniel Sichel and Stephen Oliner, *The Resurgence of Growth in the Late 1990s: Is Information Technology the Story?* Federal Reserve Board, Washington, DC, Report 2000-20; see also www.federalreserve.gov/pubs/feds/2000/200020/200020pap.pdf.

Marvin Sirbu and J. D. Tygar, "NetBill: An Internet commerce system optimized for network delivered services," *Proc. IEEE COMPCON '95*, pp. 20–25 (1995).

Sloan Digital Sky Survey, Website: www.sdss.org.

Alan Smeaton, "Indexing, browsing and searching of digital video," *Annual Review of Information Science and Technology*, vol. 36, pp. 371–407 (2004).

C. G. M. Snoek and M. Worring, "Multimodal video indexing: A review of the state of the art," *Multimedia Tools and Applications* (forthcoming 2003).

Mike Sosteric, Yuwei Shi, and Oliver Wenker, "The upcoming revolution in the scholarly communication system," *Journal of Electronic Publishing*, vol. 7, no. 2 (Dec. 2001).

Karen Sparck-Jones and Martin Kay, *Linguistics and Information Science*, Academic Press, NY (1973).

Karen Sparck-Jones, "Language and Information: Old Ideas, New Achievements," Website: www.cl.cam.ac.uk/users/ksj/GHlect02.pdf; see related article (with Steve Robertson) LM vs. PM: Where's the Relevance? at http://la.lti.cs.cmu.edu/callan/Workshops/lmir01/WorkshopProcs/OtherPages/TableOfContents.html; see also related paper in *Language Modeling for Information Retrieval*, W. Croft and J. Lafferty (eds.), Kluwer, Hingham, Mass. (2003).

Diomidis Spinellis, "The decay and failure of web references," *Comm. ACM*, vol. 46, no. 1, pp. 71–77 (Jan. 2003).

A. Spink, D. Wolfram, B. J. Jansen, and T. Saracevic, "Searching the Web: The public and their queries," *J. Amer. Soc. Inf. Sci.*, vol. 52, no. 3, pp. 226–234 (2001).

S. N. Srihari, S. W. Lam, J. J. Hull, R. K. Srihari, and V. Govindaraju, "Intelligent data retrieval from raster images of documents," *Digital Libraries '94 Proceedings*, pp. 34–40 (June 19–21, 1994).

Craig Stanfill, R. Thau, and D. Waltz, "A parallel indexed algorithm for information retrieval," *Proc. 12th ACM SIGIR Conference*, pp. 88–97 (1989).

Craig Stanfill and R. Thau, "Information retrieval on the connection machine: 1 to 8192 gigabytes," *Information Processing & Management*, vol. 27, no. 4, pp. 285–310 (1991).

Craig Stanfill and Brewster Kahle, "Parallel free-text search on the Connection machine system," *Commun. ACM*, vol. 29, no. 12, pp. 1229–39 (1986).

The Stanford University Digital Libraries Project, Website: www.diglib.stanford.edu/diglib/pub/ (1995).

Bill Steele, "Online Physics Archive that is Transforming Global Science Communication, 'arXiv.org,' is Moving from Los Alamos to Cornell University," Cornell press release (July 16, 2001).

R. M. Stein, "Browsing through terabytes," *BYTE*, vol. 16, no. 5, pp. 157–164 (May 1991).

Scott Stevens, Michael Christel, and Howard Wactlar, "Informedia: Improving access to digital video," *Interactions*, vol. 1, no. 4, pp. 67–71 (Oct. 1994).

Douglas R. Stinson, *Cryptography: Theory and Practice*, CRC Press, Boca Raton, FL (1995).

David Stipp, "2001 is just around the corner, where's HAL?" *Fortune* (November 13, 1995).

A. Stolcke, H. Bratt, J. Butzberger, H. Franco, V. R. Rao Gadde, M. Plauché, C. Richey, E. Shriberg, K. Sönmez, F. Weng, and J. Zheng, "The SRI March 2000 Hub-5 Conversational Speech Transcription System," *Proc. NIST Speech Transcription Workshop* (2000).

David W. Stowe, "Just Do It," *Lingua Franca*, pp. 32–42 (Nov./Dec. 1995).

Danny Sullivan, "Google IPO to happen, files for public offering," April 29, 2004, at http://www.searchenginewatch.com/searchday/article.php/3347471.

Danny Sullivan, Searches per Day, Search Engine Watch, Website: www.searchengine watch.com/reports/article.php/2156461.

Y. Sure and V. Iosif, "First results of a Semantic Web technologies evaluation," *DOA'02* (Distributed Objects and Applications), Website: http://ai.kaist.ac.kr/ˆsjchol/ semantic-web/FedConfInd-SureIosif-submission.pdf (Oct. 2002).

Don R. Swanson, "Two medical literatures that are logically but not bibliographically connected," *J. Amer. Soc. Inf. Sci.*, vol. 38, no. 4, pp. 228–233 (July 1987).

Don R. Swanson, "Analysis of unintended connections between disjoint science literatures," *Proc. 14th ACM SIGIR Conference*, pp. 280–289 (Oct. 1991).

Don R. Swanson and N. R. Smalheiser, "An interactive system for finding complementary literatures: A stimulus to scientific discovery," *Artificial Intelligence*, vol. 91, no. 2, pp. 183–203 (1997).

Don R. Swanson, N. R. Smalheiser, and A. Bookstein, "Information discovery from complementary literatures: Categorizing viruses as potential weapons," *J. American Society for Information Science and Technology*, vol. 52, no. 10, pp. 797–812 (August 2001).

Aldrin Sweeney, "Should you publish in electronic journals?" *Journal of Electronic Publishing*, vol. 6, no. 2 (Dec. 2000).

Gregory Tassey, The Economic Impacts of Inadequate Infrastructure for Software Testing (report prepared by RTI for NIST), NIST Website: www.nist.gov/ director/prog-ofc/report02-3.pdf (May 2002).

G. Taubes, "E-mail withdrawal prompts spasm," *Science*, vol. 262, no. 5131, pp. 173–174 (Oct. 8, 1993).

David Taubman and Michael Marcellin, *Jpeg2000: Image Compression Fundamentals, Standards and Practice*, Kluwer, Hingham, MA (2001); see also www.jpeg.org.

J. M. Tenenbaum, C. Medich, A. M. Schiffman, and W. T. Wong, "CommerceNet: Spontaneous electronic commerce on the Internet," *Proc. IEEE COMPCON'95*, pp. 38–43 (1995).

Carol Tenopir and Donald King, "Designing electronic journals with 30 years of lessons from print," *Journal of Electronic Publishing*, vol. 4, no. 2 (Dec. 1998).

Carol Tenopir and Donald King, "Trends in scientific scholarly journal publishing in the United States," *Journal of Scholarly Publishing*, vol. 28, no. 3, pp. 135–171 (1997).

Carol Tenopir et al., "Patterns of journal use by scientists through three evolutionary phases," *D-Lib Magazine*, vol. 9, no. 5 (May 2003).

B. N. Tou, M. D. Williams, R. Fikes, A. Henderston, and T. Malone, "Rabbit: An intelligent database assistant," *Proc. AAAI Conference*, pp. 314–318 (Aug. 1982).

Yuen-Hsien Tseng and Douglas Oard, "Document Image Retrieval Techniques for Chinese," *Proceedings of the Fourth Symposium on Document Image Understanding Technology*, pp. 151–158 (April 23–25, 2001).

Karen Turko, *Preservation Activities in Canada*, Commission on Preservation and Access, Washington, DC (Feb. 1996).

University of Sheffield Workshop, *Generating Electronic Text in the Humanities*, Sheffield, United Kingdom (June 1995).

Hal Varian, "The future of electronic journals," *Scholarly Communication and Technology* (March 1997).

Hal Varian and Carl Shapiro, *Information Rules: A Strategic Guide to the Network Economy*, Harvard Business School Press, Cambridge, MA (1998).

Victor Vianu, "A Web odyssey: From Codd to XML," *SIGMOD Record*, vol. 32, no. 2, pp. 68–77 (2003).

Ellen Voorhees, "Variations in relevance judgments and the measurement of retrieval effectiveness," *Information Processing and Management*, vol. 36, no. 5, pp. 697–716 (2000).

Ellen Voorhees and Lori Buckland, *The Eleventh Text Retrieval Conference*, NIST Special Publication SP 500-251, National Institute of Standards and Technology (NIST), Gaithersberg, Md. see also http://trec.nist.gov/pubs/trec11/ t11_proceedings.html (2003).

Howard Wactlar et al., Informedia Digital Video Library, Website: http://www.informedia.cs.cmu/edu.

Howard Wactlar, T. Kanade, M. A. Smith, and S. M. Stevens, "Intelligent access to digital video: Informedia project," *IEEE Computer*, vol. 29, no. 5, pp. 46–52 (May 1996).

Alex Waibel, "Interactive translation of conversational speech," *IEEE Computer*, vol. 29, no. 7, pp. 41–48 (July 1996).

Thomas Walker, "Market-driven free access to journal articles," *The Scientist*, vol. 15, no. 12, p. 43 (June 11, 2001); see also www.thescientist.com/yr2001/jun/opin_010611.html.

Mary Waltham, Why Do Publications Cost So Much? Website: www.marywaltham.com/Denver_SLA.ppt (Nov. 21, 2002).

Dacheng Wang and S. N. Srihari, "Classification of newspaper image blocks using texture analysis," *Computer Vision, Graphics, and Image Processing*, vol. 47, pp. 327–352 (1989).

Marlie Wasserman, "How much does it cost to publish a monograph?" *The Specialized Scholarly Monograph in Crisis, or How Can I get Tenure If You Won't Publish My Book? AAUP Conference* (Sept. 11–12, 1997).

Paul Welsh, "Costly computer rage," *BBC News* (May 27, 1999); see also http://news.bbc.co.uk/1/hi/business/the_economy/shill/353563.stm.

Lynn Wilcox, Don Kimber, and Francine Chen, "Audio indexing using speaker identification," *Information Science and Technologies Laboratory Report*, ISTL-QCA-1994-05-04, Xerox Palo Alto Research Center, Palo Alto, CA (1994).

Karen Wilhoit, "Outsourcing cataloging at Wright State University," *Serials Review*, vol. 20, no. 3, pp. 70–73 (1994).

John Wilkins, *An Essay Towards a Real Character and a Philosophical Language*, originally published in 1668 for S. Gellibrand, London, reprinted 1968 by Scolar Press, London.

Martha Williams, "Database publishing statistics," *Publishing Research Quarterly*, vol. 11, no. 3, pp. 3–9 (Sept. 1995).

Martha Williams, "The state of databases today: 1996," *Gale Directory of Databases*, Kathleen Lopez Nolan (ed.), Gale Research, Detroit, MI (1996).

Martha Williams, "The state of databases today: 2001," *Gale Directory of Databases*, Gale Research, Detroit, Mich., vol. 1, p. xvii–xxx (2001).

Ian Witten, Alistair Moffat, and Timothy Bell, *Managing Gigabytes: Compressing and Indexing Documents and Images*, 2nd ed., Morgan Kaufmann, San Francisco (1999).

Ian Witten and David Bainbridge, *How to Build a Digital Library*, Morgan Kaufmann, San Francisco (2003).

Barbara Wolff, "UW Press reorganizes, reflecting publishing trends nationwide," *University Communications*, University of Wisconsin-Madison (May 6, 1999); see also www.news.wisc.edu/894.html.

David Worthington, "WordPerfect vies for a comeback," *BetaNews* (March 5, 2004); see also www.betanews.com/article.php3?sid=1078475558.

Christopher Yang, Hsinchun Chen, and Kay Hong, "Exploring the World Wide Web with self-organizing map," *Proc. Int'l. World Wide Web Conference*, Poster Session number 189, Honolulu, HI, Website: http://www2002.org/CDRom/poster/189.pdf (2002).

Richard Yevich and Susan Lawson, "Introducing object-relational OS/390," *DB2 Magazine* (Spring 2000); see also www.db2mag.com/db_area/archives/2000/q1/yevich.shtml.

Hong-Jiang Zhang, Atreyi Kankanhalli, and Stephen Smoliar, "Automatic partitioning of full-motion video," *Multimedia Systems*, vol. 1, pp. 10–28 (1993).

Jason Zinoman, "On stage and off: His role is not soda jerk," *The New York Times* (March 12, 2004).

Justin Zobel, Steffen Heinz, and Hugh E. Williams, "In-memory hash tables for accumulating text vocabularies," *Information Processing Letters*, vol. 80, no. 6, pp. 271–277 (2001).

Index